THE COLLECTED WORKS OF
G. K. CHESTERTON

III

THE COLLECTED WORKS OF G. K. CHESTERTON

III

WHERE ALL ROADS LEAD

THE CATHOLIC CHURCH AND CONVERSION

WHY I AM A CATHOLIC

THE THING: WHY I AM A CATHOLIC

THE WELL AND THE SHALLOWS

THE WAY OF THE CROSS

With Introduction and Notes by
James J. Thompson, Jr.

IGNATIUS PRESS   SAN FRANCISCO

Cover by Darlene Lawless O'Rourke

ISBN 978-0-89870-310-8 (HB)
ISBN 978-0-89870-311-5 (SB)
Library of Congress catalogue number 85-81511
Printed in the United States of America

CONTENTS

General Editors' Introduction   9

A Note on the Texts   11

A Note on the Notes   13

Introduction by James J. Thompson, Jr.   15

WHERE ALL ROADS LEAD   25

    I   The Youth of the Church   27
    II   The Youth of the Church (*continued*)   32
    III   The Case for Complexity   37
    IV   The History of a Half-Truth   41
    V   The History of a Half-Truth (*continued*)   46
    VI   A Note on Comparative Religion   51
    VII   A Note on Comparative Religion (*continued*)   55

THE CATHOLIC CHURCH AND CONVERSION   59

    Foreword   61
    I   Introductory: A New Religion   64
    II   The Obvious Blunders   70
    III   The Real Obstacles   84
    IV   The World Inside Out   99
    V   The Exception Proves the Rule   110
    VI   A Note on Present Prospects   121

WHY I AM A CATHOLIC   125

THE THING: WHY I AM A CATHOLIC   133

    I   Introduction   135
    II   The Sceptic as a Critic   138

III	Is Humanism a Religion?	146
IV	The Drift from Domesticity	157
V	Logic — and Lawn Tennis	165
VI	Obstinate Orthodoxy	169
VII	The Usual Article	179
VIII	Why I Am a Catholic	184
IX	What Do They Think?	191
X	The Mask of the Agnostic	196
XI	The Early Bird in History	203
XII	Protestantism: A Problem Novel	210
XIII	A Simple Thought	215
XIV	The Call to the Barbarians	220
XV	On the Novel with a Purpose	225
XVI	The Revolt against Ideas	230
XVII	The Feasts and the Ascetic	236
XVIII	Who Are the Conspirators?	240
XIX	The Hat and the Halo	245
XX	On Two Allegories	250
XXI	The Protestant Superstitions	255
XXII	On Courage and Independence	260
XXIII	The Nordic Hindoo	267
XXIV	A Spiritualist Looks Back	271
XXV	The Roots of Sanity	277
XXVI	Some of Our Errors	282
XXVII	The Slavery of the Mind	289
XXVIII	Inge versus Barnes	292
XXIX	What We Think About	297
XXX	The Optimist as a Suicide	305
XXXI	The Outline of the Fall	309
XXXII	The Idols of Scotland	314
XXXIII	If They Had Believed	319

XXXIV   Peace and the Papacy   325
XXXV   The Spirit of Christmas   330

THE WELL AND THE SHALLOWS   337

        Introductory Note   339
        An Apology for Buffoons   341
        My Six Conversions   357
            I   The Religion of Fossils   357
           II   When the World Turned Back   362
          III   The Surrender upon Sex   367
           IV   The Prayer-Book Problem   372
            V   The Collapse of Materialism   377
           VI   The Case of Spain   382
          VII   The Well and the Shallows   387
        The Return to Religion   392
        The Reaction of the Intellectuals   400
        Levity — or Levitation   408
        The Case for Hermits   411
        Killing the Nerve   415
        The Case of Claudel   418
        The Higher Nihilism   421
        The Ascetic at Large   424
        The Backward Bolshie   427
        The Last Turn   430
        The New Luther   435
        Babies and Distributism   439
        Three Foes of the Family   442
        The Don and the Cavalier   445
        The Church and Agoraphobia   451
        Back in the Fog   454
        The Historic Moment   457
        Mary and the Convert   460
        A Century of Emancipation   464
        Trade Terms   477

Frozen Free Thought   480
Shocking the Modernists   486
A Grammar of Knighthood   489
Reflections on a Rotten Apple   493
Sex and Property   501
St. Thomas More   505
The Return of Caesar   510
Austria   514
The Scripture Reader   517
An Explanation   520
Why Protestants Prohibit   523
Where is the Parodox?   528

THE WAY OF THE CROSS   535

GENERAL EDITORS' INTRODUCTION

Throughout the early months of 1922, Frances Chesterton noticed that her husband, Gilbert, was very fidgety. She knew that this was his habit when he had to make a great decision. During this period, G. K. C. wrote to his friend Father O'Connor:

> . . . I write with a more personal motive; do you happen to have a holiday about the end of next week or thereabouts and would it be possible for you to come south and see our new house—or old studio? This sounds a very abrupt invitation; but I write in great haste, and am troubled about many things. I want to talk to you about them; especially the most serious ones, religious and concerned with my own rather difficult position. Most of the difficulty has been my own fault, but not all; some of my difficulties would commonly be called duties; though I ought perhaps to have learned sooner to regard them as lesser duties. I mean that a Pagan or Protestant or Agnostic might even have excused me; but I have grown less and less of a Pagan or Protestant, and can no longer excuse myself. There are lots of things for which I never did excuse myself; but I am thinking now of particular points that might really be casuistical. Anyhow, you are the person that Frances and I think of with most affection, of all who could help in such a matter. Could you let me know if any time such as I name, or after, could give us the joy of seeing you?

Father O'Connor arrived at Top Meadow on July 26th and served as Chesterton's sounding board. During that week, Gilbert decided to embrace Catholicism. On July 30, 1922, with Dom Ignatius Rice officiating, he was baptized in the dance room of the Railway Hotel which served as the Roman Catholic Church in Beaconsfield.

Concerning the events of that day, Chesterton wrote:

> When people ask me, or indeed anybody else, "Why did you join the Church of Rome?" the first essential answer, if it is partly an elliptical answer, is "To get rid of my sins." For there is no other religious system that does really profess to get rid of people's sins. It is confirmed by the logic, which to many seems startling, by which the Church deduces that sin confessed and adequately repented is actually abolished; and that the sinner does really begin again as if he had never sinned. . . .

9

This volume of Chesterton's major religious works contains his writing on the Theology of Conversion. We also include *The Way of the Cross* which is a commentary on the Stations of the Cross. The introduction and footnotes were prepared by James J. Thompson, Jr. Himself a convert, Mr. Thompson is an editor of the *New Oxford Review* and author of *Christian Classics Revisited.*

There exist theological essays, reviews and commentaries penned by Chesterton that are not found in the first three volumes of the *Collected Works.* It is our intention to publish a volume at the end of this series that will contain these writings.

GEORGE J. MARLIN
RICHARD P. RABATIN
JOHN L. SWAN
    General Editors

JOSEPH SOBRAN
    Consulting Editor

PATRICIA AZAR
JOE MYSAK
REV. RANDALL PAINE, O.R.C.
    Associate Editors

BARBARA D. MARLIN
    Assistant

A NOTE ON THE TEXTS

Where All Roads Lead is taken from the original text published in the November 1922 issue of *The Catholic World*, volume CXVI, number 692.

The first American edition of *The Catholic Church and Conversion* is used in this volume. It was published in New York by Macmillan Press in 1926.

Why I Am a Catholic is a brief essay taken from the first edition of *Twelve Modern Apostles and Their Creed*, published in 1926 by Duffield and Company in New York.

The Thing: Why I Am a Catholic was originally published in 1929 by Sheed and Ward. The American edition published by Dodd Mead in 1930 is used in this volume.

The first edition of *The Well and the Shallows* is used in this volume. It was published by Sheed and Ward in 1935.

The Way of the Cross was published in 1935 by Hodder and Stoughton. It contains a commentary by G. K. Chesterton and interpretive drawings of the Stations of the Cross by Frank Brangwyn. The text and drawings found in this volume are from the first edition.

A NOTE ON THE NOTES

Chesterton never used footnotes, and he would be surprised and amused that we are propping up some of his pages with these little annotations. We have decided, however, both in deference to G. K. and for the training of the reader, to let the vast majority of the pages stand on their own and leave a host of generally familiar names and references unannotated. As a rule, therefore, notes are furnished only for references clearly crucial to the context and of sufficient obscurity to send even the well-educated reader to the encyclopedia, lest the thread of narrative or argument be lost.

INTRODUCTION

In 1926, four years after his conversion to Catholicism, Chesterton noted in *The Catholic Church and Conversion* that "the Church is a house with a hundred gates; and no two men enter at exactly the same angle." He might have said a thousand or ten thousand, or simply an infinitude, for each convert's experience is unique. What better mark of the Universal Church? It proffers that which each person most needs and can find nowhere else.

Does this mean that converts are prickly individualists, each nursing his own predilections and holding nothing in common with those who stride through the other ninety-nine gates? Do those who seek an authoritative moral standard share nothing with believers who crave a majestic liturgy? Do those for whom the Faith evokes a soul-shivering emotional response lapse into silence when approached by converts who enter the Church because it consecrates human reason? Do those who admire Catholicism's guarding of tradition form a company shut off from new Catholics who find in the Church an everfresh source of renewal? Is the Church a true community of believers, or is it only an umbrella under which mutually exclusive individuals can find shelter?

For Chesterton, two essentials lay at the heart of conversion; without these, a man misses the point of becoming a Catholic. "One is that he believes it to be the solid objective truth, which is true whether he likes it or not; and the other that he seeks liberation from his sins." That is why Chesterton became a Catholic, and these two fundamentals should undergird the decision of any man to enter the Church. Without these, observed Chesterton, a man may profess to be a Catholic, but he deludes himself.

II

Admitting this unity at the core of conversion, one can still assert that each convert's experience — that which convinces him to affirm Chesterton's twofold test — *is* unique. The "angle" of entry varies ever so slightly for each person. Nowhere did Chesterton describe in detail his own angle; his *Autobiography*, published in the year of his death, disappoints those who hope to find in it a clearly demarcated map of Chesterton's particular route to Rome. But sprinkled throughout his writings (both before and after his conversion) are hints, allusions and insights that disclose Chesterton's personal story. Then, too, bold and candid autobiographical passages occasionally pierce the skin of reticence and reveal Chesterton's wrestlings with the imperative question: Why not Rome?

To trace the path that he traversed from the free-thinking Victorian ethos of his youth to his entry into the Church in 1922 would be to compose Chesterton's spiritual biography, a book that has yet to be written. But the story can at least be adumbrated. By the early twentieth century he had found refuge in the Anglican Church, specifically in an Anglo-Catholicism that prides itself on preserving the true Catholic faith in opposition to the perversions of Rome. Chesterton did not rest comfortably for long in this way-station; a decade or more before his embrace of Roman Catholicism he discerned the inadequacy of the Anglo-Catholic compromise. Why it took him so long to make the final step to Rome remains something of a mystery, although various writers attribute the delay to his reluctance to open a spiritual chasm between himself and his wife, who remained at this time staunchly committed to the Anglican Church.

The urgent need to act pressed upon Chesterton. He was a divided man, heart and mind pushing him toward Rome, loyalty to his wife demanding continued obedience to Canterbury. One looks for the crucial shock of recognition, for that moment of crisis when the command to act would no longer be denied. It appears in a passage in *The Well and the Shallows* that illumines the leitmotif of Chesterton's spiritual journey. In its rich texture and resonant beauty it rises out of the entire body of his writings with an exultant cry of joy, thanksgiving and relief.

Returning in 1920 from a voyage to the Holy Lands, the Chestertons debarked for a spell at the Adriatic seaport of Brindisi, far down the coast of the Italian peninsula. There, on Easter Sunday, a revelation flashed into Chesterton's consciousness, irradiating his being in the refulgent light of implacable Truth. Recalling the event later, he wrote:

. . . Men need an image, single, coloured and clear in outline, an image to be called up instantly in the imagination, when what is Catholic is to be distinguished from what claims to be Christian or even what in one sense is Christian. Now I can scarcely remember a time when the image of Our Lady did not stand up in my mind quite definitely, at the mention or the thought of all these things. I was quite distant from these things, and then doubtful about these things; and then disputing with the world for them, and with myself against them; for that is the condition before conversion. But whether the figure was distant, or was dark and mysterious, or was a scandal to my contemporaries, or was a challenge to myself—I never doubted that this figure was the figure of the Faith; that she embodied, as a complete human being still only human, all that the Thing had to say to humanity. The instant I remembered the Catholic Church, I remembered her; when I tried to forget the Catholic Church, I tried to forget her; when I finally saw what was nobler than my fate, the freest and hardest of all my acts of freedom, it was in front of a gilded and very gaudy little image of her in the port of Brindisi, that I promised the thing that I would do, if I returned to my own land.

III

For Chesterton, as for all who enter the Church, conversion signified commencement, not culmination; to *be* a Catholic, not to *become* one, is the grave and exigent challenge that confronts the believer. One truly fathoms Catholicism only from the inside; one comprehends it fully only as life within the Faith exfoliates into a Catholic sensibility and vision of the world. As Chesterton commented in *The Thing*, "conversion is the beginning of an active, progressive and even adventurous life of the intellect." The important question to ask of Chesterton (and of all converts) is not: Why did he become a Catholic? Rather: What kind of Catholic did he become?

Historicity and universality—always and everywhere—quickened Chesterton's Catholic sensibility. Because it has weathered the ages, the Faith has acquired the wisdom that comes with experience. The Church has watched empires rise and fall, has witnessed social transformations of cataclysmic import, has adjusted its sights to meet the comings and goings of economic systems and political arrangements.

The Church has prevailed over everything devised by the mind of man in the course of two thousand years. Man's creations are ephemeral—a mere wink in the vastness of time; the Rock endures.

This is not to argue for tradition alone, for Chesterton apprehended a truth beyond tradition: the Church is old, but it is ever new. It understands the past, but of greater consequence, it speaks to the present and anticipates the future. Chesterton's friend Hilaire Belloc proclaimed that "the Faith is Europe and Europe is the Faith." The Church's universality prevented Chesterton from adopting such a constricted view. "The Catholic philosophy," he wrote in *The Catholic Church and Conversion*, "is a universal philosophy found to fit anywhere with human nature and the nature of things." In time and space—always and everywhere—the Church was, is and shall be—"world without end, Amen."

Chesterton's appreciation of historicity and universality made him truly catholic, but one does not need to be Catholic to be catholic. The secular humanitarians and internationalists of Chesterton's day advanced their own claim to catholicity. "The nature of things": that is where Chesterton's Catholicism engendered the most telling effect upon his thinking. By becoming a Catholic he did not suddenly grasp a new reality, for he had worked out many of these ideas before his reception into the Church. Formal allegiance to the Faith enabled him to deepen his apprehension of "the nature of things," and invited him to render fully this perception of the world.

"Beef and beer" and "pigs is pigs"—two phrases cherished by Chesterton—convey the essence of his Catholic vision. The latter of these appears in *The Thing* in a playful account of a confrontation between a crusty English farmer and a spokesman for the science of economics. The economist marshalls the arcana of his trade to explain the mysteries of the market: the value of a pig rises and falls; two pigs may be better than three—a pig is not invariably just a pig. The farmer—rooted in a common sense that strikes the economist as a willful marriage of ignorance and obduracy—retorts adamantly: "Pigs is pigs!"

This rejoinder symbolized to Chesterton the workings of God-given reason and the divinely blessed perceptions of the senses.

Man's mind connects with what is *out there*, with the created order. In observing the rise of neo-paganism in the heart of the Christian West, Chesterton remarked in *The Well and the Shallows*: "And what is lost in that society is not so much religion as reason; the ordinary common daylight of intellectual instinct that has guided the children of men." In his outlook, Chesterton's farmer is a good Thomist, the economist an example of right reason gone haywire.

The farmer can rely upon his senses and "intellectual instinct" because the created order is just that: created by God. And it is good. "Beef and beer" symbolized this goodness, and the term bodied forth the robust pleasure man derives from savoring the Creator's beneficence. Throughout his career Chesterton turned repeatedly to the attack on Manichaeanism, Gnosticism and all varieties of the age-old dualistic heresy that imputes evil to the creation. For Chesterton, the material world brimmed with divinity. "Heaven has *descended* into the world of matter," he wrote in *The Thing*; "the supreme spiritual power is now operating by the machinery of matter, dealing miraculously with the souls and bodies of men. It blesses all the five senses. . . ." In the "divine materialism of the Mass" the Church daily reminds the faithful of the goodness of creation and the divinity that permeates the sensory world.

Catholicism enabled Chesterton to shatter the tedious and futile debate between optimists and pessimists. Both are partly right and partly wrong; the Church elevates the debate to a higher plane, exposes the inadequacy of both arguments, and melds the two into a coherent doctrine of man and the cosmos. Though flawed by sin, man and his world are inherently good, and the material creation has been redeemed from the stain of evil. Eat your beef and drink your beer in thanksgiving for God's blessings, and rejoice that sin and death — marks of the Fall — have been defeated.

IV

Long before he made his profession of faith, Chesterton's antagonists had accused him of defending the Catholic Church. With his embrace of the Faith there could be no doubt that he was the Church's champion, dedicating his pen to her defense. *The Catholic*

Church and Conversion, *The Thing* and *The Well and the Shallows* testify to both the urgency and the cogency of that endeavor. The Church commanded little respect and scant popularity in Chesterton's England. The historic Catholic families had always labored under the suspicions of their Protestant countrymen; to the small number of native Catholics had been added a group equally disdained by Protestants: the Irish who in the nineteenth century had flocked to England's port cities and factory towns. Refuting anti-Catholic calumnies was itself enough to occupy one man. Chesterton undertook this task, but to it he added an assault on the Church's historic enemies, ranging from the ever-recurring heresies of the age of the Church Fathers to the more recent phenomena of Calvinism and the myriad sectarianisms that had debouched from the Reformation.

Despite the importance of these longstanding foes, it was the modern age — Chesterton's own era — that furnished the main target for his slashing wit, razor-keen logic and piercing analysis. In defense of the Faith he tangled with all contenders: Darwinists, materialists, Spiritualists, Theosophists, atheists, agnostics, determinists, socialists, drumbeaters for capitalism, narrowminded nationalists (and equally procrustean internationalists), racists and secular humanitarians — a disparate crew, held together only by their shared belief in the iniquity — or at best, irrelevance — of the Catholic Church. No one ever charged Chesterton with backing off from a scrap with the paladins of modern thought.

Controversialists can easily sink into bitterness, especially when the creed they champion, as with Catholicism in England, is despised and mistrusted. In defense of a good cause, a good man can be transmogrified into a crotchety, dyspeptic misanthrope. Chesterton never succumbed to this temptation. He refused to relinquish his boyish high spirits and sanguine temperament; to him, contending for the Faith was immense fun. He exemplified the laughing apologist, chortling merrily as he pricked pomposities, exposed illogic and smashed ramshackle arguments. Although he took the Faith seriously, he never made the mistake of assuming that one Gilbert Keith Chesterton should be treated with a grave demeanor.

Chesterton usually liked his adversaries as persons, and they generally responded to him in a kindred spirit. For over three decades he conducted a running dispute with George Bernard Shaw; had they ever exhausted their substantive disagreements, they probably would have initiated a round of fierce polemics over the weather. Yet the two remained fast friends, each recognizing in the other qualities that transcended intellectual differences. H. G. Wells, another of Chesterton's regular sparring partners, represented, in Chesterton's eyes, a prime example of a man inebriated with modern progressivism. The two men pounced upon one another with gusto, yet Chesterton lauded Wells as a jewel in England's literary crown. In his fracases with William Inge, Anglican dean of St. Paul's Cathedral, Chesterton frequently lost patience with the dean's brassbound modernism, but his frustration never boiled over into vitriol. Only one opponent — Ernest Barnes, Anglican Bishop of Birmingham — consistently elicited Chesterton's unmitigated ire. But the bishop paraded a combination of invincible ignorance and flagrant chuckleheadedness that would have tried the patience and charity of our Lord himself.

Like some slightly daft medieval knight, Chesterton galloped directly into the enemy encampment and, with a laugh, threw down the gauntlet. His friend Belloc, an equally courageous apologist for the Faith, was more akin to the commander who rallies the troops to cling to their post in the face of a withering bombardment. Chesterton evinced a deftness of touch that Belloc lacked. He would prick an opponent with a swift rapier-thrust — wounding, but rarely storming in to maim permanently or to kill. Belloc would grasp a broadsword in both hands and lop off heads. Belloc's militant triumphalism precluded the kind of affable, but nonetheless serious, badinage that Chesterton loved to engage in with his adversaries. There is in Belloc a strain of ferocity, even anger and bitterness, so notably absent in Chesterton. Chesterton traded quips with his opponents; Belloc thundered the word of Truth.

Belloc's polemics appealed most to the already-convinced; his message confirmed them in their faith and steeled them to do battle with the Church's detractors. Chesterton, by contrast, spoke more to those in the opposing camp who might be entertaining doubts

about the unalloyed righteousness of their own cause. He understood the mind of the agnostic, the atheist and the half-believer in a
way that Belloc did not, and he sought, with a clever turn of phrase
here, a telling explanation there, to pick them off one by one and
spirit them into the Church. He realized that one does not bludgeon
a man into belief; those who seek converts must often practice the
subtlest of stratagems, lest they drive away the not-quite-convinced.
As he remarked in *The Catholic Church and Conversion* (with an allusion to his own experience in coming to the Faith): "There is many a
convert who has reached a stage at which no word from any Protestant or pagan could any longer hold him back. Only the word of a
Catholic can keep him from Catholicism."

V

Did converts swarm into the Church because of Chesterton's
writings? The answer must surely be no. For one thing, in predom-
inantly Protestant lands converts rarely "swarm"; the metaphor
must be altered to something more apt — say, for example, "trickle."
Moreover, one can rarely establish an unmistakable cause-and-effect
relationship in conversion: Read a book, join the Church. But this
much can be said: Chesterton presented the Church's best face to an
antagonistic and indifferent world. His form of apologetics, not
Belloc's, better advances the cause into hostile territory. Chesterton
may not have won large numbers of his fellow Englishmen to Catholicism, but they could never ignore him or dismiss him as a
crank, as they frequently did with Belloc. Yet one feels certain that it
did happen at times: the reading of one of Chesterton's books initiated in someone's mind that delicate and circuitous train of
thought that led him, by fits and starts, to approach one of those
hundred gates, and, with uneasiness and trepidation, call to the
keeper for admission.

Even conceding this much, the skeptic can reply: "That is all well
and good, but Chesterton has been dead for over fifty years. Surely
the passage of a half-century has dated him beyond reclamation."
This argument cannot be dismissed casually. How many books published before World War II survive today? Products of a specific

time, place and set of circumstances, they are imprisoned in the intellectual milieu of the moment, of interest only to the historian who brushes away the cobwebs and peers into a long-unopened book in hopes of recapturing an outmoded way of thinking.

Chesterton refuses such incarceration. The mere fact that Ignatius Press has chosen to reprint his collected works indicates that potential readers still exist. But as the old adage goes, the proof is in the pudding—and a rich one it is. To read him now is to revel in the same delight that his contemporaries felt. This transcends matters of stylistic charm and literary grace, however, for the issues that Chesterton wrestled with are as germane today as they were fifty years ago. A cursory glance down the list of opponents he challenged—modernists, materialists, Darwinists, secular humanitarians, agnostics, atheists, socialists, dabblers in the occult, to name only a few—convinces one of his continued relevance, for these foes of the Faith have fortified their sway over the minds of men in the last half-century. The Church endures, but so do her enemies. But her defenders do, too, and in the twentieth century she has never found a more cogent and engaging one than Gilbert Keith Chesterton.

James J. Thompson, Jr.
Brentwood, Tennessee

WHERE ALL ROADS LEAD

1922

I

THE YOUTH OF THE CHURCH

Until about the end of the nineteenth century, a man was expected to give his reasons for joining the Catholic Church. Today a man is really expected to give his reasons for not joining it. This may seem an exaggeration; but I believe it to stand for a subconscious truth in thousands of minds. As for the fundamental reasons for a man doing it, there are only two that are really fundamental. One is that he believes it to be the solid objective truth, which is true whether he likes it or not; and the other that he seeks liberation from his sins. If there be any man for whom these are not the main motives, it is idle to inquire what were his philosophical or historical or emotional reasons for joining the old religion; for he has not joined it at all.

But a preliminary word or two may well be said about the other matter; which may be called the challenge of the Church. I mean that the world has recently become aware of that challenge in a curious and almost creepy fashion. I am literally one of the least, because one of the latest, of a crowd of converts who have been thinking along the same lines as I. There has been a happy increase in the number of Catholics; but there has also been, if I may so express it, a happy increase in the number of non-Catholics; in the sense of conscious non-Catholics. The world has become conscious that it is

ORIGINAL EDITOR'S NOTE. — We know that the readers of *The Catholic World* will rejoice with us in the fact that we commence, in this number, a series of articles by Mr. G. K. Chesterton, on his recent conversion. For many years, we have considered him as a near neighbor and a good friend. But now he has become "one of the family." In the Editorial Comment of last month, we said, among other things, that there are those "who think of the Catholic Church merely as 'the old Church.' But the miracle of the Church is that she is the oldest and the youngest." It gives us a particular joy to have Mr. Chesterton mention this "miracle" as one of the "strongest of all the purely intellectual forces that dragged him towards the truth." All Catholics will welcome him to the Fold, but we think that none can greet him more cordially than those who enjoy *The Catholic World.* For we and he are of the same spirit. The articles will be published synchronously in America and in England. On the other side of the ocean they will run in *Blackfriars.*

not Catholic. Only lately it would have been about as likely to brood on the fact that it was not Confucian. And all the array of reasons for not joining the Church of Rome marked but the beginning of the ultimate reason for joining it.

At this stage, let it be understood, I am speaking of a reaction and rejection which was, as mine would once have been, honestly, if conventionally, convinced. I am not speaking now of the stage of mere self-deception or sulky excuses; though such a stage there may be before the end. I am remarking that even while we truly think that the reasons are reasonable, we tacitly assume that the reasons are required. Far back at the beginning of all our changes, if I may speak for many much better than myself, there was the idea that we must have reasons for not joining the Catholic Church. I never had any reasons for not joining the Greek Church, or the religion of Mahomet, or the Theosophical Society, or the Society of Friends. Doubtless, I could have discovered and defined the reasons, had they been demanded; just as I could have found the reasons for not going to live in Lithuania, or not being a chartered accountant, or not changing my name to Vortigern Brown, or not doing a thousand other things that it had never occurred to me to do. But the point is, that I never felt the presence or pressure of the possibility at all; I heard no distant and distracting voice calling me to Lithuania or to Islam; I had no itch to explain to myself why my name was not Vortigern, or why my religion was not Theosophy. That sort of presence and pressure of the Church I believe to be universal and ubiquitous today; not only among Anglicans, but among Agnostics. I repeat that I do not mean that they have no real objections; on the contrary, I mean that they have begun really to object; they have begun to kick and struggle.

One of the most famous modern masters of fiction and social philosophy, perhaps the most famous of all, was once listening to a discussion between a High Church curate and myself about the Catholic theory of Christianity. About half-way through it, the great novelist began to dance wildly about the room with characteristic and hilarious energy, calling out, "I'm not a Christian! I'm not a Christian!" flapping about like one escaped as from the net of the fowler.

He had the sense of a huge vague army making an encircling movement, and heading him and herding him in the direction of Christianity, and ultimately Catholicism. He felt he had cut his way out
of the encirclement, and was not caught yet. With all respect for his
genius and sincerity, he had the air of one delightedly doing a bolt,
before anybody could say to him: "Why do we not join the Catholic
Church?"

Now, I have noted first this common consciousness of the challenge of the Church, because I believe it to be connected with
something else. That something else is the strongest of all the purely
intellectual forces that dragged me towards the truth. It is not merely
the survival of the faith, but the singular nature of its survival. I have
called it by a conventional phrase "the old religion." But it is not an
old religion; it is a religion that refuses to grow old. At this moment
of history, it is a very young religion; rather especially a religion of
young men. It is much newer than the new religions; its young men
are more fiery, more full of their subject, more eager to explain and
argue than were the young Socialists of my own youth. It does not
merely stand firm like an old guard; it has recaptured the initiative,
and is conducting the counter-attack. In short, it is what youth
always is rightly or wrongly; it is aggressive. It is this atmosphere of
the aggressiveness of Catholicism that has thrown the old intellectuals on the defensive. It is this that has produced the almost morbid
self-consciousness of which I have spoken. The converts are truly
fighting, in those words which recur like a burden at the opening of
the Mass, for a thing which giveth joy to their youth. I cannot
understand how this unearthly freshness in something so old can
possibly be explained, except on the supposition that it is indeed
unearthly.

A very distinguished and dignified example of this paganism at
bay is Mr. W. B. Yeats. He is a man I never read or hear without
stimulation; his prose is even better than his poetry, and his talk is
even better than his prose. But exactly in this sense he is at bay; and
indeed especially so; for, of course, the hunt is up in Ireland in much
fuller cry than in England. And if I wanted an example of the pagan
defense at its best, I could not ask for a clearer statement than the

following passage from his delightful memoirs in the *Mercury;* it refers to the more mournful poems of Lionel Johnson and his other Catholic friends:

> I think it (Christianity) but deepened despair and multiplied temptation. . . . Why are these strange souls born everywhere today, with hearts that Christianity, as shaped by history, cannot satisfy? Our love letters wear out our love; no school of painting outlasts its founders, every stroke of the brush exhausts the impulse; pre-Raphaelitism had some twenty years; Impressionism, thirty, perhaps. Why should we believe that religion can never bring round its antithesis? Is it true that our air is disturbed, as Melarmé said, "by the trembling of the veil of the temple," or "that our whole age is seeking to bring forth a sacred book?" Some of us thought that book near towards the end of last century, but the tide sank again.

Of course, there are many minor criticisms of all this. The faith only multiplies temptation in the sense that it would multiply temptation to turn a dog into a man. And it certainly does not deepen despair, if only for two reasons; first, that despair to a Catholic is itself a spiritual sin and blasphemy; and, second, that the despair of many pagans, often including Mr. Yeats, could not possibly be deepened. But what concerns me in these introductory remarks, is his suggestion about the duration of movements. When he gently asks why Catholic Christianity should last longer than other movements, we may well answer even more gently: "Why, indeed?" He might gain some light on why it should, if he would begin by inquiring why it does. He seems curiously unconscious that the very contrast he gives is against the case he urges. If the proper duration of a movement is twenty years, what sort of a movement is it that lasts nearly two thousand? If a fashion should last no longer than Impressionism, what sort of a fashion is it that lasts about fifty times as long? Is it just barely conceivable that it is not a fashion?

But it is exactly here that the first vital consideration recurs; which is not merely the fact that the thing remains, but the manner in which it returns. By the poet's reckoning of the chronology of such things, it is amazing enough that one such thing has so survived. It is much more amazing that it should have not survival, but revival, and revival with that very vivacity for which the poet admits he has looked elsewhere, and admits being disappointed when he looked elsewhere. If he was expecting new things, surely he ought not to be indifferent to something that seems unaccountably to be as good as new. If the tide sank again, what about the other tide that obviously rose again? The truth is that, like many such pagan prophets, he expected to get something, but he certainly never expected to get what he got. He was expecting a trembling in the veil of the temple; but he never expected that the veil of the most ancient temple would be rent. He was expecting the whole age to bring forth a sacred book; but he certainly never expected it to be a Mass book.

Yet this is really what has happened, not as a fancy or a point of opinion, but as a fact of practical politics. The nation to which his genius is an ornament has been filled with a fury of fighting, of murder and of martyrdom. God knows it has been tragic enough; but it has certainly not been without that religious exaltation that has so often been the twin of tragedy. Everyone knows that the revolution has been full of religion, and of what religion? Nobody has more admiration than I for the imaginative resurrections which Mr. Yeats himself has effected, by the incantation of Celtic song. But I doubt if Deirdre was the woman on whom men called in battle; and it was not, I think, a portrait of Oisin that the Black-and-Tan turned in shame to the wall.

THE YOUTH OF THE CHURCH (*continued*)

When the Master-Builder spoke apprehensively of the younger generation knocking at the door, it certainly never occurred to him to
apprehend that it might be the church door. And yet, even in the
figure of Ibsen, might have been found signs of so strange a sequel.
The very words, Master-Builder, are but a tradition from a mediaeval system, and it is that very system which some would now
make a rough model for the modern system. And if the Master-
Builder had been driven by his ruthless lady friend to make a tour of
Europe, looking for the tallest towers to climb, he would soon have
discovered what people of what period had the right to be called
masters of building. He would have found himself in the tracks of
many a master, who not only climbed his own tower, but carved his
own angels or devils at the four corners of it, hanging as on wings
above the void.

The artists and art critics of the rising generation had already
begun knocking at the church door fifty years ago, in the time of
Ruskin and William Morris. In our own time, a yet younger generation of art students are justifying their bold, or possibly bald, simplifications by yet severer doctrines drawn from the Primitives. The
new artists may be, in a chronological sense, Post-Impressionists,
but they are also, in a strict historical sense, Pre-Raphaelites. But
this youngest generation knocks at the door of the Master-Builder,
not only to ask about the church of which he was a builder, but also
about the guild in which he was a master. Mediaevalism provokes a
study, not merely artistic, like Morris and Ruskin, but as economic
as that of Mr. and Mrs. Sidney Webb. Let it be understood that I am
not here discussing whether these views are accurate; I am only
pointing out that, whatever they are, they are not merely antiquated. We may denounce or delight in the school of Mr. Eric Gill;
but if we denounce it, it will not be merely for being too mediaeval;
it is much more likely to be for being very much too modern. We

may quarrel or sympathize with the Guild Socialists; but we cannot deny that they do, in fact, think they are advancing a modern thing like Socialism by adding to it an ancient word like guild. We cannot deny that these men would, in fact, be stared at, guyed or made game of merely as advanced and even anarchical innovators. The rising generation is not necessarily right; but this generation is certainly rising. Its enthusiasms cannot be dismissed as emotions of elderly regret.

I could give, of course, any number of other examples, but it is sufficient for this summary to say that there are now not only movements, but new movements on our side. I deliberately refrain from dwelling on that with which I have been rather more concerned, along with my brother and many of my friends; but which Mr. Belloc stood alone in England in preaching twenty years ago. Mr. Belloc and my brother were not exactly pallid aesthetic reactionaries seeking peace in the ruins of the past. The Distributism which they preached is now solidifying into a political party all over Europe. But in Europe, as distinct from England, the movement had older roots; and the glory of it, under God, goes without question to the great Pope, Leo XIII. Here I only note briefly the facts of the present, to show that they are part of a series that can as clearly be traced in the past. It is not true, as the rationalist histories imply, that through the ages orthodoxy has grown old slowly. It is rather heresy that has grown old quickly.

The Reformation grew old amazingly quickly. It was the Counter-Reformation that grew young. In England, it is strange to note how soon Puritanism turned into Paganism, or perhaps ultimately into Philistinism. It is strange to note how soon the Puritans degenerated into Whigs. By the end of the seventeenth century, English politics had dried up into a wrinkled cynicism that might have been as old as Chinese etiquette. It was the Counter-Reformation that was full of the fire and even of the impatience of youth. It was in the Catholic figures of the sixteenth and seventeenth centuries that we find the spirit of energy and, in the only noble sense, of novelty. It was people like St. Teresa who reformed; people like Bossuet who challenged; people like Pascal who questioned; people like Suarez who speculated. The counter-attack was like a charge of the old spears of chivalry. And, indeed, the comparison is very relevant to the generalization. I believe that this renovation, which has certainly happened in our own time, and which certainly happened in a time so recent as the Reformation, has really happened again and again in the history of Christendom.

Working backwards on the same principle, I will mention at least two examples which I suspect to have been similar: the case of Islam and the case of Arianism. The Church had any number of opportunities of dying, and even of being respectfully interred. But the younger generation always began once again to knock at the door; and never louder than when it was knocking at the lid of the coffin, in which it had been prematurely buried. Islam and Arianism were both attempts to broaden the basis to a sane and simple Theism, the former supported by great military success and the latter, by great imperial prestige. They ought to have finally established a new system, but for the one perplexing fact, that the old system preserved the only seed and secret of novelty. Anyone reading between the lines of the twelfth century record, can see that the world was permeated by potential Pantheism and Paganism; we can see it in the dread of the Arabian version of Aristotle, in the rumors about great men being Moslems in secret. Old men, seeing the simple faith of the Dark Ages dissolving, might well have thought that the fading of Christendom into Islam would be the next thing to happen. If so, the old men would have been very much surprised at what did happen.

What did happen was a roar like thunder from thousands and thousands of young men, throwing all their youth into one exultant counter-charge: the Crusades. The actual effect of the danger from the younger religion was the renewal of our own youth. It was the sons of St. Francis, the Jugglers of God, wandering singing over all the roads of the world; it was the Gothic going up like a flight of arrows; it was the rejuvenation of Europe. And though I know less of the older period, I suspect that the same was true of Athanasian orthodoxy in revolt against Arian officialism. The older men had submitted to a compromise, and St. Athanasius led the younger like a divine demagogue. The persecuted carried into exile the sacred fire. It was a flaming torch that could be cast out, but could not be trampled out.

Whenever Catholicism is driven out as an old thing, it always returns as a new thing. It suggests some parable in which an old man should be driven forth from the fireside to wander in the storm like Lear, but should return as a young man at the head of a mob, to thunder at the door like Laertes. The parable could not merely be a human tragedy, even a Shakespearean tragedy. It would have to be, in the most exact sense of the words, a divine comedy. In other words, that tragedy could only be a miracle play. That particular state of things could not be rendered in any story except a supernatural story; or, as the skeptic would put it, a fairy story. It would be easy enough to make a human tragedy about the old man being right, or about the young man being wrong, or even about the young man being punished for being wrong. But, probably, the chief punishment of the young man would be the death of the old man. It would be that he had to weep with unavailing repentance beside a grave. It would not be that the old man would suddenly jump up out of the grave, and hit him a hearty thwack over the head. That sort of punishment is only possible in a divine comedy; but that sort of punishment is exactly the sort of poetical justice which has, age after age, marked the revivals of our religion. What the realists call real life does not exhibit anything so lively as that. That sort of story is something much livelier than a ghost story; it is not so much like any tales of ghosts as like the old tales of the gods; and that also is very much to the point.

It is not a survival. It is not impossible to imagine that some very old thing might manage to survive. The Druids, let us say, if the course of religious conflicts had been different, might conceivably have lingered through some local traditions for two thousand years to the present time. It is not easy to imagine even this; but it is not impossible. But if it were true, the Druids would look lingering; the Druids would look two thousand years old; in short, the Druids would look like Druids. The Catholic priests do not look in the least like Druids. It is not a question of how many stones of Stonehenge are still standing, and how many have fallen over, or been knocked over. The stones of the Catholic Stonehenge *were* knocked over; they always are knocked over; and they always are laboriously put up again. The point is that as many of the Druidic stones as fell, still lie where they fell, and will lie there forever. There has not been a Druidic revolution every two or three hundred years, with young Druids, crowned with fresh mistletoe, dancing in the sun on Salisbury Plain. Stonehenge has not been re-built in every style of architecture from the rude round Norman to the last rococo of the Renaissance. The sacred place of the Druids is safe from what is called the vandalism of restoration.

This, then, is the vital distinction, upon which I have dwelt before going further, because its comprehension concerns the argument later on. It is not endurance, but the *kind* of recovery. Doubtless, there are, in every such transition, groups of good, and even glorious, Catholics, who have held to their religion rather as a thing of the past; and I have far too much admiration for their religious loyalty to insist here on any regrets for their reactionary politics. It is possible to look back to the passing of the monk, merely as one looks back to the passing of the Stuarts; it is possible to look back to the passing of the Stuarts merely as one looks back to the passing of the Druids. But Catholicism is not a thing that faded with the final failure of the Jacobites; rather it is a thing that returned with a rush after the relative failure of the Jacobins. There may have been ecclesiastics surviving from the Dark Ages who did not understand the new movement of the Middle Ages; there certainly were good Catholics who did not see the need for the great raid of the Jesuits or the reforms of St. Teresa; and they were most probably much better people than we are.

But the rejuvenation does recur; and it is the first fact with which I have wished to start my argument. Its effect on the question of the seat of authority and the limits of communion I may proceed to consider at another time. But, for the moment, I am content to say that we live in one of these recurrent periods of Catholicism on the march; and to draw a more simple moral from it. The real honor is due to those who were with it when its cause seemed hopeless; and no credit, beyond that of common intelligence, really belongs to anyone who has joined it when it is so evidently the hope of the world.

III

THE CASE FOR COMPLEXITY

I began with the power of the Church to grow young suddenly, when she is expected to grow old slowly, and remarked that this power in a creed was one which I could only conceive as thus regularly recurrent under two conditions: first, that it was really true; and, second, that the power in it was more than mortal. In the ultimate sense, these are undoubtedly the reasons for what is a revolution that really returns like the revolution of a wheel. But among the secondary and superficial causes of this rejuvenation may be specially noted, I fancy, the very fact of which religious reformers have so constantly complained; I mean the complexity of the creeds. There is a sense in which the Faith is the simplest of religions; but there is another sense in which it really is, by far, the most complicated. And what I am emphasizing here is that, contrary to many modern notions, it owes its victory over modern minds to its complexity and not its simplicity. It owes its most recent revivals to the very fact that it is the one creed that is still not ashamed of being complicated.

We have had during the last few centuries a series of extremely simple religions; each indeed trying to be more simple than the last. And the manifest mark of all these simplifications was, not only that they were finally sterile, but that they were very rapidly stale. A man had said the last word about them when he had said the first. Atheism is, I suppose, the supreme example of a simple faith. The man says there is no God; if he really says it in his heart, he is a certain sort of man so designated in Scripture. But, anyhow, when he has said it, he has said it; and there seems to be no more to be said. The conversation seems likely to languish. The truth is that the atmosphere of excitement, by which the atheist lived, was an atmosphere of thrilled and shuddering theism, and not of atheism at all; it was an atmosphere of defiance and not of denial. Irreverence is a very servile parasite of reverence; and has starved with its starving lord. After this first fuss about the merely aesthetic effect of blasphemy, the whole thing vanishes into its own void. If there were not God, there would be no atheists. It is easy to say this of the nineteenth century negation, for that sort of atheism is already one of the dead heresies. But what is not always noticed is that all the more modern forms of theism have the same blank. Theism is as negative as atheism. To say with the optimists that God is good, and therefore everything is good; or with the universalists that God is Love, and therefore everything is love; or with the Christian Scientists that God is Spirit, and therefore everything is spirit; or, for that matter, with the pessimists that God is cruel, and therefore everything is a beastly shame; to say any of these things is to make a remark to which it is difficult to make any reply, except "Oh;" or possibly, in a rather feeble fashion, "Well, well." The statement is certainly, in one sense, very complete; possibly a little too complete; and we find ourselves wishing it were a little more complex. And that is exactly the point. It is not complex enough to be a living organism. It has no vitality because it has no variety of function.

One broad characteristic belongs to all the schools of thought that are called broad-minded; and that is that their eloquence ends in a sort of silence not very far removed from sleep. One mark distinguishes all the wild innovations and insurrections of modern intellectualism; one note is apparent in all the new and revolutionary religions that have recently swept the world; and that note is dullness. They are too simple to be true. And, meanwhile, any one Catholic peasant, while holding one small bead of the rosary in his fingers, can be conscious, not of one eternity, but of a complex and almost a conflict of eternities; as, for example, in the relations of Our Lord and Our Lady, of the fatherhood and the childhood of God, of the motherhood and the childhood of Mary. Thoughts of that kind have, in a supernatural sense, something analogous to sex; they breed. They are fruitful and multiply; and there is no end to them. They have innumerable aspects; but the aspect that concerns the argument here is this, that a religion which is rich in this sense always has a number of ideas in reserve. Besides the ideas that are being applied to a particular problem or a particular period, there are a number of rich fields of thought which are, in that sense, lying fallow. Where a new theory, invented to meet a new problem, rapidly perishes with that problem, the old things are always waiting for other problems when they shall, in their turn, become new. A new Catholic movement is generally a movement to emphasize some Catholic idea that was only neglected in the sense that it was not till then specially needed; but when it is needed, nothing else can meet the need. In other words, the only way really to meet all the human needs of the future is to pass into the possession of all the Catholic thoughts of the past; and the only way to do that is really to become a Catholic.

In these notes, I do not intend to say anything in very direct criticism of the Anglican Church or the Anglo-Catholic theory, because I know it in my own case to be the worst possible way of going to work. The Church drew me out of Anglicanism, as the very idea of Our Lady drew me long before out of ordinary Protestantism, by being herself, that is, by being beautiful. I was converted by the positive attractions of the things I had not yet got, and not by negative disparagements of such things as I had managed to get already. When those disparagements were uttered, they generally had, almost against my will, the opposite effect to that intended; the effect of a slight setback. I think, in my heart, I was already hoping that Roman Catholics would really prove to have more charity and humility than anybody else, and anything that even seemed to savor of the opposite was judged by too sensitive a standard in the mood of that moment. I am, therefore, very anxious not to make that sort of mistake myself. It would be easy to put in a much shorter and sharper fashion the conclusion to which I, and every other convert, have eventually come. It would be easy to argue merely that our whole position was a common contradiction; since we were always arguing that England had suffered in a thousand ways from being Protestant, and yet, at the same time, arguing that she had remained Catholic. It would be easy, and in a sense only too true, to call the whole thing a piece of English half-conscious hypocricy; the attempt to remedy a mistake without admitting it. Nor do I deny that there are High Churchmen who provoke, and perhaps deserve this tone, by talking as if Catholicism had never been betrayed and oppressed. To them, indeed, one is tempted to say that St. Peter denied his Lord; but at least he never denied that he had denied Him.

But of most souls in such a transition the truth is far more subtle, and of all I knew far more sympathetic; and I have deliberately approached this problem by a route that may seem circuitous, but which I believe to be the right approach in such a problem of subtlety and sympathy. The first fact to be pointed out, I think, to the honest and doubtful Anglican is that this power of resurrection in the Church does depend on this possession of reserves in the Church. To have this power, it is necessary to possess the whole past of the religion, and not merely those parts of it that seemed obviously needed in the nineteenth century by the men of the Oxford Movement, or in the twentieth century by the men of the Anglo-Catholic Congress. They did discover the need of Catholic things, but they did discover the need of one thing at a time. They took their pick in the fields of Christendom, but they did not possess the fields; and, above all, they did not possess the fallow fields. They could not have all the riches, because they could not have all the reserves of the religion.

We hear a great many predictions of the future, which are only rather dull extensions of the present. Very few moderns have dared to imagine the future as anything but modern. Most of them have gone mad with the attempt to imagine their great-grandchildren as exactly like themselves, only more so. But the Church is Futurist in the only sane sense, just as she is Individualist in the only sane sense, or Socialist in the only sane sense. That is, she is prepared for problems which are utterly different from the problems of today. Now, I think the truth about the man who calls himself, as I did, an Anglo-Catholic, may most fairly and sympathetically be stated thus. He is, of course, in strict definition a heretic, but he is not a heresiarch. He is not merely founding a heresy of the moment. But he is merely *fighting* a heresy at the moment. Even when he is defending orthodoxy, as he so often is, he is only defending it upon certain points against certain fallacies. But the fallacies are merely fashions, and the next fashion will be quite different. And then *his* orthodoxy will be old-fashioned, but not ours.

IV

THE HISTORY OF A HALF-TRUTH

In fundamentals, the Church rejoices in being unchangeable; but she is sometimes charged with being too stiff and stationary, even in those externals that are the legitimate sphere of change. And in one sense, I think this is, indeed, true; if we mean by the Church its mortal machinery. The Church cannot change quite so fast as the charges against her do. She is sometimes caught napping and still disproving what was said about her on Monday, to the neglect of the completely contrary thing that is said about her on Tuesday. She does sometimes live pathetically in the past, to the extent of innocently supposing that the modern thinker may think to-day what he thought yesterday. Modern thought does outstrip her, in the sense that it disappears, of itself, before she has done disproving it. She is slow and belated, in the sense that she studies a heresy more seriously than the heresiarch does.

Most of us could point out examples of this error, if it be an error, so far as the external controversial machinery of Catholicism is concerned. There are Catholics who are still answering Calvinists, though there are no Calvinists to answer. There are admirable apologists assuming that the average Englishman blames the Church for distrusting the Bible; though nowadays he is much more likely to blame her for trusting it. There are those who have to apologize, in the Greek if not in the English sense, for the exalted place which our theology gives to a woman; as if our fashionable feminists still held the views of John Knox about the monstrous regiment of women. There are even some who excuse the ancient Christian hierarchy for using ritual, when all the Baptists in Balham have already become ritualists. In short, in this merely conventional and external sense, we can agree that the Catholic has been too much of a conservative. Catholicism, in the sense of most ordinary Catholics, did deserve the charge which so many Protestants brought against it. Catholicism was ignorant; it did not even know that Protestantism was dead.

But, though this fluctuation marks all the modern movements, the case is not quite the same if we turn from movements to men; and, assuredly, the Church is much more interested in the men than she is in the movements. The meanest man is immortal, and the mightiest movement is temporal, not to say temporary. But even in a secular sense, and on this social plane, there is a difference of some importance. Heresy follows heresy very rapidly in the course of a century, but not so rapidly in the life of one heretic, still less of one heresiarch; unless he is an utterly irresponsible fool. And a great heresiarch is seldom so great a fool as that. The great heresiarch generally sticks to his great heresy, even if his own son generally abandons it. The new heaven and the new earth are generally new enough to last for a lifetime. The Cosmos will not collapse for about twenty or thirty years. At any rate, the man who manufactured the Cosmos will not admit that it has collapsed. In short, while the faddist philosophy is amazingly fickle if we take history as a whole, the individual faddists are not fickle, but fixed. They have thrown away their lives on one theory, we might say on one thought. The faddist is faithful to his fad; he was the first to hold it, and he will probably be the last.

And with this, I reach a passage in my argument in which I cannot avoid a certain egotism. There is one most dismal and deplorable phrase current in the press, a phrase which probably meant something when it began among the Nonconformists; but it has lingered, and even luxuriantly multiplied, among those Nonconformists who cannot conform even to a Nonconformist religion. I mean the heart-rending habit of saying that this or that writer or speaker has "a message." Of course, it is only a case of using conventional phrases without noticing their content, and turning all sentences into strings of dead words. For that seems to be the chief result of compulsory education and unlimited printing. Huxley has a message; Haeckel has a message; Bernard Shaw has a message. It is only necessary to ask the logical question, "From whom?" to raise a thousand things that the writers have never thought of. And it is typical of the confusion, that the same person who says that Haeckel has a message probably goes on to say that he is an entirely original thinker. It may be doubted, in any case, whether the professor desires to be regarded as a messenger boy. But, anyhow, we, none of us, desire a messenger boy who originates his own message. It is true that Professor Haeckel might transform messages according to his own fancy, since he makes up embryological diagrams exactly as he chooses. But, normally, a man with a message is merely a messenger; and the term as applied to a religious or moral teacher must be a very extreme and even extraordinary assertion of his direct inspiration by God. To say that an ordinary modern moralist has a message is a confusion of thought. To say that an atheist has a message is a contradiction in terms.

The admirers of such a man are more serious when they say that he is original. And yet, it is true to say that the one thing that these original men never have, is originality. That is, they hardly ever begin with the origin, or even attempt to be an origin themselves. These revolutionists are always reactionaries, in the literal sense that they are always in a reaction against something else. Thus, Tolstoy was reacting against modern militarism and imperialism; Bernard Shaw was reacting against modern capitalism and conventionalism. In a world of really peaceful peasants, Tolstoy's occupation would be gone. In a world of Bolshevism and bobbed hair, Bernard Shaw has really nothing to say, except that his own movement has gone much further than he wished it to. But neither can be truly original in the sense of beginning at the beginning, like a man who has to make a world. It is, therefore, not easy to find a proper phrase for this sort of intellectual individualism; and the phrases current are very clumsy, whether the people who use them talk of messages or of originality, or soar into the sublime and starry nonsense of talking about an original message. But it may be a more modest and exact attempt to suggest — what such people really mean to say — that these intellectual leaders have something to say. They have necessary and neglected truths that want explaining, and they themselves happen to be very well fitted to explain them.

[Text missing in original sources.]

to the impersonal argument, it is true that there was a time when I was in danger of this sort of individual distinction. There was a time when some people suffered from the delusion that I had a message. I do not know if any went the atrocious length of calling it an original message. But I do not think I am merely misled by vanity, when I say that I do think I might have managed to launch one of those things that are called messages, one of those great modern messages from nobody to everybody, which are only delivered to about one person in ten million. It is possible that I might have found a sort of self-expression in a sort of small intellectual sect, of those who were willing to think, for about ten years, that I was maintaining a new or a neglected truth. In other words, the very little I thought I had to say, was at one time in some real danger of becoming a complete philosophy. I can only explain my escape from such a disaster by the mercy of God; and it is true that even in those days, there was something in my mind, as there is in every man's, telling me that what I wanted was not new truth or neglected truth, but truth. And to have turned my one truth into a system, in the manner of the modern pioneers, would have been nothing more or less than giving my one truth the chance to turn into a falsehood. The moment it had become a complete philosophy, it would have revealed itself as an incomplete philosophy.

I am here taking my own case only because I know it best; but I think the story may have a moral for many who fear that the Catholic religion is likely to destroy individual ideas, because it is able to digest them.

When I first read the *Penny Catechism*, my mind was arrested by an expression which seemed exactly to sum up and define, in a higher context and on a higher plane, something that I had been trying to realize and express through all my struggles with the sects and schools of my youth. It was the statement that the two sins against hope are presumption and despair. It referred, of course, to the highest of all hopes, and therefore the deepest of all despairs; but we all know that these shining mysteries have shadows on the earth below. And what is true of the most mystical hope, is exactly true of the most ordinary human cheerfulness and courage. The heresies that have attacked human happiness in my time, have all been variations either of presumption or of despair; which, in the controversies

THE HISTORY OF A HALF-TRUTH

45

of modern culture, are called optimism and pessimism. And if I wanted to write an autobiography in a sentence (and I hope I shall never write a longer one), I should say that my literary life has lasted from a time when men were losing happiness in despair, to a time when they are losing it by presumption. I began to think for myself about the time when all thinking was supposed to lead to despair, or to what was called pessimism. Like the other individuals I have mentioned, I was merely a reactionary, because my thought was merely a reaction; but it was a reaction which, in those days, I might have been contented to call optimism. I ask the reader's indulgence, if I explain next how I came to call it by a more intelligent name.

V

THE HISTORY OF A HALF-TRUTH (*continued*)

By this time it must be obvious that every single thing in the Catholic Church which was condemned by the modern world has now been reintroduced by the modern world, and always in a lower form. The Puritans rejected art and symbolism, and the decadents brought them back again, with all the old appeal to sense and an additional appeal to sensuality. The rationalists rejected supernatural healing, and it was brought back by Yankee charlatans who not only proclaimed supernatural healing, but forbade natural healing. Protestant moralists abolished the confessional and the psychoanalysts have reëstablished the confessional, with every one of its alleged dangers and not one of its admitted safeguards. The Protestant patriots resented the intervention of an international faith, and went on to solve an empire entangled in international finance. Having complained that the family was insulted by monasticism, they have lived to see the family broken in pieces by bureaucracy; having objected to fasts being appointed for anybody during any exceptional interval, they have survived to see teetotalers and vegetarians trying to impose a fast on everybody for ever.

All this, as I say, has become obvious, but there is a further development of the truth with which I am more especially dealing here; it concerns not so much the case of these general movements which may almost be called vulgar errors, but rather the case of certain individual ideas that are the private inspiration of individuals. As I said in the last issue, a young man may, without any very offensive vanity, come to the conclusion that he has something to say. He may think that a truth is missed in the current controversies, and that he himself may remind the world of it in a tolerably lucid or pointed fashion. It seems to me that there are two courses that he can follow; and I wish to suggest them here, because there must be a good many young men in that position, because I have been in it myself, and because I may be said in some sense to have followed both courses, first one and then the other.

He can take his truth, or half-truth, into the bustle and confusion of the modern world, of general secular society, and pit it against all the other notions that are being urged in the same way. He can have the honor of a controversy with Mr. Bernard Shaw, the most generous of pugilists, who is ready to take on all comers; he can review the books of Maeterlinck and Bergson; it is only too probable that he will write a book himself. In that case it is likely enough that he may be hailed by journalists as having a "message"; it is, at any rate, probable that he will have a vogue; but it is not very clear that anything will happen to his idea in the long run. There is no umpire to judge whether he beat Shaw or Shaw beat him; there is no record of his ephemeral, though possibly excellent, commentary on Bergson and Maeterlinck; his own book will be out of print like any other; and even though he may have done as well as he could reasonably expect for himself, it is not clear that he has done very much for the world; especially when the world is in a mood that permits nothing but fashions and forgetfulness. But there is a much greater danger in his position. Even supposing that his truth does become a tradition, it will only harden into a heresy. For it can only harden as the half-truth that it is; and even if it was true in its lifetime, it will have become false when it is fossilized. Sometimes a few touches from fanatical followers can turn it into a most extravagant and horrible falsehood. It is to illustrate this that I have taken as an example, at the risk of seeming egotistical, the intellectual motive which I remember to have been strongest in my own case.

Literary criticism is largely a string of labels; and at some time, early in my scribbling days, somebody called me an optimist. But he was speaking in the spirit of the time; and when he called me an optimist, he simply meant that I was not a pessimist. He certainly assumed that everybody with any intellectual pretensions was a pessimist. For in my early youth it was Schopenhauer's hour and the power of darkness, and there lay on the whole intellectual and artistic world a load of despair. The liveliest claim that could be made was to call oneself a decadent, and demand the right to rot. The decadents said in substance that everything was bad except beauty.

Some of them seemed rather to say that everything was bad except badness. Now the first movement of my mind was simply an impulse to say that being rotten was emphatically all rot. But I began to make for myself a sort of rudimentary philosophy about the thing, which was founded on the first principle that it is, after all, a precious and wonderful privilege to exist at all. It was simply what I should express now by saying that we must praise God for creating us out of nothing. But I expressed it then in a little book of poems, now happily extinct, which described (for example) the babe unborn as promising to be good if he were only allowed to be anything, or which asked what terrible transmigrations of martyrdom I had gone through before birth, to be made worthy to see a dandelion. In short, I thought, as I think still, that merely to exist for a moment, and see a white patch of daylight on a gray wall, ought to be an answer to all the pessimism of that period. But I did do it chiefly as a rebellion against the pessimism of that period. Like every rebel, I was a reactionary; that is, I was mainly reacting against something else.

Now I do think that this sort of notion might have counted for something among the other modern notions, which is not saying much. I mean that something might have been done, as a literary theme, with the notion of a new optimism founded not on everything, but rather on anything. But suppose it had really been preached as a new optimism, and taken up as a new fashion of thought or feeling. What awful and abominable nonsense it would have become before it had gone out of fashion again! I did not intend it for a nine days' wonder, but rather, so to speak, for a seven days' wonder; for a weekly and daily recognition of the seven days' wonder of creation. But long before it had got to the ninth or the seventh day, somebody would have seen its promising possibilities in the direction of perversion or insanity.

And as a matter of fact, the vista of possibilities for that innocent idea is perfectly appalling. That idea could easily, as a matter of fact, be turned into an instrument for the destruction of all that I hold most dear. If I had another intellectual passion running parallel to my revulsion from fashionable pessimism, it was a revulsion from fashionable plutocracy. As I could then only express the former by saying I was an optimist, so I could then only express the latter by saying I was a socialist. But as a fact, this fancy of mine, the philosophy of wonder and gratitude, could be used so as not only to smash all socialism, but the very mildest plea for social reform. The optimism of wonder might easily be the tool of every tyranny and usury and insolent corruption that ever oppressed the poor. The tyrant had only to say that people ought to be only too thankful if he left them alive. He had only to say that a man without political or legal rights should be only too happy because he could look at a dandelion. He had only to say that a man unjustly imprisoned should be satisfied to see the patch of daylight on the prison wall.

Now I only give that as one small instance, because I know it best, of what might happen to a half-truth when it has the chance to succeed as a heresy. There must be a thousand other similar cases of similar theories; but the moral is that the half-truth must be linked up with the whole truth; and who is to link it up? Herod, the tyrant, must not massacre babies because they would have been glad of a few months of life when they were babes unborn. A man must not be a slave on the plea that even a slave can see a dandelion. A man must not be thrown into jail in defiance of justice because he will still see a patch of daylight on the wall. In a word, wonder and humility and gratitude are good things, but they are not the only good things; and there must be something to make the poet who praises them admit that justice and mercy and human dignity are good things too. Knowing something of the nature of a modern poet, captured by a modern fancy, I can see only one thing in the world that is in the least likely to do it.

I have said that there are two courses for the young man specializing in the half-truth; I have given a personal example of him and the possibility of his horrible end. The other course is that he should take his half-truth into the culture of the Catholic Church, which really is a culture and where it really will be cultivated. For that place is really a garden; and the noisy world outside, nowadays, is none the less a wilderness because it is a howling wilderness. That is, he can take his idea where it will be valued for what is true in it, where it will be balanced by other truths and often supported by better arguments.

In other words, it will become a part, however small a part, of a permanent civilization, which uses its moral riches as science uses its store of facts. Thus, in the idle instance I have given, there is nothing true in that old childish mood of mine which the Catholic Church in any way condemns. She does not condemn a love of poetry or fantasy; she does not condemn, but rather commends, a sentiment of gratitude for the breath of life. Indeed, it is a spirit in which many Catholic poets have rather specialized, and its first and finest appearance, perhaps, is in the great Canticle of St. Francis. But in that sane spiritual society, I know that optimism will never be turned into an orgy of anarchy or a stagnation of slavery, and that there will not fall on any one of us the ironical disaster of having discovered a truth only to disseminate a lie.

VI

A NOTE ON COMPARATIVE RELIGION

I was being escorted the other day over the Roman foundations of an ancient British city, by a professor who said something that seems to me a satire on a good many other professors. I think it very probable that this professor saw the joke, though he maintained an iron gravity; but I do not know whether he saw that it was a joke against a great deal of historical science and comparative religion. I drew his attention to a bas-relief or molding representing the head of the sun with the usual halo of rays, but with the difference that the face in the disk, instead of being boyish like Apollo, was bearded like Neptune or Jupiter. "Yes," he said, with a certain delicate exactitude, "that is supposed to represent the local sun-god Sul. The best authorities identify Sul with Minerva; but this has been held to show that the identification is not complete."

That is what we call a powerful understatement. And it struck me that it was singularly like a large number of parallels I have come across in what is called comparative religion, on which I would add a postscript to these notes. Many professors identifying things remind me of this identification of Minerva with the Bearded Woman of Mr. Barnum. It is, indeed, an example of the modern world being madder than any satires on it; for long ago Mr. Belloc invented an imaginary don, who said that a bust of Ariadne had been proved by modern research to represent Silenus. And when the professors "identify" the Catholic creeds with various heathen tendencies, I do not say there is nothing in what they say; I confine myself to saying, with the restraint of the professor, that the identification is not complete.

The skeptics never give us the advantage of their skepticism. In other words, they never apply it where it does really apply. Mr. H. G. Wells, for instance, did at one time carry it to a length which was not so much skepticism about religion, but rather skepticism about thought, or even skepticism about skepticism. He suggested that there are no categories at all; that every separate thing is separate in the sense of absolutely unique. He implied that one star differeth from another, not only in glory, but in starriness or stellar quality; that one lamp-post differeth from another, so that we cannot really say even that there are ten lamp-posts in the street. But even when he had claimed that all classifications are false, he himself proceeded to fall back on something that really is a false classification. It really is like making a list of stars, of which one is in fact a firework, and another a meteoric stone, and another a street-lamp, and in that sense a lamp-post. In his *Outline of History* and other recent works on religion, he puts what he calls Christianity in its place in a list with other religions. He compares its moral effect with that of the Moslem religion, its moral origin with that of the Buddhist religion. But oddly enough, as it happens, this is at least one case in which his original skeptical argument would really apply. The skeptical truth might be stated in various ways. In one sense we might say that there is no such thing as the Buddhist religion or even the Moslem religion. In another sense we might say that if these are religions, then Christianity is not a religion. Indeed, this last suggestion, though more or less symbolical, does get near the truth about the matter. For the truth is, to use his favorite expression in his former phase, truly and indeed "unique." Christianity is not a religion; it is a Church. There may be a Moslem religion; but it would not come natural to anybody to talk about the Moslem Church. There may be a Buddhist religion; but nobody would call it the Buddhist Church. Even in avoiding the title they would be admitting the title. Anybody who hates the idea of a Church has the idea of a Church. It stands for a combination of things that are nevertheless one thing; and that one thing is really one. There is only one species and there is only one example. So that Mr. H. G. Wells, after telling us that every lamp-post is unique and every tenpenny nail is unique, has passed over the one and only unique thing in the world, and never noticed it was there.

I say that the very idea of a Catholic Church is *sui generis*, apart from claims to embody it. I am not now talking about the comparisons with Christian heresies, but of the comparison with heathen religions. It does, indeed, illustrate the incongruous and incomparable assortment of rival religions, that one of them does actually belong to this other category. One of the heathen religions really is a Christian heresy. The more we know of the great Moslem movement, the more we see that it was really a post-Christian revision, a subsequent simplification rather like the Arian movement. Of the other things that we call Eastern religions, many existed before Christianity, and almost any might have existed without Christianity. I take it as certain that Islam would never have existed without Christianity. I take it to be as clear as that Calvinism or Lollardism or Lutheranism would never have existed without Christianity. Nor was the Moslem movement in the modern sense anti-Christian. It gave to Christ as high a moral position as is given by most Unitarians, and indeed a more supernatural status than is given by some Broad Churchmen. To do Mohammed justice, his main attack was against the idolatries of Asia. Only he thought, just as the Arians did and just as the Unitarians do, that he could attack them better with a greater approximation to plain theism. What distinguishes his heresy from anything like an Arian or Albigensian heresy is that, as it sprang up on the borders of Christendom, it could spread outwards to a barbaric world. And even in this, some might venture to find a parallel in the Protestantism of Germany.

Now we might apply this principle of differentiation to each of the rival religions in turn. Each of them is not only in a different category from the Catholic Church, but in a different category from the others. Islam, if it is to go into a class at all, ought not to go into a class of Islam, Christianity, Confucianism, and Brahmanism, but rather into a class of Islam, Manichaeanism, Pelagianism, and Protestantism. In the same way Buddha ought not really to go into a class of Buddha, Christ, Mohammed, and the rest; but rather into some such class as Buddha, Pythagoras, Plato, and so on. He belongs to a class of philosophical mystics for whom what we commonly call religion was really only symbolical, and the main matter was a metaphysical unification. He may have had some of the virtues of a saint, but he was in reality a sage. He may have been what we call an idealist; he was also something very like a pessimist. But anyhow he was not a Church and did not found a Church. To consider what he did found we should have to go back to the foundations in

Brahmanism; and when we do so, we find that this, in its turn, is not another variation of the same thing, but an utterly different sort of thing with variations of its own. It is rather an old popular mythology, like our own old pagan mythology. At the back of it Brahmanism is probably nature-worship; and Buddhism is certainly the very opposite of nature-worship. It would be truer to call it an iconoclasm directed to destroying the idol called nature. Finally, it is fairly clear that Confucianism is not a religion, unless the English public-school system is a religion, or the Kultur of imperial Germany was a religion. In a sense they may be so described, since everything rests on a conscious or unconscious religion, or negation of religion. But nobody would call any of them a Church; and nobody can compare them with a Church calling itself dogmatic and divine. All these desperate things, of which one is an imitation and another a doubt and another a book of etiquette, have nothing in common except that they are none of them Churches; and that they are all examples of the various things in which men might be expected to experiment in the absence of a Church.

I have thought it advisable to add this note on a matter that affects many inquirers, though it is not one that ever especially affected me. I have always felt that the mere smell of these Oriental moralities was really very different from that of Christian morality; and that the moral savor is always the main thing for us and not always for them. But I do think it something of a curiosity of literature that Mr. Well's own category of religions should so obviously wither away at the touch of Mr. Wells's own question about categories. And I do think it is a simple and solid historical fact about the Catholic Church, that its character is as extraordinary as its claim. It is not merely the only thing that deserves a particular kind of service; it is really the only thing that asks for it. It is quite possible to be a pagan and hate the Church; it is equally possible to be a pessimist and hate the universe. But there is one Church exactly as there is one universe; and no wise man will wander about looking for another.

VII

A NOTE ON COMPARATIVE RELIGION (*Continued*)

Since writing in the last issue I have seen something in a popular publication which constitutes a sort of commentary on what I wrote; something that is in form a contradiction and in fact a confirmation. I remarked that Mr. Wells, who had previously maintained that things could not really be assimilated to each other at all, had afterwards assimilated the historic religions to each other a great deal too much. I pointed out that what we call the world's religions differ not only in the sense in which they are true, but in the sense in which they are religious. They differ not only in what they succeed in doing, but in what they profess to do. One of the most interesting of them, Buddhism, is in some sense the subject of a passage in the current publication called *The Outline of Literature*, and there Mr. Wells himself is quoted as an authority on the gospel of Buddha. He begins by saying, "The fundamental teaching of Gautama, as it is now being made plain to us by the study of original sources, is clear and simple, and in the closest harmony with modern ideas." This may be very consoling; but a man who has turned over a reasonable amount of modern journalism and controversy may still feel impelled to ask: "Which modern ideas?" Even in the work of Mr. Wells alone, there is so large and rich a variety of modern ideas as to make it a little difficult to be in the closest harmony with all of them.

We all have a vague popular impression about Buddhism, that it advises abnegation, the extinction of the ego, and so on; but these phrases might mean several different things. Certainly they might be in close harmony with modern ideas. They might be in harmony with the modern ideas of Schopenhauer, who said the will to live was a snare that kept us living against our reason. It might be in harmony with the modern ideas of Swinburne, when he said that life is a weary river, of which the best we can say is that somewhere it reaches the sea of death. It might be in harmony with the modern ideas of Mr. A. E. Housman, who wants to know why he was waked up to live, and how soon he may die and go to sleep again.

These are all modern ideas; but they do not seem very bright and bustling ones for people who have to set about making a World State or even writing an Outline of History. Indeed, I can imagine few people less likely to be content with them than Mr. Wells. He therefore proceeds to consider whether Buddhism is pessimism and what it really is. This is his version: "Until a man has overcome every sort of personal craving his life is trouble and his end sorrow. There are three principal forms the craving of life takes, and all are evil. The first is the desire to gratify the senses, sensuousness. The second is the desire for personal immortality. The third is the desire for prosperity, worldliness. . . . But when they are indeed overcome and no longer rule a man's life, when the first personal pronoun has vanished from his private thoughts, then he has reached the higher wisdom, Nirvana, serenity of soul. For Nirvana does not mean, as many people wrongly believe, extinction, but the extinction of the futile personal aims that necessarily make life base or pitiful or dreadful."

Now I cannot claim more than the most general knowledge about Buddha and Buddhism, and it is likely enough that Mr. Wells knows more about them than I do. But it is not necessary to understand Buddhism, but only to understand logic, in order to see that there is an internal difficulty here. For it cannot be doubted that in some sense Nirvana is offered as an ultimate and eternal goal of the spirit. Whether or no Nirvana is non-existence, and whether or no Buddhism denies individual existence after death, nobody denies that it promises Nirvana after death. To deny that would be to make nonsense of almost every sentence in which the word "Nirvana" is used. But if the soul does in some way find this peace after death, and if at the same time there is no personal immortality after death, why then Nirvana *is* extinction, and there, in every sense, is an end of the matter. If that is Nirvana, non-existence is Nirvana. If that is a good thing, non-existence is a good thing. The Buddhist may not extinguish himself in life, but anyhow, he is extinguished in death. He might, indeed, prepare for such extinction by effacement of self on earth. But his model would hardly be the moral ideal of Mr.

Wells. He will hardly tell a man that if he is unselfish, he will be almost as happy as a corpse; or, in a literal sense, as good as dead. He will hardly tell people that they ought to try to be as benevolent as nonentity and as kind-hearted as nobody. To pursue that ideal during this life is really, by an equally exact rendering of another and more vulgar phrase, to look like nothing on earth.

As a matter of fact, I fancy many Western theosophists would deny that Buddhism refuses any sort of personal immortality. And I suspect that some Eastern Buddhists would admit that it does, and defend it by saying that the personal immortality would be inevitably evil because it was personal. But then *they* would argue rationally, and would add that our life here also is inevitably evil because it is personal. They would probably say that the evil was not in being selfish, but in having a self. In that sense the evil would be in having a soul. When the self is lost in death, so much the better; or, in our language, if the soul is extinguished at death, so much the better. Some at least do hold this, and they would regard Mr. Wells's rebuke to mere selfishness as mere sentimentalism. But anyhow, Nirvana cannot be both the liberation from self, only to be found after death, and also the sensible serenity that can be enjoyed by everybody during life. Surely, the great sage of the East did not use words quite so loosely as that.

As a matter of fact, it is a great sage of the West who is using words loosely. The difficulty is due to an element in much of Mr. Wells's work: perhaps the one weakness that really lessens his great and admirable gift. He cannot altogether conceal a certain contrary spirit; he cannot avoid scoring off things, one might almost say scratching at things. Subconsciously, no doubt, he makes Buddha the ally of modern ideas, as a sort of balance against Catholic ideas. He therefore wishes to prove that Buddha was a modern skeptic, without admitting that he was a modern pessimist. He wants to invoke Buddhism against the Christian desire of eternal life, without invoking him against the human desire of life. About the world beyond, therefore, Buddha becomes the Nihilist of a starless night; but about the world around us he becomes only the amiable altruist, the Nonconformist who has joined an Ethical Society. Thus does great

Gautama turn up trim and tidy, and eminently fitted to attend a tin suburban chapel full of vegetarians and agnostics. I venture to think there was a good deal more in the great Indian sage, saint, or skeptic, than that. But, anyhow, Mr. Wells is trying to kill two birds with one stone, though the birds are flying in opposite directions: one being the white dove of an eternal hope and the other the black raven of despair.

THE CATHOLIC CHURCH
AND CONVERSION
1927

FOREWORD

It is with diffidence that anyone born into the Faith can approach the tremendous subject of Conversion. Indeed, it is easier for one still quite unacquainted with the Faith to approach that subject than it is for one who has had the advantage of the Faith from childhood. There is at once a sort of impertinence in approaching an experience other than one's own (necessarily more imperfectly grasped), and an ignorance of the matter. Those born into the Faith very often go through an experience of their own parallel to, and in some way resembling, that experience whereby original strangers to the Faith come to see it and to accept it. Those born into the Faith often, I say, go through an experience of scepticism in youth, as the years proceed, and it is still a common phenomenon (though not so often to be observed as it was a lifetime ago) for men of the Catholic culture, acquainted with the Church from childhood, to leave it in early manhood and never to return. But it is nowadays a still more frequent phenomenon—and it is to this that I allude—for those to whom scepticism so strongly appealed in youth to discover, by an experience of men and of reality in all its varied forms, that the transcendental truths they had been taught in childhood have the highest claims upon their matured reason.

This experience of the born Catholic may, I repeat, be called in a certain sense a phenomenon of conversion. But it differs from conversion properly so called, which rather signifies the gradual discovery and acceptance of the Catholic Church by men and women who began life with no conception of its existence: for whom it had been during their formative years no more than a name, perhaps despised, and certainly corresponding to no known reality.

Such men and women converts are perhaps the chief factors in the increasing vigor of the Catholic Church in our time. The admiration which the born Catholic feels for their action is exactly consonant to that which the Church in its earlier days showed to the martyrs. For the word "martyr" means "witness." The phenomenon of conversion apparent in every class, affecting every type of character, is the great modern *witness* to the truth of the claim of the Faith; to the fact that the Faith is reality, and that in it alone is the repose of reality to be found.

In proportion as men know less and less of the subject, in that proportion do they conceive that the entrants into the City of God are of one type, and in that proportion do they attempt some simple definition of the mind which ultimately accepts Catholicism. They will call it a desire for security; or an attraction of the senses such as is exercised by music or by verse. Or they will ascribe it to that particular sort of weakness (present in many minds) whereby they are easily dominated and changed in mood by the action of another.

A very little experience of typical converts in our time makes nonsense of such theories. Men and women enter by every conceivable gate, after every conceivable process of slow intellectual examination, of shock, of vision, of moral trial and even of merely intellectual process. They enter through the action of expanded experience. Some obtain this through travel, some through a reading of history beyond their fellows, some through personal accidents of life. And not only are the avenues of approach to the Faith infinite in number (though all converging; as must be so, since truth is one and error infinitely divided), but the individual types in whom the process of conversion may be observed differ in every conceivable fashion. When you have predicated of one what emotion or what reasoning process brought him into the fold, and you attempt to apply your predicate exactly to another, you will find a misfit. The cynic enters, and so does the sentimentalist; and the fool enters and so does the wise man; the perpetual questioner and doubter and the man too easily accepting immediate authority—they each enter after his kind. You come across an entry into the Catholic Church undoubtedly due to the spectacle, admiration and imitation of some great character observed. Next day you come across an entry into the Catholic Church out of complete loneliness, and you are astonished to find the convert still ignorant of the great mass of the Catholic effect on character. And yet again, immediately after, you will find a totally different third type, the man who enters not from loneliness, nor from the effect of another mind, but who comes in out of contempt for the insufficiency or the evil by which he has been surrounded.

The Church is the natural home of the Human Spirit.

The truth is that if you seek for an explanation of the phenomenon of conversion under any system which bases that phenomenon on illusion, you arrive at no answer to your question. If you imagine conversion to proceed from this or that or the other erroneous or particular limited and insufficient cause, you will soon discover it to be inexplicable.

There is only one explanation of the phenomenon—a phenomenon always present, but particularly arresting to the educated man outside the Catholic Church in the English-speaking countries—there is only one explanation which will account for the multiplicity of such entries and for the infinitely varied quality of the minds attracted by the great change; and that explanation is that the Catholic Church is reality. If a distant mountain may be mistaken for a cloud by many, but is recognised for a stable part of the world (its outline fixed and its quality permanent) by every sort of observer, and among these especially by men famous for their interest in the debate, for their acuteness of vision and for their earlier doubts, the overwhelming presumption is that the thing seen is a piece of objective reality. Fifty men on shipboard strain their eyes for land. Five, then ten, then twenty, make the land-fall and recognise it and establish it for their fellows. To the remainder, who see it not or who think it a bank of fog, there is replied the detail of the outline, the character of the points recognised, and that by the most varied and therefore convergent and convincing witnesses—by some who do not desire that land should be there at all, by some who dread its approach, as well as those who are glad to find it, by some who have long most ridiculed the idea that it was land at all—and it is in this convergence of witnesses that we have one out of the innumerable proofs upon which the rational basis of our religion reposes.

—Hilaire Belloc

I

INTRODUCTORY: A NEW RELIGION

The Catholic faith used to be called the Old Religion; but at the present moment it has a recognized place among the New Religions. This has nothing to do with its truth or falsehood; but it is a fact that has a great deal to do with the understanding of the modern world.

It would be very undesirable that modern men should accept Catholicism merely as a novelty; but it is a novelty. It does act upon its existing environment with the peculiar force and freshness of a novelty. Even those who denounce it generally denounce it as a novelty; as an innovation and not merely a survival. They talk of the "advanced" party in the Church of England; they talk of the "aggression" of the Church of Rome. When they talk of an Extremist they are as likely to mean a Ritualist as a Socialist. Given any normal respectable Protestant family, Anglican or Puritan, in England or America, we shall find that Catholicism is actually for practical purposes treated as a new religion, that is, a revolution. It is not a survival. It is not in that sense an antiquity. It does not necessarily owe anything to tradition. In places where tradition can do nothing for it, in places where all the tradition is against it, it is intruding on its own merits; not as a tradition but a truth. The father of some such Anglican or American Puritan family will find, very often, that all his children are breaking away from his own more or less Christian compromise (regarded as normal in the nineteenth century) and going off in various directions after various faiths or fashions which he would call fads. One of his sons will become a Socialist and hang up a portrait of Lenin; one of his daughters will become a Spiritualist and play with a planchette; another daughter will go over to Christian Science and it is quite likely that another son will go over to Rome. The point is, for the moment, that from the point of view of the father, and even in a sense of the family, all these things act after the manner of new religions, of great movements, of enthusiasms that carry young people off their feet and leave older people bewildered or annoyed. Catholicism indeed, even more than the others, is often spoken of as if it were actually one of the wild passions of youth. Optimistic aunts and uncles say that the youth will "get over it," as if it were a childish love affair or that unfortunate business with the barmaid. Darker and sterner aunts and uncles, perhaps at a rather earlier period, used actually to talk about it as an indecent indulgence, as if its literature were literally a sort of pornography. Newman remarks quite naturally, as if there were nothing odd about it at the time, that an undergraduate found with an ascetic manual or a book of monastic meditations was under a sort of cloud or taint, as having been caught with "a bad book" in his possession. He had been wallowing in the sensual pleasure of Nones or inflaming his lusts by contemplating an incorrect number of candles. It is perhaps no longer the custom to regard conversion as a form of dissipation; but it is still common to regard conversion as a form of revolt. And as regards the established convention of much of the modern world, it is a revolt. The worthy merchant of the middle class, the worthy farmer of the Middle West, when he sends his son to college, does now feel a faint alarm lest the boy should fall among thieves, in the sense of Communists; but he has the same sort of fear lest he should fall among Catholics.

Now he has no fear lest he should fall among Calvinists. He has no fear that his children will become seventeenth-century Supralapsarians,[1] however much he may dislike that doctrine. He is not even particularly troubled by the possibility of their adopting the extreme solfidian[2] conceptions once common among some of the more extravagant Methodists. He is not likely to await with terror the telegram that will inform him that his son has become a Fifth-Monarchy man,[3] any more than that he has joined the Albigensians.[4]

[1] Supralapsarianism is a variety of Calvinist predestinarianism that decreed both election and reprobation before (*supra*) the fall (*lapsus*).

[2] Solfidianism is the doctrine of justification by faith alone (*sola fide*); it totally excludes merit and good works.

[3] The Fifth-Monarchy men were Puritan radicals who flourished during the English Civil War of the 1640s. They believed that Christ would return soon to establish his reign on earth, the "Fifth Monarchy".

[4] Albigensianism, a form of Manichaean dualism, arose in southern France in the late twelfth century. In 1208 Pope Innocent III called for a crusade to stamp out the heresy; the orthodox forces prevailed by the 1220s.

He does not exactly lie awake at night wondering whether Tom at Oxford has become a Lutheran any more than a Lollard.[5] All these religions he dimly recognises as dead religions; or at any rate as old religions. And he is only frightened of new religions. He is only frightened of those fresh, provocative, paradoxical new notions that fly to the young people's heads. But amongst these dangerous juvenile attractions he does in practice class the freshness and novelty of Rome.

Now this is rather odd; because Rome is not so very new. Among these annoying new religions, one is rather an old religion; but it is the only old religion that is so new. When it was originally and really new, no doubt a Roman father often found himself in the same position as the Anglican or Puritan father. He too might find all his children going strange ways and deserting the household gods and the sacred temple of the Capitol. He too might find that one of those children had joined the Christians in their Ecclesia and possibly in their Catacombs. But he would have found that, of his other children, one cared for nothing but the Mysteries of Orpheus, another was inclined to follow Mithras, another was a Neo-Pythagorean who had learned vegetarianism from the Hindoos, and so on. Though the Roman father, unlike the Victorian father, might have the pleasure of exercising the *patria potestas*[6] and cutting off the heads of all the heretics, he could not cut off the stream of all the heresies. Only by this time most of the streams have run rather dry. It is now seldom necessary for the anxious parent to warn his children against the undesirable society of the Bull of Mithras, or even to wean him from the exclusive contemplation of Orpheus; and though we have vegetarians always with us, they mostly know more about proteids than about Pythagoras. But that other youthful extravagance is still youthful. That other new religion is once again new. That one fleeting fashion has refused to fleet; and that ancient bit of modernity is still modern. It is still to the Protestant parent now exactly what it

[5] Lollardy developed in fourteenth-century England from the teachings of John Wyclif (c. 1320–84), whose anti-clericalism and criticism of the Church's wealth and temporal power anticipated ideas that would emerge fully in the Reformation.

[6] In ancient Rome, *patria potestas* was the father's absolute authority over members of his household.

was to the pagan parent then. We might say simply that it is a nuisance; but anyhow it is a novelty. It is not simply what the father is used to, or even what the son is used to. It is coming in as something fresh and disturbing, whether as it came to the Greeks who were always seeking some new thing, or as it came to the shepherds who first heard the cry upon the hills of the good news that our language calls the Gospel. We can explain the fact of the Greeks in the time of St. Paul regarding it as a new thing, because it was a new thing. But who will explain why it is still as new to the last of the converts as it was to the first of the shepherds? It is as if a man a hundred years old entered the Olympian games among the young Greek athletes; which would surely have been the basis of a Greek legend. There is something almost as legendary about the religion that is two thousand years old now appearing as a rival of the new religions. That is what has to be explained and cannot be explained away; nothing can turn the legend into a myth. We have seen with our own eyes and heard with our own ears this great modern quarrel between young Catholics and old Protestants; and it is the first step to recognise in any study of modern conversion.

I am not going to talk about numbers and statistics, though I may say something about them later. The first fact to realise is a difference of substance which falsifies all the difference of size. The great majority of Protestant bodies to-day, whether they are strong or weak, are not strengthened in this particular fashion; by the actual attraction of their new followers to their old doctrines. A young man will suddenly become a Catholic priest, or even a Catholic monk, because he has a spontaneous and even impatient personal enthusiasm for the doctrine of Virginity as it appeared to St. Catherine or St. Clare. But how many men become Baptist ministers because they have a personal horror of the idea of an innocent infant coming unconsciously to Christ? How many honest Presbyterian ministers in Scotland really want to go back to John Knox, as a Catholic mystic might want to go back to John of the Cross? These men inherit positions which they feel they can hold with reasonable consistency and general agreement; but they do inherit them. For them religion is tradition. We Catholics naturally do not sneer at tradition; but we say that in this case it is really tradition and nothing else. Not one man in a hundred of these people would ever have joined his present communion if he had been born outside it. Not one man in a thousand of them would have invented anything like his church formulas if they had not been laid down for him. None of them has any real reason for being in their own particular church, whatever good reason they may still have for being outside ours. In other words, the old creed of their communion has ceased to function as a fresh and stimulating idea. It is at best a motto or a war cry and at the worst a catchword. But it is not meeting contemporary ideas like a contemporary idea. In their time and in their turn we believe that those other contemporary ideas will also prove their mortality by having also become mottoes and catchwords and traditions. A century or two hence Spiritualism may be a tradition and Socialism may be a tradition and Christian Science may be a tradition. But Catholicism will not be a tradition. It will still be a nuisance and a new and dangerous thing.

These are the general considerations which govern any personal study of conversion to the Catholic faith. The Church has defended tradition in a time which stupidly denied and despised tradition. But that is simply because the Church is always the only thing defending whatever is at the moment stupidly despised. It is already beginning to appear as the only champion of reason in the twentieth century, as it was the only champion of tradition in the nineteenth. We know that the higher mathematics is trying to deny that two and two make four and the higher mysticism to imagine something that is beyond good and evil. Amid all these antirational philosophies, ours will remain the only rational philosophy. In the same spirit the Church did indeed point out the value of tradition to a time which treated it as quite valueless. The nineteenth-century neglect of tradition and mania for mere documents were altogether nonsensical. They amounted to saying that men always tell lies to children but men never make mistakes in books. But though our sympathies are traditional because they are human, it is not that part of the thing which stamps it as divine. The mark of the Faith is not tradition; it is conversion. It is the miracle by which men find truth in spite of tradition and often with the rending of all the roots of humanity.

It is with the nature of this process that I propose to deal; and it is difficult to deal with it without introducing something of a personal element. My own is only a very trivial case but naturally it is the case I know best; and I shall be compelled in the pages that follow to take many illustrations from it. I have therefore thought it well to put first this general note on the nature of the movement in my time; to show that I am well aware that it is a very much larger and even a very much later movement than is implied in describing my own life or generation. I believe it will be more and more an issue for the rising generation and for the generation after that, as they discover the actual alternative in the awful actualities of our time. And Catholics when they stand up together and sing "Faith of our Fathers" may realise almost with amusement that they might well be singing "Faith of our Children." And in many cases the return has been so recent as almost to deserve the description of a Children's Crusade.

II

THE OBVIOUS BLUNDERS

I have noted that Catholicism really is in the twentieth century what it was in the second century; it is the New Religion. Indeed its very antiquity preserves an attitude of novelty. I have always thought it striking and even stirring that in the venerable invocation of the "Tantum Ergo," which for us seems to come loaded with accumulated ages, there is still the language of innovation; of the antique document that must yield to a new rite. For us the hymn is something of an antique document itself. But the rite is always new.

But if a convert is to write of conversion he must try to retrace his steps out of that shrine back into that ultimate wilderness where he once really believed that this eternal youth was only the "Old Religion." It is a thing exceedingly difficult to do and not often done well, and I for one have little hope of doing it even tolerably well. The difficulty was expressed to me by another convert who said, "I cannot explain why I am a Catholic; because now that I am a Catholic I cannot imagine myself as anything else." Nevertheless, it is right to make the imaginative effort. It is not bigotry to be certain we are right; but it is bigotry to be unable to imagine how we might possibly have gone wrong. It is my duty to try to understand what H. G. Wells can possibly mean when he says that the mediaeval Church did not care for education but only for imposing dogmas; it is my duty to speculate (however darkly) on what can have made an intelligent man like Arnold Bennett[7] stone-blind to all the plainest facts about Spain; it is my duty to find if I can the thread of connected thought in George Moore's[8] various condemnations of Catholic Ireland; and it is equally my duty to labour till I understand the strange mental state of G. K. Chesterton when he really assumed that the Catholic Church was a sort of ruined abbey, almost as deserted as Stonehenge.

[7] Arnold Bennett (1867–1931) was an English novelist, journalist and playwright.
[8] George Moore (1852–1933) was an Irish novelist who contributed to the Irish literary flowering of the early twentieth century.

I must say first that, in my own case, it was at worst a matter of slights rather than slanders. Many converts far more important than I have had to wrestle with a hundred devils of howling falsehood; with a swarm of lies and libels. I owe it to the liberal and Universalist atmosphere of my family, of Stopford Brooke[9] and the Unitarian preachers they followed, that I was always just sufficiently enlightened to be out of the reach of Maria Monk.[10] Nevertheless, as this is but a private privilege for which I have to be thankful, it is necessary to say something of what I might be tempted to call the obvious slanders, but that better men than I have not always seen that the slander was obvious. I do not think that they exercise much influence on the generation that is younger than mine. The worst temptation of the most pagan youth is not so much to denounce monks for breaking their vow as to wonder at them for keeping it. But there is a state of transition that must be allowed for in which a vague Protestant prejudice would rather like to have it both ways. There is still a sort of woolly-minded philistine who would be content to consider a friar a knave for his unchastity and a fool for his chastity. In other words, these dying calumnies are dying but not dead; and there are still enough people who may still be held back by such crude and clumsy obstacles that it is necessary to some extent to clear them away. After that we can consider what may be called the real obstacles, the real difficulties we find, which, as a fact, are generally the very opposite of the difficulties we are told about. But let us consider the evidence of all these things being black, before we go on to the inconvenient fact of their being white.

The usual protest of the Protestant, that the Church of Rome is afraid of the Bible, did not, as I shall explain in a moment, have any great terrors for me at any time. This was by no merit of my own, but by the accident of my age and situation. For I grew up in a

[9] Stopford Brooke (1832–1916), a prominent Anglican preacher in Ireland, repudiated his church in 1880 because he could no longer accept its teachings.

[10] In 1836 Maria Monk, claiming to have escaped from a convent in Montreal, published the salacious *Awful Disclosures of Maria Monk*. Although her tale was quickly exposed as a hoax, the book became a standard weapon used by anti-Catholics.

world in which the Protestants, who had just proved that Rome did
not believe the Bible, were excitedly discovering that they did not
believe the Bible themselves. Some of them even tried to combine
the two condemnations and say that they were steps of progress.
The next step in progress consisted in a man kicking his father for
having locked up a book of such beauty and value, a book which the
son then proceeded to tear into a thousand pieces. I early discovered
that progress is worse than Protestantism so far as stupidity is concerned. But most of the free-thinkers who were friends of mine happened to think sufficiently freely to see that the Higher Criticism
was much more of an attack on Protestant Bible-worship than on
Roman authority. Anyhow, my family and friends were more concerned with the opening of the book of Darwin than the book of
Daniel; and most of them regarded the Hebrew Scriptures as if they
were Hittite sculptures. But, even then, it would seem odd to worship the sculptures as gods and then smash them as idols and still go
on blaming somebody else for not having worshipped them enough.
But here again it is hard for me to know how far my own experience
is representative, or whether it would not be well to say more of
these purely Protestant prejudices and doubts than I, from my own
experience, am able to say.

The Church is a house with a hundred gates; and no two men
enter at exactly the same angle. Mine was at least as much Agnostic
as Anglican, though I accepted for a time the borderland of Anglicanism; but only on the assumption that it could really be Anglo-
Catholicism. There is a distinction of ultimate intention there which
in the vague English atmosphere is often missed. It is not a difference
of degree but of definite aim. There are High Churchmen as much as
Low Churchmen who are concerned first and last to save the
Church of England. Some of them think it can be saved by calling it
Catholic, or making it Catholic, or believing that it is Catholic; but
that is what they want to save. But I did not start out with the idea
of saving the English Church, but of finding the Catholic Church.
If the two were one, so much the better; but I had never conceived
of Catholicism as a sort of showy attribute or attraction to be tacked
on to my own national body, but as the inmost soul of the true body,

wherever it might be. It might be said that Anglo-Catholicism was simply my own uncompleted conversion to Catholicism. But it was from a position originally much more detached and indefinite that I had been converted, an atmosphere if not agnostic at least pantheistic or unitarian. To this I owe the fact that I find it very difficult to take some of the Protestant propositions even seriously. What is any man who has been in the real outer world, for instance, to make of the everlasting cry that Catholic traditions are condemned by the Bible? It indicates a jumble of topsy-turvy tests and tail-foremost arguments, of which I never could at any time see the sense. The ordinary sensible sceptic or pagan is standing in the street (in the supreme character of the man in the street) and he sees a procession go by of the priests of some strange cult, carrying their object of worship under a canopy, some of them wearing high head-dresses and carrying symbolical staffs, others carrying scrolls and sacred records, others carrying sacred images and lighted candles before them, others sacred relics in caskets or cases, and so on. I can understand the spectator saying, "This is all hocus-pocus"; I can even understand him, in moments of irritation, breaking up the procession, throwing down the images, tearing up the scrolls, dancing on the priests and anything else that might express that general view. I can understand his saying, "Your croziers are bosh, your candles are bosh, your statues and scrolls and relics and all the rest of it are bosh." But in what conceivable frame of mind does he rush in to select one particular scroll of the scriptures of this one particular group (a scroll which had always belonged to them and been a part of their hocus-pocus, if it was hocus-pocus); why in the world should the man in the street say that one particular scroll was *not* bosh, but was the one and only truth by which all the other things were to be condemned? Why should it not be as superstitious to worship the scrolls as the statues, of that one particular procession? Why should it not be as reasonable to preserve the statues as the scrolls, by the tenets of that particular creed? To say to the priests, "Your statues and scrolls are condemned by our common sense," is sensible. To say, "Your statues are condemned by your scrolls, and we are going to worship one part of your procession and wreck the rest," is not sensible from any standpoint, least of all that of the man in the street.

Similarly, I could never take seriously the fear of the priest, as of something unnatural and unholy; a dangerous man in the home. Why should a man who wanted to be wicked encumber himself with special and elaborate promises to be good? There might sometimes be a reason for a priest being a profligate. But what was the reason for a profligate being a priest? There are many more lucrative walks of life in which a person with such shining talents for vice and villainy might have made a brighter use of his gifts. Why should a man encumber himself with vows that nobody could expect him to take and he did not himself expect to keep? Would any man make himself poor in order that he might become avaricious; or take a vow of chastity frightfully difficult to keep in order to get into a little more trouble when he did not keep it? All that early and sensational picture of the sins of Rome always seemed to me silly even when I was a boy or an unbeliever; and I cannot describe how I passed out of it because I was never in it. I remember asking some friends at Cambridge, people of the Puritan tradition, why in the world they were so afraid of Papists; why a priest in somebody's house was a peril or an Irish servant the beginning of a pestilence. I asked them why they could not simply disagree with Papists and say so, as they did with Theosophists[11] or Anarchists. They seemed at once pleased and shocked with my daring, as if I had undertaken to convert a burglar or tame a mad dog. Perhaps their alarm was really wiser than my bravado. Anyhow I had not then the most shadowy notion that the burglar would convert me. That, however, I am inclined to think, is the subconscious intuition in the whole business. It must either mean that they suspect that our religion has something about it so wrong that the hint of it is bad for anybody; or else that it has something so right that the presence of it would convert anybody. To do them justice, I think most of them darkly suspect the second and not the first.

A shade more plausible than the notion that Popish priests merely seek after evil was the notion that they are exceptionally ready to seek good by means of evil. In vulgar language, it is the notion

[11] Theosophy, a syncretistic faith that combined elements from Christianity and various Asian religions, was founded in New York City in 1875 by Helena Blavatsky.

that if they are not sensual they are always sly. To dissipate this is a mere matter of experience; but before I had any experience I had seen some objections to the thing even in theory. The theory attributed to the Jesuits was very often almost identical with the practice adopted by nearly everybody I knew. Everybody in society practised verbal economies, equivocations and often direct fictions, without any sense of essential falsehood. Every gentleman was expected to say he would be delighted to dine with a bore; every lady said that somebody else's baby was beautiful if she thought it as ugly as sin; for they did not think it a sin to avoid saying ugly things. This might be right or wrong; but it was absurd to pillory half a dozen Popish priests for a crime committed daily by half a million Protestant laymen. The only difference was that the Jesuits had been worried enough about the matter to try to make rules and limitations saving as much verbal veracity as possible; whereas the happy Protestants were not worried about it at all, but told lies from morning to night as merrily and innocently as the birds sing in the trees. The fact is, of course, that the modern world is full of an utterly lawless casuistry because the Jesuits were prevented from making a lawful casuistry. But every man is a casuist or a lunatic.

It is true that this general truth was hidden from many by certain definite assertions. I can only call them, in simple language, Protestant lies about Catholic lying. The men who repeated them were not necessarily lying, because they were repeating. But the statements were of the same lucid and precise order as a statement that the Pope has three legs or that Rome is situated at the North Pole. There is no more doubt about their nature than that. One of them, for instance, is the positive statement, once heard everywhere and still heard often: "Roman Catholics are taught that anything is lawful if done for the good of the Church." This is not the fact; and there is an end of it. It refers to a definite statement of an institution whose statements are very definite; and it can be proved to be totally false. Here as always the critics cannot see that they are trying to have it both ways. They are always complaining that our creed is cut and dried; that we are told what to believe and must believe nothing else; that it is all written down for us in bulls and confessions of faith. In so far as this is true, it brings a matter like this to the point of legal and literal truth, which can be tested; and so tested, it is a lie. But even here I was saved at a very early stage by noticing a curious fact. I noticed that those who were most ready to blame priests for relying on rigid formulas seldom took the trouble to find out what the formulas were. I happened to pick up some of the amusing pamphlets of James Britten, as I might have picked up any other pamphlets of any other propaganda; but they set me on the track of that delightful branch of literature which he called Protestant Fiction. I found some of that fiction on my own account, dipping into novels by Joseph Hocking[12] and others. I am only concerned with them here to illustrate this particular and curious fact about exactitude. I could not understand why these romancers never took the trouble to find out a few elementary facts about the thing they denounced. The facts might easily have helped the denunciation, where the fictions discredited it. There were any number of real Catholic doctrines I should then have thought disgraceful to the Church. There are any number which I can still easily imagine being made to look disgraceful to the Church. But the enemies of the Church never found these real rocks of offence. They never looked for them. They never looked for anything. They seemed to have simply made up out of their own heads a number of phrases, such as a Scarlet Woman of deficient intellect might be supposed to launch on the world; and left it at that. Boundless freedom reigned; it was not treated as if it were a question of fact at all. A priest might say anything about the Faith; because a Protestant might say anything about the priest. These novels were padded with pronouncements like this one, for instance, which I happen to remember: "Disobeying a priest is the one sin for which there is no absolution. We term it a reserved case." Now obviously a man writing like that is simply imagining what might exist; it has never occurred to him to go and ask if it does exist. He has heard the phrase "a reserved case" and considers, in a poetic reverie, what he shall make it mean. He does not go and ask the nearest priest what it does mean. He does not look it up in an

---

[12] Joseph Hocking (1860–1937) was an English novelist and preacher in the United Methodist Free Church.

encyclopaedia or any ordinary work of reference. There is no doubt about the fact that it simply means a case reserved for ecclesiastical superiors and not to be settled finally by the priest. That may be a fact to be denounced; but anyhow it is a fact. But the man much prefers to denounce his own fancy. Any manual would tell him that there is no sin "for which there is no absolution"; not disobeying the priest; not assassinating the Pope. It would be easy to find out these facts and quite easy to base a Protestant invective upon them. It puzzled me very much, even at that early stage, to imagine why people bringing controversial charges against a powerful and prominent institution should thus neglect to test their own case, and should draw in this random way on their own imagination. It did not make me any more inclined to be a Catholic; in those days the very idea of such a thing would have seemed crazy. But it did save me from swallowing all the solid and solemn assertion about what Jesuits said and did. I did not accept quite so completely as others the well-ascertained and widely accepted fact that "Roman Catholics may do anything for the good of the Church"; because I had already learned to smile at equally accepted truths like "Disobeying a priest is the one sin for which there is no absolution." I never dreamed that the Roman religion was true; but I knew that its accusers, for some reason or other, were curiously inaccurate.

It is strange to me to go back to these things now, and to think that I ever took them even as seriously as that. But I was not very serious even then; and certainly I was not serious long. The last lingering shadow of the Jesuit, gliding behind curtains and concealing himself in cupboards, faded from my young life about the time when I first caught a distant glimpse of the late Father Bernard Vaughan.[13] He was the only Jesuit I ever knew in those days; and as you could generally hear him half a mile away, he seemed to be ill-selected for the duties of a curtain-glider. It has always struck me as curious that this Jesuit raised a storm by refusing to be Jesuitical (in the journalese sense I mean), by refusing to substitute smooth equivocation and verbal evasion for a brute fact. Because he talked

[13] Father Bernard Vaughan (1847–1922) was an English Jesuit famed for his preaching and his work among the poor in Manchester and London.

about "killing Germans" when Germans had to be killed, all our shifty and shamefaced morality was shocked at him. And none of those protesting Protestants took thought for a moment to realise that they were showing all the shuffling insincerity they attributed to the Jesuits, and the Jesuit was showing all the plain candour that they claimed for the Protestant.

I could give a great many other instances besides these I have given of the hidden Bible, the profligate priest or the treacherous Jesuit. I could go steadily through the list of all these more old-fashioned charges against Rome and show how they affected me, or rather why they did not affect me. But my only purpose here is to point out, as a preliminary, that they did not affect me at all. I had all the difficulties that a heathen would have had in becoming a Catholic in the fourth century. I had very few of the difficulties that a Protestant had, from the seventeenth to the nineteenth. And I owe this to men whose memories I shall always honour; to my father and his circle and the literary tradition of men like George Macdonald[14] and the Universalists of the Victorian Age. If I was born on the wrong side of the Roman wall, at least I was not born on the wrong side of the No Popery quarrel; and if I did not inherit a fully civilised faith, neither did I inherit a barbarian feud. The people I was born amongst wished to be just to Catholics if they did not always understand them; and I should be very thankless if I did not record of them that (like a very much more valuable convert) I can say I was born free.

I will add one example to illustrate this point, because it leads us on to larger matters. After a long time—I might almost say after a lifetime—I have at last begun to realise what the worthy Liberal or Socialist of Balham or Battersea really means when he says he is an Internationalist and that humanity should be preferred to the narrowness of nations. It dawned on me quite suddenly, after I had talked to such a man for many hours, that of course he had really been brought up to believe that God's Englishmen were the Chosen Race. Very likely his father or uncle actually thought they were the lost Ten Tribes. Anyhow, everything from his daily paper to his

---

[14] George Macdonald (1824–1905) was a Scottish poet and novelist.

weekly sermon assumed that they were the salt of the earth, and especially that they were the salt of the sea. His people had never thought outside their British nationality. They lived in an empire on which the sun never set, or possibly never rose. Their Church was emphatically the Church of England—even if it was a chapel. Their religion was the Bible that went everywhere with the Union Jack. And when I realised that, I realised the whole story. That was why they were excited by the exceedingly dull theory of the Internationalist. That was why the brotherhood of nations, which to me was a truism, to them was a trumpet. That was why it seemed such a thrilling paradox to say that we must love foreigners; it had in it the divine paradox that we must love enemies. That was why the Internationalist was always planning deputations and visits to foreign capitals and heart-to-heart talks and hands across the sea. It was the marvel of discovering that foreigners had hands, let alone hearts. There was in that excitement a sort of stifled cry: "Look! Frenchmen also have two legs! See! Germans have noses in the same place as we!" Now a Catholic, especially a born Catholic, can never understand that attitude, because from the first his whole religion is rooted in the unity of the race of Adam, the one and only Chosen Race. He is loyal to his own country; indeed he is generally ardently loyal to it, such local affections being in other ways very natural to his religious life, with its shrines and relics. But just as the relic follows upon the religion, so the local loyalty follows on the universal brotherhood of all men. The Catholic says, "Of course we must love all men; but what do all men love? They love their lands, their lawful boundaries, the memories of their fathers. That is the justification of being national, that it is normal." But the Protestant patriot really never thought of any patriotism except his own. In that sense Protestantism is patriotism. But unfortunately it is only patriotism. It starts with it and never gets beyond it. We start with mankind and go beyond it to all the varied loves and traditions of mankind. There never was a more illuminating flash than that which lit up the last moment of one of the most glorious of English Protestants; one of the most Protestant and one of the most English. For that is the meaning of that phrase of Nurse Cavell,[15]

[15] Edith Cavell (1865–1915) was an English nurse executed as a spy by the Germans during World War I.

herself the noblest martyr of our modern religion of nationality, when the very shaft of the white sun of death shone deep into her mind and she cried aloud, like one who had just discovered something, "I see now that patriotism is not enough."

There was this in common between the Catholics to whom I have come and the Liberals among whom I was born: neither of them would ever have imagined for a moment that patriotism was enough. But that insular idealism by which that great lady lived really had taught her unconsciously from childhood that patriotism *was* enough. Not seldom has the English lady appeared in history as a heroine; but generally as facing and defying strangers or savages, not specially as feeling them as fellows and equals. Those last words of the English martyr in Belgium have often been quoted by mere cosmopolitans; but cosmopolitans are the last people really to understand them. *They* are generally trying to prove, not that patriotism is not enough, but that it is a great deal too much. The point is here that hundreds of the most heroic and high-minded people in Protestant countries have really assumed that it is enough to be a patriot. The most careless and cynical of Catholics knows better; and so did the most vague and visionary of Universalists. Of all the Protestant difficulties, which I here find it hard to imagine, this is perhaps the most common and in many ways commendable: the fact that the normal British subject begins by being so very British. By accident I did not. The tradition I heard in my youth, the simple, the too simple truths inherited from Priestly[16] and Martineau,[17] had in them something of that grand generalisation upon men as men which, in the first of those great figures, faced the howling Jingoism of the French Wars[18] and defied even the legend of Trafalgar. It is to that tradition that I owe the fact, whether it be an advantage or a disadvantage, that I cannot worthily analyse the very heroic virtues of a

[16] Joseph Priestley (1733–1804) was an English political radical, scientist and key figure in the development of Unitarianism. Chesterton spells the name incorrectly.

[17] James Martineau (1805–1900) was an English philosopher and Unitarian minister.

[18] The French Wars were a series of conflicts between England and France that lasted from 1793 until the defeat of Napoleon in 1815.

Plymouth Brother[19] whose only centre is Plymouth. For that rationalism, defective as it was, began long ago in the same central civilisation in which the Church herself began; if it has ended in the Church it began long ago in the Republic: in a world where all these flags and frontiers were unknown; where all these state establishments and national sects were unthinkable; a vast cosmopolitan cosmos that had never heard the name of England, or conceived the image of a kingdom separate and at war; in that vast pagan peace which was the matrix of all these mysteries, which had forgotten the free cities and had not dreamed of the small nationalities; which knew only humanity, the *humanum genus,* and the name of Rome.

The Catholic Church loves nations as she loves men; because they are her children. But they certainly are her children, in the sense that they are secondary to her in time and process of production. This is, as it happens, a very good example of a fallacy that often confuses discussion about the convert. The same people who call the convert a pervert, and especially a traitor to patriotism, very often use the other catchword to the effect that he is forced to believe this or that. But it is not really a question of what a man is made to believe but of what he must believe; what he cannot help believing. He cannot disbelieve in an elephant when he has seen one; and he cannot treat the Church as a child when he has discovered that she is his mother. She is not only his mother but his country's mother in being much older and more aboriginal than his country. She is such a mother not in sentimental feeling but in historical fact. He cannot think one thing when he knows the contrary thing. He cannot think that Christianity was invented by Penda of Mercia,[20] who sent missionaries to the heathen Augustine and the rude and barbarous Gregory.[21] He cannot think that the Church first rose in the middle of the British Empire, and not of the Roman Empire. He cannot think that England existed, with cricket and fox-hunting and the

[19] The Plymouth Brethren, a millenarian sect, arose in Plymouth, England, in the 1830s.

[20] Penda of Mercia was a pagan Anglo-Saxon king of the seventh century.

[21] In 596 Pope Gregory I sent Augustine and forty monks to preach the gospel in England. Augustine became the first archbishop of Canterbury, and died in 604.

Jacobean translation[22] all complete, when Rome was founded or when Christ was born. It is no good talking about his being "free" to believe these things. He is exactly as free to believe them as he is to believe that a horse has feathers or that the sun is pea green. He cannot believe them when once he fully realises them; and among such things is the notion that the national claim upon a good patriot is in its nature more absolute, ancient and authoritative than the claim of the whole religious culture which first mapped out its territories and anointed its kings. That religious culture does indeed encourage him to fight to the last for his country, as for his family. But that is because the religious culture is generous and imaginative and humane and knows that men must have intimate and individual ties. But those secondary loyalties are secondary in time and logic to the law of universal morality which justifies them. And if the patriot is such a fool as to force the issue against that universal tradition from which his own patriotism descends, if he presses his claim to priority over the primitive law of the whole earth—then he will have brought it on himself if he is answered with the pulverising plainness of the Book of Job. As God said to the man, "Where were you when the foundations of the world were laid?"[23] We might well say to the nation, "Where were you when the foundations of the Church were laid?" And the nation will not know in the least what to answer—if it should wish to answer—but will be forced to put its hand upon its mouth, if only like one who yawns and falls asleep.

I have taken this particular case of patriotism because it concerns at least an emotion in which I profoundly believe and happen to feel strongly. I have always done my best to defend it; though I have sometimes become suspect by sympathising with other people's patriotism besides my own. But I cannot see how it can be defended except as part of a larger morality; and the Catholic morality happens to be one of the very few large moralities now ready to defend it. But the Church defends it as one of the duties of men and not as the whole duty of man; as it was in the Prussian theory of the State

[22] The Jacobean translation is the King James Version of the Bible, completed in 1611.
[23] The quotation is from Job 38:4.

and too often in the British theory of the Empire. And for this the Catholic rests, exactly as the Universalist Unitarian rested, upon the actual fact of a human unity anterior to all these healthy and natural human divisions. But it is absurd to treat the Church as a novel conspiracy attacking the State, when the State was only recently a novel experiment arising within the Church. It is absurd to forget that the Church itself received the first loyalties of men who had not yet even conceived the notion of founding such a national and separate state; that the Faith really was not only the faith of our fathers, but the faith of our fathers before they had even named our fatherland.

III

THE REAL OBSTACLES

In the last chapter I have dealt in a preliminary fashion with the Protestant case in the conventional controversial sense. I have dealt with the objections which I suspected very early of being prejudices and which I now know to be prejudices. I have dealt last and at the greatest length with what I believe to be the noblest of all the prejudices of Protestantism: that which is simply founded on patriotism. I do not think patriotism is necessarily prejudice; but I am quite sure it must be prejudice and nothing else but prejudice, unless it is covered by some common morality. And a patriotism that does not allow other people to be patriots is not a morality but an immorality. Even such a tribal prejudice, however, is a more respectable thing than most of the rags and tatters of stale slander and muddle-headedness which I am obliged to put first as the official policy of the opposition to the Church. These stale stories seem to count for a great deal with people who are resolved to keep far away from the Church. I do not believe they ever counted with anybody who had begun to draw near to it. When a man really sees the Church, even if he dislikes what he sees, he does not see what he had expected to dislike. Even if he wants to slay it he is no longer able to slander it; though he hates it at sight, what he sees is not what he looked to see; in that place he may gain a new passion but he loses his old prejudice. There drops from him the holy armour of his invincible ignorance; he can never be so stupid again. If he has a ready mind he can doubtless set his new reasons in some sort of order and even attempt to link them with his lost tradition. But the thing he hates is there; and the last chapter was wholly devoted to the study of things that are not there.

The real reasons are almost the opposite of the recognised reasons. The real difficulties are almost the opposite of the recognised difficulties. This is connected, of course, with a general fact, now so large and obvious but still not clearly comprehended and confessed.

The whole case of Protestantism against Catholicism has been turned clean round and is facing the contrary way. On practically every single point on which the Reformation accused the Church, the modern world has not only acquitted the Church of the crime, but has actually charged it with the opposite crime. It is as if the reformers had mobbed the Pope for being a miser, and then the court had not only acquitted him but had censured him for his extravagance in scattering money among the mob. The principle of modern Protestantism seems to be that so long as we go on shouting "To hell with the Pope" there is room for the widest differences of opinion about whether he should go to the hell of the misers or the hell of the spendthrifts. This is what is meant by a broad basis for Christianity and the statement that there is room for many different opinions side by side. When the reformer says that the principles of the Reformation give freedom to different points of view, he means that they give freedom to the Universalist to curse Rome for having too much predestination and to the Calvinist to curse her for having too little. He means that in that happy family there is a place for the No Popery man who finds Purgatory too tender-hearted and also for the other No Popery man who finds Hell too harsh. He means that the same description can somehow be made to cover the Tolstoyan who blames priests because they permit patriotism and the Diehard who blames priests because they represent Internationalism. After all, the essential aim of true Christianity is that priests should be blamed; and who are we that we should set narrow dogmatic limits to the various ways in which various temperaments may desire to blame them? Why should we allow a cold difficulty of the logician, technically called a contradiction in terms, to stand between us and the warm and broadening human brotherhood of all who are full of sincere and unaffected dislike of their neighbours? Religion is of the heart, not of the head; and as long as all our hearts are full of a hatred for everything that our fathers loved, we can go on flatly contradicting each other for ever about what there is to be hated.

Such is the larger and more liberal modern attack upon the Church. It is quite inconsistent with the old doctrinal attack; but it does not propose to lose the advantages arising from any sort of attack. But

in a somewhat analogous fashion, it will be found that the real difficulties of a modern convert are almost the direct contrary of those
which were alleged by the more ancient Protestants. Protestant
pamphlets do not touch even remotely any of the real hesitations
that he feels; and even Catholic pamphlets have often been concerned
too much with answering the Protestant pamphlets. Indeed the only
sense in which the priests and propagandists of Catholicism can really
be said to be behind the times is that they sometimes go on flogging
a dead horse and killing a heresy long after it has killed itself. But
even that is, properly understood, a fault on the side of chivalry. The
preacher, and even the persecutor, really takes the heresy more seriously than it is seen ultimately to deserve; the inquisitor has more
respect for the heresy than the heretics have. Still, it is true that the
grounds of suspicion or fear that do really fill the convert, and
sometimes paralyse him at the very point of conversion, have really
nothing in the world to do with this old crop of crude slanders and
fallacies, and are often the very inversion of them.

The short way of putting it is to say that he is no longer afraid of
the vices but very much afraid of the virtues of Catholicism. For instance, he has forgotten all about the old nonsense of the cunning
lies of the confessional, in his lively and legitimate alarm of the
truthfulness of the confessional. He does not recoil from its insincerity but from its sincerity; nor is he necessarily insincere in doing
so. Realism is really a rock of offence; it is not at all unnatural to
shrink from it; and most modern realists only manage to like it because they are careful to be realistic about other people. He is near
enough to the sacrament of penance to have discovered its realism
and not near enough to have yet discovered its reasonableness and its
common sense. Most of those who have gone through this experience have a certain right to say, like the old soldier to his ignorant comrade, "Yes, I was afraid; and if you were half as much
afraid, you would run away." Perhaps it is just as well that people go
through this stage before discovering how very little there is to be
afraid of. In any case, I will say little more of that example here, having a feeling that absolution, like death and marriage, is a thing that
a man ought to find out for himself. It will be enough to say that

this is perhaps the supreme example of the fact that the Faith is a paradox that measures more within than without. If that be true of the smallest church, it is truer still of the yet smaller confessional-box, that is like a church within a church. It is almost a good thing that nobody outside should know what gigantic generosity, and even geniality, can be locked up in a box, as the legendary casket held the heart of the giant. It is a satisfaction, and almost a joke, that it is only in a dark corner and a cramped space that any man can discover that mountain of magnanimity.

It is the same with all the other points of attack, especially the old ones. The man who has come so far as that along the road has long left behind him the notion that the priest will force him to abandon his will. But he is not unreasonably dismayed at the extent to which he may have to use his will. He is not frightened because, after taking this drug, he will be henceforward irresponsible. But he is very much frightened because he will be responsible. He will have somebody to be responsible to and he will know what he is responsible for; two uncomfortable conditions which his more fortunate fellow-creatures have nowadays entirely escaped. There are of course many other examples of the same principle: that there is indeed an interval of acute doubt, which is, strictly speaking, rather fear than doubt, since in some cases at least (as I shall point out elsewhere) there is actually least doubt when there is most fear.

But anyhow, the doubts are hardly ever of the sort suggested by ordinary anti-Catholic propaganda; and it is surely time that such propagandists brought themselves more in touch with the real problem. The Catholic is scarcely ever frightened of the Protestant picture of Catholicism; but he is sometimes frightened of the Catholic picture of Catholicism; which may be a good reason for not disproportionately stressing the difficult or puzzling parts of the scheme. For the convert's sake, it should also be remembered that one foolish word from inside does more harm than a hundred thousand foolish words from outside. The latter he has already learned to expect, like a blind hail or rain beating upon the Ark; but the voices from within, even the most casual and accidental, he is already prepared to regard as holy or more than human; and though this is unfair to people who only profess to be human beings, it is a fact that Catholics ought to remember. There is many a convert who has reached a stage at which no word from any Protestant or pagan could any longer hold him back. Only the word of a Catholic can keep him from Catholicism.

It is quite false, in my experience, to say that Jesuits, or any other Roman priests, pester and persecute people in order to proselytise. Nobody has any notion of what the whole story is about, who does not know that, through those long and dark and indecisive days, it is the man who persecutes himself. The apparent inaction of the priest may be something like the statuesque stillness of the angler; and such an attitude is not unnatural in the functions of a fisher of men. But it is very seldom impatient or premature and the person acted upon is quite lonely enough to realise that it is nothing merely external that is tugging at his liberty. The laity are probably less wise; for in most communions the ecclesiastical layman is more ecclesiastical than is good for his health, and certainly much more ecclesiastical than the ecclesiastics. My experience is that the amateur is generally much more angry than the professional; and if he expresses his irritation at the slow process of conversion, or the inconsistencies of the intermediate condition, he may do a great deal of harm, of the kind that he least intends to do. I know in my own case that I always experienced a slight setback whenever some irresponsible individual interposed to urge me on. It is worth while, for practical reasons, to testify to such experience, because it may guide the convert when he in his turn begins converting. Our enemies no longer really know how to attack the faith; but that is no reason why we should not know how to defend it.

Yet even that one trivial or incidental caution carries with it a reminder of what has been already noted: I mean the fact that whatever be the Catholic's worries, they are the very contrary of the Protestant's warnings. Merely as a matter of personal experience, I have been led to note here that it is not generally the priest, but much more often the layman, who rather too ostentatiously compasses sea and land to make one proselyte. All the creepy and uncanny whispers about the horror of having the priest in the home, as if he were a sort of vampire or a monster intrinsically different from mankind, vanishes with the smallest experience of the militant layman. The priest does his job, but it is much more his secular co-religionist who is disposed to explain it and talk about it. I do not object to laymen proselytising; for I never could see, even when I was practically a pagan, why a man should not urge his own opinions if he liked and that opinion as much as any other. I am not likely to complain of the evangelising energy of Mr. Hilaire Belloc or Mr. Eric Gill;[24] if only because I owe to it the most intelligent talks of my youth. But it is that sort of man who proselytises in that sort of way; and the conventional caricature is wrong again when it always represents him in a cassock. Catholicism is not spread by any particular professional tricks or tones or secret signs or ceremonies. Catholicism is spread by Catholics; but not certainly, in private life at least, merely by Catholic priests. I merely give this here out of a hundred examples, as showing once again that the old traditional version of the terrors of Popery was almost always wrong, even where it might possibly have been right. A man may say if he likes that Catholicism is the enemy; and he may be stating from his point of view a profound spiritual truth. But if he says that Clericalism is the enemy, he is repeating a catchword.

It is my experience that the convert commonly passes through three stages or states of mind. The first is when he imagines himself to be entirely detached, or even to be entirely indifferent, but in the old sense of the term, as when the Prayer Book talks of judges who will truly and indifferently administer justice. Some flippant modern person would probably agree that our judges administer justice very indifferently. But the older meaning was legitimate and even logical and it is that which is applicable here. The first phase is that of the young philosopher who feels that he ought to be fair to the Church of Rome. He wishes to do it justice; but chiefly because he sees that it suffers injustice. I remember that when I was first on the *Daily News*, the great Liberal organ of the Nonconformists, I took the trouble to draw up a list of fifteen falsehoods which I found out, by my own personal knowledge, in a denunciation of Rome by Messrs. Horton and Hocking. I

---

[24] Eric Gill (1882–1940) was an English sculptor, engraver, printer and spiritual writer who defended craftsmanship against industrial manufacturing. He converted to Catholicism in 1913.

noted, for instance, that it was nonsense to say that the Covenanters[25] fought for religious liberty when the Covenant denounced
religious toleration; that it was false to say the Church only asked
for orthodoxy and was indifferent to morality, since, if this was true
of anybody, it was obviously true of the supporters of salvation by
faith and not of salvation by works; that it was absurd to say that
Catholics introduced a horrible sophistry of saying that a man might
sometimes tell a lie, since every sane man knows he would tell a lie
to save a child from Chinese torturers; that it missed the whole
point, in this connection, to quote Ward's phrase,[26] "Make up your
mind that you are justified in lying and then lie like a trooper," for
Ward's argument was against equivocation or what people call
Jesuitry. He meant, "When the child really is hiding in the cupboard and the Chinese torturers really are chasing him with red-hot
pincers, then (and then only) be sure that you are right to deceive
and do not hesitate to lie; but do not stoop to equivocate. Do not
bother yourself to say, "The child is in a wooden house not far from
here," meaning the cupboard; but say the child is in Chiswick or
Chimbora zoo, or anywhere you choose." I find I made elaborate
notes of all these arguments all that long time ago, merely for the
logical pleasure of disentangling an intellectual injustice. I had no
more idea of becoming a Catholic than of becoming a cannibal. I
imagined that I was merely pointing out that justice should be done
even to cannibals. I imagined that I was noting certain fallacies partly
for the fun of the thing and partly for a certain feeling of loyalty to
the truth of things. But as a matter of fact, looking back on these
notes (which I never published), it seems to me that I took a tremendous amount of trouble about it if I really regarded it as a trifle; and
taking trouble has certainly never been a particular weakness of
mine. It seems to me that something was already working subconsciously to keep me more interested in fallacies about this particular topic than in fallacies about Free Trade or Female Suffrage or

[25] The Covenanters were Scotsmen who subscribed to the National Covenant of
1638, which called for the defense of Presbyterianism against corruption and error.
[26] William George Ward (1812–82) was an English moral philosopher and participant in the Oxford Movement; he converted to Catholicism in 1845.

the House of Lords. Anyhow, that is the first stage in my own case and I think in many other cases: the stage of simply wishing to protect Papists from slander and oppression, not (consciously at least) because they hold any particular truth, but because they suffer from a particular accumulation of falsehood. The second stage is that in which the convert begins to be conscious not only of the falsehood but the truth, and is enormously excited to find that there is far more of it than he would ever have expected. This is not so much a stage as a progress; and it goes on pretty rapidly but often for a long time. It consists in discovering what a very large number of lively and interesting ideas there are in the Catholic philosophy, that a great many of them commend themselves at once to his sympathies, and that even those which he would not accept have something to be said for them justifying their acceptance. This process, which may be called discovering the Catholic Church, is perhaps the most pleasant and straightforward part of the business; easier than joining the Catholic Church and much easier than trying to live the Catholic life. It is like discovering a new continent full of strange flowers and fantastic animals, which is at once wild and hospitable. To give anything like a full account of that process would simply be to discuss about half a hundred Catholic ideas and institutions in turn. I might remark that much of it consists of the act of translation; of discovering the real meaning of words, which the Church uses rightly and the world uses wrongly. For instance, the convert discovers that "scandal" does not mean "gossip"; and the sin of causing it does not mean that it is always wicked to set silly old women wagging their tongues. Scandal means scandal, what it originally meant in Greek and Latin: the tripping up of somebody else when he is trying to be good. Or he will discover that phrases like "counsel of perfection" or "venial sin," which mean nothing at all in the newspapers, mean something quite intelligent and interesting in the manuals of moral theology. He begins to realise that it is the secular world that spoils the sense of words; and he catches an exciting glimpse of the real case for the iron immortality of the Latin Mass. It is not a question between a dead language and a living language, in the sense of an everlasting language. It is a question between a dead language and a dying language; an inevitably degenerating language. It is these numberless glimpses of great ideas, that have been hidden from the convert by the prejudices of his provincial culture, that constitute the adventurous and varied second stage of the conversion. It is, broadly speaking, the stage in which the man is unconsciously trying to be converted. And the third stage is perhaps the truest and the most terrible. It is that in which the man is trying not to be converted.

He has come too near to the truth, and has forgotten that truth is a magnet, with the powers of attraction and repulsion. He is filled with a sort of fear, which makes him feel like a fool who has been patronising "Popery" when he ought to have been awakening to the reality of Rome. He discovers a strange and alarming fact, which is perhaps implied in Newman's interesting lecture on Blanco White[27] and the two ways of attacking Catholicism. Anyhow, it is a truth that Newman and every other convert has probably found in one form or another. It is impossible to be just to the Catholic Church. The moment men cease to pull against it they feel a tug towards it. The moment they cease to shout it down they begin to listen to it with pleasure. The moment they try to be fair to it they begin to be fond of it. But when that affection has passed a certain point it begins to take on the tragic and menacing grandeur of a great love affair. The man has exactly the same sense of having committed or compromised himself; of having been in a sense entrapped, even if he is glad to be entrapped. But for a considerable time he is not so much glad as simply terrified. It may be that this real psychological experience has been misunderstood by stupider people and is responsible for all that remains of the legend that Rome is a mere trap. But that legend misses the whole point of the psychology. It is not the Pope who has set the trap or the priests who have baited it. The whole point of the position is that the trap is simply the truth. The whole point is that the man himself has made his way towards the trap of truth, and not the trap that has run after the man. All steps except the last step he has taken eagerly on his own account, out

[27] Joseph Blanco White (1775–1841) was a Spanish-born priest who abandoned Catholicism, settled in England and published *Evidences Against Catholicism* in 1825.

of interest in the truth; and even the last step, or the last stage, only alarms him because it is so very true. If I may refer once more to a personal experience, I may say that I for one was never less troubled by doubts than in the last phase, when I was troubled by fears. Before that final delay I had been detached and ready to regard all sorts of doctrines with an open mind. Since that delay has ended in decision, I have had all sorts of changes in mere mood; and I think I sympathise with doubts and difficulties more than I did before. But I had no doubts or difficulties just before. I had only fears; fears of something that had the finality and simplicity of suicide. But the more I thrust the thing into the back of my mind, the more certain I grew of what Thing it was. And by a paradox that does not frighten me now in the least, it may be that I shall never again have such absolute assurance that the thing is true as I had when I made my last effort to deny it.

There is a postscript or smaller point to be added here to this paradox; which I know that many will misunderstand. Becoming a Catholic broadens the mind. It especially broadens the mind about the reasons for becoming a Catholic. Standing in the centre where all roads meet, a man can look down each of the roads in turn and realise that they come from all points of the heavens. As long as he is still marching along his own road, that is the only road that can be seen, or sometimes even imagined. For instance, many a man who is not yet a Catholic calls himself a Mediaevalist. But a man who is only a Mediaevalist is very much broadened by becoming a Catholic. I am myself a Mediaevalist, in the sense that I think modern life has a great deal to learn from mediaeval life; that Guilds are a better social system than Capitalism; that friars are far less offensive than philanthropists. But I am a much more reasonable and moderate Mediaevalist than I was when I was only a Mediaevalist. For instance, I felt it necessary to be perpetually pitting Gothic architecture against Greek architecture, because it was necessary to back up Christians against Pagans. But now I am in no such fuss and I know what Coventry Patmore[28] meant when he said calmly that it would have been quite as Catholic to decorate his mantelpiece with the

---

[28] Coventry Patmore (1823–96) was an English poet and convert to Catholicism.

Venus of Milo as with the Virgin. As a Mediaevalist I am still proudest of the Gothic; but as a Catholic I am proud of the Baroque. That intensity which seems almost narrow because it comes to the point, like a mediaeval window, is very representative of that last concentration that comes just before conversion. At the last moment of all, the convert often feels as if he were looking through a leper's window. He is looking through a little crack or crooked hole that seems to grow smaller as he stares at it; but it is an opening that looks towards the Altar. Only, when he has entered the Church, he finds that the Church is much larger inside than it is outside. He has left behind him the lop-sidedness of lepers' windows and even in a sense the narrowness of Gothic doors; and he is under vast domes as open as the Renaissance and as universal as the Republic of the world. He can say in a sense unknown to all modern men certain ancient and serene words: *Romanus civis sum*;[29] I am not a slave.

The point for the moment, however, is that there is generally an interval of intense nervousness, to say the least of it, before this normal heritage is reached. To a certain extent it is a fear which attaches to all sharp and irrevocable decisions; it is suggested in all the old jokes about the shakiness of the bridegroom at the wedding or the recruit who takes the shilling and gets drunk partly to celebrate, but partly also to forget it. But it is the fear of a fuller sacrament and a mightier army. He has, by the nature of the case, left a long way behind him the mere clumsy idea that the sacrament will poison him or the army will kill him. He has probably passed the point, though he does generally pass it at some time, when he wonders whether the whole business is an extraordinarily intelligent and ingenious confidence trick. He is not now in the condition which may be called the last phase of real doubt. I mean that in which he wondered whether the thing that everybody told him was too bad to be tolerable, is not too good to be true. Here again the recurrent principle is present; and the obstacle is the very opposite of that which Protestant propaganda has pointed out. If he still has the notion of being trapped, he has no longer any notion of being tricked. He is not afraid of finding the Church out, but rather of the Church finding him out.

---

[29] *Romanus civis sum* is Latin for "I am a citizen of Rome."

This note on the stages of conversion is necessarily very negative and inadequate. There is in the last second of time or hair's breadth of space, before the iron leaps to the magnet, an abyss full of all the unfathomable forces of the universe. The space between doing and not doing such a thing is so tiny and so vast. It is only possible here to give the reasons for Catholicism, not the cause of Catholicism. I have tried to suggest here some of the enlightenments and experiences which gradually teach those who have been taught to think ill of the Church to begin to think well of her. That anything described as so bad should turn out to be so good is itself a rather arresting process having a savour of something sensational and strange. To come to curse and remain to bless, to come to scoff and remain to pray, is always welcome in a spirit of wonder and the glow of an unexpected good.

But it is one thing to conclude that Catholicism is good and another to conclude that it is right. It is one thing to conclude that it is right and another to conclude that it is always right. I had never believed the tradition that it was diabolical; I had soon come to doubt the idea that it was inhuman, but that would only have left me with the obvious inference that it was human. It is a considerable step from that to the inference that it is divine. When we come to that conviction of divine authority, we come to the more mysterious matter of divine aid. In other words, we come to the unfathomable idea of grace and the gift of faith; and I have not the smallest intention of attempting to fathom it. It is a theological question of the utmost complexity; and it is one thing to feel it as a fact and another to define it as a truth. One or two points about the preliminary dispositions that prepare the mind for it are all that need be indicated here. To begin with, there is one sense in which the blackest bigots are really the best philosophers. The Church really is like Antichrist in the sense that it is as unique as Christ. Indeed, if it be not Christ it probably is Antichrist; but certainly it is not Moses or Mahomet or Buddha or Plato or Pythagoras. The more we see of humanity, the more we sympathise with humanity, the more we shall see that when it is simply human it is simply heathen; and the names of its particular local gods or tribal prophets or highly respectable sages are

a secondary matter compared with that human and heathen character. In the old paganism of Europe, in the existing paganism of Asia,
there have been gods and priests and prophets and sages of all sorts;
but not another institution of this sort. The pagan cults die very
slowly; they do not return very rapidly. They do not make the sort
of claim that is made at a crisis; and then make the same claim again
and again at crisis after crisis throughout the whole history of the
earth. All that people fear in the Church, all that they hate in her, all
against which they most harden their hearts and sometimes (one is
tempted to say) thicken their heads, all that has made people consciously and unconsciously treat the Catholic Church as a *peril,* is the
evidence that there is something here that we cannot look on at languidly and with detachment, as we might look on at Hottentots
dancing at the new moon or Chinamen burning paper in porcelain
temples. The Chinaman and the tourist can be on the best of terms
on a basis of mutual scorn. But in the duel of the Church and the
world is no such shield of contempt. The Church will not consent to
scorn the soul of a coolie or even a tourist; and the measure of the
madness with which men hate her is but their vain attempt to despise.

Another element, far more deep and delicate and hard to describe,
is the immediate connection of what is most awful and archaic with
what is most intimate and individual. It is a miracle in itself that anything so huge and historic in date and design should be so fresh in
the affections. It is as if a man found his own parlour and fireside in
the heart of the Great Pyramid. It is as if a child's favourite doll turned
out to be the oldest sacred image in the world, worshipped in
Chaldea or Nineveh. It is as if a girl to whom a man made love in a
garden were also, in some dark and double fashion, a statue standing
for ever in a square. It is just here that all those things which were
regarded as weakness come in as the fulness of strength. Everything
that men called sentimental in Roman Catholic religion, its keepsakes, its small flowers and almost tawdry trinkets, its figures with
merciful gestures and gentle eyes, its avowedly popular pathos and
all that Matthew Arnold meant by Christianity with its "relieving
tears"—all this is a sign of sensitive and vivid vitality in anything so
vast and settled and systematic. There is nothing quite like this

warmth, as in the warmth of Christmas, amid ancient hills hoary with such snows of antiquity. It can address even God Almighty with diminutives. In all its varied vestments it wears its Sacred Heart upon its sleeve. But to those who know that it is full of these lively affections, like little leaping flames, there is something of almost ironic satisfaction in the stark and primitive size of the thing, like some prehistoric monster; in its spires and mitres like the horns of giant herds or its colossal cornerstones like the four feet of an elephant. It would be easy to write a merely artistic study of the strange externals of the Roman religion, which should make it seem as uncouth and unearthly as Aztec or African religion. It would be easy to talk of it as if it were really some sort of mammoth or monster elephant, older than the Ice Age, towering over the Stone Age; his very lines traced, it would seem, in the earthquakes or landslides of some older creation, his very organs and outer texture akin to unrecorded patterns of vegetation and air and light—the last residuum of a lost world. But the prehistoric monster is in the Zoölogical Gardens and not in the Natural History Museum. The extinct animal is still alive. And anything outlandish and unfamiliar in its form accentuates the startling naturalness and familiarity of its mind, as if the Sphinx began suddenly to talk of the topics of the hour. The super-elephant is not only a tame animal but a pet; and a young child shall lead him.

This antithesis between all that is formidable and remote and all that is personally relevant and realistically tender is another of those converging impressions which meet in the moment of conviction. But of all these things, that come nearest to the actual transition of the gift of faith, it is far harder to write than of the rationalistic and historical preliminaries of the enquiry. It is only with those preliminary dispositions towards the truth that I claim to deal here. In the chapters that follow I propose to touch upon two of the larger considerations of this class, not because they are in themselves any larger than many other immense aspects of so mighty a theme, but because they happen to balance each other and form a sort of antithesis very typical of all Catholic truth. In the first of the two chapters I shall try to point out how it is that when we praise the

Church for her greatness we do not merely mean her largeness but, in a rather notable and unique sense, her universality. We mean her power of being cosmos and containing other things. And in the second chapter I shall point out what may seem to disturb this truth but really balances it. I mean the fact that we value the Church because she is a Church Militant; and sometimes even because she militates against ourselves. She is something more than the cosmos, in the sense of completed nature or completed human nature. She proves that she is something more by sometimes being right where they are wrong. These two aspects must be considered separately, though they come together to form the full conviction that comes just before conversion. But in this chapter I have merely noted down a few points or stages of the conversion considered as a practical process; and especially those three stages of it through which many a Protestant or Agnostic must have passed. Many a man, looking back cheerfully on them now, will not be annoyed if I call the first, patronising the Church; and the second, discovering the Church; and the third, running away from the Church. When those three phases are over, a larger truth begins to come into sight; it is much too large to describe and we will proceed to describe it.

IV

THE WORLD INSIDE OUT

The first fallacy about the Catholic Church is the idea that it is a church. I mean that it is a church in the sense in which the Nonconformist newspapers talk about The Churches. I do not intend any expression of contempt about The Churches; nor is it an expression of contempt to say that it would be more convenient to call them the sects. This is true in a much deeper and more sympathetic sense than may at first appear; but to begin with, it is certainly true in a perfectly plain and historical sense, which has nothing to do with sympathy at all. Thus, for instance, I have much more sympathy for small nationalities than I have for small sects. But it is simply a historical fact that the Roman Empire was the Empire and that it was not a small nationality. And it is simply a historical fact that the Roman Church is the Church and is not a sect. Nor is there anything narrow or unreasonable in saying that the Church is the Church. It may be a good thing that the Roman Empire broke up into nations; but it certainly was not one of the nations into which it broke up. And even a person who thinks it fortunate that the Church broke up into sects ought to be able to distinguish between the little things he likes and the big thing he has broken. As a matter of fact, in the case of things so large, so unique and so creative of the culture about them as were the Roman Empire and the Roman Church, it is not controversial but simply correct to confine the one word to the one example. Everybody who originally used the word "Empire" used it of that Empire; everybody who used the word "Ecclesia" used it of that Ecclesia. There may have been similar things in other places, but they could not be called by the same name for the simple reason that they were not named in the same language. We know what we mean by a Roman Emperor; we can if we like talk of a Chinese Emperor, just as we can if we like take a particular sort of a Mandarin and say he is equivalent to a Marquis. But we never can be certain that he is exactly equivalent; for the thing we are thinking about is peculiar to

99

our own history and in that sense stands alone. Now in that, if in no other sense, the Catholic Church stands alone. It does not merely belong to a class of Christian churches. It does not merely belong to a class of human religions. Considered quite coldly and impartially, as by a man from the moon, it is much more *sui generis* than that. It is, if the critic chooses to think so, the ruin of an attempt at a Universal Religion which was bound to fail. But calling the wreckers to break up a ship does not turn the ship into one of its own timbers; and cutting Poland up into three pieces does not make Poland the same as Posen.

But in a much more profound and philosophical sense this notion that the Church is one of the sects is the great fallacy of the whole affair. It is a matter more psychological and more difficult to describe. But it is perhaps the most sensational of the silent upheavals or reversals in the mind that constitute the revolution called conversion. Every man conceives himself as moving about in a cosmos of some kind; and the man of the days of my youth walked about in a kind of vast and airy Crystal Palace[30] in which there were exhibits set side by side. The cosmos, being made of glass and iron, was partly transparent and partly colourless; anyhow, there was something negative about it; arching over all our heads, a roof as remote as a sky, it seemed to be impartial and impersonal. Our attention was fixed on the exhibits, which were all carefully ticketed and arranged in rows; for it was the age of science. Here stood all the religions in a row — the churches or sects or whatever we called them; and towards the end of the row there was a particularly dingy and dismal one, with a pointed roof half fallen in and pointed windows most broken with stones by passers-by; and we were told that this particular exhibit was the Roman Catholic Church. Some of us were sorry for it and even fancied it had been rather badly used; most of us regarded it as dirty and disreputable; a few of us even pointed out that many details in the ruin were artistically beautiful or architecturally important. But most people preferred to deal at other and more business-like booths; at the Quaker shop of Peace and Plenty or the Salvation Army store where the showman beats the big drum outside.

[30] The Crystal Palace was a vast building erected in London in 1851 to house the first international exhibition of the products and machines of the industrial age.

Now conversion consists very largely, on its intellectual side, in the discovery that all that picture of equal creeds inside an indifferent cosmos is quite false. It is not a question of comparing the merits and defects of the Quaker meeting-house set beside the Catholic cathedral. It is the Quaker meeting-house that is inside the Catholic cathedral; it is the Catholic cathedral that covers everything like the vault of the Crystal Palace; and it is when we look up at the vast distant dome covering all the exhibits that we trace the Gothic roof and the pointed windows. In other words, Quakerism is but a temporary form of Quietism[31] which has arisen technically outside the Church as the Quietism of Fenelon appeared technically inside the Church. But both were in themselves temporary and would have, like Fenelon, sooner or later to return to the Church in order to live. The principle of life in all these variations of Protestantism, in so far as it is not a principle of death, consists of what remained in them of Catholic Christendom; and to Catholic Christendom they have always returned to be recharged with vitality. I know that this will sound like a statement to be challenged; but it is true. The return of Catholic ideas to the separated parts of Christendom was often indeed indirect. But though the influence came through many centres, it always came from one. It came through the Romantic Movement, a glimpse of the mere picturesqueness of mediaevalism; but it is something more than an accident that Romances, like Romance languages, are named after Rome. Or it came through the instinctive reaction of old-fashioned people like Johnson or Scott or Cobbett,[32] wishing to save old elements that had originally been Catholic against a progress that was merely Capitalist. But it led them to denounce that Capitalist progress and become, like Cobbett, practical foes of Protestantism without being practising followers of Catholicism. Or it came from the Pre-Raphaelites[33] or

[31] Quietism was a seventeenth-century form of mystical contemplation. François Fénelon (1651–1715), archbishop of Cambrai, championed it in France.

[32] William Cobbett (1763–1835) was an English political radical and agricultural reformer, whose best-known book was *Rural Rides* (1830).

[33] The Pre-Raphaelite Brotherhood, a movement to infuse art with morality, flourished in mid-nineteenth-century England. Its members, most prominent of whom were William Holman Hunt, John Everett Millais and Dante Gabriel Rossetti, contended that the degeneration of Western art had begun in the Renaissance with Raphael.

the opening of continental art and culture by Matthew Arnold and Morris[34] and Ruskin and the rest. But examine the actual make-up of the mind of a good Quaker or Congregational minister at this moment, and compare it with the mind of such a dissenter in the Little Bethel before such culture came. And you will see how much of his health and happiness he owes to Ruskin and what Ruskin owed to Giotto; to Morris and what Morris owed to Chaucer; to fine scholars of his own school like Philip Wicksteed, and what they owe to Dante and St. Thomas. Such a man will still sometimes talk of the Middle Ages as the Dark Ages. But the Dark Ages have improved the wallpaper on his wall and the dress on his wife and all the whole dingy and vulgar life which he lived in the days of Stiggins[35] and Brother Tadger. For he also is a Christian and lives only by the life of Christendom.

It is not easy to express this enormous inversion which I have here tried to suggest in the image of a world turned inside out. I mean that the thing which had been stared at as a small something swells out and swallows everything. Christendom is in the literal sense a continent. We come to feel that it contains everything, even the things in revolt against itself. But it is perhaps the most towering intellectual transformation of all and the one that it is hardest to undo even for the sake of argument. It is almost impossible even in imagination to reverse that reversal. Another way of putting it is to say that we have come to regard all these historical figures as characters in Catholic history, even if they are not Catholics. And in a certain sense, the historical as distinct from the theological sense, they never do cease to be Catholic. They are not people who have really created something entirely new, until they actually pass the border of reason and create more or less crazy nightmares. But nightmares do not last; and most of them even now are in various stages of waking up. Protestants are Catholics gone wrong; that is what is really meant by saying they are Christians. Sometimes they have gone very wrong; but not often have they gone right ahead with their own particular wrong. Thus a Calvinist is a Catholic

---

[34] William Morris (1834–96) was an English poet, novelist, artist and prominent advocate of socialism.

[35] Stiggins was a character in Dickens' *The Pickwick Papers.*

THE WORLD INSIDE OUT 103

obsessed with the Catholic idea of the sovereignty of God. But when
he makes it mean that God wishes particular people to be damned,
we may say with all restraint that he has become a rather morbid
Catholic. In point of fact he is a diseased Catholic; and the disease
left to itself would be death or madness. But, as a matter of fact, the
disease did not last long, and is itself now practically dead. But every
step he takes back towards humanity is a step back towards Catholicism. Thus a Quaker is a Catholic obsessed with the Catholic idea
of gentle simplicity and truth. But when he made it mean that it is a
lie to say "you" and an act of idolatry to take off your hat to a lady,
it is not too much to say that whether or not he had a hat off, he certainly had a tile loose. But as a matter of fact he himself found it
necessary to dispense with the eccentricity (and the hat) and to leave
the straight road that would have led him to a lunatic asylum. Only
every step he takes back towards common sense is a step back
towards Catholicism. In so far as he was right he was a Catholic;
and in so far as he was wrong he has not himself been able to remain
a Protestant.

To us, therefore, it is henceforth impossible to think of the Quaker as
a figure at the beginning of a new Quaker history or the Calvinist as the
founder of a new Calvinistic world. It is quite obvious to us that they
are simply characters in our own Catholic history, only characters who
caused a great deal of trouble by trying to do something that we could
do better and that they did not really do at all. Now some may suppose
that this can be maintained of the older sects like Calvinists and
Quakers, but cannot be maintained of modern movements like those of
Socialists or Spiritualists. But they will be quite wrong. The covering or
continental character of the Church applies just as much to modern
manias as to the old religious manias; it applies quite as much to Materialists or Spiritualists as to Puritans. In all of them you find that some
Catholic dogma is, first, taken for granted; then exaggerated into an error; and then generally reacted against and rejected as an error, bringing the individual in question a few steps back again on the home-
ward road. And this is almost always the mark of such a heretic; that
while he will wildly question any other Catholic dogma, he never
dreams of questioning his own favourite Catholic dogma and does

not even seem to know that it could be questioned. It never occurred to the Calvinist that anybody might use his liberty to deny or limit the divine omnipotence, or to the Quaker that anyone could question the supremacy of simplicity. That is exactly the situation of the Socialist. Bolshevism and every shade of any such theory of brotherhood is based upon one unfathomably mystical Catholic dogma; the equality of men. The Communists stake everything on the equality of man, as the Calvinists staked everything on the omnipotence of God. They ride it to death as the others rode their dogma to death, turning their horse into a nightmare. But it never seems to occur to them that some people do not believe in the Catholic dogma of the mystical equality of men. Yet there are many, even among Christians, who are so heretical as to question it. The Socialists get into a great tangle when they try to apply it; they compromise with their own ideals; they modify their own doctrine; and so find themselves, like the Quakers and the Calvinists, after all their extreme extravagances, a day's march nearer Rome.

In short, the story of these sects is not one of straight lines striking outwards and onwards, though if it were they would all be striking in different directions. It is a pattern of curves continually returning into the continent and common life of their and our civilisation; and the summary of that civilisation and central sanity is the philosophy of the Catholic Church. To us, Spiritualists are men studying the existence of spirits, in a brief and blinding oblivion of the existence of evil spirits. They are, as it were, people just educated enough to have heard of ghosts but not educated enough to have heard of witches. If the evil spirits succeed in stopping their education and stunting their minds, they may of course go on for ever repeating silly messages from Plato and doggerel verses from Milton. But if they do go a step or two further, instead of marking time on the borderland, their next step will be to learn what the Church could have taught. To us, Christian Scientists are simply people with one idea, which they have never learnt to balance and combine with all the other ideas. That is why the wealthy business man so often becomes a Christian Scientist. He is not used to ideas and one idea goes to his head, like one glass of wine to a starving man. But the Catholic Church is used to living with ideas and walks among all those very dangerous wild beasts with the poise and the lifted head of a lion-tamer. The Christian Scientist can go on monotonously repeating his one idea and remain a Christian Scientist. But if ever he really goes on to any other ideas, he will be so much the nearer to being a Catholic.

When the convert has once seen the world like that, with one balance of ideas and a number of other ideas that have left it and lost their balance, he does not in fact experience any of the inconveniences that he might reasonably have feared before that silent but stunning revolution. He is not worried by being told that there is something in Spiritualism or something in Christian Science. He knows there is something in everything. But he is moved by the more impressive fact that he finds everything in something. And he is quite sure that if these investigators really are looking for everything, and not merely looking for anything, they will be more and more likely to look for it in the same place. In that sense he is far less worried about them than he was when he thought that one or other of them might be the only person having any sort of communication with the higher mysteries and obviously rather capable of making a mess of it. He is no more likely to be overawed by the fact that Mrs. Eddy[36] achieved spiritual healing or Mr. Home[37] achieved bodily levitation than a fully dressed gentleman in Bond Street would be overawed by the top-hat on the head of a naked savage. A top-hat may be a good hat but it is a bad costume. And a magnetic trick may be a sufficient sensation but it is a very insufficient philosophy. He is no more envious of a Bolshevist for making a revolution than of a beaver for making a dam; for he knows his own civilisation can make things on a pattern not quite so simple or so monotonous. But he believes this of his civilisation and his religion and not merely of himself. There is nothing supercilious about his attitude; because he is well aware that he has only scratched the surface of the spiritual estate that is now open to him. In other words, the convert does not in the least abandon investigation or even

[36] Mary Baker Eddy (1821–1910) was the American founder of Christian Science.
[37] Daniel Home (1833–86) was a noted English Spiritualist.

adventure. He does not think he knows everything, nor has he lost curiosity about the things he does not know. But experience has taught him that he will find nearly everything somewhere inside that estate and that a very large number of people are finding next to nothing outside it. For the estate is not only a formal garden or an ordered farm; there is plenty of hunting and fishing on it, and, as the phrase goes, very good sport.

For this is one of the very queerest of the common delusions about what happens to the convert. In some muddled way people have confused the natural remarks of converts, about having found moral peace, with some idea of their having found mental rest, in the sense of mental inaction. They might as well say that a man who has completely recovered his health, after an attack of palsy or St. Vitus' dance, signalises his healthy state by sitting absolutely still like a stone. Recovering his health means recovering his power of moving in the right way as distinct from the wrong way; but he will probably move a great deal more than before. To become a Catholic is not to leave off thinking, but to learn how to think. It is so in exactly the same sense in which to recover from palsy is not to leave off moving but to learn how to move. The Catholic convert has for the first time a starting-point for straight and strenuous thinking. He has for the first time a way of testing the truth in any question that he raises. As the world goes, especially at present, it is the other people, the heathen and the heretics, who seem to have every virtue except the power of connected thought. There was indeed a brief period when a small minority did some hard thinking on the heathen or heretical side. It barely lasted from the time of Voltaire to the time of Huxley. It has now entirely disappeared. What is now called free thought is valued, not because it is free thought, but because it is freedom from thought; because it is free thoughtlessness.

Nothing is more amusing to the convert, when his conversion has been complete for some time, than to hear the speculations about when or whether he will repent of the conversion; when he will be sick of it, how long he will stand it, at what stage of his external exasperation he will start up and say he can bear it no more. For all this is founded on that optical illusion about the outside and the inside which I have tried to sketch in this chapter. The outsiders, stand by and see, or think they see, the convert entering with bowed head a sort of small temple which they are convinced is fitted up inside like a prison, if not a torture-chamber. But all they really know about it is that he has passsed through a door. They do not know that he has not gone into the inner darkness, but out into the broad daylight. It is he who is, in the beautiful and beatific sense of the word, an outsider. He does not want to go into a larger room, because he does not know of any larger room to go into. He knows of a large number of much smaller rooms, each of which is labelled as being very large; but he is quite sure he would be cramped in any of them. Each of them professes to be a complete cosmos or scheme of all things; but then so does the cosmos of the Clapham Sect[38] or the Clapton Agapemone.[39] Each of them is supposed to be domed with the sky or painted inside with all the stars. But each of these cosmic systems or machines seems to him much smaller and even much simpler than the broad and balanced universe in which he lives. One of them is labelled Agnostic; but he knows by experience that it has not really even the freedom of ignorance. It is a wheel that must always go round without a single jolt of miraculous interruption — a circle that must not be squared by any higher Mathematics of mysticism; a machine that must be scoured as clean of all spirits as if it were the avowed machine of materialism. In living in a world with two orders, the supernatural and the natural, the convert feels he is living in a larger world and does not feel any temptation to crawl back into a smaller one. One of them is labelled Theosophical or Buddhistic; but he knows by experience that it is only the same sort of wearisome wheel used for spiritual things instead of material things. Living in a world where he is free to do anything, even to go to the devil, he does not see why he should tie himself to the wheel of a mere destiny. One of them is labelled

[38] The Clapham Sect was a group of English reformers who crusaded against various social evils, especially the international slave trade. The group, which originated in the 1790s, took its name from its meeting place, Henry Thornton's house in Clapham Common. Its most significant member was William Wilberforce (1759–1833).

[39] The Clapton Agapemone was a nineteenth-century English communal sect headed by Henry Prince.

Humanitarian; but he knows that such humanitarians have really far less experience of humanity. He knows that they are thinking almost entirely of men as they are at this moment in modern cities, and have nothing like the huge human interest of what began by being preached to legionaries in Palestine and is still being preached to peasants in China. So clear is this perception that I have sometimes put it to myself, as something between a melancholy meditation and a joke. "Where *should* I go now, if I did leave the Catholic Church?" I certainly would not go to any of those little social sects which only express one idea at a time, because that idea happens to be fashionable at the moment. The best I could hope for would be to wander away into the woods and become, *not* a Pantheist (for that is also a limitation and a bore) but rather a pagan, in the mood to cry out that some particular mountain peak or flowering fruit tree was sacred and a thing to be worshipped. That at least would be beginning all over again; but it would bring me back to the same problem in the end. If it was reasonable to have a sacred tree it was not unreasonable to have a sacred crucifix; and if the god was to be found on one peak he may as reasonably be found under one spire. To find a new religion is sooner or later to have found one; and why should I have been discontented with the one I had found? Especially, as I said in the first words of this essay, when it is the one old religion which seems capable of remaining new.

I know very well that if I went upon that journey I should either despair or return; and that none of the trees would ever be a substitute for the real sacred tree. Paganism is better than pantheism, for paganism is free to imagine divinities, while pantheism is forced to pretend, in a priggish way, that all things are equally divine. But I should not imagine any divinity that was sufficiently divine. I seem to know that weary return through the woodlands; for I think in some symbolic fashion I have walked that road before. For as I have tried to confess here without excessive egotism, I think I am the sort of man who came to Christ from Pan and Dionysus and not from Luther or Laud;[40] that the conversion I understand is that of the pagan and not the Puritan; and upon that antique conversion is

---

[40] William Laud (1573–1645), archbishop of Canterbury and persecutor of the Puritans, was executed for his support of King Charles I.

founded the whole world that we know. It is a transformation far more vast and tremendous than anything that has been meant for many years past, at least in England and America, by a sectarian controversy or a doctrinal division. On the height of that ancient empire and that international experience, humanity had a vision. It has not had another; but only quarrels about that one. Paganism was the largest thing in the world and Christianity was larger; and everything else has been comparatively small.

V

THE EXCEPTION PROVES THE RULE

The Catholic Church is the only thing which saves a man from the degrading slavery of being a child of his age. I have compared it with the New Religions; but this is exactly where it differs from the New Religions. The New Religions are in many ways suited to the new conditions; but they are only suited to the new conditions. When those conditions shall have changed in only a century or so, the points upon which alone they insist at present will have become almost pointless. If the Faith has all the freshness of a new religion, it has all the richness of an old religion; it has especially all the reserves of an old religion. So far as that is concerned, its antiquity is alone a great advantage, and especially a great advantage for purposes of renovation and youth. It is only by the analogy of animal bodies that we suppose that old things must be stiff. It is a mere metaphor from bones and arteries. In an intellectual sense old things are flexible. Above all, they are various and have many alternatives to offer. There is a sort of rotation of crops in religious history; and old fields can lie fallow for a while and then be worked again. But when the new religion or any such notion has sown its one crop of wild oats, which the wind generally blows away, it is barren. A thing as old as the Catholic Church has an accumulated armoury and treasury to choose from; it can pick and choose among the centuries and brings one age to the rescue of another. It can call in the old world to redress the balance of the new.

Anyhow, the New Religions are suited to the new world; and this is their most damning defect. Each religion is produced by contemporary causes than can be clearly pointed out. Socialism is a reaction against Capitalism. Spiritualism is a reaction against Materialism; it is also in its intensified form merely the trail of the tragedy of the Great War. But there is a somewhat more subtle sense in which the very fitness of the new creeds makes them unfit; their very acceptability makes them inaccessible. Thus they all profess to be progressive because the peculiar boast of their peculiar period was progress; they claim to be democratic because our political system still rather pathetically claims to be democratic. They rushed to a reconciliation with science, which was often only a premature surrender to science. They hastily divested themselves of anything considered dowdy or old-fashioned in the way of vesture or symbol. They claimed to have bright services and cheery sermons; the churches competed with the cinemas; the churches even became cinemas. In its more moderate form the mood was merely one of praising natural pleasures, such as the enjoyment of nature and even the enjoyment of human nature. These are excellent things and this is an excellent liberty; and yet it has its limitations.

We do not really want a religion that is right where we are right. What we want is a religion that is right where we are wrong. In these current fashions it is not really a question of the religion allowing us liberty; but (at the best) of the liberty allowing us a religion. These people merely take the modern mood, with much in it that is amiable and much that is anarchical and much that is merely dull and obvious, and then require any creed to be cut down to fit that mood. But the mood would exist even without the creed. They say they want a religion to be social, when they would be social without any religion. They say they want a religion to be practical, when they would be practical without any religion. They say they want a religion acceptable to science, when they would accept the science even if they did not accept the religion. They say they want a religion like this because they are like this already. They say they want it, when they mean that they could do without it.

It is a very different matter when a religion, in the real sense of a binding thing, binds men to their morality when it is not identical with their mood. It is very different when some of the saints preached social reconciliation to fierce and raging factions who could hardly bear the sight of each others' faces. It was a very different thing when charity was preached to pagans who really did not believe in it; just as it is a very different thing now, when chastity is preached to new pagans who do not believe in it. It is in those cases that we get the real grapple of religion; and it is in those cases that we get the peculiar and solitary triumph of the Catholic faith. It is not in merely being right when we are right, as in being cheerful or hopeful or humane. It is in having been right when we were wrong, and in the fact coming back upon us afterwards like a boomerang. One word that tells us what we do not know outweighs a thousand words that tell us what we do know. And the thing is all the more striking if we not only did not know it but could not believe it. It may seem a paradox to say that the truth teaches us more by the words we reject than by the words we receive. Yet the paradox is a parable of the simplest sort and familiar to us all; any example might be given of it. If a man tells us to avoid public houses, we think him a tiresome though perhaps a well-intentioned old party. If he tells us to use public houses, we recognise that he has a higher morality and presents an ideal that is indeed lofty, but perhaps a little too simple and obvious to need defence. But if a man tells us to avoid the one particular public house called The Pig and Whistle, on the left hand as you turn round by the pond, the direction may seem very dogmatic and arbitrary and showing insufficient process of argument. But if we then fling ourselves into The Pig and Whistle and are immediately poisoned with the gin or smothered in the feather-bed and robbed of our money, we recognise that the man who advised us did know something about it and had a cultivated and scientific knowledge of the public houses of the district. We think it even more, as we emerge half-murdered from The Pig and Whistle, if we originally rejected his warning as a silly superstition. The warning itself is almost more impressive if it was not justified by reasons, but only by results. There is something very notable about a thing which is arbitrary when it is also accurate. We may very easily forget, even while we fulfil, the advice that we thought was self-evident sense. But nothing can measure our mystical and unfathomable reverence for the advice that we thought was nonsense.

As will be seen in a moment, I do not mean in the least that the Catholic Church is arbitrary in the sense of never giving reasons; but I do mean that the convert is profoundly affected by the fact that, even when he did not see the reason, he lived to see that it was reasonable. But there is something even more singular than this, which it will be well to note as a part of the convert's experience. In many cases, as a matter of fact, he did originally have a glimpse of the reasons, even if he did not reason about them; but they were forgotten in the interlude when reason was clouded by rationalism. The point is not very easy to explain, and I shall be obliged to take merely personal examples in order to explain it. I mean that we have often had a premonition as well as a warning; and the fact often comes back to us after we have disregarded both. It is worth noting in connection with conversion, because the convert is often obstructed by a catchword which says that the Church crushes the conscience. The Church does not crush any man's conscience. It is the man who crushes his conscience and then finds out that it was right, when he has almost forgotten that he had one.

I will take two examples out of the new movements: Socialism and Spiritualism. Now it is perfectly true that when I first began to think seriously about Socialism, I was a Socialist. But it is equally true, and more important than it sounds, that before I had ever heard of Socialism I was a strong anti-Socialist. I was what has since been called a Distributist, though I did not know it. When I was a child and dreamed the usual dreams about kings and clowns and robbers and policemen, I always conceived all contentment and dignity as consisting in something compact and personal; in being king of the castle or captain of the pirate ship or the man who owned the shop or the robber who was safe in the cavern. As I passed through boyhood I always imagined battles for justice as being the defence of special walls and houses and high defiant shrines; and I embodied some of those crude but coloured visions in a story called *The Napoleon of Notting Hill*. All this happened, in fancy at least, when I had never heard of Socialism and was a much better judge of it.

Shades of the prison-house began to close and with them came a merely mechanical discussion as to how we were all to get out of prison. *Then* indeed, in the darkness of the dungeon, was heard the voice of Mr. Sidney Webb,[41] telling us that we could only conceivably

[41] Sidney Webb (1859–1947) was one of the founders in 1884 of the Fabian Society, an organization dedicated to establishing socialism in England through non-revolutionary, parliamentary means.

get out of our Capitalist captivity with the patent Chubb key[42] of Collectivism. Or to use a more exact metaphor, he told us that we could only escape from our dark and filthy cells of industrial slavery by melting all our private latchkeys into one gigantic latchkey as large as a battering ram. We did not really like giving up our little private keys or local attachments or love of our own possessions; but we were quite convinced that social justice must be done somehow and could only be done socialistically. I therefore became a Socialist in the old days of the Fabian Society; and so I think did everybody else worth talking about—except the Catholics. And the Catholics were an insignificant handful, the dregs of a dead religion, essentially a superstition. About this time appeared the Encyclical on Labour by Leo XIII;[43] and nobody in our really well-informed world took much notice of it. Certainly the Pope spoke as strongly as any Socialist could speak when he said that Capitalism "laid on the toiling millions a yoke little better than slavery." But as the Pope was not a Socialist it was obvious that he had not read the right Socialist books and pamphlets; and we could not expect the poor old gentleman to know what every young man knew by this time—that Socialism was inevitable. That was a long time ago, and by a gradual process, mostly practical and political, which I have no intention of describing here, most of us began to realise that Socialism was not inevitable; that it was not really popular; that it was not the only way, or even the right way, of restoring the rights of the poor. We have come to the conclusion that the obvious cure for private property being given to the few is to see that it is given to the many; not to see that it is taken away from everybody or given in trust to the dear good politicians. Then, having discovered that fact as a fact, we look back at Leo XIII and discover in his old and dated document, of which we took no notice at the time, that he was saying then exactly what we are saying now. "As many as possible of the working classes should become owners." That is what I mean by the justification

[42] The Chubb key is used in a lock invented by an Englishman named Chubb.

[43] Pope Leo XIII reigned from 1878 to 1903. His encyclical on labour, *Rerum novarum* (1891), supported the rights of labor, called for a just wage and defended trade unions.

of arbitrary warning. If the Pope had said then exactly what we said and wanted him to say, we should not have really reverenced him then and we should have entirely repudiated him afterwards. He would only have marched with the million who accepted Fabianism; and with them he would have marched away. But when he saw a distinction we did not see then, and do see now, that distinction is decisive. It marks a disagreement more convincing than a hundred agreements. It is not that he was right when we were right, but that he was right when we were wrong.

The superficial critic of these things, noting that I am no longer a Socialist, will always say, "Of course, you are a Catholic and you are not allowed to be a Socialist." To which I answer emphatically, No. That is missing the whole point. The Church anticipated my experience; but it was experience and not only obedience. I am quite sure now from merely living in this world, and seeing something of Catholic peasants as well as Collectivist officials, that it is happier and healthier for most men to become owners than for them to give up all ownership to those officials. I do not follow the State Socialist in his extreme belief in the State; but I have not ceased to be credulous about the State merely because I have become credulous about the Church. I believe less in the State because I know more of the statesmen. I cannot believe small property to be impossible after I have seen it. I cannot believe State management to be impeccable after I have seen it. It is not any authority, except what St. Thomas calls the authority of the senses, which tells me that the mere community of goods is a solution that is too much of a simplification. The Church has taught me, but I could not unteach myself; I have learned because I have lived, and I could not unlearn it. If I ceased to be a Catholic I could not again be a Communist.

As it happens, my story was almost exactly the same in connection with Spiritualism. There again I was modern when I was young, but not when I was very young. While I had a vague but innocent nursery religion still hanging about me, I regarded the first signs of these psychic and psychological things with mere repugnance. I hated the whole notion of mesmerism and magnetic tricks with the mind; I loathed their bulging eyes and stiff attitudes and unnatural trances and the whole bag of tricks. When I saw a girl I admired set down to crystal-gazing, I was furious; I hardly knew why. Then came the period when I wanted to know why, when I examined my own reasons and found I had none. I saw that it was inconsistent in science to revere research and forbid psychical research. I saw that men of science were more and more accepting these things and I went along with my scientific age. I was never exactly a Spiritualist, but I almost always defended Spiritualism. I experimented with a planchette, quite enough to convince myself finally that some things do happen that are not in the ordinary sense natural. I have since come to think, for reasons that would require too much space to detail, that it is not so much supernatural as unnatural and even antinatural. I believe the experiments were bad for me; I believe they are bad for the other experimentalists. But I found out the fact long before I found out the Catholic Church or the Catholic view of that question. Only, as I have said, when I do find it out, I find it rather impressive; for it is not the religion that was right when I was right, but the religion that was right when I was wrong.

But I wish to note about both those cases that the common cant in the matter is emphatically not true. It is not true that the Church crushed my natural conscience; it is not true that the Church asked me to give up my individual ideal. It is not true that Collectivism was ever my *ideal*. I do not believe it was ever really anybody else's ideal. It was not an ideal but a compromise; it was a concession to practical economists who told us that we could not prevent poverty except by something uncommonly like slavery. State Socialism never came natural to us; it never convinced us that it was natural; it convinced us that it was necessary. In exactly the same way Spiritualism never came as something natural but only as something necessary. Each told us that it was *the only way* into the promised land, in the one case of a future life and the other of life in the future. We did not like government departments and tickets and registers; but we were told there was no other way of reaching a better society. We did not like dark rooms and dubious mediums and ladies tied up with rope, but we were told there was no other way to reach a better world. We were ready to crawl down a municipal drain-pipe or through a spiritual sewer, because it was the only way to better things; the only way even to prove that there were better things. But the drain-pipe had never figured in our dreams like a tower of ivory or a house of gold, or even like the robbers' tower of our romantic boyhood or the solid and comfortable house of our matured experience. The Faith had not only been true all along, but it had been true to the first and the last things, to our unspoilt instincts and our conclusive experience; and it had condemned nothing but an interlude of intellectual snobbishness and surrender to the persuasions of pedantry. It had condemned nothing but what we ourselves should have come to condemn, though we might have condemned it too late.

The Church therefore never made my individual ideal impossible; it would be truer to say that she was the first to make it possible. The Encyclical's ideal had been much nearer my own instinct than the ideal I had consented to substitute for it. The Catholic suspicion of table-rapping was much more like my own original suspicion than it was like my own subsequent surrender. But in those two cases it is surely clear that the Catholic Church plays exactly the part that she professes to play: something that knows what we cannot be expected to know, but should probably accept if we really knew it. I am not in this case, any more than in the greater part of this study, referring to the things that are really best worth knowing. The supernatural truths are connected with the mystery of grace and are a matter for theologians; admittedly a rather delicate and difficult matter even for them. But though the transcendental truths are the most important they are not those that best illustrate this particular point, which concerns the decisions which can be more or less tested by experience. And of all those things that can be tested by experience I could tell the same story: that there was a time when I thought the Catholic doctrine was meaningless, but that even that was not the very earliest time, which was a time of greater simplicity, when I had a sort of glimpse of the meaning though I had never even heard of the doctrine. The world deceived me and the Church would at any time have undeceived me. The thing that a man may really shed at last like a superstition is the fashion of this world that passes away.

I could give many other examples, but I fear they would inevitably tend to be egotistical examples. Throughout this brief study I am under the double difficulty that all roads lead to Rome, but that each pilgrim is tempted to talk as if all roads had been like his own road. I could write a great deal, for instance, about my early wrestlings with the rather ridiculous dilemma which was put to me in my youth by the optimist and the pessimist. I promptly and properly refused to be a pessimist; and I therefore fell into the way of calling myself an optimist. Now I should not call myself either, and what is more important I can see that virtue may be entangled in both. But I think it is entangled; and I think that an older and simpler truth can loosen the tangle. But the point in the present connection is this; that before I had ever heard of optimists or pessimists I was something much more like what I am now than could be covered by either of those two pedantic words. In my childhood I assumed that cheerfulness was a good thing, but I also assumed that it was a bad thing not to protest against things that are really bad. After an interlude of intellectual formalism and false antithesis, I have come back to being able to think what I could then only feel. But I have realised that the protest can rise to a much more divine indignation and that the cheerfulness is but a faint suggestion of a much more divine joy. It is not so much that I have found I was wrong as that I have found out why I was right.

In this we find the supreme example of the exception that proves the rule. The rule, of which I have given a rough outline in the previous chapter, is that the Catholic philosophy is a universal philosophy found to fit anywhere with human nature and the nature of things. But even when it does not fit in with human nature it is found in the long run to favour something yet more fitting. It generally suits us, but where it does not suit us we learn to suit it, so long as we are alive enough to learn anything. In the rare cases where a reasonable man can really say that it cuts across his intelligence, it will generally be found that it is true, not only to truth, but even to his deepest instinct for truth. Education does not cease with conversion, but rather begins. The man does not cease to study because he has become convinced that certain things are worth studying; and these things include not only the orthodox values but even the orthodox vetoes. Strangely enough, in a sense, the forbidden fruit is often more fruitful than the free. It is more fruitful in the sense of a fascinating botanical study of why it is really poisonous. Thus, for the sake of an example, all healthy people have an instinct against usury; and the Church has only confirmed that instinct. But to learn how to define usury, to study what it is and to argue why it is wrong, is to have a liberal education, not only in political economy, but in the philosophy of Aristotle and the history of the Councils of Lateran.[44] There almost always is a human reason for all the merely human advice given by the Church to humanity; and to find out the principle of the thing is, among other things, one of the keenest of intellectual pleasures. But in any case the fact remains that the Church is right in the main in being tolerant in the main; but that where she is intolerant she is most right and even more reasonable. Adam lived in a garden where a thousand mercies were granted to him; but the one inhibition was the greatest mercy of all.

In the same way, let the convert, or still more the semi-convert, face any one fact that does seem to him to deface the Catholic scheme as a falsehood; and if he faces it long enough he will probably find that it is the greatest truth of all. I have found this myself in that extreme logic of free will which is found in the fallen angels and the possibility of perdition. Such things are altogether beyond my imagination, but the lines of logic go out towards them in my reason. Indeed, I can undertake to justify the whole Catholic theology, if I be granted to start with the supreme sacredness and value of two things: Reason and Liberty. It is an illuminating comment on current anti-Catholic talk that they are the two things which most people imagine to be forbidden to Catholics.

But the best way of putting what I mean is to repeat what I have already said, in connection with the satisfying scope of Catholic universality. I cannot picture these theological ultimates and I have not the authority or learning to define them. But I still put the matter to myself thus: Supposing I were so miserable as to lose the Faith, could I go back to that cheap charity and crude optimism

---

[44] The Councils of Lateran were five general councils of the Church, held at St. John Lateran church in Rome between 1123 and 1512.

which says that every sin is a blunder, that evil cannot conquer or does not even exist? I could no more go back to those cushioned chapels than a man who has regained his sanity would willingly go back to a padded cell. I might cease to believe in a God of any kind; but I could not cease to think that a God who had made men and angels free was finer than one who coerced them into comfort. I might cease to believe in a future life of any kind; but I could not cease to think it was a finer doctrine that we choose and make our future life than that it is fitted out for us like an hotel and we are taken there in a celestial omnibus as compulsory as a Black Maria.[45] I know that Catholicism is too large for me, and I have not yet explored its beautiful or terrible truths. But I know that Universalism is too small for me; and I could not creep back into that dull safety, who have looked on the dizzy vision of liberty.

[45] The Black Maria was a van used in England to transport prisoners.

VI

A NOTE ON PRESENT PROSPECTS

On reconsidering these notes I find them to be far too personal; yet I do not know how any conception of conversion can be anything else. I do not profess to have any particular knowledge about the actual conditions and calculations of the Catholic movement at the moment. I do not believe that anybody else has any knowledge of what it will be like the next moment. Statistics are generally misleading and predictions are practically always false. But there is always a certain faint tradition of the thing called common sense; and so long as a glimmer of it remains, in spite of all journalism and State instruction, it is possible to appreciate what we call a reality. Nobody in his five wits will deny that at this moment conversion is a reality. Everybody knows that his own social circle, which fifty years ago would have been a firm territory of Protestantism, perhaps hardening into rationalism or indifference but doing even that slowly and without conscious convulsion, has just lately shown a curious disposition to collapse softly and suddenly, first in one unexpected place and then in another, making great holes in that solid land and letting up the leaping flames of what was counted an extinct volcano. It is in everybody's experience, whether he is sad or glad or mad or merely indifferent, that these conversions seem to come of themselves in the most curious and apparently accidental quarters; Tom's wife, Harry's brother, Fanny's funny sister-in-law who went on the stage, Sam's eccentric uncle who studied military strategy—of each of these isolated souls we hear suddenly that it is isolated no longer. It is one with the souls militant and triumphant.

Against these things (which we know as facts and do not merely read as statistics) there is admittedly something to be set. It is what is commonly called leakage; and with a paragraph upon this point I will close these pages. Father Ronald Knox,[46] with that felicity that is so

[46] Monsignor Ronald Knox (1888–1957) was one of the most famous Anglican converts to Catholicism in twentieth-century England. He served as Catholic chaplain at Oxford University (1926–39), produced a fresh translation of the Vulgate Bible, authored detective stories and became one of England's most articulate Catholic apologists.

good that the wit almost seems like good luck, has remarked that the Catholic Church really does have to get on by hook or crook. That is, by the hook of the fisherman and the crook of the shepherd; and it is the hook that has to catch the convert and the crook that has to keep him. He said in this connection that the conversions to the Church just now were so numerous that they would be obvious and overwhelming, like a landslide, if it were not that they were neutralised in mere numbers, or rather lessened in their full claim of numbers, by a certain amount of falling away in other directions. Now the first fact to realise is that it is in other directions, in totally different directions. Some people, especially young people, abandon practicing Catholicism. But none of them abandon it for Protestantism. All of them practically abandon it for paganism. Most of them abandon it for something that is really rather too simple to be called an *ism* of any kind. They abandon it for things and not theories; and when they do have theories they may sometimes be Bolshevist theories or Futurist[47] theories, but they are practically never the theological theories of Protestantism. I will not say they leave Catholicism for beer and skittles; for Catholicism has never discouraged those Christian institutions as Protestantism sometimes has. They leave it to have a high old time; and considering what a muddle we have made of modern morality, they can hardly be blamed. But this reaction, which is only that of a section, is in its nature a reaction of the young and as such I do not think it will last. I know it is the cant phrase of the old rationalists that their reason prevents a return to the Faith, but it is false: it is no longer reason but rather passion.

This may sound a sweeping statement, but if it be examined it will be found not unjust, and certainly not unsympathetic. Nothing is more notable if we really study the characteristics of the rising generation than the fact that they are *not* acting upon any exact and definite philosophy, such as those which have made the revolutions of the past. If they are anarchical, they are not anarchist. The dogmatic anarchism of the middle of the nineteenth century is not the creed they hold, or

[47] Futurism, whose major proponent was the Italian Filippo Marinetti (1876–1944), was an avant-garde artistic and literary movement that arose just before World War I. It celebrated dynamism, violence and the machine age.

even the excuse they offer. They have a considerable negative revolt against religion, a negative revolt against negative morality. They have a feeling, which is not unreasonable, that to commit themselves to the Catholic citizenship is to take responsibilities that continually act as restraints. But they do not maintain anything like a contrary system of spiritual citizenship, or moral responsibility. For instance, it is perfectly natural that they should want to act naturally. But they do not want to act naturally according to any intellectual theory of the reliability of Nature. On the contrary, their young and brilliant literary representatives are very prone to press upon us the crudity and cruelty of Nature. That is the moral of Mr. Aldous Huxley, and of many others. State to them any of the consistent theories of the supreme claim of Nature upon us, such as the pantheistic idea of God in all natural things; or the Nietzschean theory that nature is evolving something with superior claims to our own; or any other definable defence of the natural process itself, and they will almost certainly reject it as something unproved or exploded. They do not want to have an exact imitation of the laws of the physical universe; they want to have their own way, a much more intelligible desire. But the result is that they are, after all, at a disadvantage in face of those other young people who have satisfied their reason by a scheme that makes the universe reasonable.

For that is the very simple explanation of the affair. In so far as there is really a secession among the young, it is but a part of the same process as that conversion of the young, of which I wrote in the first chapter. The rising generation sees the real issue; and those who are ready for it rally, and those who are not ready for it scatter. But there can be but one end to a war between a solid and a scattered army. It is not a controversy between two philosophies, as was the Catholic and the Calvinist, or the Catholic and the Materialist. It is a controversy between philosophers and philanderers. I do not say it in contempt; I have much more sympathy with the person who leaves the Church for a love-affair than with one who leaves it for a long-winded German theory to prove that God is evil or that children are a sort of morbid monkey. But the very laws of life are against the endurance of a revolt that rests on nothing but natural passion; it is bound to change in its proportion with the coming of experience; and, at the worst, it will become a battle between bad Catholics and good Catholics, with the great dome over all.

WHY I AM A CATHOLIC
1926

WHY I AM A CATHOLIC

The difficulty of explaining "why I am a Catholic" is that there are ten thousand reasons all amounting to one reason: that Catholicism is true. I could fill all my space with separate sentences each beginning with the words, "It is the only thing that . . ." As, for instance, (1) It is the only thing that really prevents a sin from being a secret. (2) It is the only thing in which the superior cannot be superior; in the sense of supercilious. (3) It is the only thing that frees a man from the degrading slavery of being a child of his age. (4) It is the only thing that talks as if it were the truth; as if it were a real messenger refusing to tamper with a real message. (5) It is the only type of Christianity that really contains every type of man; even the respectable man. (6) It is the only large attempt to change the world from the inside; working through wills and not laws; and so on.

Or I might treat the matter personally and describe my own conversion; but I happen to have a strong feeling that this method makes the business look much smaller than it really is. Numbers of much better men have been sincerely converted to much worse religions. I would much prefer to attempt to say here of the Catholic Church precisely the things that cannot be said even of its very respectable rivals. In short, I would say chiefly of the Catholic Church that it is catholic. I would rather try to suggest that it is not only larger than me, but larger than anything in the world; that it is indeed larger than the world. But since in this short space I can only take a section, I will consider it in its capacity of a guardian of the truth.

The other day a well-known writer, otherwise quite well-informed, said that the Catholic Church is always the enemy of new ideas. It probably did not occur to him that his own remark was not exactly in the nature of a new idea. It is one of the notions that Catholics have to be continually refuting, because it is such a very old idea. Indeed, those who complain that Catholicism cannot say anything new, seldom think it necessary to say anything new about Catholicism. As a matter of fact, a real study of history will show it to be curiously contrary to the fact. In so far as the ideas really are ideas, and in so far as any such ideas can be new, Catholics have continually suffered through supporting them when they were really new; when they were much too new to find any other support. The Catholic was not only first in the field but alone in the field; and there was as yet nobody to understand what he had found there.

Thus, for instance, nearly two hundred years before the Declaration of Independence and the French Revolution, in an age devoted to the pride and praise of princes, Cardinal Bellarmine and Suarez the Spaniard laid down lucidly the whole theory of real democracy. But in that age of Divine Right they only produced the impression of being sophistical and sanguinary Jesuits, creeping about with daggers to effect the murder of kings. So, again, the Casuists of the Catholic schools said all that can really be said for the problem plays and problem novels of our own time, two hundred years before they were written. They said that there really are problems of moral conduct; but they had the misfortune to say it two hundred years too soon. In a time of tub-thumping fanaticism and free and easy vituperation, they merely got themselves called liars and shufflers for being psychologists before psychology was the fashion. It would be easy to give any number of other examples down to the present day, and the case of ideas that are still too new to be understood. There are passages in Pope Leo's *Encyclical on Labor* which are only now beginning to be used as hints for social movements much newer than socialism. And when Mr. Belloc wrote about the Servile State, he advanced an economic theory so original that hardly anybody has yet realized what it is. A few centuries hence, other people will probably repeat it, and repeat it wrong. And then, if Catholics object, their protest will be easily explained by the well-known fact that Catholics never care for new ideas.

Nevertheless, the man who made that remark about Catholics meant something; and it is only fair to him to understand it rather more clearly than he stated it. What he meant was that, in the modern world, the Catholic Church is in fact the enemy of many influential fashions; most of which still claim to be new, though many of them are beginning to be a little stale. In other words, in so far as he meant that the Church often attacks what the world at any given moment supports, he was perfectly right. The Church does often set herself against the fashion of this world that passes away; and she has experience enough to know how very rapidly it does pass away. But to understand exactly what is involved, it is necessary to take a rather larger view and consider the ultimate nature of the ideas in question, to consider, so to speak, the idea of the idea.

Nine out of ten of what we call new ideas are simply old mistakes. The Catholic Church has for one of her chief duties that of preventing people from making those old mistakes; from making them over and over again forever, as people always do if they are left to themselves. The truth about the Catholic attitude towards heresy, or as some would say, towards liberty, can best be expressed perhaps by the metaphor of a map. The Catholic Church carries a sort of map of the mind which looks like the map of a maze, but which is in fact a guide to the maze. It has been compiled from knowledge which, even considered as human knowledge, is quite without any human parallel. There is no other case of one continuous intelligent institution that has been thinking about thinking for two thousand years. Its experience naturally covers nearly all experiences; and especially nearly all errors. The result is a map in which all the blind alleys and bad roads are clearly marked, all the ways that have been shown to be worthless by the best of all evidence: the evidence of those who have gone down them.

On this map of the mind the errors are marked as exceptions. The greater part of it consists of playgrounds and happy hunting-fields, where the mind may have as much liberty as it likes; not to mention any number of intellectual battle-fields in which the battle is indefinitely open and undecided. But it does definitely take the responsibility of marking certain roads as leading nowhere or leading to destruction, to a blank wall, or a sheer precipice. By this means, it does prevent men from wasting their time or losing their lives upon paths that have been found futile or disastrous again and again in the past, but which might otherwise entrap travelers again and again in the future. The Church does make herself responsible for warning her people against these; and upon these the real issue of the case depends. She does dogmatically defend humanity from its worst foes, those hoary and horrible and devouring monsters of the old mistakes.

Now all these false issues have a way of looking quite fresh, especially to a fresh generation. Their first statement always sounds harmless and plausible. I will give only two examples. It sounds harmless to say, as most modern people have said: "Actions are only wrong if they are bad for society." Follow it out, and sooner or later you will have the inhumanity of a hive or a heathen city, establishing slavery as the cheapest and most certain means of production, torturing the slaves for evidence because the individual is nothing to the State, declaring that an innocent man must die for the people, as did the murderers of Christ. Then, perhaps, you will go back to Catholic definitions, and find that the Church, while she also says it is our duty to work for society, says other things also which forbid individual injustice. Or again, it sounds quite pious to say, "Our moral conflict should end with a victory of the spiritual over the material." Follow it out, and you may end in the madness of the Manicheans, saying that a suicide is good because it is a sacrifice, that a sexual perversion is good because it produces no life, that the devil made the sun and moon because they are material. Then you may begin to guess why Catholicism insists that there are evil spirits as well as good; and that materials also may be sacred, as in the Incarnation or the Mass, in the sacrament of marriage or the resurrection of the body.

Now there is no other corporate mind in the world that is thus on the watch to prevent minds from going wrong. The policeman comes too late, when he tries to prevent men from going wrong. The doctor comes too late, for he only comes to lock up a madman, not to advise a sane man on how not to go mad. And all other sects and schools are inadequate for the purpose. This is not because each of them may not contain a truth, but precisely because each of them does contain a truth; and is content to contain a truth. None of the others really pretends to contain the truth. None of the others, that is, really pretends to be looking out in all directions at once. The Church is not merely armed against the heresies of the past or even of the present, but equally against those of the future, that may be the exact opposite of those of the present. Catholicism is not ritualism; it may in the future be fighting some sort of superstitious and

idolatrous exaggeration of ritual. Catholicism is not asceticism; it
has again and again in the past repressed fanatical and cruel exaggerations of asceticism. Catholicism is not mere mysticism; it is even
now defending human reason against the mere mysticism of the
Pragmatists. Thus, when the world went Puritan in the seventeenth
century, the Church was charged with pushing charity to the point
of sophistry, with making everything easy with the laxity of the
confessional. Now that the world is not going Puritan but Pagan, it
is the Church that is everywhere protesting against a Pagan laxity in
dress or manners. It is doing what the Puritans wanted done when it
is really wanted. In all probability, all that is best in Protestantism
will only survive in Catholicism; and in that sense all Catholics will
still be Puritans when all Puritans are Pagans.

Thus, for instance, Catholicism, in a sense little understood,
stands outside a quarrel like that of Darwinism at Dayton. It stands
outside it because it stands all around it, as a house stands all around
two incongruous pieces of furniture. It is no sectarian boast to say it
is before and after and beyond all these things in all directions. It is
impartial in a fight between the Fundamentalist and the theory of
the Origin of Species, because it goes back to an origin before that
Origin; because it is more fundamental than Fundamentalism. It
knows where the Bible came from. It also knows where most of the
theories of Evolution go to. It knows there were many other Gospels besides the Four Gospels, and that the others were only eliminated by the authority of the Catholic Church. It knows there are
many other evolutionary theories besides the Darwinian theory; and
that the latter is quite likely to be eliminated by later science. It does
not, in the conventional phrase, accept the conclusions of science,
for the simple reason that science has not concluded. To conclude is
to shut up; and the man of science is not at all likely to shut up. It
does not, in the conventional phrase, believe what the Bible says, for
the simple reason that the Bible does not say anything. You cannot
put a book in the witness-box and ask it what it really means. The
Fundamentalist controversy itself destroys Fundamentalism. The
Bible by itself cannot be a basis of agreement when it is a cause
of disagreement; it cannot be the common ground of Christians

when some take it allegorically and some literally. The Catholic refers it to something that can say something, to the living, consistent, and continuous mind of which I have spoken; the highest mind of man guided by God.

Every moment increases for us the moral necessity for such an immortal mind. We must have something that will hold the four corners of the world still, while we make our social experiments or build our Utopias. For instance, we must have a final agreement, if only on the truism of human brotherhood, that will resist some reaction of human brutality. Nothing is more likely just now than that the corruption of representative government will lead to the rich breaking loose altogether, and trampling on all the traditions of equality with mere pagan pride. We must have the truisms everywhere recognized as true. We must prevent mere reaction and the dreary repetition of the old mistakes. We must make the intellectual world safe for democracy. But in the conditions of modern mental anarchy, neither that nor any other ideal is safe. Just as Protestants appealed from priests to the Bible, and did not realize that the Bible also could be questioned, so republicans appealed from kings to the people, and did not realize that the people also could be defied. There is no end to the dissolution of ideas, the destruction of all tests of truth, that has become possible since men abandoned the attempt to keep a central and civilized Truth, to contain all truths and trace out and refute all errors. Since then, each group has taken one truth at a time and spent the time in turning it into a falsehood. We have had nothing but movements; or in other words, monomanias. But the Church is not a movement but a meeting-place; the trysting-place of all the truths in the world.

THE THING:
WHY I AM A CATHOLIC

1929

I

INTRODUCTION

It will be naturally objected to the publication of these papers that they are ephemeral and that they are controversial. In other words, the normal critic will at once dismiss them as too frivolous and dislike them as too serious. The rather one-sided truce of good taste, touching all religious matters, which prevailed until a short time ago, has now given place to a rather one-sided war. But the truce can still be invoked, as such terrorism of taste generally is invoked, against the minority. We all know the dear old Conservative colonel who swears himself red in the face that he is not going to talk politics, but that damning to hell all those bloody blasted Socialists is not politics. We all have a kindly feeling for the dear old lady living at Bath or Cheltenham who would not dream of talking uncharitably about anybody, but who does certainly think the Dissenters are too dreadful or that Irish servants are really impossible. It is in the spirit of these two very admirable persons that the controversy is now conducted in the Press on behalf of a Progressive Faith and a Broad and Brotherly Religion. So long as the writer employs vast and universal gestures of fellowship and hospitality to all those who are ready to abandon their religious beliefs, he is allowed to be as rude as he likes to all those who venture to retain them. The Dean of St. Paul's[1] permits himself genially to call the Catholic Church a treacherous and bloody corporation; Mr. H. G. Wells is allowed to compare the Blessed Trinity to an undignified dance; the Bishop of Birmingham to compare the Blessed Sacrament to a barbarous blood-feast. It is felt that phrases like these cannot ruffle that human peace and harmony which all such humanitarians desire; there is nothing in these expressions that could possibly interfere with brotherhood and the sympathy that is the bond of society; we may be sure of this, for we have the word of the writers themselves that

[1] William Inge (1860–1954) was dean of St. Paul's Anglican cathedral, London, from 1911 to 1934.

their whole aim is to generate an atmosphere of liberality and love. If, therefore, any unlucky interruption mar the harmony of the occasion, if it is really impossible for these fraternal festivities to pass off without some silly disturbance, or somebody making a scene, it is obvious that the blame must lie with a few irritable and irritating individuals, who cannot accept these descriptions of the Trinity and the Sacrament and the Church as soothing their feelings or satisfying their ideas.

It is explained very clearly in all such statements that they are accepted by all intelligent people except those who do not accept them. But as I myself, in my political experience, have ventured to doubt the right of the Tory colonel to curse his political opponents and say it is not politics, or of the lady to love everybody and loathe Irishmen, I have the same difficulty in admitting the right of the most liberal and large-minded Christian to see good in all religions and nothing but evil in mine. But I know that to publish replies to this effect, particularly direct replies given in real controversy, will be regarded by many as a provocation and an impertinence.

Well, I must in this matter confess to being so old-fashioned as to feel something like a point of honour. I think I may say that I am normally of the sort to be sociable and get on easily with my fellows; I am not so much disposed to quarrel as to argue; and I value more than I can easily say the generally genial relations I have kept with those who differ from me merely in argument. I am very fond of England even as it is, quite apart from what it was or might be; I have a number of popular tastes, from detective stories to the defence of public houses; I have been on many occasions on the side of the majority, as for instance in the propaganda of English patriotism during the Great War. I could even find in these sympathies a sufficient material for popular appeals; and, in a more practical sense, I should enjoy nothing more than always writing detective stories, except always reading them. But if in this much too lucky and even lazy existence I find that my co-religionists are being pelted with insults for saying that their religion is right, it would ill become me not to put myself in the way of being insulted. Many of them have had far too hard a life, and I have had far too easy a life, for me not to count it a privilege to be the object of the same curious controversial methods. If the Dean of St. Paul's really does believe, as he most undoubtedly does say, that the most devout and devoted rulers of the Catholic Church, when they accepted (realistically and even reluctantly) the fact of a modern miracle, were engaged in a "lucrative imposture," I should very much prefer to believe that he accuses me along with better men than myself of becoming an impostor merely for filthy lucre. If the word "Jesuit" is still to be used as synonymous with the word "liar," I should prefer that the same simple translation should apply to the word "Journalist," of which it is much more often true. If the Dean accuses Catholics as Catholics of desiring innocent men to die in prison (as he does), I should much prefer that he should cast me for some part in that terrific and murderous melodrama; it might in any case be material for a detective story. In short, it is precisely because I do sympathize and agree with my Protestant and agnostic fellow countrymen, on about ninety-nine subjects out of a hundred, that I do feel it a point of honour not to avoid their accusations on these points, if they really have such accusations to bring. I am very sorry if this little book of mine seems to be controversial on subjects about which everybody is allowed to be controversial except ourselves. But I am afraid there is no help for it; and if I assure the reader that I have tried to start putting it together in an unimpaired spirit of charity, it is always possible that the charity may be as one-sided as the controversy. Anyhow, it represents my attitude towards this controversy; and it is quite possible that everything is wrong with it, except that it is right.

II

THE SCEPTIC AS A CRITIC

It takes three to make a quarrel. There is needed a peacemaker. The full potentialities of human fury cannot be reached until a friend of both parties tactfully intervenes. I feel myself to be in some such position in the recent American debate about Mr. Mencken's *Mercury*[2] and the Puritans; and I admit it at the beginning with an embarrassment not untinged with terror. I know that the umpire may be torn in pieces. I know that the self-appointed umpire ought to be torn in pieces. I know, above all, that this is especially the case in anything which in any way involves international relations.

Perhaps the only sound criticism is self-criticism. Perhaps this is even more true of nations than of men. And I can quite well understand that many Americans would accept suggestions from their fellow countrymen which they would rightly refuse from a foreigner. I can only plead that I have endeavoured to carry out the excellent patriotic principle of "See England First" in the equally patriotic paraphrase of "Criticize England First." I have been engaged upon it long enough to be quite well aware that there are evils present in England that are relatively absent from America; and none more conspicuously absent, as Mr. Belloc has pointed out to the surprise of many, than the real, servile, superstitious, and mystical adoration of Money.

But what makes me so objectionable on the present occasion is that I feel a considerable sympathy with both sides. This offensive attitude I will endeavour to disguise, as far as possible, by tactfully distributed abuse of such things as I really think are abuses, and a gracefully simulated disgust with this or that part of each controversial case. But the plain truth is, that if I were an American, I should very frequently rejoice at the *American Mercury's* scoring off somebody

---

[2] Henry Louis Mencken (1880–1956), an American journalist and author, was a caustic critic of American society and literature. He founded and edited the *American Mercury* (1924).

or something; nor would my modest fireside be entirely without mild rejoicings when the *American Mercury* was scored off. But I do definitely think that both sides, and perhaps especially the iconoclastic side, need what the whole modern world needs — a fixed spiritual standard even for their own intellectual purposes. I might express it by saying that I am very fond of revolutionists, but not very fond of nihilists. For nihilists, as their name implies, have nothing to revolt about.

On this side of the matter there is little to be added to the admirably sane, subtle, and penetrating article by Mr. T. S. Eliot;* especially that vital sentence in it in which he tells Professor Irving Babbitt[3] (who admits the need of enthusiasm) that we cannot have an enthusiasm for having an enthusiasm. I think I know, incidentally, what we must have. Professor Babbitt is a very learned man; and I myself have little Latin and less Greek. But I know enough Greek to know the meaning of the second syllable of "enthusiasm," and I know it to be the key to this and every other discussion.

Let me take two examples, touching my points of agreement with the two sides. I heartily admire Mr. Mencken, not only for his vivacity and wit, but for his vehemence and sometimes for his violence. I warmly applaud him for his scorn and detestation of Service; and I think he was stating a historical fact when he said, as quoted in *The Forum*: "When a gang of real estate agents, bond salesmen, and automobile dealers gets together to sob for Service, it takes no Freudian to surmise that someone is about to be swindled." I do not see why he should not call a spade a spade and a swindler a swindler. I do not blame him for using vulgar words for vulgar things. But I do remark upon two ways in which the fact of his philosophy being negative makes his criticism almost shallow. First of all, it is obvious that such a satire is entirely meaningless unless swindling is a sin. And it is equally obvious that we are instantly swallowed up in the abysses of "moralism" and "religionism," if it is a sin. And the second point, if less obvious, is equally important — that his healthy instinct against greasy hypocrisy does not really enlighten him about the heart of that hypocrisy.

---

* "The Humanism of Irving Babbitt", *The Forum* for July 1928.

[3] Irving Babbitt (1865–1933) was professor of French literature at Harvard from 1894 to 1933, and a leading figure in the New Humanism.

What is the matter with the cult of Service is that, like so many modern notions, it is an idolatry of the intermediate, to the oblivion of the ultimate. It is like the jargon of the idiots who talk about Efficiency without any criticism of Effect. The sin of Service is the sin of Satan: that of trying to be first where it can only be second. A word like Service has stolen the sacred capital letter from the thing which it was once supposed to serve. There is a sense in serving God, and an even more disputed sense in serving man; but there is no sense in serving Service. To serve God is at least to serve an ideal being. Even if he were an imaginary being, he would still be an ideal being. That ideal has definite and even dogmatic attributes — truth, justice, pity, purity, and the rest. To serve it, however imperfectly, is to serve a particular concept of perfection. But the man who rushes down the street waving his arms and wanting something or somebody to serve, will probably fall into the first bucket-shop or den of thieves and usurers, and be found industriously serving *them*. There arises the horrible idea that industry, reliability, punctuality, and business activity are good things; that mere readiness to serve the powers of this world is a Christian virtue. That is the case against Service, as distinct from the curse against Service, so heartily and inspiringly hurled by Mr. Mencken. But the serious case cannot be stated without once more raising the real question of whether mankind ought to serve anything; and of whether they had not better try to define what they intend to serve. All these silly words like Service and Efficiency and Practicality and the rest fail because they worship the means and not the end. But it all comes back to whether we do propose to worship the end; and preferably the right end.

Two other characteristic passages from Mr. Mencken will serve to show more sharply this curious sense in which he misses his own point. On the one hand, he appears to state most positively the purely personal and subjective nature of criticism; he makes it individual and almost irresponsible. "The critic is first and last simply trying to express himself; he is trying to achieve thereby for his own inner ego the grateful feeling of a function performed, a tension relieved, a katharsis attained, which Wagner achieved when he wrote *Die Walküre*, and a hen achieves every time she lays an egg." That is all consistent enough as far as it goes; but unfortunately Mr. Mencken appears to go on to something quite inconsistent with it. According to the quotation, he afterwards bursts into a song of triumph because there is now in America not only criticism, but controversy. "To-day for the first time in years there is strife in American criticism . . . ears are bitten off, noses are bloodied. There are wallops both above and below the belt."

Now, there may be something in his case for controversy; but it is quite inconsistent with his case for creative self-expression. If the critic produces the criticism *only* to please himself, it is entirely irrelevant that it does not please somebody else. The somebody else has a perfect right to say the exact opposite to please himself, and be perfectly satisfied with himself. But they cannot controvert because they cannot compare. They cannot compare because there is no common standard of comparison. Neither I nor anybody else can have a controversy about literature with Mr. Mencken, because there is no way of criticizing the criticism, except by asking whether the critic is satisfied. And there the debate ends, at the beginning: for nobody can doubt that Mr. Mencken is satisfied.

But not to make Mr. Mencken a mere victim of the *argumentum ad hominem*, I will make the experiment in a viler body and offer myself for dissection. I daresay a great deal of the criticism I write really is moved by a mood of self-expression; and certainly it is true enough that there is a satisfaction in self-expression. I can take something or other about which I have definite feelings — as, for instance, the philosophy of Mr. Dreiser,[4] which has been mentioned more than once in this debate. I can achieve for my own inner ego the grateful feeling of writing as follows:

"He describes a world which appears to be a dull and discolouring illusion of indigestion, not bright enough to be called a nightmare; smelly, but not even stinking with any strength; smelling of the stale gas of ignorant chemical experiments by dirty, secretive schoolboys — the sort of boys who torture cats in corners; spineless and spiritless like a broken-backed worm; loathsomely slow and laborious

[4] Theodore Dreiser (1871–1945) was an American novelist whose naturalist fiction dealt with the dispossessed and criminal and the grimmer realities of American life.

like an endless slug; despairing, but not with dignity; blaspheming, but not with courage; without wit, without will, without laughter or uplifting of the heart; too old to die, too deaf to leave off talking, too blind to stop, too stupid to start afresh, too dead to be killed, and incapable even of being damned, since in all its weary centuries it has not reached the age of reason."

That is what I feel about it; and it certainly gives me pleasure to relieve my feelings. I have got it off my chest. I have attained a katharsis. I have laid an egg. I have produced a criticism, satisfying all Mr. Mencken's definitions of the critic. I have performed a function. I feel better, thank you.

But what influence my feelings can be expected to have on Mr. Dreiser, or anybody who does not admit my standards of truth and falsehood, I do not quite see. Mr. Dreiser can hardly be expected to say that his chemistry is quackery, as I think it—quackery without the liveliness we might reasonably expect from quacks. He does not think fatalism base and servile, as I do; he does not think free will the highest truth about humanity, as I do. He does not believe that despair is itself a sin, and perhaps the worst of sins, as Catholics do. He does not think blasphemy the smallest and silliest sort of pride, as even pagans do. He naturally does not think his own picture of life a false picture, resembling real life about as much as a wilderness of linoleum would resemble the land of all the living flowers, as I do. But he would not think it falser for being like a wilderness. He would probably admit that it was dreary, but think it correct to be dreary. He would probably own that he was hopeless, but not see any harm in being hopeless. What I advance as accusations, he would very probably accept as compliments.

Under these circumstances, I do not quite see how I, or anyone with my views, could have a *controversy* with Mr. Dreiser. There does not seem to be any way in which I could prove him wrong, because he does not accept my view of what is wrong. There does not seem to be any way in which he could prove himself right, because I do not share his notions of what is right. We might, indeed, meet in the street and fall on each other; and while I believe we are both heavy men, I doubt not that he is the more formidable. The very possibility of our being reduced to this inarticulate explanation may possibly throw some light on Mr. Mencken's remarkable description of the new literary life in America. "Ears are bitten off," he says; and this curious form of cultural intercourse might really be the only solution, when ears are no longer organs of hearing and there are no organs except organs of self-expression. He that hath ears to hear and will not hear may just as well have them bitten off. Such deafness seems inevitable in the creative critic, who is as indifferent as a hen to all noises except her own cackling over her own egg. Anyhow, hens do not criticize each other's eggs, or even pelt each other with eggs, in the manner of political controversy. We can only say that the novelist in question has undoubtedly laid a magnificently large and solid egg — something in the nature of an ostrich's egg; and after that, there is really nothing to prevent the ostrich from hiding its head in the sand, achieving thereby for its own inner ego the grateful feeling of a function performed. But we cannot argue with it about whether the egg is a bad egg, or whether parts of it are excellent.

In all these instances, therefore, because of the absence of a standard of utimate values, the most ordinary functions really cannot be performed. They not only cannot be performed with "a grateful feeling," or a katharsis, but in the long run they cannot be performed at all. We cannot really denounce the Service-mongering bond salesman as a swindler, because we have no certain agreement that it is shameful to be a swindler. A little manipulation of some of Mr. Mencken's own individualistic theories about mentality as superior to moralism might present the swindler as a superman. We cannot really argue for or against the mere ideal of Service, because neither side has really considered what is to be served or how we are to arrive at the right rules for serving it. Consequently, in practice, it may turn out that the State of Service is merely the Servile State. And finally, we cannot really argue about that or anything else, because there are no rules of the game of argument. There is nothing to prove who has scored a point and who has not. There cannot be "strife in American criticism"; the professors cannot be "forced to make some defence." That would require plaintiffs and defendants to appear before some tribunal and give evidence according to some tests of truth. There can be a disturbance, but there cannot be a discussion.

In plain words, the normal functions of man — effort, protest, judgment, persuasion, and proof — are found in fact to be hampered and hamstrung by these negations of the sceptic even when the sceptic seems at first to be only denying some distant vision or some miraculous tale. Each function is found in fact to refer to some end, to some test, to some way of distinguishing between use and misuse, which the mere sceptic destroys as completely as he could destroy any myth or superstition. If the function is only performed for the satisfaction of the performer, as in the parable of the critic and the egg, it becomes futile to discuss whether it is an addled egg. It becomes futile to consider whether eggs will produce chickens or provide breakfast. But even to be certain of our own sanity in applying the tests, we do really have to go back to some aboriginal problem, like that of the old riddle of the priority of egg or chicken; we do really, like the great religions, have to begin *ab ovo*. If those primordial sanities can be disturbed, the whole of practical life can be disturbed with them. Men can be frozen by fatalism, or crazed by anarchism, or driven to death by pessimism; for men will not go on indefinitely acting on what they feel to be a fable. And it is in this organic and almost muscular sense that religion is really the help of man — in the sense that without it he is ultimately helpless, almost motionless.

Mr. Mencken and Mr. Sinclair Lewis and the other critics in the *Mercury* movement are so spirited and sincere, they attack so vigorously so many things that ought to be attacked, they expose so brilliantly many things that really are impostures, that in discussing matters with them a man will have every impulse to put his cards on the table. It would be affectation and almost hypocrisy in me to ignore, in this place, the fact that I do myself believe in a special spiritual solution of this problem, a special spiritual authority above this chaos. Nor, indeed, is the idea altogether absent, as an idea, from many other minds besides my own. The Catholic philosophy is mentioned in terms of respect, and even a sort of hope, both by Professor Babbitt* and Mr.

* Babbitt mentions it in "The Critic and American life", *The Forum* for February 1928.

T. S. Eliot. I do not misunderstand their courtesies, or seek to lure them a step further than they desire to go. But, as a matter of fact, by a series of faultlessly logical steps, Mr. Eliot led Professor Babbitt so near to the very gates of the Catholic Church that in the end I felt quite nervous, so to speak, for fear they should both take another unintentional step and fall into it by accident.

I have a particular reason for mentioning this matter in conclusion—a reason that is directly related to this curious effect of scepticism in weakening the normal functions of the human being. In one of the most brilliant and amusing of Mr. Sinclair Lewis's recent books there is a passage which I quote from memory, but I think more or less correctly. He said that the Catholic Faith differs from current Puritanism in that it does not ask a man to give up his sense of beauty, or his sense of humour, or his pleasant vices (by which he probably meant smoking and drinking, which are not vices at all), but that it does ask a man to give up his life and soul, his mind, body, reason, and all the rest. I ask the reader to consider, as quietly and impartially as possible, the statement thus made; and put it side by side with all those other facts about the gradual fossilizing of human function by the fundamental doubts of our day.

It would be far truer to say that the Faith gives a man back his body and his soul and his reason and his will and his very life. It would be far truer to say that the man who has received it receives all the old human functions which all the other philosophies are already taking away. It would be nearer to reality to say that he alone will have freedom, that he alone will have will, because he alone will believe in free will; that he alone will have reason, since ultimate doubt denies reason as well as authority; that he alone will truly act, because action is performed to an end. It is at least a less unlikely vision that all this hardening and hopeless despair of the intellect will leave him at last the only walking and talking citizen in a city of paralytics.

III

IS HUMANISM A RELIGION?

I have just been reading Mr. Norman Foerster's[5] book on "American Criticism"; and I hope it is no disrespect to the bulk of the book, a series of very thoughtful studies on American thinkers, if I say that the whole point of it is in the last chapter; which propounds a certain problem or challenge to modern thought. It is the problem of whether what he calls Humanism can satisfy humanity. Of his other topics it would be easy to talk for ever. He generally says the right thing; he sometimes says the last word, in that suggestive or provocative style that tempts somebody to say one word more. In my own estimate of his subjects, Whitman would be very much larger and Lowell very much smaller. About Emerson he seems both sensitive and just; and Emerson certainly had distinction; but just that dry sort of distinction to which I should always be afraid of being unfair. A Puritan tried to be a Pagan; and succeeded in being a Pagan who hesitated about whether he ought to go and see a girl dancing. But all these things are stimulating but secondary to the question which I will take the liberty of attacking separately and attempting to answer seriously. I fear that answering it seriously must mean answering it personally. The question really is whether Humanism can perform all the functions of religion; and I cannot but regard it in relation to my own religion. It is only just to say that Humanism is quite different from Humanitarianism. It means, as explained here, something like this. Modern science and organization are in a sense only too natural. They herd us like the beasts along lines of heredity or tribal doom; they attach man to the earth like a plant instead of liberating him, even like a bird, let alone an angel. Indeed, their latest psychology is lower than the level of life. What is subconscious is sub-human and, as it were, subterranean:

---

[5] Norman Foerster (1887–1972) was an American literary critic and a proponent of the New Humanism.

or something less than earthly. This fight for culture is above all a fight for consciousness: what some would call self-consciousness: but anyhow against mere subconsciousness. We need a rally of the really *human* things; will which is morals, memory which is tradition, culture which is the mental thrift of our fathers. Nevertheless, my first duty is to answer the question put to me; and I must answer it in the negative.

I do not believe that Humanism can be a complete substitute for Superhumanism. I do not believe it because of a certain truth to me so concrete as to be called a fact. I know it sounds very like something that has often been said in conventional or superficial apologetics. But I do not mean it in that vague sense; so far from inheriting it as a convention, I have rather recently collided with it as a discovery. I have realized it relatively late in life, and realized that it is indeed that whole story and moral of my own lifetime. But even a few years ago, when most of my moral and religious views were pretty finally formed, I should not have seen it quite sharply and clearly; as I see it now.

The fact is this: that the modern world, with its modern movements, is living on its Catholic capital. It is using, and using up, the truths that remain to it out of the old treasury of Christendom; including, of course, many truths known to pagan antiquity but crystallized in Christendom. But it is *not* really starting new enthusiasms of its own. The novelty is a matter of names and labels, like modern advertisement; in almost every other way the novelty is merely negative. It is not starting fresh things that it can really carry on far into the future. On the contrary, it is picking up old things that it cannot carry on at all. For these are the two marks of modern moral ideals. First, that they were borrowed or snatched out of ancient or mediaeval hands. Second, that they wither very quickly in modern hands. That is, very briefly, the thesis I maintain; and it so happens that the book called *American Criticism* might almost have been meant for a text-book to prove my point.

I will begin with a particular example with which the book also deals. My whole youth was filled, as with a sunrise, with the sanguine glow of Walt Whitman. He seemed to me something like a crowd turned to a giant, or like Adam the First Man. It thrilled me to hear of somebody who had heard of somebody, who saw him in the street; it was as if Christ were still alive. I did not care about whether his unmetrical poetry were a wise form or no, any more than whether a true Gospel of Jesus were scrawled on parchment or stone. I never had a hint of the evil some enemies have attributed to him; if it was there, it was not there for me. What I saluted was a new equality, which was not a dull levelling but an enthusiastic lifting; a shouting exultation in the mere fact that men were men. Real men were greater than unreal gods; and each remained as mystic and majestic as a god, while he became as frank and comforting as a comrade. The point can be put most compactly in one of Whitman's own phrases; he says somewhere that old artists painted crowds, in which one head had a nimbus of gold-coloured light; "but I paint hundreds of heads, but paint no head without its nimbus of gold-coloured light." A glory was to cling about men as men; a mutual worship was to take the form of fellowship; and the least and lowest of men must be included in this fellowship; a hump-backed negro half-wit, with one eye and homicidal mania, must not be painted without his nimbus of gold-coloured light. This might seem only the final expansion of the movement begun a century before with Rousseau and the Revolutionists; and I was brought up to believe, and did believe, that the movement was the beginning of bigger and better things. But these were songs before sunrise: and there is no comparison between even sunrise and the sun. Whitman was brotherhood in broad daylight, showing endless varieties of radiant and wonderful creatures, all the more sacred for being solid. Shelley had adored Man, but Whitman adored Men. Every human face, every human feature, was a matter of mystical poetry, such as lit like chance torchlight, hitherto, a face here and there in the crowd. A king was a man treated as all men should be treated. A god was a man worshipped as all men should be worshipped. What could they do against a race of gods and a republic of kings; not verbally but veritably the New World?

Well . . . here is what Mr. Foerster says about the present position of the founder of the new world of democracy: "Our present science lends little support to an inherent 'dignity of man' or to his 'perfectibility.'

It is wholly possible that the science of the future will lead us away from democracy towards some form of aristocracy. The millennial expectations that Whitman built upon science and democracy, we are now well aware, rested upon insecure foundations. . . . The perfection of nature, the natural goodness of man, 'the great pride of man in himself' offset with an emotional humanitarianism — these are the materials of a structure only slightly coloured with modernity. His politics, his ethics, his religion belong to the past, even that facile 'religiousness' which he hoped would suffuse and complete the work of science and democracy. . . . In the essentials of his prophecy, Whitman, we must conclude, has been falsified by the event." This is a very moderate and fair statement; it would be easy to find the same thing in a much fiercer statement. Here is a monumental remark by Mr. H. L. Mencken: "They (he means certain liberal or ex-liberal thinkers) have come to realize that the morons whom they sweated to save do not want to be saved, and are not worth saving." That is the New Spirit, if there is any New Spirit. "I will make unconquerable cities, with their arms about each other's necks," cried Walt Whitman, "by the love of comrades, by the lifelong love of comrades." I like to think of the face of Mr. Mencken of Baltimore, if some casual comrade from Pittsburg tried to make him unconquerable by putting an arm round his neck. But the idea is dead for much less ferocious people than Mr. Mencken. It is dead in a man like Aldous Huxley, who complained recently of the "gratuitous" romancing of the old republican view of human nature. It is dead in the most humane and humorous of our recent critics. It is dead in so many wise and good men today, that I cannot help wondering whether, under modern conditions of his favourite "science," it would not be dead in Whitman himself.

It is not dead in me. It remains real for me, not by any merit of mine, but by the fact that this mystical idea, while it has evaporated as a mood, still exists as a creed. I am perfectly prepared to assert, as firmly as I should have asserted in my boyhood, that the humpbacked and half-witted negro is decorated with a nimbus of gold-coloured light. The truth is that Whitman's wild picture, or what he thought was a wild picture, is in fact a very old and orthodox picture.

There are, as a matter of fact, any number of old pictures in which whole crowds are crowned with haloes, to indicate that they have all attained Beatitude. But for Catholics it is a fundamental dogma of the Faith that all human beings, without any exception whatever, were specially made, were shaped and pointed like shining arrows, for the end of hitting the mark of Beatitude. It is true that the shafts are feathered with free will, and therefore throw the shadow of all the tragic possibilities of free will; and that the Church (having also been aware for ages of that darker side of truth, which the new sceptics have just discovered) does also draw attention to the darkness of that potential tragedy. But that does not make any difference to the gloriousness of the potential glory. In one aspect it is even a part of it; since the freedom is itself a glory. In that sense they would still wear their haloes even in hell.

But the point is that anyone believing that all these beings were made to be blessed, and multitudes of them probably well on their way to be blessed, really has a sound philosophic reason for regarding them all as radiant and wonderful creatures, or seeing all their heads in haloes. That conviction does make every human face, every human feature, a matter of mystical poetry. But it is not at all like modern poetry. The most modern of modern poetry is not the poetry of reception, but of rejection, or rather, of repulsion. The spirit that inhabits most recent work might be called a fury of fastidiousness. The new man of letters does not get his effect by saying that for him a hump-backed negro has a halo. He gets his effect by saying that, just as he was about to embrace finally the fairest of women, he was nauseated by a pimple above her eyebrow or a stain of grease on her left thumb. Whitman tried to prove that dirty things were really clean, as when he glorified manure as the matrix of the purity of grass. His followers in free verse try to prove that clean things are really dirty; to suggest something leprous and loathsome about the thick whiteness of milk, or something prickly and plague-stricken about the unaccountable growth of hair. In short, the whole mood has changed, as a matter of poetry. But it has not changed as a matter of theology; and that is the argument for having an unchanging theology. The Catholic theology has nothing to do with democracy, for or against, in the sense of a machinery of voting or a criticism of particular political privileges. It is not committed to support what Whitman said for democracy, or even what Jefferson or Lincoln said for democracy. But it is absolutely committed to contradict what Mr. Mencken says against democracy. There will be Diocletian persecutions, there will be Dominican crusades, there will be rending of all religious peace and compromise, or even the end of civilization and the world, before the Catholic Church will admit that one single moron, or one single man, " is not worth saving."

I have therefore found in my middle age this curious fact about the lesson of my life, and that of all my generation. We all grew up with a common conviction, lit by the flames of the literary genius of Rousseau, of Shelley, of Victor Hugo, finding its final flare up and conflagration in the universalism of Walt Whitman. And we all took it for granted that all our descendants would take it for granted. I said the discovery of brotherhood seemed like the discovery of broad daylight; of something that men could never grow tired of. Yet even in my own short lifetime, men have already grown tired of it. We cannot now appeal to the love of equality as an *emotion*. We cannot now open a new book of poems, and expect it to be about the life-long love of comrades, or "Love, the beloved Republic, that feeds upon freedom and lives." We realize that in most men it has died, because it was a mood and not a doctrine. And we begin to wonder too late, in the wise fashion of the aged, how we could ever have expected it to last as a mood, if it was not strong enough to last as a doctrine. And we also begin to realize that all the real strength there was in it, which is the only strength that remains in it, was the original strength of the doctrine. What really happened was this: that the men of the eighteenth century, many of them in a just impatience with corrupt and cynical priests, turned on those priests and said in effect, "Well, I suppose you call yourselves Christians; so you can't actually *deny* that men are brothers or that it is our duty to help the poor." The very confidence of their challenge, the very ringing note in the revolutionary voice, came from the fact that the Christian reactionaries were in a false position as Christians. The democratic demand one because it seemed unanswerable. And it seemed unanswerable, not in the least because it is unanswerable, but because even decadent Christians dared not give the answer. Mr. H. L. Mencken will always be happy to oblige with the answer.

Now, it was just here that, for me, the business began to be odd and interesting. For, looking back on older religious crises, I seem to see a certain coincidence; or rather, a set of things too coincident to be called a coincidence. After all, when I come to think of it, all the other revolts against the Church, before the Revolution and especially since the Reformation, had told the same strange story. Every great heretic had always exhibited three remarkable characteristics in combination. First, he picked out some mystical idea from the Church's bundle or balance of mystical ideas. Second, he used that one mystical idea against all the other mystical ideas. Third (and most singular), he seems generally to have had no notion that his own favourite mystical idea was a mystical idea, at least in the sense of a mysterious or dubious or dogmatic idea. With a queer uncanny innocence, he seems always to have taken this one thing for granted. He assumed it to be unassailable, even when he was using it to assail all sorts of similar things. The most popular and obvious example is the Bible. To an impartial pagan or sceptical observer, it must always seem the strangest story in the world; that men rushing in to wreck a temple, overturning the altar and driving out the priest, found there certain sacred volumes inscribed "Psalms" or "Gospels"; and (instead of throwing them on the fire with the rest) began to use them as infallible oracles rebuking all the other arrangements. If the sacred high altar was all wrong, why were the secondary sacred documents necessarily all right? If the priest had faked his Sacraments, why could he not have faked his Scriptures? Yet it was long before it even occurred to those who brandished this one piece of Church furniture to break up all the other Church furniture that anybody could be so profane as to examine this one fragment of furniture itself. People were quite surprised, and in some parts of the world are still surprised, that anybody should dare to do so.

Again, the Calvinists took the Catholic idea of the absolute knowledge and power of God; and treated it as a rocky irreducible truism so solid that anything could be built on it, however crushing or cruel. They were so confident in their logic, and its one first principle of predestination, that they tortured the intellect and imagination with dreadful deductions about God, that seemed to turn Him into a demon. But it never seems to have struck them that somebody might suddenly say that he did not believe in the demon. They were quite surprised when people called "infidels" here and there began to say it. They had assumed the Divine foreknowledge as so fixed, that it must, if necessary, fulfil itself by destroying the Divine mercy. They never thought anybody would deny the knowledge exactly as they denied the mercy. Then came Wesley and the reaction against Calvinism; and Evangelicals seized on the very Catholic idea that mankind has a sense of sin; and they wandered about offering everybody release from his mysterious burden of sin. It is a proverb, and almost a joke, that they address a stranger in the street and offer to relax his secret agony of sin. But it seldom seemed to strike them, until much later, that the man in the street might possibly answer that he did not want to be saved from sin, any more than from spotted fever or St. Vitus's Dance; because these things were not in fact causing him any suffering at all. They, in their turn, were quite surprised when the result of Rousseau and the revolutionary optimism began to express itself in men claiming a purely human happiness and dignity; a contentment with the comradeship of their kind; ending with the happy yawp of Whitman that he would not "lie awake and weep for his sins."

Now the plain truth is that Shelley and Whitman and the revolutionary optimists were themselves doing exactly the same thing all over again. They also, though less consciously because of the chaos of their times, had really taken out of the old Catholic tradition one particular transcendental idea; the idea that there is a spiritual dignity in man as man, and a universal duty to love men as men. And they acted in exactly the same extraordinary fashion as their prototypes, the Wesleyans and the Calvinists. They took it for granted that this spiritual idea was absolutely self-evident like the sun and moon; that nobody could ever destroy that, though in the name of it they destroyed everything else. They perpetually hammered away at their human divinity and human dignity, and inevitable love for all human beings; as if these things were naked natural facts. And now they are quite surprised when new and restless realists suddenly explode, and begin to say that a pork-butcher with red whiskers and a wart on his nose does not strike them as particularly divine or dignified, that they are not conscious of the smallest sincere impulse to love him, that they could not love him if they tried, or that they do not recognize any particular obligation to try.

It might appear that the process has come to an end, and that there is nothing more for the naked realist to shed. But it is not so; and the process can still go on. There are still traditional charities to which men cling. There are still traditional charities for them to fling away when they find they are only traditional. Everybody must have noticed in the most modern writers the survival of a rather painful sort of pity. They no longer honour all men, like St. Paul and the other mystical democrats. It would hardly be too much to say that they despise all men; often (to do them justice) including themselves. But they do in a manner pity all men, and particularly those that are pitiable; by this time they extend the feeling almost disproportionately to the other animals. This compassion for men is also tainted with its historical connection with Christian charity; and even in the case of animals, with the example of many Christian saints. There is nothing to show that a new revulsion from such sentimental religions will not free men even from the obligation of pitying the pain of the world. Not only Nietzsche, but many Neo-Pagans working on his lines, have suggested such hardness as a higher intellectual purity. And having read many modern poems about the Man of the Future, made of steel and illumined with nothing warmer than green fire, I have no difficulty in imagining a literature that should pride itself on a merciless and metallic detachment. Then, perhaps, it might be faintly conjectured that the last of the Christian virtues had died. But so long as they lived they were Christian.

I do not therefore believe that Humanism and Religion are rivals on equal terms. I believe it is a rivalry between the pools and the fountain; or between the firebrands and the fire. Each of these old intellectuals snatched one firebrand out of the undying fire; but the point is that though he waved the torch very wildly, though he would have used the torch to burn down half the world, the torch went out very soon. The Puritans did not really perpetuate their sublime exultation in helplessness; they only made it unpopular. We did not go on indefinitely looking at the Brooklyn crowds with the eye of Whitman; we have come with singular rapidity to regard them with the eye of Dreiser. In short, I distrust spiritual experiments outside the central spiritual tradition; for the simple reason that I think they do not last, even if they manage to spread. At the most they stand for one generation; at the commonest for one fashion; at the lowest for one clique. I do not think they have the secret of continuity; certainly not of corporate continuity. For an antiquated, doddering old democrat like myself may be excused for attaching some slight importance to that last question; that of covering the common life of mankind. How many Humanists are there supposed to be among the inferior crowd of human beings? Are there to be, for instance, no more than there were Greek philosophers in an ordinary rabble of jolly pagan polytheistic Greeks? Are there to be no more than there were men concentrated on the Culture of Matthew Arnold, among the mobs who followed Cardinal Manning[6] or General Booth?[7] I do not in the least intend to sneer at Humanism; I think I understand the intellectual distinction it draws, and I have tried to understand it in a spirit of humility; but I feel a faint interest in how many people out of the battered and bewildered human race are actually expected to understand it. And I ask with a certain personal interest; for there are three hundred million people in the world who accept the mysteries that I accept and live by the faith I hold. I really want to know whether it is anticipated that there will be three hundred million Humanists in Humanity. The sanguine may say that Humanism will be the religion of the next generation, just as Comte said that Humanity would be the God of the next generation; and so in one sense it was. But it is not the God of this generation. And the question is what will be the religion of the next generation after that, or all the other generations (as a certain ancient promise ran) even unto the end of the world.

[6] Henry Edward Manning (1808–92), a convert to Catholicism, became archbishop of Westminster in 1865 and a cardinal ten years later.
[7] William Booth (1829–1912), an Englishman, founded the Salvation Army.

Humanism, in Mr. Foerster's sense, has one very wise and worthy character. It is really trying to pick up the pieces; that is, to pick up all the pieces. All that was done before was first blind destruction and then random and scrappy selection; as if boys had broken up a stained-glass window and then made a few scraps into coloured spectacles, the rose-coloured spectacles of the republican or the green or yellow spectacles of the pessimist and the decadent. But Humanism as here professed will stoop to gather all it can; for instance, it is great enough to stoop and pick up the jewel of humility. Mr. Foerster does understand, as the eighteenth and nineteenth centuries did not understand, the case for humility. Matthew Arnold, who made something of the same stand for what he called Culture in the mid-nineteenth century, attempted something of the same preservation of chastity; which he would call, in a rather irritating manner, "pureness." But before we call either Culture or Humanism a substitute for religion, there is a very plain question that can be asked in the form of a very homely metaphor. Humanism may try to pick up the pieces; but can it stick them together? Where is the *cement* which made religion corporate and popular, which can prevent it falling to pieces in a debris of individualistic tastes and degrees? What is to prevent one Humanist wanting chastity without humility, and another humility without chastity, and another truth or beauty without either? The problem of an enduring ethic and culture consists in finding an arrangement of the pieces by which they remain related, as do the stones arranged in an arch. And I know only one scheme that has thus proved its solidity, bestriding lands and ages with its gigantic arches, and carrying everywhere the high river of baptism upon an aqueduct of Rome.

IV

THE DRIFT FROM DOMESTICITY

In the matter of reforming things, as distinct from deforming them, there is one plain and simple principle; a principle which will probably be called a paradox. There exists in such a case a certain institution or law; let us say, for the sake of simplicity, a fence or gate erected across a road. The more modern type of reformer goes gaily up to it and says, "I don't see the use of this; let us clear it away." To which the more intelligent type of reformer will do well to answer: "If you don't see the use of it, I certainly won't let you clear it away. Go away and think. Then, when you can come back and tell me that you *do* see the use of it, I may allow you to destroy it."

This paradox rests on the most elementary common sense. The gate or fence did not grow there. It was not set up by somnambulists who built it in their sleep. It is highly improbable that it was put there by escaped lunatics who were for some reason loose in the street. Some person had some reason for thinking it would be a good thing for somebody. And until we know what the reason was, we really cannot judge whether the reason was reasonable. It is extremely probable that we have overlooked some whole aspect of the question, if something set up by human beings like ourselves seems to be entirely meaningless and mysterious. There are reformers who get over this difficulty by assuming that all their fathers were fools; but if that be so, we can only say that folly appears to be a hereditary disease. But the truth is that nobody has any business to destroy a social institution until he has really seen it as an historical institution. If he knows how it arose, and what purposes it was supposed to serve, he may really be able to say that they were bad purposes, or that they have since become bad purposes, or that they are puposes which are no longer served. But if he simply stares at the thing as a senseless monstrosity that has somehow sprung up in his path, it is he and not the traditionalist who is suffering from an illusion. We might even say that he is seeing things in a nightmare. This principle applies to a thousand things, to trifles as well as true institutions, to convention as well as to conviction. It was exactly the sort of person, like Joan of Arc, who did know why women wore skirts, who was most justified in not wearing one; it was exactly the sort of person like St. Francis, who did sympathize with the feast and the fireside, who was most entitled to become a beggar on the open road. And when, in the general emancipation of modern society, the Duchess says she does not see why she shouldn't play leapfrog, or the Dean declares that he sees no valid canonical reason why he should not stand on his head, we may say to these persons with patient benevolence: "Defer, therefore, the operation you contemplate until you have realized by ripe reflection what principle or prejudice you are violating. Then play leapfrog and stand on your head and the Lord be with you."

Among the traditions that are being thus attacked, not intelligently but most unintelligently, is the fundamental human creation called the Household or the Home. That is a typical thing which men attack, not because they can see through it, but because they cannot see it at all. They beat at it blindly, in a fashion entirely haphazard and opportunist; and many of them would pull it down without even pausing to ask why it was ever put up. It is true that only a few of them would have avowed this object in so many words. That only proves how very blind and blundering they are. But they have fallen into a habit of mere drift and gradual detachment from family life; something that is often merely accidental and devoid of any definite theory at all. But though it is accidental it is none the less anarchical. And it is all the more anarchical for not being anarchist. It seems to be largely founded on individual irritation; an irritation which varies with the individual. We are merely told that in this or that case a particular temperament was tormented by a particular environment; but nobody even explained how the evil arose, let alone whether the evil is really escaped. We are told that in this or that family Grandmamma talked a great deal of nonsense, which God know is true; or that it is very difficult to have intimate intellectual relations with Uncle Gregory without telling him he is a fool, which is indeed the case. But nobody seriously considers the remedy, or even the malady; or whether the existing individualistic dissolution is a remedy at all. Much of this business began with the influence of Ibsen, a very powerful dramatist and an exceedingly feeble philosopher. I suppose that Nora of The Doll's House was intended to be an inconsequent person; but certainly her most inconsequent action was her last. She complained that she was not yet fit to look after children, and then proceeded to get as far as possible from the children, that she might study them more closely.

There is one simple test and type of this neglect of scientific thinking and the sense of a social rule; the neglect which has now left us with nothing but a welter of exceptions. I have read hundreds and thousands of times, in all the novels and newspapers of our epoch, certain phrases about the just right of the young to liberty, about the unjust claim of the elders to control, about the conception that all souls must be free or all citizens equal, about the absurdity of authority or the degradation of obedience. I am not arguing those matters directly at the moment. But what strikes me as astounding, in a logical sense, is that not one of these myriad novelists and newspaper-men ever seems to think of asking the next and most obvious question. It never seems to occur to them to inquire what becomes of the opposite obligation. If the child is free from the first to disregard the parent, why is not the parent free from the first to disregard the child? If Mr. Jones, Senior, and Mr. Jones, Junior, are only two free and equal citizens, why should one citizen sponge on another citizen for the first fifteen years of his life? Why should the elder Mr. Jones be expected to feed, clothe and shelter out of his own pocket another person who is entirely free of any obligations to him? If the bright young thing cannot be asked to tolerate her grandmother, who has become something of a bore, why should the grandmother or the mother have tolerated the bright young thing at a period of her life when she was by no means bright? Why did they laboriously look after her at a time when her contributions to the conversation were seldom epigrammatic and not often intelligible? Why should Jones Senior stand drinks and free meals to anybody so unpleasant as Jones Junior, especially in the immature phases of his existence? Why should he not throw the baby out of the window;

or at any rate, kick the boy out of doors? It is obvious that we are dealing with a real relation, which may be equality, but is certainly not similarity.

Some social reformers try to evade this difficulty, I know, by some vague notions about the State or an abstraction called Education eliminating the parental function. But this, like many notions of solid scientific persons, is a wild illusion of the nature of mere moonshine. It is based on that strange new superstition, the idea of infinite resources of organization. It is as if officials grew like grass or bred like rabbits. There is supposed to be an endless supply of salaried persons, and of salaries for them; and they are to undertake all that human beings naturally do for themselves; including the care of children. But men cannot live by taking in each other's baby-linen. They cannot provide a tutor for each citizen; who is to tutor the tutors? Men cannot be educated by machinery; and though there might be a Robot bricklayer or scavenger, there will never be a Robot schoolmaster or governess. The actual effect of this theory is that one harassed person has to look after a hundred children, instead of one normal person looking after a normal number of them. Normally that normal person is urged by a natural force, which costs nothing and does not require a salary; the force of natural affection for his young, which exists even among the animals. If you cut off that natural force, and substitute a paid bureaucracy, you are like a fool who should pay men to turn the wheel of his mill, because he refused to use wind or water which he could get for nothing. You are like a lunatic who should carefully water his garden with a watering-can, while holding up an umbrella to keep off the rain.

It is now necessary to recite these truisms; for only by doing so can we begin to get a glimpse of that *reason* for the existence of the family, which I began this essay by demanding. They were all familiar to our fathers, who believed in the links of kinship and also in the links of logic. Today our logic consists mostly of missing links; and our family largely of absent members. But, anyhow, this is the right end at which to begin any such inquiry; and *not* at the tail-end or the fag-end of some private muddle, by which Dick has become discontented or Susan has gone off on her own. If Dick or Susan wish to destroy the family because they do not see the use of it, I say as I said in the beginning; if they do not see the use of it, they had much better preserve it. They have no business even to think of destroying it until they have seen the use of it.

But it has other uses, besides the obvious fact that it means a necessary social work being done for love when it cannot be done for money; and (one might almost dare to hint) presumably to be repaid with love since it is never repaid in money. On that simple side of the matter the general situation is easy to record. The existing and general system of society, subject in our own age and industrial culture to very gross abuses and painful problems, is nevertheless a normal one. It is the idea that the commonwealth is made up of a number of small kingdoms, of which a man and a woman become the king and queen and in which they exercise a reasonable authority, subject to the common sense of the commonwealth, until those under their care grow up to found similar kingdoms and exercise similar authority. This is the social structure of mankind, far older than all its records and more universal than any of its religions; and all attempts to alter it are mere talk and tomfoolery.

But the other advantage of the small group is now not so much neglected as simply not realized. Here again we have some extraordinary delusions spread all over the literature and journalism of our time. Those delusions now exist in such a degree that we may say, for all practical purposes, that when a thing has been stated about a thousand times as obviously true, it is almost certain to be obviously false. One such statement may be specially noted here. There is undoubtedly something to be said against domesticity and in favour of the general drift towards life in hotels, clubs, colleges, communal settlements and the rest; or for a social life organized on the plan of the great commercial system of our time. But the truly extraordinary suggestion is often made that this escape from the home is an escape into greater freedom. The change is actually offered as favourable to liberty.

To anybody who can think, of course, it is exactly the opposite. The domestic division of human society is not perfect, being human. It does not achieve complete liberty; a thing somewhat difficult to do or even to define. But it is a mere matter of arithmetic that it puts a larger number of people in supreme control of something, and able to shape it to their personal liking, than do the vast organizations that rule society outside; whether those systems are legal or commercial or even merely social. Even if we were only considering the parents, it is plain that there are more parents than there are policemen or politicians or heads of big businesses or proprietors of hotels. As I shall suggest in a moment, the argument actually applies indirectly to the children as well as directly to the parents. But the main point is that the world *outside* the home is now under a rigid discipline and routine and it is only inside the home that there is really a place for individuality and liberty. Anyone stepping out of the front-door is obliged to step into a procession, all going the same way and to a great extent even obliged to wear the same uniform. Business, especially big business, is now organized like an army. It is, as some would say, a sort of mild militarism without bloodshed; as I should say, a militarism without the military virtues. But anyhow, it is obvious that a hundred clerks in a bank or a hundred waitresses in a teashop are more regimented and under rule than the same individuals when each has gone back to his or her own dwelling or lodging, hung with his or her favourite pictures or fragrant with his or her favourite cheap cigarettes. But this, which is so obvious in the commercial case, is no less true even in the social case. In practice, the pursuit of pleasure is merely the pursuit of fashion. The pursuit of fashion is merely the pursuit of convention; only that it happens to be a new convention. The jazz dances, the joy rides, the big pleasure parties and hotel entertainments, do not make any more provision for a *really* independent taste than did any of the fashions of the past. If a wealthy young lady wants to do what all the other wealthy young ladies are doing, she will find it great fun, simply because youth is fun and society is fun. She will enjoy being modern exactly as her Victorian grandmother enjoyed being Victorian. And quite right too; but it is the enjoyment of convention, not the enjoyment of liberty. It is perfectly healthy for all young people of all historic periods to herd together, to a reasonable extent, and enthusiastically copy each other. But in that there is nothing particularly fresh and certainly nothing particularly free. The girl who likes shaving her head and powdering her nose and wearing short skirts will find the world organized for her and will march happily with the procession. But a girl who happened to like having her hair down to her heels or loading herself with barbaric gauds and trailing garments or (most awful of all) leaving her nose in its natural state — she will still be well advised to do these things on her own premises. If the Duchess does want to play leapfrog, she must not start suddenly leaping in the manner of a frog across the ballroom of the Babylon Hotel, when it is crowded with the fifty best couples professionally practising the very latest dance, for the instruction of society. The Duchess will find it easier to practice leapfrog to the admiration of her intimate friends in the old oak-panelled hall of Fitzdragon Castle. If the Dean must stand on his head, he will do it with more ease and grace in the calm atmosphere of the Deanery than by attempting to interrupt the program of some social entertainment already organized for philanthropic purposes.

If there is this impersonal routine in commercial and even in social things, it goes without saying that it exists and always must exist in political and legal things. For instance, the punishments of the State must be sweeping generalizations. It is only the punishments of the home that can possibly be adapted to the individual case; because it is only there that the judge can know anything of the individual. If Tommy takes a silver thimble out of a work-basket, his mother may act very differently according as she knows that he did it for fun or for spite or to sell to somebody, or to get somebody into trouble. But if Tomkins takes a silver thimble out of a shop, the law not only can but must punish him according to the rule made for all shoplifters or stealers of silver. It is only the domestic discipline that can show any sympathy or especially any humour. I do not say that the family always does do this: but I say that the state never ought to attempt it. So that even if we consider the parents alone as independent princes, and the children merely as subjects, the relative freedom of the family can and often does work to the advantage of those subjects. But so long as the children are children, they will always be the subjects of somebody. The question is whether they are to be distributed naturally under their natural princes, as the old phrase went, who normally feel for them what nobody else will feel, a natural affection. It seems to me clear that this normal distribution gives the largest amount of liberty to the largest number of people.

My complaint of the anti-domestic drift is that it is unintelligent. People do not know what they are doing; because they do not know what they are undoing. There are a multitude of modern manifestations, from the largest to the smallest, ranging from a divorce to a picnic party. But each is a separate escape or evasion; and especially an evasion of the point at issue. People ought to decide in a philosophical fashion whether they desire the traditional social order or not; or if there is any particular alternative to be desired. As it is they treat the public question merely as a mess or medley of private questions. Even in being anti-domestic they are much too domestic in their test of domesticity. Each family considers only its own case and the result is merely narrow and negative. Each case is an exception to a rule that does not exist. The family, especially in the modern state, stands in need of considerable correction and reconstruction; most things do in the modern state. But the family mansion should be preserved or destroyed or rebuilt; it should not be allowed to fall to pieces brick by brick because nobody has any historic sense of the object of bricklaying. For instance, the architects of the restoration should rebuild the house with wide and easily opened doors, for the practice of the ancient virtue of hopitality. In other words, private property should be distributed with sufficiently decent equality to allow of a margin for festive intercourse. But the hospitality of a house will always be different from the hospitality of a hotel. And it will be different in being more individual, more independent, more interesting than the hospitality of a hotel. It is perfectly right that the young Browns and the young Robinsons should meet and mix and dance and make asses of themselves, according to the design of their Creator. But there will always be some difference between the Browns entertaining the Robinsons and the Robinsons entertaining the Browns. And it will be a difference to the advantage of variety, of personality, of the potentialities of the mind of man; or, in other words, of life, liberty and the pursuit of happiness.

V

LOGIC—AND LAWN TENNIS

When we say that we doubt the intellectual improvement produced by Protestantism and Rationalism and the modern world, there generally arises a very confused controversy, which is a sort of tangle of terminology. But, broadly speaking, the difference between us and our critics is this. They mean by growth an increase of the tangle; whereas we mean by thought a disentangling of the tangle. Even a short and simple length of straight and untangled wire is worth more to us than whole forests of mere entanglement. That there are more topics talked about, or more terms used, or more people using them, or more books and other authorities cited—all this is nothing to us if people misuse the terms, misunderstand the topics, invoke the authorities at random and without the use of reason; and finally bring out a false result. A peasant who merely says, "I have five pigs; if I kill one I shall have four pigs," is thinking in an extremely simple and elementary way; but he is thinking as clearly and correctly as Aristotle or Euclid. But suppose he reads or half-reads newspapers and books of popular science. Suppose he starts to call one pig the Land and another pig Capital and a third pig Exports, and finally brings out the result that the more pigs he kills the more he possesses; or that every sow that litters decreases the number of pigs in the world. He has learnt economic terminology, merely as a means of becoming entangled in economic fallacy. It is a fallacy he could never have fallen into while he was grounded in the divine dogma that Pigs is Pigs. Now for that sort of intellectual instruction and advancement we have no use at all; and in that sense only it is true that we prefer the ignorant peasant to the instructed pedant. But that is not because we think ignorance better than instruction or barbarism better than culture. It is merely that we think a short length of the untangled logical chain is better than an interminable length of it that is interminably tangled. It is merely that we prefer a man to do a sum of simple addition right than a sum of long division wrong.

Now what we observe about the whole current culture of journalism and general discussion is that people do not know how to begin to think. Not only is their thinking at third and fourth hand, but it always starts about three-quarters of the way through the process. Men do not know where their own thoughts came from. They do not know what their own words imply. They come in at the end of every controversy and know nothing of where it began or what it is all about. They are constantly assuming certain absolutes, which, if correctly defined, would strike even themselves as being not absolutes but absurdities. To think thus is to be in a tangle; to go on thinking is to be in more and more of a tangle. And at the back of all there is always something understood; which is really something misunderstood.

For instance, I read an article by the admirable Mr. Tilden,[8] the great tennis-player, who was debating what is wrong with English Tennis. "Nothing can save English Tennis," he said, except certain reforms of a fundamental sort, which he proceeded to explain. The English, it appears, have a weird and unnatural way of regarding tennis as a game, or thing to be enjoyed. He admitted that this has been part of a sort of amateur spirit in everything which is (as he very truly noted) also a part of the national character. But all this stands in the way of what he called saving English Tennis. He meant what some would call making it perfect, and others would call making it professional. Now, I take that as a very typical passage, taken from the papers at random, and containing the views of a keen and acute person on a subject that he thoroughly understands. But what he does not understand is the thing which he supposes to be understood. He thoroughly knows his subject and yet he does not know what he is talking about; because he does not know what he is taking for granted. He does not realize the relation of means and ends, or axioms and inferences, in his own philosophy. And nobody would probably be more surprised and even legitimately indignant than he, if I were to say that the first principles of his philosophy appear to be as follows: (1) There is in the nature of things a certain absolute and divine Being, whose name is

[8] William Tilden (1893–1953) was the dominant amateur tennis player in the world in the 1920s.

Mr. Lawn Tennis. (2) All men exist for the good and glory of this Mr. Tennis and are bound to approximate to his perfections and ful-fil his will. (3) To this higher duty they are bound to surrender their natural desire for enjoyment in this life. (4) They are bound to put this loyalty first; and to love it more passionately than patriotic tradition, the preservation of their own national type and national culture; not to mention even their national virtues. That is the creed or scheme of doctrine that is here developed without being defined. The only way for us to save the game of Lawn Tennis is to prevent it from being a game. The only way to save English Tennis is to pre-vent it from being English. It does not occur to such thinkers that some people may possibly like it because it is English and enjoy it because it is enjoyable. There is some abstract divine standard in the thing, to which it is everybody's duty to rise, at any sacrifice of pleasure or affection. When Christians say this of the sacrifices made for Christ, it sounds rather a hard saying. But when tennis-players say it about the sacrifices demanded by tennis, it sounds quite or-dinary and casual in the confusion of current thought and expres-sion. And nobody notices that a sort of human sacrifice is being of-fered to a sort of new and nameless god.

In the good old days of Victorian rationalism it used to be the con-ventional habit to scoff at St. Thomas Aquinas and the mediaeval theo-logians; and especially to repeat perpetually a well-worn joke about the man who discussed how many angels could dance on the point of a nee-dle. The comfortable and commercial Victorians, with their money and merchandise, might well have felt a sharper end of the same needle, even if it was the other end of it. It would have been good for their souls to have looked for that needle, not in the haystack of mediaeval metaphysics, but in the neat needle-case of their own favourite pocket Bible. It would have been better for them to meditate, not on how many angels could go on the point of a needle, but on how many camels could go through the eye of it. But there is another comment on this curious joke or catchword, which is more relevant to our purpose here. If the mediaeval mystic ever did argue about angels standing on a needle, at least he did not argue as if the object of angels was to stand on a needle; as if God had created all the Angels and Archangels, all the

Thrones, Virtues, Powers and Principalities, solely in order that there might be something to clothe and decorate the unseemly nakedness of the point of a needle. But that is the way that modern rationalists reason. The mediaeval mystic would not even have said that a needle exists to be a standing-ground for angels. The mediaeval mystic would have been the first to say that a needle exists to make clothes for men. For mediaeval mystics, in their dim transcendental way, were much interested in the real reasons for things and the distinction between the means and the end. They wanted to know what a thing was really for, and what was the dependence of one idea on another. And they might even have suggested, what so many journalists seem to forget, the paradoxical possibility that Tennis was made for Man and not Man for Tennis.

The Modernists were peculiarly unfortunate when they said that the modern world must not be expected to tolerate the old syllogistic methods of the Schoolmen. They were proposing to scrap the one mediaeval instrument which the modern world will most immediately require. There would have been a far better case for saying that the revival of Gothic architecture has been sentimental and futile; that the Pre-Raphaelite movement[9] in art was only an eccentric episode; that the fashionable use of the world "Guild" for every possible sort of social institution was affected and artificial; that the feudalism of Young England was very different from that of Old England. But of this method of clean-cut deduction, with the definition of the postulates and the actual answering of the question, is something of which the whole of our newspaper-flattered society is in sharp and instant need; as the poisoned are in need of medicine. I have here taken only one example which happened to catch my eye out of a hundred thousand that flash past every hour. And as Tennis, like every other good game, has to be played with the head as well as the hand, I think it highly desirable that it should be occasionally discussed at least as intelligently as it is played.

[9] The Pre-Raphaelite Brotherhood, a movement to infuse art with morality, flourished in mid-nineteenth-century England. Its members, most prominent of whom were William Holman Hunt, John Everett Millais and Dante Gabriel Rossetti, contended that the degeneration of Western art had begun in the Renaissance with Raphael.

VI

OBSTINATE ORTHODOXY

I have been asked to explain something about myself which seems to be regarded as very extraordinary. The problem has been presented to me in the form of a cutting from a very flattering American article, which yet contained a certain suggestion of wonder. So far as I can understand, it is thought extraordinary that a man should be ordinary. I am ordinary in the correct sense of the term; which means the acceptance of an order; a Creator and the Creation, the common sense of gratitude for Creation, life and love as gifts permanently good, marriage and chivalry as laws rightly controlling them, and the rest of the normal traditions of our race and religion. It is also thought a little odd that I regard the grass as green, even after some newly-discovered Slovak artist has painted it grey; that I think daylight very tolerable in spite of thirteen Lithuanian philosophers sitting in a row and cursing the light of day; and that, in matters more polemical, I actually prefer weddings to divorces and babies to Birth Control. These eccentric views, which I share with the overwhelming majority of mankind, past and present, I should not attempt to defend here one by one. And I only give a general reply for a particular reason. I wish to make it unmistakably plain that my defence of these sentiments is not sentimental. It would be easy to gush about these things; but I defy the reader, after reading this, to find the faintest trace of the tear of sensibility. I hold this view not because it is sensibility, but because it is sense.

On the contrary, it is the sceptics who are the sentimentalists. More than half the "revolt" and the talk of being advanced and progressive is simply a weak sort of snobbishness which takes the form of a worship of Youth. Some men of my generation delight in declaring that they are of the Party of the Young and defending every detail of the latest fashions or freaks. If I do not do that, it is for the same reason that I do not dye my hair or wear stays. But even when it is less despicable than that, the current phrase that everything must be done for youth, that the rising generation is all that matters, is in sober fact a piece of pure sentimentalism. It is also, within reason, a perfectly natural piece of sentiment. All healthy people like to see the young enjoying themselves; but if we turn that pleasure into a principle, we are sentimentalists. If we desire the greatest happiness of the greatest number, it will be obvious that the greatest number, at any given moment, are rather more likely to be between twenty-five and seventy than to be between seventeen and twenty-five. Sacrificing everything to the young will be like working only for the rich. They will be a privileged class and the rest will be snobs or slaves. Moreover, the young will always have a fair amount of fun under the worst conditions; if we really wish to console the world, it will be much more rational to console the old. This is what I call facing facts; and I have continued to believe in most of these traditions because they are facts. I could give a great many other examples; for instance, chivalry. Chivalry is not the romantic, but the realistic, view of the sexes. It is so realistic that the real reasons for it cannot always be given in print.

If those called free-thinkers are sentimentalists, those called free-lovers are open and obvious sentimentalists. We can always convict such people of sentimentalism by their weakness for euphemism. The phrase they use is always softened and suited for journalistic appeals. They talk of free love when they mean something quite different, better defined as free lust. But being sentimentalists they feel bound to simper and coo over the word "love." They insist on talking about Birth Control when they mean less birth and no control. We could smash them to atoms, if we could be as indecent in our language as they are immoral in their conclusions. And as it is with morals, so it is with religion. The general notion that science establishes agnosticism is a sort of mystification produced by talking Latin and Greek instead of plain English. Science is the Latin for knowledge. Agnosticism is the Greek for ignorance. It is not self evident that ignorance is the goal of knowledge. It is the ignorance and not the knowledge that produces the current notion that free thought weakens theism. It is the real world, that we see with our own eyes, that obviously unfolds a plan of things that fit into each other. It is only a remote and misty legend that ever pretended to explain it by the automatic advantage of the "fit." As a fact, modern evolutionists, even when they are still Darwinians, do not pretend that the theory explains all varieties and adaptations. Those who know are rather rescuing Darwin at the expense of Darwinism. But it is those who do not know who doubt or deny; it is typical that their myth is actually called the Missing Link. They actually know nothing of their own argument except that it breaks down somewhere. But it is worth while to ask why this loose legend has such power over many; and I will proceed to my suggestion. I have not changed my mind; nor, indeed, have they changed their mind. They have only changed their mood.

What we call the intellectual world is divided into two types of people—those who worship the intellect and those who use it. There are exceptions; but, broadly speaking, they are never the same people. Those who use the intellect never worship it; they know too much about it. Those who worship the intellect never use it; as you can see by the things they say about it. Hence there has arisen a confusion about intellect and intellectualism; and, as the supreme expression of that confusion, something that is called in many countries the Intelligentsia, and in France more especially, the Intellectuals. It is found in practice to consist of clubs and coteries of people talking mostly about books and pictures, but especially new books and new pictures; and about music, so long as it is very modern music; or what some would call very unmusical music. The first fact to record about it is that what Carlyle said of the world is very specially true of the intellectual world—that it is mostly fools. Indeed, it has a curious attraction for complete fools, as a warm fire has for cats. I have frequently visited such societies, in the capacity of a common or normal fool, and I have almost always found there a few fools who were more foolish than I had imagined to be possible to man born of woman; people who had hardly enough brains to be called half-witted. But it gave them a glow within to be in what they imagined to be the atmosphere of intellect; for they worshipped it like an unknown god. I could tell many stories of that world. I remember a venerable man with a very long beard who seemed to live at one of these clubs. At intervals he would hold up his hand as if for silence and preface his remarks by saying, "A Thought." And then he would say something that sounded as if a cow had suddenly spoken in a drawing-room. I remember once a silent and much-enduring man (I rather think it was my friend Mr. Edgar Jepson, the novelist) who could bear it no longer and cried with a sort of expiring gasp, "But, Good God, man, you don't call that a *thought*, do you?" But that was pretty much the quality of the thought of such thinkers, especially of the free thinkers. Out of this social situation arises one sort of exception to the rule. Intelligence does exist even in the Intelligentsia. It does sometimes happen that a man of real talent has a weakness for flattery, even the flattery of fools. He would rather say something that silly people think clever than something which only clever people could perceive to be true. Oscar Wilde was a man of this type. When he said somewhere that an immoral woman is the sort of woman a man never gets tired of, he used a phrase so baseless as to be perfectly pointless. Everybody knows that a man may get tired of a whole procession of immoral women, especially if he is an immoral man. That was "a Thought"; otherwise something to be uttered, with uplifted hand, to people who could not think at all. In their poor muddled minds there was some vague connection between wit and cynicism; so they never applauded him so warmly as a wit, as when he was cynical without being witty. But when he said, "A cynic is a man who knows the price of everything and the value of nothing,"[10] he made a statement (in excellent epigrammatic form) which really meant something. But it would have meant his own immediate dethronement if it could have been understood by those who only enthroned him for being cynical.

Anyhow, it is in this intellectual world, with its many fools and few wits and fewer wise men, that there goes on perpetually a sort of ferment of fashionable revolt and negation. From this comes all that is called destructive criticism; though, as a matter of fact, the new critic is generally destroyed by the next critic long before he has had any chance of destroying anything else. When people say solemnly

[10] Wilde's quotation is from *Lady Windermere's Fan* (1892).

that the world is in revolt against religion or private property or patriotism or marriage, they mean that *this* world is in revolt against them; or rather, is in permanent revolt against everything. Now, as a matter of fact, this world has a certain excuse for being always in that state of excitement, apart from mere fuss and mere folly. The reason is rather an important one; and I would ask anyone who really does want to think, and especially to think freely, to pause upon it seriously for a moment. It arises from the fact that these people are so much concerned with the study of Art. It collapses into mere drivelling and despair, because they try to transfer their treatment of art to the treatment of morals and philosophy. In this they make a bad blunder in reasoning. But then, as I have explained, intellectuals are not very intellectual.

The Arts exist, as we should put it in our primeval fashion, to show forth the glory of God; or, to translate the same thing in terms of our psychology, to awaken and keep alive the sense of wonder in man. The success of any work of art is achieved when we say of any subject, a tree or a cloud or a human character, "I have seen that a thousand times and I never saw it before." Now for this purpose a certain variation of *venue* is natural and even necessary. Artists change what they call their attack; for it is to some extent their business to make it a surprise attack. They have to throw a new light on things; and it is not surprising if it is sometimes an invisible ultra-violet ray or one rather resembling a black ray of madness or death. But when the artist extends the eccentric experiment from art to real life, it is quite different. He is like an absent-minded sculptor turning his chisel from chipping at the bust to chipping at the bald head of the distinguished sitter. And these anarchic artists do suffer a little from absence of mind.

Let us take a practical case for the sake of simplicity. Many moderns will be heard scoffing at what they would call "chocolate-box art"; meaning an insipid and sickly art. And it is easy to call up the sort of picture that might well make anybody ill. I will suppose, for the sake of argument, that we are looking sadly at the outside of a chocolate-box (now, I need hardly say, empty) and that we see painted on it in rather pallid colours a young woman with golden ringlets gazing from a balcony and holding a rose in the spot-light caused by a convenient ray of moonlight. Any similar touches may be added to the taste or distaste of the critic; she may be convulsively clasping a letter or conspicuously wearing an engagement ring or languidly waving farewell to a distant gentleman in a gondola; or anything else I can think of, calculated to cause pain to the sensitive critic. I sympathize with the critic's feeling; but I think he goes quite wrong in his thinking.

Now, what do we mean when we say that this is a silly picture, or a stale subject, or something very difficult to bear, even when we are fortified by chocolates to endure it? We mean it is possible to have too much of a good thing; to have too many chocolate-boxes, as to have too many chocolates. We mean that it is not a picture, but a picture of a picture. Ultimately it is a picture of innumerable pictures; not a real picture of a rose or a girl or a beam of moonlight. In other words, artists have copied artists, right away back to the first sentimental pictures of the Romantic Movement.

But roses have not copied roses. Moonbeams have not imitated each other. And though a woman may copy women in externals, it is only in externals and not in existence; her womanhood was not copied from any other woman. Considered as realities, the rose and the moon and the woman are simply themselves. Suppose that scene to be a real one, and there is nothing particularly imitative about it. The flower is unquestionably fresh as the young woman is unquestionably young. The rose is a real object, which would smell as sweet by any other name, or by no name. The girl is a particular person, whose personality is entirely new to the world and whose experiences are entirely new to herself. If she does indeed choose to stand in that attitude on that balcony holding that botanical specimen (which seems improbable), we have no right to doubt that she has her own reasons for doing so. In short, when once we conceive the thing as reality, we have no reason whatever to dismiss it as mere repetition. So long as we are thinking of the thing as copied mechanically and for money, as a piece of monotonous and mercenary ornament, we naturally feel that the flower is in a special sense an artificial flower and that the moonlight is all moonshine. We feel inclined to welcome even wild variations in the decorative style; and to admire the new artist who will paint the rose black, lest we should forget that it is a deep red, or the moonshine green, that we may realize it is something more subtle than white. But the moon is the moon and the rose is the rose; and we do not expect the real things to alter. Nor is there any reason to expect the rules about them to alter. Nor is there any reason, so far as this question is concerned, to expect the woman to alter her attitude either about the beauty of the rose or the obligations of the engagement-ring. These things, considered as real things, are quite unaffected by the variation of artistic attack in fictitious things. The moon will continue to affect the tides, whether we paint it blue or green or pink with purple spots. And the man who imagines that artistic revolutions must always affect morals is like a man who should say, "I am so bored with seeing pink roses painted on chocolate-boxes that I refuse to believe that roses grow well in a clay soil."

In short, what the critics would call romanticism is in fact the only form of realism. It is also the only form of rationalism. The more a man uses his reason upon realities, the more he will see that the realities remain much the same, though the representations are very different. And it is only the representations that are repetitions. The sensations are always sincere; the individuals are always individual. If the real girl is experiencing a real romance, she is experiencing something old, but not something stale. If she has plucked something from a real rose-tree, she is holding a very ancient symbol, but a very recent rose. And it is exactly in so far as a man *can* clear his head, so as to see actual things as they are, that he will see these things as permanently important as they are. Exactly in so far as his head is confused with current fashions and aesthetic modes of the moment, he will see nothing about it except that it is like a picture on a chocolate-box, and not like a picture at the Post-Futurist Gallery. Exactly in so far as he is thinking about real people, he will see that they are really romantic. Exactly in so far as he is thinking only about pictures and poems and decorative styles, he will think that romance is a false or old-fashioned style. He can only see people as imitating pictures; whereas the real people are not imitating anything. They are only being themselves — as they will always be. Roses remain radiant and mysterious, however many pink rosebuds are sprinkled like pips over cheap wallpapers. Falling in love remains radiant and mysterious, however threadbare be the thousandth repetition of a rhyme as a valentine or a cracker-motto. To see this fact is to live in a world of facts. To be always thinking of the banality of bad wallpapers and valentines is to live in a world of fictions.

Now the main truth about all this sceptical revolt, and all the rest of it, is that it was born in a world of fictions. It came from the Intelligentsia, who were perpetually discussing novels and plays and pictures instead of people. They insisted on putting "real life" on the stage and never saw it in the street. They professed to be putting realism into their novels when there was less and less of it in their conversation, as compared with the conversation of the common people. And that perpetual experiment, and shifting of the standpoint, which was natural enough in an artist seeking for certain effects (as it is natural in a photographer hovering round and focussing and fussing with his camera), was wholly inapplicable to any study of the permanent rules and relations of society. When these people began to play about with morals and metaphysics, they simply produced a series of mad worlds where they might have been harmlessly producing a series of mad pictures. Pictures are always meant to catch a certain aspect, at a certain angle, in a certain light; sometimes in light that is almost as brief as lightning. But when the artists became anarchists and began to exhibit the community and the cosmos by these flashes of lightning, the result was not realism but simply nightmare. Because a particular painter, for a particular purpose, might paint the red rose black, the pessimist deduced that the red rose of love and life was really as black as it was painted. Because one artist, from one angle, seized a momentary impression of moonlight as green, the philosopher solemnly put on a pair of green spectacles and declared that it was now a solid scientific certainty that the moon must be crawling with maggots, because it was made of green cheese.

In short, there might have been some value in the old cry of art for the artists; if it had meant that the artists would confine themselves to the medium of art. As a fact, they were always meddling with the medium of morals and religion; and they imported into them the unrest, the changing moods and the merely experimental tricks of their own trade. But a man with a solid sense of reality can see that this is utterly unreal. Whatever the laws of life and love and human relations may be, it is monstrously improbable that they ought to be changed with every fashion in poetry any more than with every fashion in pantaloons. It is insane that there should be a new pattern of hearts or heads whenever there is a new pattern of hats. These things are realities, like a high tide or a clay soil; and you do not get rid of high tides and clay soils by calling roses and moonlight old-fashioned and sentimental. I will venture to say, therefore, and I trust without undue vanity, that I have remained rooted in certain relations and traditions, not because I am a sentimentalist or even a romanticist; but because I am a realist. And I realize that morals must not change with moods, as Cubism[11] must not mean chopping up real houses into cubes, or Vorticism[12] swallowing real ships in whirlpools.

I have not changed my views of these things because there has never been any reason to change them. For anybody impelled by reason and not by running with a crowd will, for instance, perceive that there are always the same arguments for a Purpose and therefore a Personality in things, if he is a thinking person. Only it is now made easy for him to admit vaguely that there may be a Purpose, while denying that there is a Personality, so long as he happens to be a very unthinking person. It is quite as certain as it ever was that life is a gift of God immensely valuable and immensely valued; and anybody can prove it by putting a pistol to the head of a pessimist. Only a certain sort of modern does not like any problem presented to his head; and would dislike a plain question almost as much as a pistol. It is obvious common sense, and obviously consonant to real life, that romantic love is normal to youth and has its natural development in marriage and parenthood as the corresponding conditions of

[11] Cubism was an avant-garde movement in painting that arose in France in the first decade of the twentieth century. Its key figures were Pablo Picasso and Georges Braque.

[12] Vorticism was an avant-garde literary and artistic movement launched in England on the eve of World War I by Wyndham Lewis and Ezra Pound.

age. None of the nonsense talked about this, that or the other individual irritation or licence has ever made any difference to that solid social truth, for anyone who cares whether things are true, apart from whether they are trite. It is the man who cannot see that a thing is true, although it is trite, who is very truly a victim of mere words and verbal associations. He is the fool who has grown so furious with paper roses that he will not believe that the real rose has a root; nor (till he discovers it with an abrupt and profane ejaculation) that it has a thorn.

The truth is that the modern world has had a mental breakdown; much more than a moral breakdown. Things are being settled by mere associations because there is a reluctance to settle them by arguments. Nearly all the talk about what is advanced and what is antiquated has become a sort of giggling excitement about fashions. The most modern of the moderns stare at a picture of a man making love to a lady in a crinoline with exactly the same sort of vacant grin with which yokels stare at a stranger in an outlandish sort of hat. They regard their fathers of another age exactly as the most insular would regard the foreigners from another country. They seem mentally incapable of getting any further than the statement that our girls are shingled and short-skirted while their silly old great-grandmothers wore ringlets and hoops. That seems to satisfy all their appetite for satire; they are a simple race, a little like savages. They are exactly like the sort of cockney tripper who would roar with laughter because French soldiers wore red trousers and blue coats, while English soldiers were dressed properly in blue trousers and red coats. I have not altered my lines of thought for people who think in this fashion. Why should I?

VII

THE USUAL ARTICLE

The Editor of an evening paper published recently what he announced as, and even apologized for as, "an unusual article." He anxiously guarded himself from expressing any opinion on the dreadful and dangerous views which the unusual article set forth. Needless to say, before I had read five lines of the unusual article, I knew it was a satisfactory sample of the usual article. It was even a careful and correct copy of the usual article; a sort of prize specimen, as if a thing could be unusually usual. I had read the article before, of course — thousands and thousands of times (as it seems to me) — and had always found it the same; but never before, somehow, had it seemed so exactly the same.

There are things of which the world today is subconsciously very weary. It does not always know what they are; for they commonly bear large though faded labels, describing them as the New Movement or the Latest Discovery. For instance, men are already as tired of the Socialist State as if they had been living in it for a thousand years. But there are some things on which boredom is becoming acute. It is now very near the surface; and may suddenly wake up in the form of suicide or murder or tearing newpapers with the teeth. So it is with this familiar product, the Usual Article. It is not only too usual; it has become intolerably, insupportably, unbearably usual. It is appropriately described as "A Woman's Cry to the Churches." And I beg to announce that, though I am of a heavy and placid habit, and have never been accused of any such feminine graces as hysteria, yet, if I have to read this article three more times, I shall scream. My scream will be entitled, "A Man's Cry to the Newspapers."

I will repeat somewhat hurriedly what the lady in question cried; for the reader knows it already by heart. The message of Christ was perfectly "simple": that the cure of everything is Love; but since He was killed (I do not quite know why) for making this remark, great temples have been put up to Him and horrid people called priests have given the world nothing but "stones, amulets, formulas, shibboleths." They also "quarrel eternally among themselves as to the placing of a button or the bending of a knee." All this gives no comfort to the unhappy Christian, who apparently wishes to be comforted only by being told that he has a duty to his neighbour. "How many men in the time of their passing get comfort out of the thought of the Thirty-Nine Articles,[13] Predestination, Transubstantiation, the doctrine of eternal punishment, and the belief that Christ will return on the Seventh Day?" The items make a curious catalogue; and the last item I find especially mysterious. But I can only say that, if Christ was the giver of the original and really comforting message of love, I should have thought it *did* make a difference whether He returned on the Seventh Day. For the rest of that singular list, I should probably find it necessary to distinguish. I certainly never gained any deep and heartfelt consolation from the thought of the Thirty-Nine Articles. I never heard of anybody in particular who did. Of the idea of Predestination there are broadly two views; the Calvinist and the Catholic; and it would make a most uncommon difference to *my* comfort, if I held the former instead of the latter. It is the difference between believing that God knows, as a fact, that I choose to go to the devil; and believing that God has given me to the devil, without my having any choice at all. As to Transubstantiation, it is less easy to talk currently about that; but I would gently suggest that, to most ordinary outsiders with any common sense, there would be a considerable practical difference between Jehovah pervading the universe and Jesus Christ coming into the room.

But I touch rapidly and reluctantly on these examples, because they exemplify a much wider question of this interminable way of talking. It consists of talking as if the moral problem of man were perfectly simple, as everyone knows it is not; and then depreciating attempts to solve it by quoting long technical words, and talking about senseless ceremonies without inquiring about their sense. In other words, it is exactly as if somebody were to say about the science of medicine: "All I ask is Health; what could be simpler than the

[13] The Thirty-nine Articles are the fundamental statement of doctrine of the Anglican Church. The document received its definitive form in 1571.

beautiful gift of Health? Why not be content to enjoy for ever the glow of youth and the fresh enjoyment of being fit? Why study dry and dismal sciences of anatomy and physiology; why inquire about the whereabouts of obscure organs of the human body? Why pedantically distinguish between what is labelled a poison and what is labelled an antidote, when it is so simple to enjoy Health? Why worry with a minute exactitude about the number of drops of laudanum or the strength of a dose of chloral, when it is so nice to be healthy? Away with your priestly apparatus of stethoscopes and clinical thermometers; with your ritualistic mummery of feeling pulses, putting out tongues, examining teeth, and the rest! The god Aesculapius came on earth solely to inform us that Life is on the whole preferable to Death; and this thought will console many dying persons unattended by doctors."

In other words, the Usual Article, which is now some ten thousand issues old, was always stuff and nonsense even when it was new. There may be, and there has been, pedantry in the medical profession. There may be, and there has been, theology that was thin or dry or without consolation for men. But to talk as if it were possible for any science to attack any problem, without developing a technical language, and a method always methodical and often minute, merely means that you are a fool and have never really attacked a problem at all. Quite apart from the theory of a Church, if Christ had remained on earth for an indefinite time, trying to induce men to love one another, He would have found it necessary to have some tests, some methods, some way of dividing true love from false love, some way of distinguishing between tendencies that would ruin love and tendencies that would restore it. You cannot make a success of anything, even loving, entirely without thinking. All this is so obvious that it would seem unnecessary to repeat it; and yet it is necessary to repeat it, because it is the flat contradiction of it that is now incessantly repeated. Its flatness stretches around us like a vast wilderness on every side.

It is a character of the Usual Article that it alludes occasionally to the New Religion; but always in a rather timid and remote fashion. It suggests that there will be a better and broader belief; though it seldom touches on the belief, but only on the broadness. There is never in it by any chance anything resembling even the note of the true innovator. For the true innovator must be in some sense a legislator. We may put it in a hostile fashion, by saying that the revolutionist always becomes the tyrant. We may put it in a friendly fashion, by saying that the reformer must return to the idea of form. But anybody really founding a new religion, even a false religion, must have a certain quality of responsibility. He must make himself responsible for saying that some things shall be forbidden and some permitted; that there shall be a certain plan or system that must be defended from destruction. And all the things in any way resembling new religions, to do them justice, do show this quality and suffer this disadvantage. Christian Science is theoretically based on peace and almost on the denial of struggle. But for all that there has been not a little struggle in the councils of that creed; and the relations of all the successors of Mrs. Eddy[14] have by no means been relations of peace. I do not say it as a taunt, but rather as a tribute; I should say that these proceedings did prove that the people involved were trying to found a real religion. It is a compliment to Christian Scientists to say that they also had their tests and their creeds, their anathemas and their excommunications, their encyclicals and their heresy-hunts. But it is a compliment to Christian Scientists which they can hardly use as an insult to Christians. Communism, even in its final form of Marxian materialism, had some of the qualities of a fresh and sincere faith. It had one of them at least: that it did definitely expel men for denying the creed. Both the Communist and the Christian Scientist were under this grave disadvantage; that they did turn a faith into a fact. There is such a thing as a Bolshevist government and it governs, even if it misgoverns. There are such things as Christian Science healers; there probably is such a thing as Christian Science healing, even if we do not fully admit that the healing is health. There is a Church in active operation; and for that reason it exhibits all the dogmas and differences charged against the Church of Christ. But the philosophy expressed in the Usual Article

[14] Mary Baker Eddy (1821–1910) was the American founder of Christian Science.

avoids all these disadvantages by never coming into the world of reality at all. Its god is afraid to be born; its scripture is afraid to be written; it only manages to remain as the New Religion by always coming tomorrow and never today. It puffs itself out with spiritual pride, because it does not impose what it cannot even invent. It shines with Pharisaical self-satisfaction, because there are no crimes committed for its creed and no creed to be the motive of its crimes. This sort of critic is a surgeon who never performs an unsuccessful operation because he never operates; a soldier who never falls because he never fights. Anybody can talk for ever about a non-existent religion which shall be free from all the evils of existence. Anybody can dream of that entirely humane and harmonious Christianity, whose Christ is never born and never crucified. It is so easy to do, that half a hundred people in the papers and the public discussions have been doing nothing else for the last twenty or thirty years. But it is every bit as futile as applied to a spiritual idea as it would be if applied to a scientific theory or a political program; and I only mention it because I have just heard it for the hundredth time; and feel a faint hope that I may be mentioning it for the last time.

VIII

WHY I AM A CATHOLIC

A leading article in a daily paper was recently devoted to the New Prayer Book;[15] without having anything very new to say about it. For it mostly consisted in repeating for the nine-hundredth-and-ninety-nine-thousandth time that what the ordinary Englishman wants is a religion without dogma (whatever that may be), and that the disputes about Church matters were idle and barren on both sides. Only, suddenly remembering that this equalization of both sides might possibly involve some slight concession or consideration for our side, the writer hastily corrected himself. He proceeded to suggest that though it is wrong to be dogmatic, it is essential to be dogmatically Protestant. He suggested that the ordinary Englishman (that useful character) was quite convinced, in spite of his aversion to all religious differences, that it was vital to religion to go on differing from Catholicism. He is convinced (we were told) that "Britain is as Protestant as the sea is salt." Gazing reverently at the profound Protestantism of Mr. Michael Arlen[16] or Mr. Noel Coward,[17] or the latest nigger dance in Mayfair, we might be tempted to ask: If the salt lose its savour, wherewith shall it be salted? But since we may rightly deduce from this passage that Lord Beaverbrook[18] and Mr. James Douglas and Mr. Hannen Swaffer,[19] and all their following, are indeed stern and unbending Protestants (and as we know that

[15] The New Prayer Book is the 1928 revision of the *Book of Common Prayer*.

[16] Michael Arlen (1895–1956) was a Bulgarian-born (of Armenian extraction) English novelist, whose most popular novel, *The Green Hat*, appeared in 1924.

[17] Sir Noel Coward (1899–1973) was an English actor, playwright and composer famous for his witty comedies of manners.

[18] William Max Aitken, Lord Beaverbrook (1879–1964), was a Canadian-born English newspaper magnate and politician.

[19] Hannen Swaffer (1879–1962) was an English journalist known for his gossip columns and drama criticism. He was a prominent figure among English Spiritualists.

Protestants are famous for the close and passionate study of the Scriptures, unhindered by Pope or priest), we might even take the liberty of interpreting the saying in the light of a less familiar text. It is possible that in comparing Protestantism to the salt of the sea they were haunted with some faint memory of another passage, in which the same Authority spoke of one single and sacred fountain that is of living water, because it is of life-giving water, and really quenches the thirst of men; while all other pools and puddles are distinguished from it by the fact that those who drink of them will thirst again. It is a thing that does occasionally happen to people who prefer to drink salt water.

This is perhaps a somewhat provocative way of opening the statement of my strongest conviction; but I would respectfully plead that the provocation came from the Protestant. When Protestantism calmly claims to rule all the souls in the tone of Britannia ruling all the seas, it is permissible to retort that the very quintessence of such salt can be found thickest in the stagnation of the Dead Sea. But it is still more permissible to retort that Protestantism is claiming what no religion at this moment can possibly claim. It is calmly claiming the allegiance of millions of agnostics, atheists, hedonistic pagans, independent mystics, psychic investigators, theists, theosophists,[20] followers of Eastern cults and jolly fellows living like the beasts that perish. To pretend that all these are Protestants is considerably to lower the prestige and significance of Protestantism. It is to make it merely negative; and salt is not negative.

Taking this as a text and test of the present problem of religious choice, we find ourselves faced from the first with a dilemma about the traditional religion of our fathers. Protestantism as here named is either a negative or a positive thing. If Protestantism is a positive thing, there is no doubt whatever that it is dead. In so far as it really was a set of special spiritual beliefs it is no longer believed. The genuine Protestant creed is now hardly held by anybody—least of all by the Protestants. So completely have they lost faith in it, that they have mostly forgotten what it was. If almost any modern man be asked whether we save our souls solely through our theology, or

[20] Theosophy, a syncretistic faith that combined elements from Christianity and various Asian religions, was founded in New York City in 1875 by Helena Blavatsky.

whether doing good (to the poor, for instance) will help us on the road to God, he would answer without hesitation that good works are probably more pleasing to God than theology. It would probably come as quite a surprise to him to learn that, for three hundred years, the faith in faith alone was the badge of a Protestant, the faith in good works the rather shameful badge of a disreputable Papist. The ordinary Englishman (to bring in our old friend once more) would now be in no doubt whatever on the merits of the long quarrel between Catholicism and Calvinism. And that was the most important and intellectual quarrel between Catholicism and Protestantism. If he believes in a God at all, or even if he does not, he would quite certainly prefer a God who has made all men for joy, and desires to save them all, to a God who deliberately made some for involuntary sin and immortal misery. But that was the quarrel; and it was the Catholic who held the first and the Protestant who held the second. The modern man not only does not share, he does not even understand, the unnatural aversion of the Puritans to all art and beauty in relation to religion. Yet that was the real Protestant protest; and right into the Mid-Victorian time Protestant matrons were shocked at a white gown, let alone a coloured vestment. On practically every essential count on which the Reformation actually put Rome in the dock, Rome has since been acquitted by the jury of the whole world.

It is perfectly true that we can find real wrongs, provoking rebellion, in the Roman Church just before the Reformation. What we cannot find is one of those real wrongs that the Reformation reformed. For instance, it was an abominable abuse that the corruption of the monasteries sometimes permitted a rich noble to play the patron and even play at being the Abbot, or draw on the revenues supposed to belong to a brotherhood of poverty and charity. But all that the Reformation did was to allow the same rich noble to take over *all* the revenue, to seize the whole house and turn it into a palace or a pig-sty, and utterly stamp out the last legend of the poor brotherhood. The worst things in worldly Catholicism were made worse by Protestantism. But the best things remained somehow through the era of corruption; nay, they survived even the era of reform. They survive today in all Catholic countries, not only in the colour and poetry and popularity of religion, but in the deepest lessons of practical psychology. And so completely are they justified, after the judgment of four centuries, that every one of them is now being copied, even by those who condemned it; only it is often caricatured. Psycho-analysis is the Confessional without the safeguards of the Confessional; Communism is the Franciscan movement without the moderating balance of the Church; and American sects, having howled for three centuries at the Popish theatricality and mere appeal to the senses, now "brighten" their services by super-theatrical films and rays of rose-red light falling on the head of the minister. If we had a ray of light to throw about, we should not throw it on the minister.

Next, Protestantism may be a negative thing. In other words, it may be a new and totally different list of charges against Rome; and only in continuity because it is still against Rome. That is very largely what it is; and that is presumably what the *Daily Express* really meant, when it said that our country and our countrymen are soaked in Protestantism as in salt. In other words, the legend that Rome is wrong anyhow, is still a living thing, though all the features of the monster are now entirely altered in the caricature. Even this is an exaggeration, as applied to the England of today; but there is still a truth in it. Only the truth, when truly realized, can hardly be very satisfactory to honest and genuine Protestants. For, after all, what sort of a tradition is this, that tells a different story every day or every decade, and is content so long as all the contradictory tales are told against one man or one institution? What sort of holy cause is it to inherit from our ancestors, that we should go on hating something and being consistent only in hatred; being fickle and false in everything else, even in our reason for hating it? Are we really to settle down seriously to make up a new set of stories against the bulk of our fellow-Christians. Is that Protestantism; and is that worth comparing to patriotism or the sea?

Anyhow, that was the situation I found myself facing when I began to think of these things, the child of a purely Protestant ancestry and, in the ordinary sense, of a Protestant household. But as a fact my family, having become Liberal, was no longer Protestant.

I was brought up a sort of Universalist and Unitarian; at the feet of that admirable man, Stopford Brooke.[21] It was not Protestantism save in a very negative sense. Often it was the flat contrary of Protestantism, even in that sense. For instance, the Universalist did not believe in hell; and he was emphatic in saying that heaven was a happy state of mind—"a temper." But he had the sense to see that most men do not live or die in a state of mind so happy that it will alone ensure them a heaven. If heaven is a temper, it is certainly not a universal temper; and a good many people pass through this life in a devil of a temper. If all these were to have heaven, solely through happiness, it seemed clear that something must happen to them first. The Universalist therefore believed in a progress after death, at once punishment and enlightenment. In other words, he believed in Purgatory; though he did not believe in Hell. Right or wrong, he obviously and flatly contradicted the Protestant, who believed in Hell but not in Purgatory. Protestantism, through its whole history, had waged ceaseless war on this one idea of Purgatory or Progress beyond the grave. I have come to see in the complete Catholic view much deeper truths on all three ideas; truths concerned with will and creation and God's most glorious love of liberty. But even at the start, though I had no thought of Catholicism, I could not see why I should have any concern with Protestantism; which had always said the very opposite of what a Liberal is now expected to say.

I found, in plain words, that there was no longer any question of clinging to the Protestant faith. It was simply a question of whether I should cling to the Protestant feud. And to my enormous astonishment, I found a large number of my fellow Liberals eager to go on with the Protestant feud, though they no longer held the Protestant faith. I have no title to judge them; but to me, I confess, it seemed like a rather ugly breach of honour. To find out that you have been slandering somebody about something, to refuse to apologize, and to make up another more plausible story against him, so that you can carry on the spirit of the slander, seemed to me at the start a rather poor way of behaving. I resolved at least to consider the

[21] Stopford Brooke (1832–1916), a prominent Anglican preacher in Ireland, repudiated Anglicanism in 1880 because he could no longer accept its teachings.

original slandered institution on its own merits and the first and most obvious question was: Why were Liberals so very illiberal about it? What was the meaning of the feud, so constant and so inconsistent? That question took a long time to answer and would now take much too long a time to record. But it led me at last to the only logical answer, which every fact of life now confirms; that the thing is hated, as nothing else is hated, simply because it is, in the exact sense of the popular phrase, like nothing on earth.

There is barely space here to indicate this one thing out of the thousand things that confirm the same fact and confirm each other. I would undertake to pick up any topic at random, from pork to pyrotechnics, and show that it illustrates the truth of the only true philosophy; so realistic is the remark that all roads lead to Rome. Out of all these I have here only taken one fact; that the thing is pursued age after age by an unreasonable hatred that is perpetually changing its reason. Now of nearly all the dead heresies it may be said that they are not only dead, but damned; that is, they are condemned or would be condemned by common sense, even outside the Church, when once the mood and mania of them is passed. Nobody now wants to revive the Divine Right of Kings which the first Anglicans advanced against the Pope. Nobody now wants to revive the Calvinism which the first Puritans advanced against the King. Nobody now is sorry that the Iconoclasts were prevented from smashing all the statues of Italy. Nobody now is sorry that the Jansenists[22] failed to destroy all the dramas in France. Nobody who knows anything about the Albigensians[23] regrets that they did not convert the world to pessimism and perversion. Nobody who really understands the logic of the Lollards[24] (a much more sympathetic set of people) really wishes that they had succeeded in taking

[22] Jansenism, an extreme form of Augustinianism that emphasizes human depravity and predestination, rose to prominence in seventeenth-century France. Pope Clement XI condemned it in *Unigenitus Dei Filius* (1713).

[23] Albigensianism, a form of Manichaean dualism, flourished in southern France in the late twelfth century. In 1208 Pope Innocent III called for a crusade to stamp out the heresy; the orthodox forces prevailed by the 1220s.

[24] Lollardy developed in fourteenth-century England from the teachings of John Wyclif (c. 1320–84), whose anti-clericalism and criticism of the Church's wealth and temporal power anticipated ideas that would emerge fully in the Reformation.

away all political rights and privileges from everybody who was not in a state of grace. "Dominion founded on Grace" was a devout ideal; but considered as a plan for disregarding an Irish policeman controlling the traffic in Piccadilly, until we have discovered whether he has confessed recently to his Irish priest, it is wanting in actuality. In nine cases out of ten the Church simply stood for sanity and social balance against heretics who were sometimes very like lunatics. Yet at each separate moment the pressure of the prevalent error was very strong; the exaggerated error of a whole generation, like the strength of the Manchester School[25] in the 'fifties, or of Fabian Socialism[26] as a fashion in my own youth. A study of the true historical cases commonly shows us the spirit of the age going wrong, and the Catholics at least relatively going right. It is a mind surviving a hundred moods.

As I say, this is only one aspect; but it was the first that affected me and it leads on to others. When a hammer has hit the right nail on the head a hundred times, there comes a time when we think it was not altogether by accident. But these historical proofs would be nothing without the human and personal proofs, which would need quite a different sort of description. It is enough to say that those who know the Catholic practice find it not only right, but always right when everything else is wrong; making the Confessional the very throne of candour where the world outside talks nonsense about it as a sort of conspiracy; upholding humility when everybody is praising pride; charged with sentimental charity when the world is talking a brutal utilitarianism; charged with dogmatic harshness when the world is loud and loose with vulgar sentimentalism—as it is today. At the place where the roads meet there is no doubt of the convergence. A man may think all sorts of things, most of them honest and many of them true, about the right way to turn in the maze at Hampton Court.[27] But he does not think he is in the centre; he knows.

[25] The Manchester School, of mid-nineteenth-century England, was a school of political economy associated with John Bright and Richard Cobden; it advocated free trade and government nonintervention in the economy.

[26] Fabian Socialism was an English form of nonrevolutionary, parliamentary socialism. It took its name from the Fabian Society, founded in 1884 by Sidney and Beatrice Webb, George Bernard Shaw and others.

[27] Hampton Court was built in the early sixteenth century by Cardinal Wolsey on the Thames River near London, and was later favored as a residence of English kings.

IX

WHAT DO THEY THINK?

All science, even the divine science, is a sublime detective story. Only it is not set to detect why a man is dead; but the darker secret of why he is alive. The Catholic Church remains in the best sense a mystery even to believers. It would be foolish of them to complain if it is a riddle to unbelievers. But in a more practical sense we may well ask a question. What do they think it really is? What do they think we think it really is? What do they think it is all about, or even supposed to be all about? That problem becomes darker and darker for me, the more I stare at it. It becomes black as midnight, for instance, when I stare at such a sentence as I saw recently in *Truth*, a singularly intelligent and often a highly valuable paper. It stated that Rome tolerates, in her relation with the Russian Uniats,[28] "strange heresies and even bearded and wedded clergy."

In that one extraordinary phrase, what formless monster begins to take form in their visions? In those eight words it is not too much to say that every term is startling in its inconsequence. As somebody tumbling down the stairs bumps upon every step, the writer comes a crash upon every word. The word "strange" is strange enough. The word "heresy" is stranger. Perhaps at first sight the word "bearded," with its joyous reminiscences of the game of Beaver, may appear the most funny. "Wedded" is also funny. Even the "and" between bearded and wedded is funny. But by far the funniest and most fantastic thing in all that fantastic sentence is the word "even."

It is not everybody who can thus bestrew a page with comic conjunctions and farcical particles of speech. Only a wild unreason, about the whole way the thing hangs together, could thus make even the joints and hinges of that rickety statement rattle and creak with laughter. We can hardly say of this version of the Roman Catholic faith that it is a false version, or that it differs from the true

[28] Russian Uniates are Eastern-rite Catholics loyal to the papacy.

version, or even that it differs from our version. What *is* the version; and how can it be even their version? There is in the world, they would tell us, a powerful and persecuting superstition, intoxicated with the impious idea of having a monopoly of divine truth, and therefore cruelly crushing and exterminating everything else as error. It burns thinkers for thinking, discoverers for discovering, philosophers and theologians who differ by a hair's breadth from its dogmas; it will tolerate no tiny change or shadow of variety even among its friends and followers; it sweeps the whole world with one encyclical cyclone of uniformity; it would destroy nations and empires for a word, so wedded is it to its fixed idea that its own word is the Word of God. When it is thus sweeping the world, it comes to a remote and rather barbarous region somewhere on the borders of Russia; where it stops suddenly; smiles broadly; and tells the people there that they can have the strangest heresies they like. Strange heresies, by the standard of strangeness likely to exist in an experience so long as that of the Roman Church, may well be very strange indeed. The Church is no stranger to heresies that involved human sacrifice, or the worship of demons, or the practice of perversions. We might well suppose, therefore, that the Church says benevolently to these fortunate Slavs, "By all means worship Baphomet and Beelzebub; say the Lord's Prayer backwards; continue to drink the blood of infants—nay, even," and here her voice falters, till she rallies with an effort of generous resolution, "—yes, even, if you really must, grow a beard." And then, I suppose, we must call up yet darker and more dreadful visions, of the heretic hiding himself in secret places, in caverns of witchcraft or sealed gardens of black magic, while the blasphemous beard is grown. Nobody explains why these particular Eastern Europeans should be regarded with so much favour, or why a number of long hairs on the chin should be regarded with so much disfavour. It is presumably a problem on which this intolerant spiritual tyranny will suffer no question to be asked.

Does the reader realize the despair that falls upon the hapless Catholic journalist at such moments; or how wild a prayer he may well send up for the intercession of St. Francis of Sales?[29] What is

---

[29] St. Francis de Sales (1567–1622) was bishop of Geneva and the patron saint of journalists.

he to say; or at what end of that sentence is he to begin? What is the good of his laboriously beginning to explain that a married clergy is a matter of discipline and not doctrine, that it can therefore be allowed locally without heresy—when all the time the man thinks a beard as important as a wife and more important than a false religion? What is the sense of explaining to him the peculiar historical circumstances that have led to preserving some local habits in Kiev or Warsaw, when the man at any moment may receive a mortal shock by seeing a bearded Franciscan walking through Wimbledon or Walham Green? What we want to get at is the mind of the man who can think so absurdly about us as to suppose we could have a horror of heresy, and then a weakness for heresy, and then a greater horror of hair. To what does he attribute all the inconsistent nonsense and inconsequent bathos that he associates with us? Does he think we are all joking; or all dreaming; or all out of our minds; or what does he think? Until we have got at that, we have really got very little further.

The notion that he merely thinks the Church is all nonsense is not very consistent with the way in which he talks about her in other aspects; as when he says she has always resisted such and such changes, which he perhaps approves; or that she can be counted on as an influence for such and such principles, which he perhaps dislikes; or that she is forbidden to accept this doctrine or committed to defending that. But what he can possibly suppose to be the principle upon which she accepts or rejects doctrines I never can imagine. And the more we really come in contact with the puzzle, the more we shall feel, I think, something quite unique and even creepy about it. It is like the old fable of the five blind men who tried to explore an elephant; a fable that used to be told as a sort of farce; but which I can well imagine being told by Maeterlinck[30] or some modern mystic so as to make the flesh creep with mysteries. The thing is at once so obvious and so invisible; so public and so impalpable; so universal and so secret. They say so much about it; and they say so little. They see so much of it; and they see so little. There is a sort of colossal contradiction, such as can only be conceived between different dimensions

[30] Maurice Maeterlinck (1862–1949) was a Belgian Symbolist playwright.

or different planes of thought, in the co-existence of such familiar fact and such utterly unknown truth. Indeed, there is only one combination of words I know of, which ever did exactly express so huge a human and historical paradox; and they also are familiar and unfathomable: "The light shone in the darkness and the darkness comprehended it not."[31]

Some part of the difficulty is doubtless due to the odd way in which so many people are at once preoccupied with it and prejudiced against it. It is queer to observe so much ignorance with so little indifference. They love talking about it and they hate hearing about it. It would seem that they especially hate asking about it. If, for instance, a man contributing to *Truth*, in the middle of educated London, really were a little puzzled by Rome making an exception of the Uniats, and were perhaps especially puzzled by an exception to the celibacy of the clergy (I omit his dark and inscrutable broodings on the subject of Beavers) might it not have occurred to him to go and ask some Catholic priest, or for that matter, some Catholic layman, and thus gain some sort of rough idea of the relative importance attached in our system to celibacy and heresy and hair on the face? Could he not have gained a glimpse of the usual order of hierarchy of these ideas, which would have prevented him from writing the staggering word "and" or the stunning word "even"? But I am inclined to suspect that even this omission, negative as it may seem, has in it something deeper than mere negligence. I fancy that there is more than meets the eye in this curious controversial attitude; the desire to ask rhetorical questions and not to ask real questions; the wish to heckle and not to hear. It may well be connected with more mystical aspects of the whole question, on which I am certainly not going to speculate, since they are admittedly the most subtle problems of the trained theologian; all those questions about the will to believe and the operations of grace; and the fact that something more than reason is needed to bring any of us into the most reasonable of all philosophies.

But apart from these mysteries, I think there is another reason that is human and historical. The thing that causes Catholic philosophy

---

[31] The quotation is from John 1:5.

to be neglected is the very thing that really makes it impossible to neglect. It is the fact that it was something left for dead; and now rather incredibly come to life. An ordinary man would not mind very much whether he knew the exact ritual with which Roman augurs examined the entrails of beasts or watched the movements of birds; because he is certain that the world will not go back to that Roman religion. The world was once almost as certain that it would not go back to this other Roman religion. A man would not be very much ashamed of having put the metals in the wrong order in the imaginary formula of an alchemist, described in a historical romance; because he is convinced that alchemists can only return in romance and can never return in history. There was a time when he felt quite as safe about abbots as about alchemists. That time has already passed. That mere confident contempt, as I have said, has already been succeeded by a rather restless curiosity. But mental habits overlap; and the dead momentum of the old disregard of facts goes along side by side with a new movement of anxiety about possibilities. They would not be so ignorant about it if they had not decided that it was dead. They would not be so irritated about it if they had not discovered that it was alive. For ignorance accumulates like knowledge; and these newly aroused critics are the inheritors of the accruing interest of four hundred years of an ignorance that became an indifference. At this moment they are no longer indifferent; but they are still ignorant. They have been awakened suddenly in the watches of the night, and what they see they can neither deny nor understand. For they see one that was dead walking; and the blaze of that living death blasts or obliterates all the older details of life; and all the fables they have believed and all the facts they have forgotten are alike swallowed up in the miracle they can neither believe nor forget.

X

THE MASK OF THE AGNOSTIC

Sir Arthur Keith,[32] in his recent remarks on the soul, let the cat out of the bag. He let it out of that very prim and proper professional bag which is carried by the "medical man" whom he described as conscientiously compelled to assert that the life of the soul ceases with the breath of the body. Perhaps the figure which fits in so well with the bag is less fortunate in the case of the cat; a mystic animal, whose nine lives might rather be supposed to represent immortality, at least in the form of reincarnation. But anyhow, he let the cat out of the bag; in the sense of revealing a secret which such wise men would be wiser to keep. It is the secret that such scientists do not speak as scientists, but simply as materialists. That is, they do not give their conclusions, but simply their opinions; and very shaky sort of opinions some of them are.

Not long ago, in his famous address on Anthropoids to the Congress at Leeds, Sir Arthur Keith said that he spoke simply as the foreman of a jury. It is true that he had not apparently consulted the jury; and it was rapidly made clear that the jury violently disagreed; which is unusual in a jury after the foreman has delivered the verdict. Still, in using this image he meant to claim complete impartiality of a judicial sort. He meant that a juryman is bound by oath to go entirely by the facts and the evidence, without fear or favour. And this effect would be a hundred times more effective if we were left free to imagine that the juryman's personal sympathies might be on the other side; or at least, if we did not know that they were very keenly on the one side. Sir Arthur should have been careful to preserve the impression that, speaking strictly and solely as an anthropologist, he was forced to accept the natural selection of anthropoids. He should then have left it to be inferred that, merely as a private

[32] Arthur Keith (1866–1955) was conservator of the Hunterian Museum of the Royal College of Surgeons from 1908 to 1933; he was an anatomist, an anthropologist and a defender of Darwinism.

person, he might be yearning for seraphic visions and celestial hopes; he might be searching the Scriptures or awaiting the Apocalypse. For all it was any business of ours, or any business of anybody's, he might be in private life a Mormon multiplying the stars in his heavenly crown or a Holy Roller continually convulsed by the Holy Ghost. The point was that the facts forced the Darwinian conclusion upon him. And a man of that sort, being forced to accept them, would be a real witness because a reluctant witness. In the trial of Darwin the man might feel for the plaintiff, but the juryman would be forced to find for the defendant.

And now Sir Arthur Keith has thrown the whole of that imperial impartiality away. He has gone out of his way to dogmatize and lay down the law about the soul; which has nothing to do with his subject, except in so far as it is everybody's subject. But while it does not relate to what is his subject, it has told everybody which is his side. It has turned the foreman of the jury into a very unmistakable advocate for that side. Indeed, such a partisan is more like a party to the suit than an advocate; since it is the whole point that as a private person he has long had the private prejudice. Henceforth it is obvious that Keith deciding for Darwin is simply like Bradlaugh[33] deciding for Darwin, or Ingersoll[34] deciding for Darwin, or any atheist on a stool in Hyde Park deciding for Darwin. When *they* choose the side of natural selection, we can all agree that it is a very natural selection.

As to the conclusion itself, it seems almost incredibly inconclusive. Unless Sir Arthur Keith is very badly misreported, he specially stated that spiritual existence ceases with the physical functions; and that no medical man could conscientiously say anything else. However grave be the injury called death (which indeed is often fatal), this strikes me as a case in which it is quite unnecessary to call in a medical man at all. There is always a certain irony, even in the simple pages of my favourite detective stories, in the fact that everybody rushes for a doctor as soon as they are quite certain that a

[33] Charles Bradlaugh (1833–91) was an English journalist, politician and freethinker.
[34] Robert G. Ingersoll (1833–99) was America's most famous agnostic in the late nineteenth century.

man is dead. But in the detective story there may at least be something to be learnt by the doctor from the dead body. In the doctrinal
speculation there is nothing whatever; and it does but confuse the
eternal detective story for the doctor of medicine to pretend to be a
doctor of divinity. The truth is that all this business about "a
medical man" is mere bluff and mystagogy. The medical man "sees"
that the mind has ceased with the body. What the medical man sees
is that the body can no longer kick, talk, sneeze, whistle or dance a
jig. And a man does not need to be very medical in order to see that.
But whether the principle of energy, that once made it kick, talk,
sneeze, whistle and dance, does or does not still exist on some other
plane of existence — a medical man knows no more about that than
any other man. And when medical men were clear-headed, some of
them (like an ex-surgeon named Thomas Henry Huxley) said they
did not believe that medical men or any men could know anything
about it. That is an intelligent position; but it does not seem to be
Sir Arthur Keith's position. He has been put up publicly to *deny* that
the soul survives the body; and to make the extraordinary remark
that any medical man must say the same. It is as if we were to say
that any competent builder or surveyor must deny the possibility of
the Fourth Dimension; because he has learnt the technical secret that
a building is measured by length, breadth and height. The obvious
query is — Why bring in a surveyor? Everybody knows that everything is in fact measured by three dimensions. Anybody who thinks
there is a fourth dimension thinks so in spite of being well aware
that things are generally measured by three. Or it is as if a man were
to answer a Berkleyan metaphysician, who holds all matter to be an
illusion of mind, by saying, "I can call the evidence of an intelligent
navvy who actually has to deal with solid concrete and cast iron; and
he will tell you they are quite real." We should naturally answer that
we do not need a navvy to tell us that solid things are solid; and it is
quite in another sense that the philosopher says they are not solid.
Similarly, there is nothing to make a medical man a materialist, except what might make any man a materialist. And it is when a man
has absorbed all that obvious materialism that he begins to use his
mind. And, as some hold, does not stop.

This very unphilosophical irruption into philosophy was, how-ever, in one way enlightening. It threw a light backwards on the speaker's previous proclamation on things on which he has more right to speak. Even in those things he betrayed a curious simplicity common among such official scientists. The truth is that they be-come steadily less scientific and more official. They develop that thin disguise that is the daily wear of politicians. They perform before us the most artful tricks with the most artless transparency. It is like watching a child trying to hide something. They are perpetually try-ing to bluff us with big words and learned allusions; on the assump-tion that we have never learnt anything—even of their own funny little ways. Every leader-writer who thunders "Galileo" at us assumes that we know even less about Galileo than he does. Every preacher of popular science who throws a long word at us thinks we shall have to look it up in the dictionary and hopes we shall not study it seriously even in the encyclopaedia. Their use of science is rather like the use made of it by the heroes of certain adventure stories, in which the white men terrify the savages by predicting an eclipse or producing an electric shock. These are in a sense true demonstrations of science. They are in a sense right in saying that they are scientists. Where they are perhaps wrong is in supposing that we are savages.

But it is rather amusing for us who watch the preparations for giving us an electric shock, when we are seriously expected to be shocked by the shock. It is rather a joke when we, the benighted savages, are ourselves not only quite capable of predicting the eclipse, but capable of predicting the prediction. Now, among these facts that have been familiar to us for a long time is the fact that men of science stage and prepare their effects exactly as politicians do. They also do it rather badly—exactly as politicians do. Neither of these two modern mystagogues has yet realized how transparent his tricks have become. One of the most familiar and transparent of them is what is known as the "official contradiction." It is a strange symbolic way of declaring that something has happened by denying that it has happened. So whitewashing reports are published after political scandals as regularly as bluebooks. So the Right Honour-able Gentleman hopes it is not necessary for him to contradict what he feels sure the Honourable Member could not have intended to insinuate. So a Cabinet Minister is put up to deny from a platform that there is any change in the Government's policy about Damascus. And so Sir Arthur Keith is put up to deny that there is any change in the scientific attitude about Darwin.

And when we hear that, we all give a sort of sigh of satisfaction; for we all know exactly what *that* means. It means more or less the opposite of what it says. It means that there has been a devil of a row about Damascus inside the Party, or, in other words, that there is beginning to be a devil of a scandal about discredited Darwinians inside the scientific world. The curious thing is that in the latter case the officials are not only solemn in uttering the official contradiction, but much more simple in supposing that nobody will realize that it is official. In the case of the similar legal fiction in politics, the politicians by this time not only know the truth, but often know that we know the truth. Everybody knows by this time, by the gossip that is repeated everywhere, exactly what is meant by the absolute agreement on everything which binds the Prime Minister and all his colleagues. The Prime Minister does not really expect us to believe that he is the holy and beloved king of a brotherhood of knights sworn to a faith and giving their hearts to him alone. But Sir Arthur Keith does really expect us to believe that he is the foreman of a jury containing all the different men of science, all absolutely agreed that Darwin's particular opinion was "eternal." That is what I mean by childish concealment; and the artless or transparent trick. That is why I say that they do not even know how much we know.

For the politician is less pompously absurd than the anthropologist, even if we test it by what they both call Progress; which is mostly only another word for Time. We all know the official optimism which always defends the present government. But this is like an official defence of all the past governments. If a man were to say that the politics of Palmerston[35] were eternal, we should think him a little out of date. Yet Darwin was prominent at about the same date as Palmerston; and is quite equally dated. If Mr. Lloyd

[35] Henry John Temple, Lord Palmerston (1784–1865), was prime minister of Great Britain almost continuously from 1855 to 1865.

George were to get up and say that the great Liberal Party had not receded from one single position taken up by Cobden and Bright,[36] the only true Tribunes of the People, we should reluctantly conclude (if such a thing be conceivable) that he was talking party claptrap to people ignorant of the history of the party. If a social reformer were to affirm solemnly that all social philosophy was still proceeding strictly on the principles of Herbert Spencer, we should know it was doing nothing of the sort, and that only an absolutely fossilized official could pretend that it was. Yet Darwin and Spencer were not only contemporaries but comrades and allies; and the Darwinian biology and the Spencerian sociology were regarded as parts of the same movement, which our grandfathers regarded as a very modern movement. Even considered *a priori* as a matter of probability it therefore seems rather unlikely that the science of that generation was any more infallible than its ethics and politics. Even on the principles Sir Arthur professes, it seems very queer that there should now be no more to be said about Darwinism than he said about it. But we do not need to appeal to those principles or those probabilities. We can appeal to the facts. As it happens, we do know something about the facts; and Sir Arthur Keith does not seem to know that we know.

It was in a Catholic paper that certain statements were made about Darwinism today; statements which Sir Arthur Keith himself went out of his way to contradict; and about which Sir Arthur Keith himself was proved sensationally and disastrously wrong. Probably the story is now known to all readers of that paper; but it will possibly never come to the knowledge of most other journalists, and it certainly will not be recorded in most of the other papers. Touching this cosmic controversy, most of the other papers are emphatically party papers; and they support the party leader when he publishes the official contradiction. They will not let the public know how triumphantly his other contradiction was contradicted.

When Mr. Belloc stated that these Darwinians were out of date and ignorant of recent biology, he quoted among a great many other

[36] Richard Cobden (1804–65) and John Bright (1811–99) were Englishmen who fought for free trade and the repeal of the Corn Laws in the 1840s.

recent authorities the French biologist Vialleton as denying the possibility of natural selection in a particular case connected with reptiles and birds. Sir Arthur Keith, coming to the rescue of Mr. H. G. Wells, and eager to prove that he and Mr. Wells were not out of date or ignorant of recent biology, proceeded to contradict Mr. Belloc flatly. He said that there was no such statement in Vialleton's book; in other words, he accused Mr. Belloc of having misquoted or misrepresented Vialleton's book. It then appeared, to the amazement of everybody, and especially of Mr. Belloc, that Sir Arthur Keith did not even know of the existence of the book. He was referring only to an early and elementary work by the same author published long ago. That was the last he had ever read Vialleton. The important book, of which even I, a mere unscientific man in the street, had heard at least something, had never come to his ears at all. In short, the general charge, that Darwinians are out of date in their information, was proved about as completely as anything controversial can ever be proved in this world.

Now, when a thing like that has happened, above all when it has happened to us, in the pages of a paper in which I write, in the experience of one of my own friends, how can it be expected that people in our position should take seriously the speech at the opening of the British Association at Leeds? How can we keep a straight face when the President strikes an attitude as if pointing to the stars and declaring Darwinism equally eternal? That sort of thing is not meant for us; but for the reporters; just as the true story of Wells and Belloc is generally kept out of the reports.

XI

THE EARLY BIRD IN HISTORY

St. Joan of Arc, a star and a thunderbolt, strange as a meteoric stone whose very solidity is not of this earth, may be compared also to a diamond among pebbles; the one white stone of history. Like a diamond, she is clear but not simple, as some count simplicity; but having many facets or aspects. There is one aspect of the discussion on St. Joan which I have never seen specially noted, and it seems to be worth a note. It concerns that common and current charge against the Catholic Church that she is, as the phrase goes, always behind the times.

When I became a Catholic, I was quite prepared to find that in many respects she really was behind the times. I was very tolerant of the idea of being behind the times, having had long opportunities of studying the perfectly ghastly people who were abreast of the times; or the still more pestilent people who were in advance of the times. I was prepared to find Catholicism rather Conservative, and in that sense slow; and so, of course, in some aspects it is. I knew that being in the movement generally meant only being in the fashion. I knew that fashions had an extraordinary way of being first omnipresent and oppressive and then suddenly blank and forgotten. I knew how publicity seems fixed like a spotlight and vanishes like a lightning-flash. I had seen the whole public imagination filled with a succession of Krugers[37] and Kaisers, who were to be hanged next week and about whom nobody cared a hang next month. I have lived through an overwhelming illusion that there was nobody in the world except General Gordon[38] or Captain Dreyfus[39] or

[37] Krugers is an allusion to Paul Kruger (1825–1904), president of the South African Republic; he was deposed by the British in the Boer War of 1899–1902.

[38] Charles George Gordon (1833–85) was an English general known as "Chinese" Gordon for having quelled a rebellion in Taiping in 1864. He died at the siege of Khartoum in the Sudan.

[39] Alfred Dreyfus (1859–1935) was a French army officer wrongly convicted in 1894 of spying for the Germans. He was later exonerated; but at the turn of the century his case engendered bitterness in France between "Dreyfusards", largely of the Left, and "anti-Dreyfusards", who came mainly from the ranks of Catholics and royalists.

the elephant Jumbo at the Zoo. If there is something in the world
that takes no notice of these world-changes, I confess to finding a
certain comfort in its indifference. I think it was just as well, from
every point of view, that the ecclesiastical authorities delayed a decision about Darwinism or even Evolution; and declined altogether to
be excited in that universal excitement. There were many, even
among the sympathetic, who seemed to think that Catholics ought to
put up an altar to the Missing Link, as Pagans did to the Unknown
God. But Catholics prefer to wait until they know what they are doing; and would prefer to learn a little more about a thing besides the
fact that nobody can find it. And of course it is true that in some matters, judged by the feverish pace of recent fashion, the Church has
always been slow as well as sure. But there is another side of the truth,
and one which is more commonly missed. As it happens, both sides
are strikingly illustrated in the story of the status of St. Joan.

If we go back to the very beginning of a story, we very often find
that the Church did actually do something which her foes ignored
and even her friends forgot. Then other social tendencies set in,
other questions occupied the world, the tides of time and change
passed over the whole business; and when that business came again
to the surface, the world had the impression that the Church was
dealing with it after a very long delay. But the world itself had never
dealt with it at all. The world, as a matter of fact, had never woken
up to the fact at all, until it woke up with a start and began to abuse
the Church for not having woken up before. During all those long
intervening ages, the world had really been much more asleep than
the Church. The Church, a very long time ago, had done something; and the world had done nothing. The case of St. Joan of Arc
is one curious example.

The Canonization of St. Joan came very slowly and very late. But
the Rehabilitation of St. Joan came very promptly and very early. It
is a very exceptional example of rapid reparation for a judicial crime
or a miscarriage of justice. There have been any number of these
judicial crimes in history. There have been any number of heroes and
martyrs whom history regards as having suffered for their virtues.
It has almost passed into a popular proverb, especially in modern

times; as in the words of the American popular poet: "Right for ever on the scaffold, wrong for ever on the throne."[40] But I can hardly remember another example of the throne paying so prompt a salute to the scaffold. The condemnation of St. Joan was reversed by the Pope in the lifetime of her contemporaries, at the appeal of her brothers; about as soon as anybody could have expected anything of the sort to be reversed. I do not know if the Athenian Republic did as much for Socrates or the Florentine for Savonarola; but I am pretty certain that nobody could have got the Carthaginians to apologize thus to Regulus[41] or the Antiochi to Maccabaeus.[42] The only really fair way of considering the fashionable subject of the crimes of Christendom would be to compare them with the crimes of heathenism; and the normal human practice of the Pagan world. And while it may be a weakness of human beings, of every age and creed, to stone the prophets and then build their sepulchres, it is really very seldom that the sepulchre is built even as quickly as that. When those who build the sepulchre are really and truly the representatives or inheritors of those who threw the stones, it does not generally happen for hundreds of years. To take the parallel passions of the secular side of the Middle Ages, we should be considerably surprised to learn that when the head of William Wallace[43] had been stuck on a spike by Edward the First, his remains had been respectfully interred and his character cleared by Edward the Third. We should be considerably surprised if the courts of Queen Elizabeth had gone out of their way to repudiate and quash the case against Thomas More. It is generally long afterwards, when the actual ambitions and rivalries are dead, when the feuds and family interests have long been forgotten, that a rather sentimental though sincere tenderness is shown to the dead enemy. In the nineteenth century the English do make a romance about Wallace and a statue of

[40] The quotation is from James Russell Lowell's *The Present Crisis* (1844).

[41] Marcus Atilius Regulus was a Roman general in the First Punic War (264–241 B.C.); he suffered a crushing defeat at the hands of the Carthaginians in 256.

[42] Judas Maccabaeus (d. 160 B.C.) was a Jewish patriot who led a rebellion against Antiochus Epiphanes, the Seleucid ruler of Palestine.

[43] William Wallace (c. 1272–1305) was a Scotsman executed by the English for rebellion against the crown.

Washington. In the nineteenth and twentieth centuries the English do produce a fine enthusiasm and a number of excellent books about St. Joan. And I for one hope to see the day when this measure of magnanimity shall be filled up where it has been most wanting; and some such payment made for the deepest debt of all. I should like to see the day when the English put up a statue of Emmet[44] beside the statue of Washington; and I wish that in the Centenary of Emancipation there were likely to be as much fuss in London about the figure of Daniel O'Connell[45] as there was about that of Abraham Lincoln.

But I mean the comment here in a rather larger sense; and in a larger sense it is an even stronger case. I mean that if we take the tale of St. Joan as a test, the really remarkable thing is not so much the slowness of the Church to appreciate her, as the slowness of everybody else. The world, especially the wisest men of the world, were extraordinarily late in realizing what a remarkable thing had happened; very much later than the rather rigid religious officials of the fifteenth century. That rigidity of fifteenth century religion was very soon broken up, partly by good and partly by bad forces. Comparatively soon after St. Joan's ashes were thrown into the Seine, quite soon after the Rehabilitation, the Renaissance had really begun. Very soon after that the Reformation had begun. The Renaissance produced a number of large and liberal views on all sorts of things. The Reformation produced numberless narrow views, divided among all sorts of sects. But at least there were plenty of differences and varied points of view, many of them now loosened from anything that may have been restrictive in the mediaeval discipline. Human reason and imagination, left to themselves, might at least have made as much of Jeanne d'Arc as of John Huss. As a fact, human reason and imagination, left to themselves, made extraordinarily little of her. Humanism and Humanitarianism and, in a general sense, Humanity, did not really rehabilitate Joan until about five hundred years after the Church had done so.

[44] Robert Emmet (1778–1803) was an Irish nationalist executed by the English for rebellion.

[45] Daniel O'Connell (1775–1847) was an Irishman who led the fight for Catholic Emancipation, a movement that culminated in a Parliamentary act of 1829 that granted political and civil rights to Catholics.

The history of what great men have said about this great woman is a very dismal tale. The greatest man of all, Shakespere, has an unfortunate pre-eminence by his insular insults in *Henry the Sixth*. But the thing went on long after Shakespere; and was far worse in people who had far less excuse than Shakspere. Voltaire was a Frenchman; he was a great Frenchman; he professed an admiration for many French heroes; he certainly professed to be a reformer and a friend of freedom; he most certainly might have seized on any mediaeval miscarriage of justice that might be turned to anti-clerical account. What Voltaire wrote about St. Joan it will be most decent to pass over in silence. But it is the same all along the line; it is the same far later in rationalistic history than Voltaire. Byron had with all his faults a sensibility to the splendid and heroic, especially in the matter of nations struggling to be free. He was far less insular than any other English poet; he had far more comprehension of France and of the Continent; and he is still comprehended and admired there. He called St. Joan of Arc a fanatical strumpet. That was the general tone of human culture, of history as taught and talked in the age of reason. Mr. Belloc has noted that, so strong was this secular social pressure, that even a Catholic, when he wished to be moderate, like Lingard,[46] was more or less sceptical, not indeed of the morality, but certainly of the miraculous mission of St. Joan. It is true that Schiller was sympathetic, though sentimental—and therefore out of touch. But it was not till nearly the end of the nineteenth century, not fully until the beginning of the twentieth century, that ordinary men of genius awoke to the recognition of one of the most wonderful women of genius in the history of the world. One of the first really popular attempts at a rationalist rehabilitation came, of all people in the world, from Mark Twain. His notion of the Middle Ages was as provincial as the Yankee at the Court of King Arthur; but it is to the credit of this rather crude genius, of the late culture of a new country, that he did catch the flame from the pyre of Rouen, which so many cultivated sceptics had found cold. Then came a patronizing pamphlet by Anatole France;[47]

[46] John Lingard (1771–1851) was an English Catholic priest who authored a multi-volume history of England.

[47] Anatole France was the pseudonym of the French novelist François Anatole Thibault (1844–1924).

which I for one think rather more insulting than the ribald verse of Voltaire. Then came the last great attempt; wrong in many ways in its contention, but conspicuously spirited and sincere — the play of *St. Joan.* On the whole, nobody can say that humanists and rationalists have been very early in the field. This heroine had to wait about five centuries for Bernard Shaw.

Now, in that comparison, nobody can say that the Church comes off very badly in comparison with the world. The truth is that the ecclesiastical apology to the martyr came so early that everybody had forgotten all about it, long before the rest of the world began to consider the question at all. And though I have taken here the particular case of St. Joan of Arc, I believe that something of the same sort could be traced through a great many other affairs in human history.

It is true of those who gave the Jesuits a bad name and hanged them; and the hanging was not always metaphorical. The simplified version of it is to say that the Jesuits, especially in their capacity of Casuists, suffered almost entirely from being two hundred years before their time. They tried to start in a cautious way what is now surging up on every side of us in a chaotic way; all that is implied in talking about problem novels and problem plays. In other words, they recognized that there really are problems in moral conduct; not problems about whether the moral law should be obeyed, but problems about how in a particular case the moral law really applies. But they were not remembered as pioneers who had begun to ask the questions of Ibsen and Hardy and Shaw. They were remembered only as wicked conspirators who had not always believed in the Divine Right of Kings. They pioneered early enough to be execrated by an earlier generation; but too early to be thanked by a later generation. Protestants have eagerly supported Pascal against them, without taking the trouble to discover that any number of the things that Pascal denounced are things that any modern man would defend. For instance, Pascal blamed the infamous Jesuits for saying that a girl might in some conditions marry against the wish of her parents. The Jesuits would have had all modern novels, let alone problem novels, on their side. But they were too early in the field to have anybody on their side. Moreover, they wished to fit these exceptions into the moral rule; the Moderns who did it two centuries later have produced no rule, but a welter of exceptions.

Here, again, is yet another example that occurs to me at the moment. Many have given long histories of the laborious slowness with which the idea of justice to the aborigines, to Red Indians or such races, has advanced step by step with the progress of modern humanitarian ideas. In such a history Penn, the great Quaker, appears like a primeval founder and father of the republic; and he was undoubtedly very early in the field—in the Puritan field. But Las Casas,[48] the Apostle of the Indians, actually sailed in a ship with Christopher Columbus. It would be difficult to be earlier in the American field than that. He spent his life pleading for the rights of the savages; but he did it at a time when nobody in the north would listen to such a story about a saint of Spain. In this and in many other examples, I believe that the real history of the Catholic pioneer has been the same; to be first and to be forgotten.

[48] Bartolomé de Las Casas (1474–1566) was a Spanish Dominican who became bishop of Chiapas in Mexico.

XII

PROTESTANTISM: A PROBLEM NOVEL

I have been looking at the little book on Protestantism which Dean Inge has contributed to the sixpenny series of Sir Ernest Benn;[49] and though I suppose it has already been adequately criticized, it may be well to jot down a few notes on it before it is entirely forgotten. The book, which is called "Protestantism," obviously ought to be called "Catholicism." What the Dean has to say about any real thing recognizable as Protestantism is extraordinarily patchy, contradictory and inconclusive. It is only what he has to say about Catholicism that is clear, consistent and to the point. It is warmed and quickened by the human and hearty motive of hatred; and it makes everything else in the book look timid and tortuous by comparison. I am not going to annotate the work considered as history. There are some curious, if not conscious, falsifications of fact, especially in the form of suppressions of fact. He begins by interpreting Protestantism as a mere "inwardness and sincerity" in religion; which none of the Protestant reformers would have admitted to be Protestantism, and which any number of Catholic reformers have made the very heart and soul of their reforms inside Catholicism. It might be suggested that self-examination is now more often urged and practised among Catholics than among Protestants. But whether or no the champions of sincerity examine themselves, they might well examine their statements. Some of the statements here might especially be the subject of second thoughts. It is really a startling suppression and falsification to say that Henry the Eighth had only a few household troops; so that his people must have favoured his policy, or they would have risen against it. It seems enough to reply that they did rise against it. And *because* Henry had only a few household troops, he brought in bands of ferocious mercenaries from abroad to put down the religious revolt of his own people. It is an effort of

---

[49] Ernest Benn (1875–1914), an English author and publisher, promoted laissez-faire economics and individualism.

charity to concede even complete candour to the story-teller, who can actually use such an argument, and then keep silent upon such a sequel. Or again, it is outrageously misleading to suggest that the Catholic victims of Tudor and other tyranny were justly executed as traitors and not as martyrs to a religion. Every persecutor alleges social and secular necessity; so did Caiaphas and Annas; so did Nero and Diocletian; from the first the Christians were suppressed as enemies of the Empire; to the last the heretics were handed over to the secular arm with secular justifications. But when, in point of plain fact, a man can be hanged, drawn and quartered merely for saying Mass, or sometimes for helping somebody who has said Mass, it is simply raving nonsense to say that a religion is not being persecuted. To mention only one of many minor falsifications of this kind, it is quite true to say that Milton was in many ways more of a Humanist than a Puritan; but it is quite false to suggest that the Milton family was a typical Puritan family, in its taste for music and letters. The very simple explanation is that the Milton family was largely a Catholic family; and it was the celebrated John who specially separated himself from its creed but retained its culture. Countless other details as definitely false could be quoted; but I am much more interested in the general scope of the work—which allows itself to be so curiously pointless about Protestantism, merely in order to make a point against Catholicism.

Here is the Dean's attempt at a definition. "What is the main function of Protestantism? It is essentially an attempt to check the tendency to corruption and degradation which attacks every institutional religion." So far, so good. In that case St. Charles Borromeo,[50] for instance, was obviously a leading Protestant. St. Dominic and St. Francis, who purged the congested conventionalism of much of the monasticism around them, were obviously leading Protestants. The Jesuits who sifted legend by the learning of Bollandism,[51] were obviously leading Protestants. But most living Protestant leaders are not

[50] St. Charles Borromeo (1538–84) was cardinal-archbishop of Milan and a reformer of abuses among the clergy and laity.

[51] Bollandism takes its name from John Bolland, a Flemish Jesuit who in 1643 published the first volume of the *Acta Sanctorum*, historically reliable lives of the saints.

leading Protestants. If degradation drags down *every* institutional religion, it has presumably dragged down Protestant institutional religion. Protestants might possibly appear to purge Protestantism; but so did Catholics appear to purge Catholicism. Plainly this definition is perfectly useless as a *distinction* between Protestantism and Catholicism. For it is not a description of any belief or system or body of thought; but simply of a good intention, which all men of all Churches would profess and a few men in some Churches practise—especially in ours. But the Dean not only proves that modern Protestant institutions ought to be corrupt, he says that their primitive founders ought to be repudiated. He distinctly holds that we cannot follow Luther and Calvin.

Very well—let us go on and see whom we are to follow. I will take one typical passage towards the end of the book. The Dean first remarks, "The Roman Church has declared that there can be no reconciliation between Rome and modern Liberalism or Progress." One would like to see the encyclical or decree in which this declaration was made. Liberalism might mean many things, from the special thing which Newman denounced (and defined) to the intention of voting at a by-election for Sir John Simon.[52] Progress generally means something which the Pope has never, so far as I know, found it necessary to deny; but which the Dean himself has repeatedly and most furiously denied. He then goes on: "Protestantism is entirely free from this uncompromising preference for the Dark Ages." "The Dark Ages," of course, is cant and claptrap; we need take no notice of that. But we may perhaps notice, not without interest and amusement, that about twenty-five lines before, the Dean himself has described the popular Protestantism of America as if it were a barbarism and belated obscurantism. From which one may infer that the Dark Ages are still going on, exactly where there is Protestantism to preserve them. And considering that he says at least five times that the appeal of Protestants to the letter of Scripture is narrow and superstitious, it surely seems a little astonishing that he should sum up by declaring Protestantism, as such, to be *"entirely*

[52] John Simon (1873–1954) was an English jurist and prominent figure in the Liberal Party.

free", from this sort of darkness. Then, on top of all this welter of wordy contradictions, we have this marvelous and mysterious conclusion: "It is in this direction that Protestants may look for the beginning of what may really be a new Reformation, a resumption of the unfinished work of Sir Thomas More, Giordano Bruno and Erasmus."

In short, Protestants may look forward to a Reformation modelled on the work of two Catholics and one obscure mystic, who was not a Protestant and of whose tenets they and the world know practically nothing. One hardly knows where to begin, in criticizing this very new Reformation, two-thirds of which was apparently started by men of the Old Religion. We might meekly suggest that, if it be regrettable that the work of Sir Thomas More was "unfinished," some portion of the blame may perhaps attach to the movement that cut off his head. Is it possible, I wonder, that what the Dean really means is that we want a new Reformation to undo all the harm that was done by the old Reformation? In this we certainly have no reason to quarrel with him. We should be delighted also to have a new Reformation, of ourselves as well as of Protestants and other people; though it is only fair to say that Catholics did, within an incredibly short space of time, contrive to make something very like a new Reformation; which is commonly called the Counter-Reformation. St. Vincent de Paul[53] and St. Francis of Sales have at least as good a right to call themselves inheritors of the courtesy and charity of More as has the present Dean of St. Paul's. But putting that seventeenth century reform on one side, there is surely something rather stupendous about the reform that the Dean proposes for the twentieth century, and the patron saints he selects for it out of the sixteenth century.

For this, it seems, is how we stand. We are not to follow Luther and Calvin. But we are to follow More and Erasmus. And that, if you please, is the true Protestantism and the promise of a second Reformation. We are to copy the views and virtues of the men who found they *could* remain under the Pope, and especially of one who actually died for supremacy of the Pope. We are to throw away practically every rag of thought or theory that was held by the people who did not remain

[53] St. Vincent de Paul (1576–1660) was a French saint famed for his works of mercy.

under the supremacy of the Pope. And we are to bind up all these views in a little popular pamphlet with an orange cover and call them "Protestantism." The truth is that Dean Inge had an impossible title and an impossible task. He had to present Protestantism as Progress; when he is far too acute and cultivated a man not to suspect that it was (as it was) a relapse into barbarism and a break away from all that was central in civilization. Even by the test of the Humanist, it made religion inhuman. Even by the test of the liberal, it substituted literalism for liberalism. Even if the goal had been mere Modernism, it led its followers to it by a long, dreary and straggling detour, a wandering in the wilderness, that did not even discover Modernism till it had first discovered Mormonism. Even if the goal had been logical scepticism, Voltaire could reach it more rapidly from the school of the Jesuits than the poor Protestant provincial brought up among the Jezreelites. Every mental process, even the process of going wrong, is clearer in the Catholic atmosphere. Protestantism has done nothing for Dean Inge, except give him a Deanery which rather hampers his mental activity. It has done nothing for his real talent or scholarship or sense of ideas. It has not in history defended any of the ideas he defends, or helped any of the liberties in which he hopes. But it has done one thing: it has hurt something he hates. It has done some temporary or apparent harm to the heritage of St. Peter. It once made something that looked like a little crack in the wall of Rome. And because of *that*, the Dean can pardon anything to the Protestants—even Protestantism.

For this is the strange passion of his life; and he toils through all these pages of doubts and distinctions only for the moment when he can liberate his soul in one wild roar of monomaniac absurdity: "Let the innocent Dreyfus die in prison; let the Irishman who has committed a treacherous murder be told to leave 'politics' out of his confession; let the lucrative imposture of Lourdes . . ." That is the way to talk! It is so tiring, pretending to talk sense.

XIII

A SIMPLE THOUGHT

Most men would return to the old ways in faith and morals if they could broaden their minds enough to do so. It is narrowness that chiefly keeps them in the rut of negation. But this enlargement is easily misunderstood, because the mind must be enlarged to see the simple things; or even to see the self-evident things. It needs a sort of stretch of imagination to see the obvious objects against the obvious background; and especially the big objects against the big background. There is always the sort of man who can see nothing but the spot on the carpet, so that he cannot even see the carpet. And that tends to irritation, which he may magnify into rebellion. Then there is the kind of man who can only see the carpet, perhaps because it is a new carpet. That is more human, but it may be tinged with vanity and even vulgarity. There is the man who can only see the carpeted room; and that will tend to cut him off too much from other things, especially the servants' quarters. Finally, there is the man enlarged by imagination, who cannot sit in the carpeted room, or even in the coal-cellar, without seeing all the time the outline of the whole house against its aboriginal background of earth and sky. He, understanding that the roof is raised from the beginning as a shield against sun or snow, and the door against frost or slime, will know better and not worse than the rest the reasons of the rules within. He will know better than the first man that there ought not to be a spot on the carpet. But he will know, unlike the first man, why there is a carpet.

He will regard in the same fashion a speck or spot upon the records of his tradition or his creed. He will not explain it ingeniously; certainly he will not explain it away. On the contrary, he will see it very simply; but he will also see it very largely; and against the background of larger things. He will do what his critics never by any chance do; he will see the obvious thing and ask the obvious question. For the more I read of the modern criticisms of religion, especially of my own religion, the more I am struck by this narrow concentration and this imaginative incapacity to take in the problem as a whole, I have recently been reading a very moderate condemnation of current Catholic practices, coming from America, where the condemnation is often far from moderate. It takes the form, generally speaking, of a swarm of questions, all of which I should be quite willing to answer. Only I am vividly conscious of the big questions that are not asked, rather than of the little questions that are.

And I feel above all, this simple and forgotten fact; that whether certain charges are or are not true of Catholics, they are quite unquestionably true of everybody else. It never occurs to the critic to do anything so simple as to compare what is Catholic with what is Non-Catholic. The one thing that never seems to cross his mind, when he argues about what the Church is like, is the simple question of what the world would be like without it.

That is what I mean by being too narrow to see the house called the church against the background called the cosmos. For instance, the writer of whom I speak indulges in the millionth mechanical repetition of the charge of mechanical repetition. He says that we repeat prayers and other verbal forms without thinking about them. And doubtless there are many sympathizers who will repeat that denunciation after him, without thinking about it at all. But, before we come to explaining the Church's real teaching about such things, or quoting her numberless recommendations of attention and vigilance, or expounding the reason of the reasonable exceptions that she does allow, there is a wide, a simple and a luminous truth about the whole situation which anybody can see if he will walk about with his eyes open. It is the obvious fact that *all* human forms of speech tend to fossilize into formalism; and that the Church stands unique in history, not as talking a dead language among everlasting languages; but, on the contrary, as having preserved a living language in a world of dying languages. When the great Greek cry breaks into the Latin of the Mass, as old as Christianity itself, it may surprise some to learn that there are a good many people in church who really do say *Kyrie eleison* and mean exactly what they say. But anyhow, they mean what they say rather more than a man who begins a letter with "Dear Sir" means what he says. "Dear" is emphatically a dead word; in that place it has ceased to have any meaning.

It is exactly what the Protestants would allege of Popish rites and forms; it is done rapidly, ritually, and without any memory even of the meaning of the rite. When Mr. Jones the solicitor uses it to Mr. Brown the banker, he does not mean that the banker is dear to him, or that his heart is filled with Christian love, even so much as the heart of some poor ignorant Papist listening to the Mass. Now, life, ordinary, jolly, heathen, human life, is simply chockful of these dead words and meaningless ceremonies. You will not escape from them by escaping from the Church into the world. When the critic in question, or a thousand other critics like him, say that we are only required to make a material or mechanical attendance at Mass, he says something which is *not* true about the ordinary Catholic in his feelings about the Catholic Sacraments. But he says something which *is* true about the ordinary official attending official functions, about the ordinary Court levee or Ministerial reception, and about three-quarters of the ordinary society calls and polite visits in the town. This deadening of repeated social action may be a harmless thing; it may be a melancholy thing; it may be a mark of the Fall of Man; it may be anything the critic chooses to think. But those who have made it, hundreds and hundreds of times, a special and concentrated charge against the Church, are men blind to the whole human world they live in and unable to see anything but the thing they traduce.

There are, even in this record, any number of other cases of this queer and uncanny unconsciousness. The writer complains that priests are led blindfold into their calling and do not understand the duties involved in it. That also we seem to have heard before. But we have seldom heard it in so extraordinary a form as in his statement, that a man can be finally committed to the priesthood while he is still "a child." He would appear to have odd and elastic ideas about the duration of childhood. As Mr. Michael Williams[54] has pointed out in his most thoughtful and illuminating collection of essays, "Catholicism and the Modern Mind," this is playing about with a matter of plain fact; since a priest is twenty-four at the earliest when he takes his vows. But here again I myself am haunted by this

[54] Michael Williams (1877–1950) was a Canadian-born American journalist who established the Catholic magazine *Commonweal* in 1924.

huge and naked and yet neglected comparison between the Church and everything outside the Church. Most critics of Catholicism declare it to be destructive of patriotism; and this critic says something about the disadvantages of the Church being merely "attached to an Italian diocese." Well, I for one have always been a defender of the cult of patriotism; and nothing that I say here has any connection with what is commonly called pacifism. I think that our friends and brethren fell ten years ago in a just war against the hard heathenism of the north; I think the Prussianism they defeated was frozen with the pride of hell; and for these dead, I think it is well with them; and perhaps better than with us, who live to see how evil Peace can be.

But really—when we come to talk about the Church involving young people in vows! What are we to say to those who would pit patriotism or pagan citizenship against the Church on that issue? They conscript by violence boys of eighteen, they applaud volunteers of sixteen for saying they are eighteen, they throw them by thousands into a huge furnace and torture-chamber, of which their imaginations can have conceived nothing and from which their honour forbids them to escape; they keep them in those horrors year after year without any knowledge even of the possibility of victory; and kill them like flies by the million before they have begun to live. That is what the State does; that is what the World does; that is what their Protestant, practical, sensible, secular society does. And after that they have the astounding impudence to come and complain of us, because in dealing with a small minority of specialists, we allow a man finally to choose a charitable and peaceful life, not only long after he is twenty-one, but when he is well on towards thirty, and after he has had about ten years to think quietly whether he will do it or not!

In short, what I miss in all these things is the obvious thing: the question of how the Church compares with the world outside the Church, or opposed to the Church, or offered as a substitute for the Church. And the fact obviously is that the world will do all that it has ever accused the Church of doing, and do it much worse, and do it on a much larger scale, and do it (which is worst and most important of all) without any standards for a return to sanity or any motives for a movement of repentance. Catholic abuses can be reformed, because there is the admission of a form. Catholic sins can be expiated, because there is a test and a principle of expiation. But where else in the world today is any such test or standard found; or anything except a changing mood, which makes patriotism the fashion ten years ago and pacifism the fashion ten years afterwards?

The danger is today that men will not sufficiently enlarge their minds to take in the obvious things; and this is one of them. It is that men charge the Roman tradition with being half-heathen and then take refuge from it in a complete heathenism. It is that men complain because Christians have been infected with paganism; and then flee from the plague-spotted to take refuge with the pestilence. There is no single one of these faults alleged against the Catholic institution, which is not far more flagrant and even flamboyant in every other institution. And it is to these other institutions, the State, the School, the modern machinery of taxation and police, to which these people actually look to save them from the superstition of their fathers. That is the contradicition; that is the crashing collision; that is the inevitable intellectual disaster in which they have already involved themselves; and we have only to wait as patiently as we can, to see how long it is before they realize what has happened.

XIV

THE CALL TO THE BARBARIANS

A book was sent me the other day by a gentleman who pins his faith to what he calls the Nordic race; and who, indeed, appears to offer that race as a substitute for all religions. Crusaders believe that Jerusalem was not only the Holy City, but the centre of the whole world. Moslems bow their heads towards Mecca and Roman Catholics are notorious for being in secret communication with Rome. I presume that the Holy Place of the Nordic religion must be the North Pole. What form of religious architecture is exhibited in its icebergs, how far its vestments are modified by the white covering of Arctic animals, how the morning and evening service may be adapted to a day and a night each lasting for six months, whether their only vestment is the alb or their only service the angelus of noon, upon all these mysteries I will not speculate. But I can affirm with some confidence that the North Pole is very little troubled by heretical movements or the spread of modern doubt. Anyhow, it would seem that we know next to nothing about this social principle, except that anything is good if it is near enough to the North. And this undoubtedly explains the spiritual leadership of the Eskimo throughout history; and the part played by Spitzbergen as the spiritual arena of modern times. The only thing that puzzles me is that the Englishmen who now call themselves Nordic used to call themselves Teutonic; and very often even Germanic. I cannot think why they altered this so abruptly in the autumn of 1914. Some day, I suppose, when we have diplomatic difficulties with Norway, they will equally abruptly drop the word Nordic. They will hastily substitute some other — I would suggest Borealic. They might be called the Bores, for short.

But I only mention this book because of a passage in it which is rather typical of the tone of a good many people when they are talking about Catholic history. The writer would substitute one race for all religions; in which he certainly differs from us, who are ready to offer one religion to all races. And even here, perhaps, the comparison is not altogether to his advantage. For anybody who likes can belong to the religion; whereas it is not very clear what is to be done with the people who do not happen to belong to the race. But even among religions he is ready to admit degrees of depravity; he will distinguish between these disgusting institutions; of course, according to their degree of latitude. It is rather unfortunate for him that many Eskimos are Catholics and that most French Protestants live in the south of France; but he proceeds on his general principle clearly enough. He points out, in his pleasant way, why it is exactly that Roman Catholicism is such a degrading superstition. And he adds (which is what interests me at the moment) that this was illustrated in the Dark Ages, which were a nightmare of misery and ignorance. He then admits handsomely that Protestantism is not quite so debased and devilish as Catholicism; and that men of the Protestant nations do exhibit rudimentary traces of the human form. But this, he says, "is not due to their Protestantism, but to their Nordic common sense." They are more educated, more liberal, more familiar with reason and beauty, because they are what used to be called Teutonic; descended from Vikings and Gothic chiefs rather than from the Tribunes of Florence or the Troubadours of Provence. And in this curious idea I caught a glimpse of something much wider and more interesting; which is another note of the modern ignorance of the Catholic tradition. In speaking of things that people do not know, I have mostly spoken of things that are really within the ring or circle of our own knowledge; things inside the Catholic culture which they miss because they are outside it. But there are some cases in which they themselves are ignorant even of the things outside it. They themselves are ignorant, not only of the centre of civilization which they slander, but even of the ends of the earth to which they appeal; they not only cannot find Rome on their map, but they do not even know where to look for the North Pole.

Take, for instance, that remark about the Dark Ages and the Nordic common sense. It is tenable and tolerable enough to say that the Dark Ages were a nightmare. But it is nonsense to say that the Nordic element was anything remotely resembling sense. If the Dark

Ages were a nightmare, it was very largely because the Nordic nonsense made them an exceedingly Nordic nightmare. It was the period of the barbarian invasions; when piracy was on the high seas and civilization was in the monasteries. You may not like monasteries, or the sort of civilization that is preserved by monasteries; but it is quite certain that it was the only sort of civilization there was. But this is simply one of the things that the Nordic gentleman does not know. He imagines that the Danish pirate was talking about Tariff Reform and Imperial Preference, with scientific statistics from Australia and Alaska, when he was rudely interrupted by a monk named Bede[55] who had never heard of anything but monkish fables. He supposes that a Viking or a Visigoth was firmly founded on the principles of the Primrose League[56] and the English Speaking Union, and that everything else would have been founded on them if fanatical priests had not rushed in and proclaimed the savage cult called Christianity. He thinks that Penda of Mercia,[57] the last heathen king, was just about to give the whole world the benefits of the British Constitution, not to mention the steam engine and the works of Rudyard Kipling, when his work was blindly ruined by unlettered ruffians with such names as Augustine and Dunstan and Anselm.[58] And that is the little error which invalidates our Nordic friend's importance as a serious historian; that is why we cannot throw ourselves with utter confidence and surrender into the stream of his historical enthusiasm. The difficulty consists in the annoying detail that nothing like what he is thinking about ever happened in the world at all; that the religion of race that he proposes is exactly what he himself calls the Dark Ages. It is what some scientific persons call a purely subjective idea; or in other words, a nightmare. It is very doubtful if there ever was any Nordic race. It is quite certain that there never was any Nordic common sense. The very words "common sense" are a translation from the Latin.

[55] Bede was an eighth-century English monk and historian.

[56] The Primrose League was founded in England in 1883 to honor Benjamin Disraeli and to promote Conservative principles.

[57] Penda of Mercia was a pagan Anglo-Saxon king of the seventh century.

[58] Augustine (d. 604) was an apostle to England, Dunstan (924–988) was a monastic reformer, and Anselm (1033–1109) was a theologian. Each served as archbishop of Canterbury and each was canonized.

Now that one typical or even trivial case has a larger application. One very common form of Protestant or rationalist ignorance may be called the ignorance of what raw humanity is really like. Such men get into a small social circle, very modern and very narrow, whether it is called the Nordic race or the Rationalist Association. They have a number of ideas, some of them truisms, some of them very untrue, about liberty, about humanity, about the spread of knowledge. The point is that those ideas, whether true or untrue, are the very reverse of universal. They are not the sort of ideas that any large mass of mankind, in any age or country, may be assumed to have. They may in some cases be related to deeper realities; but most men would not even recognize them in the form in which these men present them. There is probably, for instance, a fundamental assumption of human brotherhood that is common to all humanity. But what we call humanitarianism is not common to humanity. There is a certain recognition of reality and unreality which may be called common sense. But the scientific sense of the special value of truth is not generally regarded as common sense. It is silly to pretend that priests specially persecuted a naturalist, when the truth is that all the little boys would have persecuted him in any village in the world, merely because he was a lunatic with a butterfly-net. Public opinion, taken as a whole, is much more contemptuous of specialists and seekers after truth than the Church ever was. But these critics never can take public opinion as a whole. There are a great many examples of this truth; one is the case I have given, the absurd notion that a horde of heathen raiders out of the northern seas and forests, in the most ignorant epoch of history, were not likely to be at least as ignorant as anybody else. They were, of course, much more ignorant than anybody with the slightest social connection with the Catholic Church. Other examples may be found in the story of other religions. Great tracts of the globe, covered in theory by the other religions, are often covered in practice merely by certain human habits of fatalism or pessimism or some other human mood. Islam very largely stands for the fatalism. Buddhism very largely stands for the pessimism. Neither of them knows anything of either the Christian or the humanitarian sort of hope. But an even more convincing experience is to go out into the street, or into a tube or a tram, and talk to the actual cabman, cooks and charwomen cut off from the Creed by the modern chaos. You will find that heathens are not happy, however Nordic. You will soon find that you do not need to go to Arabia for fatalism; or to the Thibetan desert for despair.

XV

ON THE NOVEL WITH A PURPOSE

I see that Mr. Patrick Braybrooke and others, writing to the *Catholic Times*, have raised the question of Catholic propaganda in novels written by Catholics. The very phrase, which we are all compelled to use, is awkward and even false. A Catholic putting Catholicism into a novel, or a song, or a sonnet, or anything else, is not being a propagandist; he is simply being a Catholic. Everybody understands this about every other enthusiasm in the world. When we say that a poet's landscape and atmosphere are full of the spirit of England, we do not mean that he is necessarily conducting an Anti-German propaganda during the Great War. We mean that if he is really an English poet, his poetry cannot be anything but English. When we say that songs are full of the spirit of the sea, we do not mean that the poet is recruiting for the Navy or even trying to collect men for the merchant service. We mean that he loves the sea; and for that reason would like other people to love it. Personally, I am all for propaganda; and a great deal of what I write is deliberately propagandist. But even when it is not in the least propagandist, it will probably be full of the implications of my own religion; because that is what is meant by having a religion. So the jokes of a Buddhist, if there were any, would be Buddhist jokes. So the love-songs of a Calvinistic Methodist, should they burst from him, would be Calvinistic Methodist love-songs. Catholics have produced more jokes and love-songs than Calvinists and Buddhists. That is because, saving their holy presence, Calvinists and Buddhists have not got so large or human a religion. But anything they did express would be steeped in any convictions that they do hold; and that is a piece of common sense which would seem to be quite self-evident; yet I foresee a vast amount of difficulty about it in the one isolated case of the Catholic Church.

To begin with, what I have said would be true of any other real religion; but so much of the modern world is full of a religiosity that is rather a sort of unconscious prejudice. Buddhism is a real religion, or at any rate, a very real philosophy. Calvinism was a real religion, with a real theology. But the mind of the modern man is a curious mixture of decayed Calvinism and diluted Buddhism; and he expresses his philosophy without knowing that he holds it. We say what it is natural to us to say; but we know what we are saying; therefore it is assumed that we are saying it for effect. He says what it is natural to him to say; but he does not know what he is saying, still less why he is saying it. So he is not accused of uttering his dogma with the purpose of revealing it to the world; for he has not really revealed it to himself. He is just as partisan; he is just as particularist; he is just as much depending on one doctrinal system as distinct from another. But he has taken it for granted so often that he has forgotten what it is. So his literature does not seem to him partisan, even when it is. But our literature does seem to him propagandist, even when it isn't.

Suppose I write a story, let us hope a short story, say, about a wood that is haunted by evil spirits. Let us give ourselves the pleasure of supposing that at night all the branches have the appearance of being hung with hundreds of corpses, like the orchard of Louis the Eleventh,[59] the spirits of travellers who have hanged themselves when they came to that spot; or anything bright and cheery like that. Suppose I make my hero, Gorlias Fitzgorgon (that noble character) make the sign of the cross as he passes this spot; or the friend who represents wisdom and experience advise him to consult a priest with a view to exorcism. Making the sign of the cross seems to me not only religiously right, but artistically appropriate and psychologically probable. It is what I should do; it is what I conceive that my friend Fitzgorgon would do; it is also ascetically apt, or, as they say, "in the picture." I rather fancy it might be effective if the traveller saw with the mystical eye, as he saw the forest of dead men, a sort of shining pattern or silver tangle of crosses hovering in the dark, where so many human fingers had made that sign upon the empty air. But though I am writing what seems to me natural and appropriate and artistic, I know that the moment I have written it, a

---

[59] Louis the Eleventh was King of France from 1461 to 1483.

great roar and bellow will go up with the word "Propaganda" coming from a thousand throats; and that every other critic, even if he is kind enough to commend the story, will certainly add: "But why does Mr. Chesterton drag in his Roman Catholicism?"

Now let us suppose that Mr. Chesterton has not this disgusting habit. Let us suppose that I write the same story, or the same sort of story, informed with a philosophy which is familiar and therefore unobserved. Let us suppose that I accept the ready-made assumptions of the hour, without examining them any more than the others do. Suppose I get into the smooth rut of newspaper routine and political catchwords; and make the man in my story act exactly like the man in the average magazine story. I know exactly what the man in the average magazine story would do. I can almost give you his exact words. In that case Fitzgorgon, on first catching a glimpse of the crowds of swaying spectres in the moon, will almost inevitably say: "But this is the twentieth century!"

In itself, of course, the remark is simply meaningless. It is far more meaningless than making the sign of the cross could ever be; for to that even its enemies attach some sort of meaning. But to answer a ghost by saying, "This is the twentieth century," is in itself quite unmeaning; like seeing somebody commit a murder and then saying, "But this is the second Tuesday in August!" Nevertheless, the magazine writer who for the thousandth time puts these words into the magazine story, has an intention in this illogical phrase. He is really depending upon two dogmas; neither of which he dares to question and neither of which he is able to state. The dogmas are: first, that humanity is perpetually and permanently improving through the process of time; and, second, that improvement consists in a greater and greater indifference or incredulity about the miraculous. Neither of these two statements can be proved. And it goes without saying that the man who uses them cannot prove them, for he cannot even state them. In so far as they are at all in the order of things that can be proved, they are things that can be disproved. For certainly there have been historical periods of relapse and retrogression; and there certainly are highly organized and scientific civilizations very much excited about the supernatural; as people are about

Spiritualism today. But anyhow, those two dogmas must be accepted on authority as absolutely true before there is any sense whatever in Gorlias Fitzgorgon saying, "But this is the twentieth century." The phrase depends on the philosophy; and the philosophy is put into the story.

Yet nobody says the magazine story is propagandist. Nobody says it is preaching that philosophy because it contains that phrase. We do not say that the writer has dragged in his progressive party politics. We do not say that he is going out of his way to turn the short story into a novel with a purpose. He does not feel as if he were going out of his way; his way lies straight through the haunted wood, as does the other; and he only makes Gorlias say what seems to him a sensible thing to say; as I make him do what seems to me a sensible thing to do. We are both artists in the same sense; we are both propagandists in the same sense and non-propagandists in the same sense. The only difference is that I can defend my dogma and he cannot even define his.

In other words, this world of today does not know that all the novels and newspapers that it reads or writes are in fact full of certain assumptions, that are just as dogmatic as dogmas. With some of those assumptions I agree, such as the ideal of human equality implied in all romantic stories from *Cinderella* to *Oliver Twist*; that the rich are insulting God in despising poverty. With some of them I totally disagree; as in the curious idea of human inequality, which is permitted about races though not about classes. "Nordic" people are so much superior to "Dagoes," that a score of Spanish desperados armed to the teeth are certain to flee in terror from the fist of any solitary gentleman who has learned all the military and heroic virtues in Wall Street or the Stock Exchange. But the point about these assumptions, true or false, is that they are left as being assumed, or alluded to, or taken naturally as they come. They are not felt as being preached; and therefore they are not called propaganda. Yet they have in practice all the double character of propaganda; they involve certain views with which everyone does not agree; and they do in fact spread those views by means of fiction and popular literature. What they do not do is to state them clearly so that they can be criticized. I do not blame the writers for putting their philosophy into their stories. I should not blame them even if they used their stories to spread their philosophy. But they do blame us; and the real reason is that they have not yet realized that we have a philosophy at all.

The truth is, I think, that they are caught in a sort of argument in a circle. Their vague philosophy says to them: "All religion is dead; Roman Catholicism is a religious sect which must be particularly dead, since it consists of mere external acts and attitudes, crossings, genuflections and the rest; which these sectarians suppose they have to perform in a particular place at a particular time." Then some Catholic will write a romance or a tragedy about the love of a man and woman, or the rivalry of two men, or any other general human affair; and they will be astonished to find that he cannot preach these things in an "unsectarian" way. They say, "Why does he drag in his religion?" They mean, "Why does he drag in his religion, which consists entirely of crossings, genuflections and external acts belonging to a particular place and time, when he is talking about the wide world and the beauty of woman and the anger and ambition of man?" In other words, they say, "When we have assumed that his creed is a small and dead thing, how dare he apply it as a universal and living thing? It has no right to be so broad, when we all know it is so narrow."

I conclude therefore that, while Mr. Braybrooke was quite right in suggesting that a novelist with a creed ought not to be ashamed of having a cause, the more immediate necessity is to find some way of popularizing our whole philosophy of life, by putting it more plainly than it can be put in the symbol of a story. The difficulty with a story is in its very simplicity and especially in its swiftness. Men do things and do not define or defend them. Gorlias Fitzgorgon makes the sign of the cross; he does not stop in the middle of the demon wood to explain why it is at once an invocation of the Trinity and a memorial of the Crucifixion. What is wanted is a popular outline of the way in which ordinary affairs are affected by our view of life, and how it is also a view of death, a view of sex, and a view of social decencies, and so on. When people understood the light that shines for us upon all these facts, they would no longer be surprised to find it shining in our fictions.

XVI

THE REVOLT AGAINST IDEAS

At the time when the *Daily Express* communiqués provided some pretty awful revelations about Mexico, the *Daily Express* correspondence column provided almost equally awful revelations about England. It gave us a glimpse of what monstrous and misshapen things are still living in our midst, veiled in red brick villas or disguised under bowler hats. The awful revelations about England were, of course, mainly psychological. It was not anarchy in the State, which is the failing of the fighting Latin peoples. It was anarchy in the mind; which is the special character of those whom we call, in moments of anger, Anglo-Saxons. A Mexican atheist would be quite capable of cutting the throat of a priest or training a cannon on a nunnery. But he would be quite incapable of arguing, as the English Protestants did in the newspaper, that it was quite right of Calles[60] to persecute this belief on this occasion, *because* it was quite wrong of Catholics to persecute any belief on any occasion. No anarchist can be as anarchical as all that. Calles might blow up St. Peter's; but he would not blame a Spaniard for having once done what he was praising a Mexican for trying to do. To that extent even Calles is more of a Catholic as well as more of a Latin. He wants to have his own way, and to prevent thousands of people from having their way; but he does not want to have it both ways. That wild sacrament, the miracle of the vanishing and reappearing cake, of the cake that is ever devoured and ever remaining—that miracle belongs to the religion of unreason and only takes place in the chapels of our own free country.

Amid a welter of such words there was a phrase in one of the letters which is of some sociological interest to us. One of these intolerant tolerationists was endeavouring to defend Calles by suggesting that only prejudice can accuse him of anarchical or antireligious extremes of opinion. It is quite unfair (it was said) to call Calles an atheist or a Bolshevist. Indeed, we may learn from all these

---

[60] Plutarcho Elias Calles (1877–1945) was president of Mexico from 1924 to 1928.

letters that Calles is probably a Wesleyan Methodist and regularly at-
tends a chapel in East Croydon. But he is even worse. They appear to
regard it as a favour to Calles to pay him the extraordinary compliment of comparing him to the sixteenth century Reformers. The correspondent here in question uses this as an argument against any alleged
anarchism in the Mexican — if he is a Mexican. "Calles and his partisans are branded as Atheists and Bolsheviks — Why? Were the English Reformers Bolsheviks? Certainly not."

Here we are happily all able to agree. With heartfelt unanimity
we can repeat, "Certainly not." The English Reformers were certainly not Bolshevists. None will withhold the handsome admission
that the English Reformers were Capitalists. Few people in history
have deserved to be described so exactly, so completely, so typically
as Capitalists. They were a great many other things besides Capitalists; some of them were cads, some gentlemen, a few honest men,
many thieves, a baser sort courtiers, a better sort monomaniacs; but
they were all Capitalists and what they created was Capitalism.
They all conducted their powerful political operations on a basis of
much accumulated capital; but they never, even with their dying
eyes, lost the light of hope and expectation; the promise and the vision of more capital.

But what concerns us nowadays is this; that it is their Capitalism that
has remained. As a matter of fact, many of them did have other ideals or
spiritual simplification which might in some ways be compared to
Communism. We should never be likely to call a man like Cranmer or
a man like Burleigh[61] a Bolshevist. We could only say, with Hamlet,
that we would he were so honest a man. But there were men in that
movement, or that muddle, who were as mad and as honest as Bolshevists. There were theoretical, and especially theological enthusiasms
which moved specially towards simplicity; like that of the Bolshevists.
But the point to fix and rivet is that *those* theories are dead. There was a
logical and even lofty scheme of thought; but it is *that* which is utterly
abandoned by modern thought. There were sincere ideals in some of
the early Protestants; but they are not the ideals of any of the modern

[61] William Cecil, Lord Burleigh (1520–98), was lord treasurer and chief minister
under Elizabeth I.

Protestants. Thus Calvinism was a clear philosophy; which is alone enough to distinguish it from Modern Thought. But in so far as they had an element of Calvinism, their Calvinism is dead. If they had had an element of Communism, as some of them might, that Communism would now be dead. Nothing but their Capitalism is alive.

We must remember that even to talk of the corruption of the monasteries is a compliment to the monasteries. For we do not talk of the corruption of the corrupt. Nobody pretends that the mediaeval institutions began in mere greed and pride. But the modern institutions did. Nobody says that St. Benedict drew up his rule of labour in order to make his monks lazy; but only that they became lazy. Nobody says that the first Franciscans practised poverty to obtain wealth; but only that later fraternities did obtain wealth. But it is quite certain that the Cecils and the Russells and the rest did from the first want to obtain wealth. That which was death to Catholicism was actually the birth of Capitalism. Since then we have had, not the inconsistency that a man who vowed to be poor became rich; but rather a shocking consistency, that the man who vowed to be rich became richer. After that there was no stopping a race of relative ambition; and a belief in bigger and bigger things. It is indeed true that the Reformers were not Communists. It might be aptly retorted that the Religious were Communists. But the more vital point is not Communism, but a certain comparative spirit. The English squire increased and the English yeoman diminished. Both found their pride in private ownership of land. But the pride was more and more in having a great estate, and not in having an estate. So, in his turn, the English shopkeeper ceased to be proud of minding his own business and could only be proud of the number of businesses he could mind. From this has come all the mercantile megalomania of today; with its universal transformation of Trades into Trusts. It is the natural conclusion of the movement away from the transformation of all Trades into Guilds. But its genesis was the change from an ideal of humility, in which many failed, to an ideal of pride in which (by its nature) only a few can succeed.

In this sense we may agree with the newspaper correspondent; that the Reformers were not Revolutionists. We can reassure that simple gentleman of our full realization that they were not Bolshevists. We can entirely absolve the Cranmers and the Cromwells of any restless desire to raise the proletariat. We can clear the great names of Burleigh and Bacon of the stain of any dangerous sympathy with the poor. The distinguishing mark of the Reformers was a profound respect for the powers that be, but an even profounder respect for the wealth that was to be; and a really unfathomable reverence for the wealth that was to be their own. Some people like that spirit, and regard it as the soundest foundation of stable government; we need not argue about it here. It is, broadly speaking, what is regarded as respectability by all those who have nothing else to respect. Certainly nobody could confuse it with revolution. But the point of historical importance could be put in another fashion, also more or less favourable to the Reformers. Capitalism was not only solid, it was in a sense candid. It set up a class to be worshipped openly and frankly because of its wealth. That is the point at the moment and the real contrast between this and the older mediaeval order. Such wealth was the abuse of the monks and abbots; it was the use of the merchants and the squires. The avaricious abbot violated his ideals. The avaricious employer had no ideals to violate. For there never has been, properly speaking, such a thing as the ideal good of Capitalism; though there are any number of good men who are Capitalists following other ideals. The Reformation, especially in England, was above all the abandonment of the attempt to rule the world by ideals, or even by ideas. The attempt had undoubtedly failed, in part because those who were supposed to be the idealists failed to uphold the ideals; and any number of people who were supposed to accept the general idea thwarted the fulfilment of the ideas. But it also fell under the attack of those who hated, not only those ideals, but any ideals. It was the result of the impatient and imperious appetites of humanity, hating to be restrained by bonds; but most of all to be restrained by invisible bonds. For the English Reformers did not really set up an opposite ideal or an alternative set of ideas. As our friend truly said, they were not Bolshevists. They set up certain very formidable things called facts. They set out almost avowedly to rule the realm merely by facts; by the fact that somebody called Russell had two hundred times more money than any of his neighbours; by the fact that somebody called Cecil had obtained the power of having any of his neighbours hanged. Facts are at least solid while they last; but the fatal thing about them is that they do not last. It is only the ideas that last. And today a man may be called Russell and have considerably less money than a man who is called Rockefeller; and history may see the amazing spectacle of a man called Cecil largely thrust out of practical politics and called an idealist and a failure.

The same progress of Capitalism that made the squires had destroyed the squires. The same commercial advance that exalted England before Europe has abased England before America. Exactly in so far as we have our affections healthily attached to this adventurous and patriotic England of the last few centuries, we shall see that our affections and attachments are bound to be betrayed. The process called practical, the attempt to rule merely by facts, has in its own nature the essence of all betrayal. We discover that facts, which seem so solid, are of all things the most fluid. As the professors and the prigs say, facts are always evolving; in other words, they are always evading or escaping or running away. Men who bow down to the wealth of a squire, because it enables him to behave like a gentleman, have to go on bowing down to the same wealth in somebody who cannot behave like a gentleman; and eventually perhaps to the same wealth not attached to any recognizable human being at all, but invested in an irresponsible company in a foreign country. Wealth does indeed take to itself wings, and even abide in the uttermost parts of the sea. Wealth becomes formless and almost fabulous; indeed, they were unconscious satirists who talked about "fabulous wealth." Great financiers buy and sell thousands of things that nobody has ever seen; and which are for all practical purposes imaginary. So ends the adventure of trusting only to facts; it ends in a fairyland of fantastic abstractions.

We must go back to the idea of government by ideas. There is just that grain of truth in the already mentioned fantasy of Communism. But there were many richer, and subtler and better balanced ideas even in the mediaeval make-up of Catholicism. I repeat that this Catholicism was ruined by Catholics as well as Protestants. Mediaeval sins hampered and corrupted mediaeval ideas, before the Reformers decided to throw away all ideas. But that was the right thing to

follow, or to try to follow; and there is not and never will be anything else to do except to try again. Many mediaeval men failed in
the attempt to live up to those ideals. But many more modern men
are more disastrously failing in the attempt to live without them.
And through that failure we shall gradually come to understand the
real advantages of that ancient scheme which only partly failed; according to which, in theory at least, the man of peace was higher
than the man of war, and poverty superior to wealth.

There is one quaint little phrase in Macaulay's[62] essay on Bacon;
that great outbreak of the Philistines against the Philosophers. In
one small sentence the great Philistine betrays the weakness of his
whole argument of utility. Speaking scornfully of the Schoolmen,
he says that St. Thomas Aquinas would doubtless (such was his simplicity) have thought it more important to engage in the manufacture of syllogisms than in the manufacture of gunpowder. Not even
the Gunpowder Plot[63] could prevent that sturdy Protestant from
assuming that gunpowder is always useful. Since his time we have
seen a good deal more gunpowder. One does not need to be a pacifist to think that gunpowder need hardly go on being useful on
quite such a grand scale. And a great part of the world has now
reached a mood of reaction, in which it is disposed to cry out, "If
there are any syllogisms that will save us from all this gunpowder,
for God's sake let us listen to them." Even logic they are prepared, in
their despair, to accept. They will not only listen to religion, they
will even perhaps listen to reason, if it will promise them a little peace.

[62] Thomas Babington Macaulay (1800–59) author of a multi-volume history of
England, was Great Britain's most acclaimed historian in the nineteenth century.
[63] The Gunpowder Plot was an alleged Catholic conspiracy in 1605 to blow up the
Houses of Parliament.

XVII

THE FEASTS AND THE ASCETIC

I was reflecting in the course of the recent feast of Christmas (which, like other feasts, is preceded by a fast) that the combination is still a puzzle to many. The Modernist, or man who boasts of being modern, is generally rather like a man who overeats himself so much on Christmas Eve that he has no appetite on Christmas Day. It is called being In Advance of the Times; and is incumbent upon all who are progressive, prophetic, futuristic and generally looking towards what Mr. Belloc calls the Great Rosy Dawn: a dawn which generally looks a good deal rosier the night before than it does the morning after.

To many people, however, who are not offensively in advance of the times the combination of these ideas does seem to be a sort of contradiction or confusion. But in real fact it is not only not so confused, but even not so complicated. The great temptation of the Catholic in the modern world is the temptation to intellectual pride. It is so obvious that most of his critics are talking without in the least knowing what they are talking about, that he is sometimes a little provoked towards the very un-Christian logic of answering a fool according to his folly. He is a little bit disposed to luxuriate in secret, as it were, over the much greater subtlety and richness of the philosophy he inherits; and only answer a bewildered barbarian so as to bewilder him still more. He is tempted to ironical agreements or even to disguising himself as a dunce. Men who have an elaborate philosophical defence of their views sometimes take pleasure in boasting of their almost babyish credulity. Having reached their own goal through labyrinths of logic, they will point the stranger only to the very shortest short cut of authority; merely in order to shock the simpleton with simplicity. Or, as in the present case, they will find a grim amusement in presenting the separate parts of the scheme as if they were really separate; and leave the outsider to make what he can of them. So when somebody says that a fast is the opposite to a feast, and yet both seem to be sacred to us, some of us will always be moved merely to say, "Yes," and relapse into an objectionable grin. When the anxious ethical inquirer says, "Christmas is devoted to merry-making, to eating meat and drinking wine, and yet you encourage this pagan and materialistic enjoyment," you or I will be tempted to say, "Quite right, my boy," and leave it at that. When he then says, looking even more worried, "Yet you admire men for fasting in caves and deserts and denying themselves ordinary pleasures; you are clearly committed, like the Buddhists, to the opposite or ascetic principle," we shall be similarly inspired to say, "Quite correct, old bean," or "Got it first time, old top," and merely propose an adjournment for convivial refreshment.

Nevertheless, it is a temptation to be resisted. Not only is it obviously our duty to explain to the other people that what seems to them contradictory is really complementary, but we are not altogether justified in any such tone of superiority. We are not right in making our geniality an expression of our despair. We are not entitled to despair of explaining the truth; nor is it really so horribly difficult to explain. The real difficulty is not so much that the critic is crude as that we ourselves are not always clear, even in our own minds, far less in our public expositions. It is not so much that they are not subtle enough to understand it, as that they and we and everybody else are not simple enough to understand it. Those two things are obviously part of one thing, if we are straightforward enough to look at the thing; and to see it simply as it is. I suggested recently that people would see the Christian story if it could only be told as a heathen story. The Faith is simply the story of a God who died for men. But, queerly enough, if we were even to print the words without a capital G, as if it were the cult of some new and nameless tribe, many would realize the idea for the first time. Many would feel the thrill of a new fear and sympathy if we simply wrote "the story of a god who died for men." People would sit up suddenly and say what a beautiful and touching pagan religion that must be.

Let us suppose, for the sake of argument, that the Church is out of the question; that we have nothing but the earth and the children of man pottering about on it, with their normal mortal tales and traditions.

Then suppose there appears on this earth a prodigy, a portent, or what is alleged to be a portent. In some way heaven has rent the veil or the gods have given some new marvel to mankind. Suppose, for instance, it is a fountain of magic water, said to be flowing at the top of a mountain. It blesses like holy water; it heals diseases; it inspires more than wine, or those who drink of it never thirst again. Well, this story may be true or false; but among those who spread it as true, it is perfectly obvious that the story will produce a number of other stories. It is equally obvious that those stories will be of two kinds. The first sort will say: "When the water was brought down to the valley there was dancing in all the villages; the young men and maidens rejoiced with music and laughter. A surly husband and wife were sprinkled with the holy water and reconciled, so that their house was full of happy children. A cripple was sprinkled and he went capering about gaily like an acrobat. The gardens were watered and became gay with flowers," and so on. It is quite equally obvious that there will be another sort of story from exactly the same source, told with exactly the same motive. "A man limped a hundred miles, till he was quite lame, to find the sacred fountain. Men lay broken and bleeding among the rocks on the mountainside in their efforts to climb after it. A man sold all his lands and the rivers running through them for one drop of the water. A man refused to turn back from it, when confronted with brigands, but was tortured and died calling for it," and so on. There is nothing in the least inconsistent between these two types of legend. They are exactly what would naturally be expected, given the original legend of the miraculous fountain. Anyone who can really look at them simply, can see that they are both equally simple. But we in our time have confused ourselves with long words for unreal distinctions; and talking incessantly about optimism and pessimism, about asceticism and hedonism, about what we call Paganism and what we think about Buddhism, till we cannot understand a plain tale when it is told. The Pagan would have understood it much better.

This very simple truth explains another fact that I have heard the learned insist on with some excitement: the emphasis and repetition touching the ascetic side of religion. It is exactly what would happen with any human story, even if it were a heathen story. We remark upon the case of the man who starves to get the water more than on the case of the man who is merely glad to get the water. We remark upon it more because it is more remarkable. Any human tradition would make more of the heroes who suffered for something than of the human beings who simply benefited by it. But that does not alter the fact that there are more human beings than heroes; and that this great majority of human beings has benefited by it. It is natural that men should marvel more at the man who deliberately lames himself than at the man who dances when he is no longer lame. But that does not alter the fact that the countries where that legend prevails are, in fact, full of dancing. I have here only suggested how very simple, after all, is the contradiction between austerity and jollity which puzzles our critics so much. There is a higher application of it to ascetics, which I may consider on another occasion. Here I will only hint at it by saying: "The more a man could *live* only on the water, the more he would prove it to be the water of life."

XVIII

WHO ARE THE CONSPIRATORS?

I came across, more or less indirectly, the other day, a lady of educated and even elegant pretensions, of the sort whom her foes would call luxurious and her friends cultured, who happened to mention a certain small West Country town, and added with a sort of hiss that it contained "a nest of Roman Catholics." This apparently referred to a family with which I happen to be acquainted. The lady then said, her voice changing to a deep note of doom, "God alone knows what is said and done behind those closed doors."

On hearing this stimulating speculation, my mind went back to what I remembered of the household in question, which was largely concerned with macaroons, and a little girl who rightly persuaded herself that I could eat an almost unlimited number of them. But when I contrasted that memory with that vision it was brought suddenly and stunningly to my mind what a vast abyss still yawns between us and many of our countrymen, and what extraordinary ideas are still entertained about us, by people who walk about the world without keepers or strait-waistcoats and are apparently, on all other subjects, sane. It is doubtless true, and theologically sound, to say that God alone knows what goes on in Catholic homes; as it is to say that God alone knows what goes on in Protestant heads. I do not know why a Catholic's doors should be any more closed than anybody else's doors; the habit is not unusual in persons of all philosophical beliefs when retiring for the night; and on other occasions depends on the weather and the individual taste. But even those who would find it difficult to believe that an ordinary Catholic is so eccentric as to bolt and padlock himself in the drawing-room or the smoking-room, whenever he strolls into those apartments, do really have a haunting idea that it is more conceivable of a Catholic than of a Calvinistic Methodist or a Plymouth Brother.[64] There does remain the stale savour of a sort of sensational romance about us; as if we

[64] The Plymouth Brethren was a millenarian sect that arose in Plymouth, England, in the 1830s.

were all foreign counts and conspirators. And the really interesting fact is that this absurd melodrama can be found among educated people; though now rather in an educated individual than in an educated class. The world still pays us this wild and imaginative compliment of imagining that we are much less ordinary than we really are. The argument, of course, is the one with which we are wearily familiar in twenty other aspects; the argument that because the evidence against us cannot be produced, it must have been concealed. It is obvious that Roman Catholics do not generally shout to each other the arrangements of a St. Bartholomew Massacre[65] across the public streets; and the only deduction any reasonable man can draw is that they do it behind closed doors. It is but seldom that the project of burning down London is proclaimed in large letters on the posters of the *Universe*; so what possible deduction can there be, except that the signals are given at the private tea-table by means of a symbolical alphabet of macaroons? It would be an exaggeration to say that it is my daily habit to leap upon aged Jews in Fleet Street and tear out their teeth; so, given my admitted monomania on the subject, it only remains to suppose that my private house is fitted up like a torture chamber for this mode of mediaeval dentistry. Catholic crimes are not plotted in public, so it stands to reason that they must be plotted in private. There is indeed a third remote and theoretical alternative; that they are not plotted anywhere; but it is unreasonable to expect our fellow-countrymen to suggest anything so fanciful as that.

Now this mysterious delusion, still far commoner than many suppose even in England, and covering whole interior spaces of America, happens to be another illustration of what I have been suggesting in an earlier essay; the fact that those who are always digging and prying for secret things about us, have never even glanced at the most self-evident things about themselves. We have only to ask ourselves, with a sort of shudder, what would have been said if we really had confessed to conspiracy as shamelessly as half our accusers have confessed to it themselves. What in the world would be said,

[65] The St. Bartholomew Massacre was the French Catholic slaughter of Protestants that began on St. Bartholomew's Day 1572.

either in America or in Europe, if we really had behaved like a secret society, in places where the groups of our enemies cannot even deny that they are secret societies? What in the world would happen if a Catholic Congress at Glasgow or Leeds really consisted entirely of hooded and white-robed delegates, all with their faces covered and their names unknown, looking out of slits in their ghastly masks of white? Yet this was, until just lately, the rigid routine of the great American organization to destroy Catholicism; an organization which recently threatened to seize all government in America. What would have been said, if there really was a definite, recognized, but entirely unknown thing, called the Secret of the Catholics; as there has been for long past a recognized but unknown reality called the Secret of the Freemasons? I daresay a great deal involved in such things is mere harmless foolery. But if we had done such things, would our critics have said it was harmless foolery? Suppose we had started to spread the propaganda of the Faith by means of a movement called "Know Nothing,"[66] because we were in the habit of always shaking our heads and shrugging our shoulders and swearing that we knew nothing of the Faith we meant to spread. Suppose our veneration for the dignity of St. Peter were wholly and solely a veneration for the denial of St. Peter; and we used it as a sort of motto or password to swear that we knew not Christ. Yet that was admittedly the policy of a whole political movement in America, which aimed at destroying the citizenship of Catholics. Suppose that the Mafia and all the murder secret associations of the Continent had been notoriously working on the Catholic side, instead of the other side. Should we ever have heard the last of it? Would not the world have rung with indignant denunciation of a disgrace clinging to all our conduct, and a treason that must never be forgot? Yet these things are done constantly, and at regular intervals, and right down to the present day, by the Anti-Catholic parties; and it is never thought necessary to recall them, or say a word of apology for them, in the writings of any Anti-Catholic partisan. It would be just our Jesuitical way to dare to look over hedges, when everybody else is only stealing horses.

[66] The Know-Nothing, or American, Party was an anti-Catholic and anti-immigrant movement that flourished in the United States in the mid-1850s.

In short, what I recently said of bigotry is even more true of secrecy. In so far as there is something merely antiquated about a certain type of doctrinal narrowness, it is much more characteristic of Dayton, Tennessee,[67] than of Louvain or Rome. And in the same way, in so far as there is something antiquated about all these antics in masks and cloaks, it has been much more characteristic of the Ku Klux Klan than of the Jesuits. Indeed, this sort of Protestant is a figure of old-fashioned melodrama in a double sense and in a double aspect. He is antiquated in the plots he attributes to us and in the plots that he practises himself.

As regards the latter, it is probable that the whole world will discover this fact a long time before he does. The anti-clerical will go on playing solemnly the pranks of Cagliostro,[68] like a medium still blindfolded in broad daylight; and will open his mouth in mysteries long after everybody in the world is completely illuminated about the illuminati. And though the almost half-witted humour of the American society, which seemed to consist entirely of beginning as many words as possible with KL, has been rather abruptly toned down by a reaction of relative sanity, I have no doubt that there is still many a noble Nordic fellow going about hugging himself over the happy secret that he is a Kleagle or a Klemperor, long after everybody has ceased to klare a klam whether he is or not. On the political side the power of these conspiracies has been practically broken in both Continents; in Italy by the Fascists and in America by a rally of reasonable and public-spirited governors of both political parties. But the point of historical interest remains: that it was the very people who accused us of mummery and mystery who surrounded all their secularizing activities with far more fantastic mysteries and mummeries; that they had not even the manhood to fight an ancient ritual with the appearance of republican simplicity, but boasted of hiding everything in a sort of comic complexity; even when there was nothing to hide. By this time such movements as

[67] Dayton, Tennessee, was the site of the Scopes anti-evolution trial of 1925.

[68] Count Alessandro Cagliostro (1743–95) was the assumed name of the Sicilian Giuseppe Balsamo, who won notoriety as an alchemist and peddler of drugs and potions.

the Ku Klux Klan have very little left which can be hidden or which is worth hiding; and it is therefore probable that our romantic curiosity about them will be considerably colder than their undying romantic curiosity about us. The Protestant lady will continue to resent the fact that God does not share with her his knowledge of the terrible significance of tea and macaroons in the Catholic home. But we shall probably in the future feel a fainter and fainter interest in whatever it is the Kleagles do behind closed—or perhaps I should say, behind Klosed Doors.

XIX

THE HAT AND THE HALO

Perhaps it is a little ungenerous to refer again to the *fiasco* of the unfortunate Bishop of Birmingham,[69] when he made an exhibition of himself on the subject of St. Francis. That he should be unable to restrain himself from attacking one whom so many free-thinkers have loved and reverenced is interesting as showing how far sectarians can go. But the tone of the attack raises a question more interesting than the personal one. It may be called broadly the question of Sentiment; but it involves the whole question of what things in life are deep and what things shallow; what is central and what is merely external. It is needless to say that people like the Bishop invariably and instinctively get them the wrong way round.

For instance, he said something to the effect that people are now seeing St. Francis in a halo of false sentiment, or through a haze of false sentiment. I am not sure which he said and I doubt whether he knew which he meant. If the Bishop had a halo it would probably be rather like a haze. But anyhow he implied that the hero-worship of St. Francis was a sort of external and extraneous thing, a dazzling distraction or a distorting medium, something added to his figure afterwards; whereas the facts about the *real* St. Francis were quite different and decidedly repulsive to a refined person. Well, the poor Bishop got all his facts about St. Francis quite wrong; and his claim to talk about the real St. Francis, even in an ordinary historical sense, was pretty rapidly shown up. But there was something behind it which interests me much more. It is the curious trick of turning everything inside out; so that the really central things become external and the merely external things central. The inmost soul of St. Francis is a haze of false sentiment; but the accidents of his historical setting, as viewed by people without any historical sense, are a sort of dreadful secret of his soul.

[69] Ernest William Barnes (1874–1953) was Anglican bishop of Birmingham from 1924 to 1953, and a leading modernist.

According to this sort of criticism, St. Francis had a great soul; which was merely a cloak for a miserable body. It is sentimental to consider what he felt like. But it is realistic to consider what he looked like. Or rather it is realistic to consider what he would have looked like to the best-dressed people in Birmingham who never saw him, or the fashionable tailor in Bond Street who never had the opportunity of making him a suit of clothes. The critic tells us what some hypothetical suburban snob of the twentieth century would have thought of the Saint he never saw; and *that* is the real truth about the Saint. We can tell him what the Saint would have thought of the suburban snob (and his thoughts would have been full of the simple and spontaneous tenderness which he showed to all small and helpless creatures) but *that* is only sentiment about St. Francis. What St. Francis himself felt about all other creatures is only a misleading and artificial addition to his character. But what some of the most limited and least imaginative of those creatures might possibly think about him, or rather about his clothes or his meals — that alone is reality.

When the admirers of St. Francis, who number myriads of Protestants and Agnostics as well as Catholics, say that they admire that great man, they mean that they admire his mind, his affections, his tastes, his point of view. They mean that, like any other poet, he puts them in a position to view the world in a certain way; and that life looked at from his mental standpoint is more inspiring or intelligible. But when the Bishop tells them that they do not know the facts about St. Francis, he does not mean that St. Francis had some other mind or some other standpoint. He means that St. Francis did not have hot and cold water laid on in the bathroom, did not put on a clean collar every morning, did not send a sufficient number of shirts to the Birmingham Imperial Laundry every week, did not have black mud smeared on his boots or white mud to stiffen his shirt front, and all the rest of it. And *that* is what he calls the truth about St. Francis! Everything else, including everything that St. Francis did do, is a haze of sentiment.

That is the deeper problem of which this foolish affair happens to be an illustration. How are we to make these superficial people

understand that we are not being sentimental about St. Francis, that
we are not presenting an elegant and poetical picture of St. Francis;
that we are not presenting irresponsible emotional ravings about St.
Francis; that we are simply presenting St. Francis? We are presenting a remarkable mind; just as Plato presented a remarkable mind,
whether it was his own or somebody else's. We think no more of
Bishop Barnes and his nonsense than a Platonist would think about
some joke in Aristophanes and Socrates catching fleas. There may
have been people who saw that mind through a haze of false sentiment; there were people who saw it through a haze of exaggerated
enthusiasm; like those heretics who made St. Francis greater than
Christ and the founder of a new dispensation. But even those fanatics were more like philosophers than a gentleman who is content to
say either of a true saint or a false god, that his taste in linen and
steam laundries was "not ours." In short, the true situation is simple
and obvious enough. It is we who are thinking about the real Francis Bernadone, even the realistic Francis Bernadone, the actual man
whose mind and mood we admire. It is the critic who is thinking of
the unreal Francis, a fantastic phantom produced by looking at him
in a Bond Street looking-glass or comparing him with the fashion-
plates of 1926. If it is well for a man to be happy, to have the way of
welcoming the thing that happens and the next man that comes
along, then St. Francis was happy; happier than most modern men.
If it be good that a man should be sympathetic, should include a
large number of things in his imaginative sympathy, should have a
hospitality of the heart for strange things and strange people, then
St. Francis was sympathetic; more sympathetic than most modern
men. If it be good that a man should be original, should add something creative and not merely customary or conventional, should do
what he thinks right in his own way and without fear of worldly
consequences in ruin or starvation, then St. Francis was original;
more original than most modern men. All these are tests at once personal and permanent; they deal with the very essence of the ego or
individual and they are not affected by changes in external fashion.
To say that these things are mere sentiment is to say that the inmost
sense of the inmost self is mere sentiment. And yet how are we to

stop superficial people from calling it mere sentiment? How are we to make them realize that it is not we who have a sentimental attachment to a mediaeval friar, but they who have an entirely sentimental attachment to certain modern conventions?

Such critics have never really thought of asking what they mean by "sentiment," still less what they mean by "false sentiment." "False" is simply a conventional term of abuse to be applied to "sentiment"; and "sentiment" is simply a conventional term of abuse to be applied to Catholicism. But it is very much more applicable nowadays to Protestantism. It is especially applicable to Bishop Barnes's own rather nebulous type of Protestantism. Men of his school always complain of our thinking too much of theology, just as they complained a few centuries before of our thinking too little of theology. But theology is only the element of reason in religion; the reason that prevents it from being a mere emotion. There are a good many broad-minded persons for whom it is only an emotion; and it would hardly be unfair to say it is only a sentiment. And we have not to look far for them in cases like these.

If a school of critics were found prepared to pay divine honours to a certain person while doubting whether he was divine, men who took off their hats in his churches while denying that he was present on his altars, who hinted that he was only a religious teacher and then hinted again that he must be served as if he were the only teacher of religion; who are always ready to treat him as a fallible individual in relation to his rivals, and then to invoke him as an infallible authority against his followers, who dismissed every text they choose to think dogmatic and then gush over every text they choose to think amiable, who heckled him with Higher Criticism about three-quarters of what he said and then grovelled before a mawkish and unmanly ideal made by misunderstanding the little which is left—if there were a school of critics in *this* relation to a historical character, we might very well admit that they were not getting to grips with it, but surrounding it with "a halo of false sentiment."

That is the vital distinction. At least we do not admit sentiment as a substitute for statement; still less as a contradiction of something that we state. There may be devotional expressions that are emotional, and even extravagantly emotional; but they do not actually distort any definition that is purely intellectual. But in the case of our critics, the confusion is in the intellect. We do not claim that all our pictorial or poetical expressions are adequate; but the fault is in the execution not in the conception. And there is a conception which is not a confusion. We do not say that every pink and blue doll from an Art Repository is a satisfactory symbol of the Mother of God. But we do say that it is less of a contradiction than exists in a person who says there is no Original Sin in anybody, and then calls it Mariolatry to say there was no Original Sin in Mary. We do not profess to admire the little varnished pictures of waxen angels or wooden children around the Communion Table. But we do most strongly profess and proclaim that they are less of a blot on the intellectual landscape than a bishop who suggests that the Host may actually be the divine Presence, but that High Church curates will do his lordship a personal favour if they take no notice of it. We are under no illusions about the literary quality of a large number of hymns in our hymn-books, or any other hymn-books. But we modestly submit that though they are doggerel they are not nonsense; and that saying that we can assert a personal God, a personal immortality, a personal divine love that extends to the least and worst, and do all this without holding "a Creed," *is* nonsense. We know that the nearest sane agnostic or atheist would agree that it is nonsense. Devotional art and literature are often out of balance or broken in expression; sometimes because the emotion is too real and too strong for the reason, the same thing which makes the love-letters of the wisest men like the letters of lunatics; sometimes from a real deficiency in the individual power of reason; but never from a theoretical repudiation of reason, like that of the Pragmatists and about three-quarters of the Modernists. And in the same way it is the very reverse of the truth to say that a mere emotional distortion of the facts has drawn the modern mind towards St. Francis. It is, on the contrary, emphatically an attraction of mind to mind; and the more purely mental the process, the less it will be interrupted by ignorant irritation against the strangeness of Italian manners or mediaeval conditions. And in this case there is no international problem. Thousands of Englishmen who know nothing but England glow with love and understanding of St. Francis. We may well feel an unaffected pity for the one unlucky Englishman who cannot understand.

XX

ON TWO ALLEGORIES

Perhaps it is only fair that the modern iconoclasm should be applied also to the ancient iconoclasts; and especially to the great Puritans, those idol-breakers who have long been idols. Mr. Belloc was recently tapping the Parliamentary statue of Cromwell with a highly scientific hammer; and Mr. Noyes[70] has suddenly assailed the image of Bunyan with something more like a sledge-hammer. In the latter case I confess to thinking the reaction excessive; I should say nothing worse of Bunyan than of many old writers; that he is best known by his best passages, and that many, who fondly believe they have read him, would be mildly surprised at some of his worst passages. But that is not peculiar to Bunyan; and I for one should be content with saying what I said some years ago. A fair and balanced view of the culture and creeds involved can best be reached by comparing the Pilgrimage of Christian with the Pilgrimage of Piers Plowman. The Puritan allegory is much neater (even if it be not always neat) than the rather bewildering mediaeval medley. The Puritan allegory is more national, in the sense that the language and style have obviously become clearer and more fixed. But the Puritan allegory is certainly much narrower than the mediaeval allegory. Piers Plowman deals with the death or resurrection of a whole human society, where men are members of each other. In the later work schism has "isolated the soul"; and it is certainly mere individualism, when it is not mere terrorism. But I will only say now what I said then; I do not want to damage the statue of John Bunyan at Bedford, where it stands facing (symbolically in more ways than one) the site of his own prison. But I do wish there were a statue of John Langland,[71] uplifted on a natural height into a more native air, and looking across all England from the Malvern hills.

[70] Alfred Noyes (1880–1958) was an English poet who converted to Catholicism in 1927.

[71] William Langland (c. 1332–c. 1400), who Chesterton mistakenly refers to as John, was the presumed poet of *The Vision of Piers Plowman*, a religious allegory representing a dream-vision of the Christian life. It is considered one of the finest examples of Middle English alliterative verse.

But there is one intellectual side issue of the debate that does interest me very much. Mr. James Douglas, who once presented himself to me as a representative of Protestant truth, and who is certainly a representative of Protestant tradition, answered Mr. Alfred Noyes in terms very typical of the present state of that tradition. He said that we should salute Bunyan's living literary genius, and not bother our heads about Bunyan's obsolete theology. Then he added the comparison which seems to me so thought-provoking: that this is after all what we do, when we admire Dante's genius and not *his* obsolete theology. Now there is a distinction to be made here; if the whole modern mind is to realize at all where it stands. If I say that Bunyan's theology *is* obsolete, but Dante's theology is *not* obsolete—then I know the features of my friend Mr. Douglas will be wreathed in a refined smile of superiority and scorn. He will say that I am a Papist and therefore of course I think the Papist dogmatism living. But the point is that he is a Protestant and he thinks the Protestant dogmatism dead. I do at least defend the Catholic theory because it can be defended. The Puritans would presumably be defending the Puritan theory—if it could be defended. The point is that it is dead for them as much as for us. It is not merely that Mr. Noyes demands the disappearance of a disfigurement; it is that Mr. Douglas says it cannot be a disfigurement because it has already disappeared. Now the Thomist philosophy, on which Dante based his poetry, has not disappeared. It is not a question of faith but of fact; anybody who knows Paris or Oxford, or the worlds where such things are discussed, will tell you that it has not disappeared. All sorts of people, including those who do not believe in it, refer to it and argue against it on equal terms.

I do not believe, for a fact, that modern men so discuss the seventeenth century sectarianism. Had I the privilege of passing a few days with Mr. Douglas and his young lions of the *Daily Express,* I doubt not that we should discuss and differ about many things. But I do rather doubt whether Mr. Douglas would every now and again cry out, as with a crow of pure delight, "Oh, I must read you this charming little bit from Calvin." I do rather doubt whether his young journalists are joyously capping each other's quotations from Toplady's[72] sermons

[72] Augustus Toplady (1740–78) was an Anglican clergyman who wrote the hymn "Rock of Ages".

on Calvinism. But eager young men do still quote Aquinas, just as they still quote Aristotle. I have heard them at it. And certain ideas are flying about, even in the original prose of St. Thomas, as well as in the poetry of Dante—or, for that matter, of Donne.

The case of Bunyan is really the opposite of the case of Dante. In Dante the abstract theory still illuminates the poetry; the ideas enlighten even where the images are dark. In Bunyan it is the human facts and figures that are bright; while the spiritual background is not only dark in spirit, but blackened by time and change. Of course it is true enough that in Dante the mere images are immensely imaginative. It is also true that in one sense some of them are obsolete; in the sense that the incidents are obsolete and the personal judgment merely personal. Nobody will ever forget how there came through the infernal twilight the figure of that insolent Troubadour, carrying his own head aloft in his hand, like a lantern to light his way. Everybody knows that such an image is poetically true to certain terrible truths about the unnatural violence of intellectual pride. But as to whether anybody has any business to say that Bertrand de Born[73] is damned, the obvious answer is No. Dante knew no more about it than I do: only he cared more about it; and his personal quarrel is an obsolete quarrel. But that sort of thing is not Dante's theology, let alone Catholic theology.

In a word; so far from his theology being obsolete, it would be much truer to say that everything is obsolete except his theology. That he did not happen to like a particular Southern gentleman is obsolete; but that was at most a private fancy, in demonology rather than theology. We come to theology when we come to theism. And if anybody will read the passage in which Dante grapples with the gigantic problem of describing the Beatific Vision, he will find it is uplifted into another world of ideas from the successful entry to the Golden City at the end of the Pilgrim's Progress. It is a Thought; which a thinker, especially a genuine freethinker, is always free to go on thinking. The images of Dante are not to be worshipped, any more than any other images. But there is an idea behind all images;

[73] Bertrand de Born (1140–1215), a knight of Provence, was condemned in Canto XXVIII of Dante's *Inferno* as a sower of discord among kinsmen.

and it is before that, in the last lines of the Paradiso, that the spirit of the poet seems first to soar like an eagle and then to fall like a stone.

There is nothing in this comparison that reflects on the genius and genuineness of Bunyan in his own line or class; but it does serve to put him in his own class. I think there was something to be said for the vigorous denunciation of Mr. Noyes; but no such denunciation is involved in this distinction. On the contrary, it would be easy to draw the same distinction between two men both at the very top of all literary achievement. It would be true to say, I think, that those who most enjoy reading Homer care more about an eternal humanity than an ephemeral mythology. The reader of Homer cares more about men than about gods. So, as far as one can guess, does Homer. It is true that if those curious and capricious Olympians did between them make up a religion, it is now a dead religion. It is the human Hector who so died that he will never die. But we should remonstrate with a critic who, after successfully proving this about Homer, should go on to prove it about Plato. We should protest if he said that the only interest of the Platonic Dialogues today is in their playful asides and very lively local colour, in the gay and graceful picture of Greek life; but that nobody troubles nowadays about the obsolete philosophy of Plato. We should point out that there is no truth in the comparison; and that if anything the case is all the other way. Plato's philosophy will be important as long as there is philosophy; and Dante's religion will be important as long as there is religion. Above all, it will be important as long as there is that lucid and serene sort of religion that is most in touch with philosophy. Nobody will say that the theology of the Baptist tinker is in that sense serene or even lucid; on many points it necessarily remains obscure. The reason is that such religion does not do what philosophy does; it does not begin at the beginning. In the matter of mere chronological order, it is true that the pilgrimage of Dante and that of Bunyan both end in the Celestial City. But it is in a very different sense that the pilgrimage of Bunyan begins in the City of Destruction. The mind of Dante, like that of his master St. Thomas, really begins as well as ends in the City of Creation. It begins as well as ends in the burning focus in which all things began. He sees his series from the right end, though he then begins it at the wrong end. But it is the whole point of a personal work like *The Pilgrim's Progress* that it does begin with a man's own private sins and private panic about them. This intense individualism gives it great force; but it cannot in the nature of things give it great breadth and range. Heaven is heaven; but the wanderer has not many other thoughts about it except that it is haven. It is typical of the two methods, each of them very real in its way, that Dante could write a whole volume, one-third of his gigantic epic, describing the things of Heaven; whereas in the case of Bunyan, as the gates of Heaven open the book itself closes.

I think it worth while to write this note on the critical remark of Mr. James Douglas, because it is a remark that would be made as readily by many other intelligent men today. But it is founded on a fallacy; on the idea that the choice between living philosophies and dead philosophies is the same as the choice between old philosophies and new. It is not true of Plato and it is not true of Dante; and, apart from whatever is our own philosophy, we should realize that some of the most ancient are the most alive.

XXI

THE PROTESTANT SUPERSTITIONS

That delightful guessing game, which has long caused innocent merriment in so many Catholic families, the game of guessing at exactly which line of an article say on Landscape or Latin Elegiacs, we shall find the Dean of St. Pauls introducing the Antidote to Antichrist; or the Popish Plot Revealed—that most familiar of our Catholic parlour games happened to be entertaining me some time ago, as a sort of substitute for a crossword puzzle, when I found I had hit on a very lucky example. I wrote above about "Catholic families," and had almost, by force of associations written "Catholic firesides." And I imagine that the Dean really does think that even in this weather we keep the home-fires burning, like the fire of Vesta,[74] in permanent expectation of relighting the fires of Smithfield.[75] Anyhow, this sort of guessing game or crossword puzzle is seldom disappointing. The Dean must by this time have tried quite a hundred ways of leading up to his beloved topic; and even concealing it, like a masked battery, until he can let loose the cannonade in a perfect tornado of temper. Then the crossword puzzle is no longer a puzzle, though the crosswords are apparent and appropriate enough; especially those devoted to the great historical process of crossing out the Cross.

In the case of this particular article, it was only towards the end of it that the real subject was allowed to leap out from an ambush upon the reader. I think it was a general article on Superstition; and, being a journalistic article of the modern type, it was of course devoted to discussing superstition without defining superstition. In an article of that enlightened sort, it seemed enough for the writer to suggest that superstition is anything that he does not happen to like. Some of the things are also things that I do not happen to like. But such a writer is not reasonable even when he is right. A man ought to have

[74] Vesta was the Roman goddess of the hearth.
[75] Smithfield was an area outside of London in the sixteenth century where heretics were burned.

some more philosophical objection to stories of ill luck than merely calling them credulity; as certainly as a man ought to have some more philosophical objection to Mass than to call it Magic. It is hardly a final refutation of Spiritualists to prove that they believe in Spirits; any more than a refutation of Deists to prove that they believe in Deity. Creed and credence and credulity are words of the same origin and can be juggled backwards and forwards to any extent. But when a man assumes the absurdity of anything that anybody else believes, we wish first to know what he believes; on what principle he believes; and, above all, upon what principle he disbelieves. There is no trace of anything so rational in the Dean's piece of metaphysical journalism. If he had stopped to define his terms, or in other words to tell us what he was talking about, such an abstract analysis would of course have filled up some space in the article. There might have been no room for the Alarum Against the Pope.

The Dean of St. Paul's got to business, in a paragraph in the second half of his article, in which he unveiled to his readers all the horrors of a quotation from Newman; a very shocking and shameful passage in which the degraded apostate says that he is happy in his religion, and in being surrounded by the things of his religion; that he likes to have objects that have been blessed by the holy and beloved, that there is a sense of being protected by prayers, sacramentals and so on; and that happiness of this sort satisfies the soul. The Dean, having given us this one ghastly glimpse of the Cardinal's spiritual condition, drops the curtain with a groan and says it is Paganism. How different from the Christian orthodoxy of Plotinus![76]

Now it was exactly that little glimpse that interested me in this matter; not so much a glimpse into the soul of the Cardinal as into the mind of the Dean. I suddenly seemed to see, in much simpler form than I had yet realized, the real issue between him and us. And the curious thing about the issue is this; that what he thinks about us is exactly what we think about him. What I for one feel most strongly, in considering a case like that of the Dean and his quotation from the Cardinal, is that the Dean is a man of distinguished intelligence and culture, that he

[76] Plotinus (c. 203–262) was the founder of Neo-platonic philosophy. Dean Inge traced his influence on Christianity in the Gifford Lectures of 1918.

is always interesting, that he is sometimes even just, or at least justified or justifiable; but that he is first and last the champion of a Superstition; the man who is really and truly defending a Superstition, as it would be understood by people who could define a Superstition. What makes it all the more amusing is that it is in a rather special sense a Pagan Superstition. But what makes it most intensely interesting, so far as I am concerned, is that the Dean is devoted to what may be called par-excellence a superstitious Superstition. I mean that it is in a special sense a *local* superstition.

Dean Inge is a superstitious person because he is worshipping a relic; a relic in the sense of a remnant. He is idolatrously adoring the broken fragment of something; simply because that something happens to have lingered out of the past in the place called England; in the rather battered form called Protestant Christianity. It is as if a local patriot were to venerate the statue of Our Lady of Walsingham[77] *only* because she was in Walsingham and without even remembering that she was in Heaven. It is still more as if he venerated a fragment chipped from the toe of the statue and forgot where it came from and ignored Our Lady altogether. I do not think it superstitious to respect the chip in relation to the statue, or the statue in relation to the saint, or the saint in relation to the scheme of theology and philosophy. But I do think it superstitious to venerate, or even to accept, the fragment because it happens to be there. And Dean Inge does accept the fragment called Protestantism because it happens to be there.

Let us for a moment consider the whole matter as philosophers should; in a universal air above all local superstitions like the Dean's. It is quite obvious that there are three or four philosophies or views of life possible to reasonable men; and to a great extent these are embodied in the great religions or in the wide field of irreligion. There is the atheist, the materialist or monist or whatever he calls himself, who believes that all is ultimately material, and all that is material is mechanical. That is emphatically a view of life; not a very bright or breezy view, but one into which it is quite possible to fit many facts

[77] Our Lady of Walsingham was a shrine erected in 1601 at Walsingham, England, to honor an apparition of the Virgin.

of existence. Then there is the normal man with the natural religion, which accepts the general idea that the world has a design and therefore a designer; but feels the Architect of the Universe to be inscrutable and remote, as remote from men as from microbes. That sort of theism is perfectly sane; and is really the ancient basis of the solid if somewhat stagnant sanity of Islam. There is again the man who feels the burden of life so bitterly that he wishes to renounce all desire and all division, and rejoin a sort of spiritual unity and peace from which (as he thinks) our separate selves should never have broken away. That is the mood answered by Buddhism and by many metaphysicians and mystics. Then there is a fourth sort of man, sometimes called a mystic and perhaps more properly to be called a poet; in practice he can very often be called a pagan. His position is this; it is a twilight world and we know not where it ends. If we do not know enough for monotheism, neither do we know enough for monism. There may be a borderland and a world beyond; but we can only catch hints of it as they come; we may meet a nymph in the forest; we may see the fairies on the mountains. We do not know enough about the natural to *deny* the preternatural. That was, in ancient times, the healthiest aspect of Paganism. That is, in modern times, the rational part of Spiritualism. All these are possible as general views of life; and there is a fifth that is at least equally possible, though certainly more positive.

The whole point of this last position might be expressed in the line of M. Cammaerts's beautiful little poem about bluebells; *le ciel est tombé par terre*. Heaven has *descended* into the world of matter; the supreme spiritual power is now operating by the machinery of matter, dealing miraculously with the bodies and souls of men. It blesses all the five senses; as the senses of the baby are blessed at a Catholic christening. It blesses even material gifts and keepsakes, as with relics or rosaries. It works through water or oil or bread or wine. Now that sort of mystical materialism may please or displease the Dean, or anybody else. But I cannot for the life of me understand why the Dean, or anybody else, does not *see* that the Incarnation is as much a part of that idea as the Mass; and that the Mass is as much a part of that idea as the Incarnation. A Puritan may think it blasphemous that God should become a wafer. A Moslem thinks it blasphemous that God should become a workman in Galilee. And he is perfectly right, from his point of view; and given his primary principle. But if the Moslem has a principle, the Protestant has only a prejudice. That is, he has only a fragment; a relic; a superstition. If it be profane that the miraculous should descend to the plane of matter, then certainly Catholicism is profane; and Protestantism is profane; and Christianity is profane. Of all human creeds or concepts, in that sense, Christianity is the most utterly profane. But why a man should accept a Creator who was a carpenter, and then worry about holy water, why he should accept a local Protestant tradition that God was born in some particular place mentioned in the Bible, merely because the Bible had been left lying about in England, and then say it is incredible that a blessing should linger on the bones of a saint, why he should accept the first and most stupendous part of the story of Heaven on Earth, and then furiously deny a few small but obvious deductions from it — that is a thing I do not understand; I never could understand; I have come to the conclusion that I shall never understand. I can only attribute it to Superstition.

XXII

ON COURAGE AND INDEPENDENCE

When we are pressed and taunted upon our obstinacy in saying the Mass in a dead language, we are tempted to reply to our questioners by telling them that they are apparently not fit to be trusted with a living language. When we consider what they have done with the noble English language, as compared with the English of the Anglican Prayer-Book, let alone the Latin of the Mass, we feel that their development may well be called degenerate.

The language called dead can never be called degenerate. Surely even they might understand our taking refuge in it, by the time that (in the vernacular) the word "immaculate" is applied only to the shirt-fronts of snobs; or "unction" means not Extreme Unction, but only unctous rectitude. It is needless to note once more how the moral qualities have lost their mystical quality; and with it all their dignity and delicacy and spontaneous spiritual appeal. Charity, that was the flaming heart of the world, has become a name for a niggardly and pompous patronage of the poor, generally amounting by this time to the enslavement of the poor.

But there are more subtle examples of this degeneration in ideal terms. And an even worse example, I think, than the cheapening of the word *charity* is the new newspaper cheapening of the word *courage*.

Any man living in complete luxury and security who chooses to write a play or a novel which causes a flutter and exchange of compliments in Chelsea and Chiswick and a faint thrill in Streatham and Surbiton, is described as "daring," though nobody on earth knows what danger it is that he dares. I speak, of course, of terrestrial dangers; or the only sort of dangers he believes in. To be extravagantly flattered by everybody he considers enlightened, and rather feebly rebuked by everybody he considers dated and dead, does not seem so appalling a peril that a man should be stared at as a heroic warrior and militant martyr because he has had the strength to endure it.

The dramatic critic of a Sunday paper, a little while ago, lashed himself into a frenzy of admiration for the "courage" of some dismal and dirty play or other, because it represented a soldier as raving like a hysterical woman against the cruelty of those who had expected him to defend his country. It may be amusing that his idea of courage should be a defence of cowardice. But it is the sort of defence of it that we have heard ten thousand times during the reaction after the War; and the courage required to utter it is exactly as great as the courage required to utter any other stale quotation from the cant and convention of the moment: such trifles as the absurdity of marriage or the sympathetic personality of Judas Iscariot. These things have become quite commonplace; but they still pretend to be courageous. So sham soldiers have been known to swagger about in uniform when the war was over.

The Catholic Church, as the guardian of all values, guards also the value of words. Her children will not fall, I hope, into this conventional and comfortable folly. We need not pretend that Catholics today are called upon to show anything worth calling courage, by the standard of the Catholics in other days. It did require some courage to be a Catholic when it involved the definite disinclination felt by most of us for being racked or ripped up with a knife. It did require some courage when there was only an intermittent possibility of being torn in pieces by a mob. Even that our subtle human psychology regards with some distaste.

But I hope we do not feel any distaste for being on the opposite side to Bishop Barnes,[78] or for being regarded with alarm and suspicion by Jix.[79] These things are almost intellectual pleasures. Indeed, they really involve a certain temptation to intellectual pride. Let us pray to be delivered from it; and let us hope that we are not left altogether without occasions for courage. But most of them will be present in private life and in other practical aspects of public life; in resisting pain or passion or defying the economic threat and tyranny of our time. But do not let us make fools of ourselves like the rationalists and the realists,

[78] Ernest William Barnes (1874–1953), an English clergyman, was a controversial proponent of modernism and pacifism. He was ordained Bishop of Birmingham in 1924.

[79] William Joynson Hicks, Lord Brentford (1865–1932), was known in the popular press as "Jix". He served as British Home Secretary from 1924 to 1929.

by posing as martyrs who are never martyred for defying tyrants who have been dead for two hundred years.

But though the name of this virtue has been vulgarized so much that it is hard to use it even where it is exact, let alone where it is in any case exaggerative, there is a somewhat analogous quality which the modern world lauds equally loudly and has lost almost more completely.

Putting aside the strict sense of a Catholic courage, the world ought to be told something about Catholic intellectual independence. It is, of course, the one quality which the world supposes that Catholics have lost. It is also, at this moment, the one quality which Catholics perceive that all the world has lost. The modern world has many marks, good as well as bad; but by far the most modern thing in it is the abandonment of individual reason, in favour of press stunts and suggestion and mass psychology and mass production. The Catholic Faith, which always preserves the unfashionable virtue, is at this moment alone sustaining the independent intellect of man.

Our critics, in condemning us, always argue in a circle. They say of mediaevalism that all men were narrow. When they discover that many of them were very broad, they insist that those men must have been in revolt, not only against mediaevalism, but against Catholicism. No Catholics were intelligent; for when they were intelligent, they cannot really have been Catholics. This circular argument appears with a slight difference in the matter of independent thought today. It consists of extending to all Catholicism what are in fact the independent ideas of different Catholics. Men start by assuming (what they have been told) that Rome rigidly suppresses *all* variety and therefore Romanists never differ on anything. Then if one of them advances an interesting view, they say that Rome must have imposed it on him and therefore on all other Roman Catholics. I myself have advanced several economic and political suggestions, for which I never dreamed of claiming anything more than that a loyal Catholic can offer them. But I would rather take any other example than my own unimportant opinions.

In any case, my own experience of the modern world tells me that Catholics are much more and not less individualistic than other men in their general opinions. Mr. Michael Williams, the spirited propagandist of Catholicism in America, gave this as a very cogent reason for refusing to found or join anything like a Catholic party in politics. He said that Catholics will combine for Catholicism, but it is quite abnormally difficult to get them to combine for anything else. This is confirmed by my own impressions and is contrasted very sharply with my recollections about most other religious groups, for instance, what we called the Free Churches, constituting what was also called the Nonconformist Conscience, represented a marvel of moral unity and the spreading of a special spiritual atmosphere. But the Free Churches were not free, whatever else they were. The most striking and even startling thing about them was the *absence* of any individual repudiations of the common ideals which the Conscience laid down. The Nonconformist Conscience was not the normal conscience; they would hardly themselves have pretended that the mass of mankind necessarily agreed with them about Drink or Armaments. But they all agreed with each other about Drink or Armaments. A Nonconformist minister standing up to defend public-houses, or public expenditure on guns and bayonets, was a much rarer thing than a heretic in much more hierarchical systems. It was broadly the fact that *all* such men supported what they called Temperance; which seemed to mean an intemperate denunciation of temperate drinking. It is almost as certain that *all* of them insisted on what they called Peace; which seemed, so far as I could make out, to mean such weakening of armament as would involve disaster and destruction in War. But the question here is not whether I disagreed with them; but whether they ever disagreed with each other. And one thing is at least certain, that on things of this sort they disagreed with each other infinitely less than Catholics do. Though the traditional culture and sacramental symbol of the vine makes most Catholics moderately favourable to fermented liquor in moderation, there have been many prominent Catholics who were teetotallers in a degree hardly to be called moderate. The great Cardinal Manning startled all his own supporters by the passion of this private conviction; just as he startled them by many other Radical eccentricities, such as making friends with Stead[80] and championing the Salvation Army.

[80] William Stead (1849–1912) was an English journalist and dabbler in psychic phenomena.

Whether he was right is not here in question; the point is that he thought he was right when his own religious world thought he was wrong, and not unfrequently told him so. You would not have found a man in the Salvation Army to defend Irish whisky, as you found a man like Father Matthew[81] to denounce it.

The same facts could be supported by a hundred facts in my own experience. Dean Inge observed the other day that Mr. Belloc was the only man in England who believed that Dreyfus was guilty. He might have added that he was nearly the only man in England who knew any of the actual facts of the case, which were suppressed in the English newspapers. In any case, the phrase is an exaggeration; for several men, like Lord Chief Justice Russell,[82] whom no one will call incompetent to judge evidence, and old Harry Labouchere,[83] whom no one will call a zealot for militarism, were of the same opinion. But substantially it is true that Mr. Belloc, in the days of his youth, found himself absolutely alone in almost any assembly of English people discussing the question. It is by no means the only occasion on which he has found himself alone. Merely from my own personal knowledge of him. I could give a list as long as this article of topics on which he was opposed to everyone else's opinion and sometimes opposed to mine. To mention only a few things, large and small, he would probably be the only person in a drawing-room saying that Lewis Carroll was overrated, that Byron and Longfellow were not overrated, that wit is superior to humour, that *Ally Sloper's Half-Holiday* was superior to *Punch,* that James the Second was chiefly notable as a stolid English patriot suspicious of French influence, that an Irish political murder might actually be as excusable as a Russian political murder (old regime), that half the modern legislation advanced in favour of Labour is part of a plan to re-establish pagan slavery, that it is the mark of the Protestant

[81] Father Theobald Matthew (1796–1856) was an Irish priest who campaigned for total abstinence from alcohol.

[82] Charles Russell, Baron Russell of Killowen (1832–1900), was Lord Chief Justice of England from 1894 to 1900.

[83] Henry du Pré Labouchere (1831–1912) was an English journalist, politician and founder of the magazine *Truth*.

culture to tolerate Catholicism and the mark of the Catholic culture to persecute it, and a variety of other opinions which would at least be largely regarded as paradoxes. And he says such things because he is a Catholic: which does not mean that other Catholics would say the same. On the contrary, each would say something quite different. It is not that they need agree with him; but that he need not agree with them. Apart from his own genius, Catholics do differ thus more than a company of Anglican public-school patriots or solid Liberal Nonconformists; to say nothing of the middle class of the Middle West, with its rigid pattern of regular guys. Catholics know the two or three transcendental truths on which they do agree; and take rather a pleasure in disagreeing on everything else. A glance at the living literature, written by other Catholics besides Mr. Belloc, will confirm what I say.

I might take, for instance, a book like the remarkable recent work of Mr. Christopher Hollis,[84] "The American Heresy." Now surely nobody in his senses will say that all Catholics are bound to believe that the Slave States ought to have won the American Civil War, that America ought never to have extended westward of Tennessee, that Andrew Jackson was a savage, or that Abraham Lincoln was a failure, that Calhoun was like a heathen Roman or that Wilson was an arrogant and dishonest schoolmaster. These opinions are not part of the Catholic order; but they are illustrations of the Catholic liberty. And they illustrate exactly the sort of liberty which the modern world emphatically has not got; the real liberty of the mind. It is no longer a question of liberty from kings and captains and inquisitors. It is a question of liberty from catchwords and headlines and hypnotic repetitions and all the plutocratic platitudes imposed on us by advertisement and journalism.

It is strictly true to say that the average reader of the *Daily Mail* and the "Outline of History"[85] is inhibited from these intellectual acts. It is true to say that he *cannot* think that Abraham Lincoln was a

[84] Christopher Hollis (1902–77) was an English author, Conservative politician and convert to Catholicism.
[85] The *Outline of History* was an immensely popular book by H. G. Wells, published in 1920.

failure. It is true to say that he *cannot* think that a republic should have refused to expand as it has expanded. He cannot move his mind to such a position, even experimentally; it means moving it out of too deep a rut, worn too smooth by the swift traffic of modern talk and journalism, all perpetually moving one way.

These modern people mean by mental activity simply an express train going faster and faster along the same rails to the same station; or having more and more railway carriages hooked on to it to be taken to the same place. The one notion that has vanished from their minds is the notion of voluntary movement even to the same end. They have fixed not only the ends, but the means. They have imposed not only the doctrines, but the words. They are bound not merely in religion, which is avowedly binding, but in everything else as well. There are formal praises of free thought; but even the praises are in a fixed form. Thousands who have never learned to think at all are urged to think whatever may take their fancy about Jesus Christ. But they are, in fact, forbidden to think in any way but one about Abraham Lincoln. That is why it is worth remarking that it is a Catholic who has thought for himself.

XXIII

THE NORDIC HINDOO

I cannot, as some do, find Dr. Barnes a very exciting Bishop merely because he is an Evolutionist in the style of fifty years ago and a Protestant persecutor in the style of eighty years ago. His views are stale enough; but I admit that his arguments are sometimes amusing.

Thus, he reached the last limit of wildness in one remark which he made in the course of explaining that the folklore of the Mediterranean had been forced upon the Nordic nations — whatever that may mean. He added abruptly that Indian and Chinese metaphysics are now much more important than ours. But, above all, he made the crowning assertion that Rome is thus stamped as Provincial.

This seems to suggest to the educational mind the construction of an examination paper in elementary general knowledge. It might run something like this:

1. From what language is the word "provincial" derived?

2. To what provinces did it generally refer?

3. If Athens, Antioch, Rome and Jerusalem were provincial towns, what was their Metropolitan city?

4. What reasons are there for supposing that Birmingham occupied this Metropolitan position from the earliest times?

5. Give a short account of the conquest of Southern Europe and the Near East by the Emperors of Birmingham.

6. At what date did the Papacy rebel against the Diocese of Birmingham?

7. Explain the old proverb, "All roads lead to Birmingham."

8. Discuss the following remark, "The most charmingly Nordic people I know are those dear Chinamen."

9. Why is the folklore of the Hindoos so much more reasonable than that of the Romans?

10. When will the Bishop of Birmingham go touring in the Provinces?

Answers must be sent in before the time of the Disestablishment of the Church of England, and priests are forbidden to give their crafty assistance to the candidates.

Really, I do not know any other way of dealing with even a pretence of seriousness with such an extraordinary remark. It was rendered even more extraordinary, of course, by the further remarks on the subject of Chinamen and Hindoos. Now we know all about the Nordic Man, so far as anybody can know anything about a person who does not exist. We know, for instance, that up to the autumn of 1914 he used to be called the Teutonic Man. Dean Inge used to be frightfully fond of him in those days; even fonder than he is now. He once quoted lavishly, and still quotes occasionally, from that great and glorious English patriot, Mr. Houston Stewart Chamberlain.[86]

We quite understood that all Nordic Men were like gods, having long golden hair and gigantic stature; and this made it all the more pleasant to realize that we ourselves were Nordic Men. Unfortunately, the Germans were even more Nordic and gigantic and beautiful to gaze upon; they said so; and they ought to know. The poor Teuton was a little unpopular for five years or so; but now he is creeping out again to feel the sun, like the kings after Napoleon's fall in Mrs. Browning's poem.[87] Like several other people, he changed his name during the War. He is now entirely Nordic and not at all Teutonic.

And, as it is, and always was, his whole profession in life to praise himself and exalt the virtue of pride, so much undervalued by Christians, it is perfectly natural that he should despise "Dagos" and talk about the lower culture of lesser breeds without the law. It is natural that he should insist that all Spaniards are cowardly bull-fighters and all Italians luxurious organ-grinders. He may be expected to point out at intervals the sluggish incompetence of Napoleon and the impotent languor of Mussolini.

All this we were used to; it was what we expected from the Nordic

---

[86] Houston Stewart Chamberlain (1855–1917) was an Englishman who espoused Nordic racial superiority. He moved to Germany, where, after his death, his theories enjoyed popularity among the Nazis.

[87] Chesterton is referring to Elizabeth Barrett Browning's "Crowned and Buried".

Man; for nobody ever expected a Nordic Man to face facts staring him in the face, or to learn anything even from his own experience. We thought we had it all clear and complete, like a mutual understanding; there was the Nordic Man who was noble because he was Protestant and had light hair; and there was the Southern Catholic who was a lower sort of animal, because he was swarthy and superstitious. But why Hindoos? O Venerable Father in God and gentle shepherd of souls, why Hindoos?

Why are we now told to learn from people who are even less light-haired and even further off from the Arctic Circle? Are they not a lower race, conquered by the earth-shaking Imperialism of Birmingham? Are they not a lesser breed without the law? Are we to go to Asia to escape from the folklore and magic? Do the dear Indians never exhibit any of the errors that deface the deplorable Romans? If the Latins are idolaters, do the Indians never have idols? If Southern Europe is attached to mythology, is Southern Asia a world of pure reason that has never been defaced by a myth?

The explanation, the only explanation that I can suggest, is the one I have already suggested; and it is in a simple word; the word *despair*. Everybody knows that when a military compaign begins to fail there is an inevitable and even pardonable temptation to every military commander on the defeated side to lower the standard of military fitness and collect soldiers from anywhere, whatever be their military quality. This has happened again and again even among the white races; something similar is constantly happening in their relation to the other races. So both the Dutch and the English in the South African quarrel have been continually tempted to make use of the natives for war as well as labour. France has been blamed from relying on dark troops; though I never could see why she should be blamed by us, who drew dark troops from all over our own Empire.

Anyhow, it is a process that defeated or embarrassed captains fall back upon regularly but often reluctantly. It is a very exact parallel to the defeat of the bishop of Birmingham and his cry for help to the Hindoos. He has reached the position in which he will accept reinforcements from anywhere except Rome. Rome must be provincial; even if it is the only place in the world that is provincial. Rome must be barbaric; if all the barbarians of the earth are called up to sack the city.

And when we have reached that point, it is not difficult to see that the very invasion and spoliation proclaim it to be a Holy City; unique and universal and towering over the tribes of men.

XXIV

A SPIRITUALIST LOOKS BACK

We hear much about new religions; many of them based on the very latest novelties of Buddha and Pythagoras. But I have come to a conclusion which I fear will offend still more. I fancy that all modern religions are counter-religions; attacks on, or alternative to the Catholic Church. They bear no likeness to the natural pagan speculations that existed before the Catholic Church, or would exist if it had never existed. The attitude of Dean Inge is certainly much more like that of Plotinus than that of Plato. But it is even more like that of Porphyry[88] than that of Plotinus. He is exactly like some pagan of the decline; it is not necessary for him to know very much about the Christian superstition; as soon as he heard of it, he hated it.

In a recent work, which I have considered in this place, he is careful to insist that the word *Protestant* had an old meaning which was not merely negative. And he has certainly fulfilled an old meaning that is positive; if the word *Protestant* means a man who doth protest too much. He is so very anxious to explain what he thinks about the Catholic Church that he cannot keep it out of any article about M. Coné[89] or Monkey Glands.

The Dean stands by himself; and must be presumably described as an Anglican, for want of anything else in particular to call him. But it is very interesting to observe that even those who seem to go out into the wilderness to stake out their own Promised Land, like the Mormons, are eventually found to be as much a mere reaction against orthodoxy as the Modernists. Their march towards the new Utopia is found to be only a rather longer and more elaborate manoeuvre of one

[88] Porphyry (233–c. 301) was a Neo-platonic philosopher, disciple of Plotinus and opponent of Christianity.
[89] This should probably read "Coué", for Émile Coué (1857–1926), a French chemist who promoted the idea that people could cure their illness through mind control. His slogan, "Every day, in every way, I am becoming better and better", was widely popular in the 1920s.

of the armies besieging the Holy City. We imagined that these new schismatics had finally gone off to pray; but we always find (a little while afterwards) that they have remained to scoff. They always come back to boo and riot in our churches when they have got tired of trying to build their own.

One who thus reveals all that he does not know, and certainly ought to know, is Sir Arthur Conan Doyle. He broke out the other day into a diatribe, which was supposed to begin with the relations of his new religion to others, but which turned with incalculable rapidity into mere abuse of his old original family religion, as if there were no other in the world.

Perhaps he is right; and there is not. But you would think a man fresh from founding a new religion might have a few new things to say about that; instead of old and negative things to say about something else. But the special strictures of Sir Arthur Conan Doyle on Catholic orthodoxy had a certain very curious character, which alone makes them worth noting at all. In themselves they are almost indescribably stale and thin and shabby; and have been thrashed threadbare in a hundred controversies. But the odd thing which I want to remark about them is this; that they are not only old, but old-fashioned, in the sense that they do not even fit into what is now fashionable. They had some meaning sixty years ago. They have no meaning at all for anybody who looks at the living world as it is—even at the world of new faiths or fads like Spiritualism. But the Spiritualist is not looking even at the Spiritualist world. He is not looking at the human world, or the heathen world, or even at the worldly world. He is looking only at the thing he hates.

For instance, he says exactly as did our Calvinist great-grandmother, that the Confessional is a most indelicate institution; and that it is highly improper for a young lady of correct deportment, in the matter of prunes and prisms, to mention such things as sins to a strange gentleman who is a celibate. Well, of course, all Catholics know the answer to that; and hundreds of Catholics have answered it to Protestants who had some sort of right or reason to ask it.

Nobody, or next to nobody, has ever had to go into so much morbid detail in confessing to a priest as in confessing to a doctor.

And the joke of it is that the Protestant great-grandmother, who objected to the gentleman priest, would have been the very first to object to a lady doctor. What matters in the confessional is the moral guilt and not the material details. But the material details are everything in medicine, even for the most respectable and responsible physician, let alone all the anarchical quacks who have been let loose to hear confessions in the name of Psychoanalysis or Hypnotic Cures. But though we all know the old and obvious answers, what I find startling is this: that our critic does not see the new and obvious situation.

What in the world is the sense of his coming with his prunes and prisms into the sort of society that surrounds us today? If a girl must not mention sin to a man in a corner of a church, it is apparently the only place nowadays in which she may not do so. She may sit side by side with him on a jury and discuss the details of the foulest and most perverted wickedness in the world, perhaps with a man's life hanging on the minuteness of the detail. She may read in novels and newspapers sins she has never heard of, let alone sins she is likely to commit or confess. She must not whisper to an impersonal presence behind a grating the most abstract allusion to the things that she hears shouted and cat-called in all the theatrical art and social conversation of the day.

Sir Arthur Conan Doyle must know as well as I do that modesty of that sort is not being regarded at all by the modern world; and that nobody dreams of attempting to safeguard it so strictly as it is safeguarded in Catholic conversation and Catholic confessions. We can say of Rome and Purity what Swinburne said, in another sense, about Rome and Liberty—"Who is against her but all men, and who is beside her but Thou?"

And yet the critic has the impudence to accuse us of the neglect of what all but we are neglecting; simply because that charge was used against us a century ago, and anything used against us can be used over and over again, until it drops to pieces. The old stick of the old grandmother is still good enough to beat the old dog with, though if the old grandmother could rise from the dead, she would think the dog the only decent object in the landscape.

I mean nothing flippant when I say that the only interesting thing about all this is its staleness. I have no unfriendly feelings towards Sir Arthur Conan Doyle, to whom we all owe so much gratitude in the realm of literature and entertainment, and who often seems to me entirely right in his manner of defending Spiritualism against Materialism. But I do realize, even if he does not realize, that, at the back of the whole business, he is not defending Spiritualism, and not attacking Materialism; he is attacking Rome.

By a deep and true ancestral instinct with him, he knows that this is ultimately the one Thing to be either attacked or defended; and that he that is not against it is for it. Unless the claim of the Church can be challenged in the modern world, it is impossible really to set up an alternative modern religion. He feels that to be a fact, and I am glad to sympathize with him. Indeed, it is because I would remain so far sympathetic that I take only one example among the doctrines he denounced; and deliberately avoid, for instance, his strangely benighted remarks on the cult of the Blessed Virgin. For I confess to a difficulty in remaining patient with blindness about that topic. But there are other parallel topics.

He has some very innocent remarks about what he considers grotesque in the sacramental system; innocent, because apparently unconscious of what everybody else in the world considers grotesque in the spiritualistic system. If any Christian service was so conducted as to resemble a really successful seance, the world might well be excused for falling back on the word "grotesque," a favourite word of Dr. Watson. Indeed, we may well question whether the institution of the Red-Headed League or the episode of the Yellow Face at the window, or any of the fantasies of Mr. Sherlock Holmes, were any more fantastic than some that have been submitted to us seriously enough by the school of Sir Arthur Conan Doyle. I do not say that this test of external extravagance ought to be final, or that no defence of such details could be made. But when Sir Arthur deliberately gibes at our ceremonies, we may at least be allowed to smile at his. Suppose any Catholic rite before the altar consisted of binding a human being hand and foot with ropes; should we ever hear the last of the horrible survival of human sacrifice? Suppose we declared that the priest went into a trance and that clouds of thick white stuff like cotton-wool came out of his mouth, as a manifestation of celestial grace; might not some of our critics be heard to murmur the word, "grotesque"? If we conducted a quiet little evening service in which a big brass trumpet careered about in the air and patted people on the head, caressed a lady with intimate gestures of affection, and generally exhibited itself as about as attractive an object as a philandering trombone or an amorous big drum, would not our critics have something to say about the unwholesome hysteria and senseless excitement of Popery? If the Spiritualist goes out of his way to challenge us to a duel in the matter of dignity, I do not really think it can be reasonably said that he is on stronger ground than we.

But I remark on all these charges, not in order to show how they recoil upon themselves, but in order to show how the Spiritualist is driven to return upon himself, and to react against his origins, and to forget all else in making war upon his mother.

The man of the modern religion does not quarrel with the modern world, as he well might, for its neglect of modesty. He quarrels with the ancient mother, who is alone teaching it any modesty at all. He does not devote himself to condemning the modern dances or the fashionable comedies for their vulgar and obvious indifference to dignity. He brings his special charge of grotesque extravagance against the only ceremonial that really retains any dignity. It seems to him, somehow, more important that the Catholic Church should be, on the most minute point, open to misunderstanding, than that the whole world should go to the devil in a dance of death before his very eyes. And he is quite right; at least, the instinct of which this is a symbol is quite right.

The world really pays the supreme compliment to the Catholic Church in being intolerant of her tolerating even the appearance of the evils which it tolerates in everything else. A fierce light does indeed beat upon that throne and blacken every blot; but the interest here is in the fact that even those who profess to be setting up new thrones or throwing new light are perpetually looking backwards at the original blaze if only to discover the blots. They have not really succeeded in getting out of the orbit of the system which they criticize. They have not really found new stars; they are still pointing at alleged spots on the sun, and thereby admitting that it is their native daylight and the centre of their solar system.

XXV

THE ROOTS OF SANITY

The Dean of St. Paul's, when he is right, is very right. He is right with all that ringing emphasis that makes him in other matters so rashly and disastrously wrong. And I cannot but hail with gratitude the scorn with which he spoke lately of all the newspaper nonsense about using monkey-glands to turn old men into young men; or into young monkeys, if that is to be the next step towards the Superman. Not unnaturally, he tried to balance his denunciation of that very experimental materialism which he is always accusing us of denouncing, by saying that this materialism is one evil extreme and that Catholicism is the other. In that connection he said some of the usual things which he commonly finds it easy to say, and we generally find it tolerably easy to answer.

For instance, it is a good example of the contradictory charges brought against Rome that the Dean apparently classes us with those who leave children entirely "unwarned" about the moral dangers of the body. Considering that we have been abused for decades on the ground that we forced on the young the infamous suggestions of the Confessional, this is rather funny.

Only the other day I noted that Sir Arthur Conan Doyle revived this charge of an insult to innocence; and I will leave Dean Inge and Sir Arthur to fight it out. And when he charges us with indifference to Eugenics and the breeding of criminals and lunatics, it is enough that he has himself to denounce the perversion of science manifested in the monkey business. He might permit others to resent equally the schemes by which men are to act like lunatics and criminals in order to avoid lunacy and crime.

There is, however, another aspect of this matter of being right or wrong, which is not so often associated with us, but which is equally consistent with our philosophy. And it has a notable bearing on the sort of questions here raised by Dean Inge. It concerns not only the matters in which the world is wrong, but rather especially the matters in which the world is right. The world, especially the modern world, has reached a curious condition of ritual or routine; in which we might almost say that it is wrong even when it is right. It continues to a great extent to do the sensible things. It is rapidly ceasing to have any of the sensible reasons for doing them. It is always lecturing us on the deadness of tradition; and it is living entirely on the life of tradition. It is always denouncing us for superstition; and its own principal virtues are now almost entirely superstitions.

I mean that when we are right, we are right by principle; and when they are right, they are right by prejudice. We can say, if they prefer it so, that they are right by instinct. But anyhow, they are still restrained by healthy prejudice from many things into which they might be hurried by their own unhealthy logic. It is easiest to take very simple and even extreme examples; and some of the extremes are nearer to us than some may fancy.

Thus, most of our friends and acquaintances continue to entertain a healthy prejudice against Cannibalism. The time when this next step in ethical evolution will be taken seems as yet far distant. But the notion that there is not very much difference between the bodies of men and animals — that is not by any means far distant, but exceedingly near. It is expressed in a hundred ways, as a sort of cosmic communism. We might almost say that it is expressed in every other way except cannibalism.

It is expressed, as in the Voronoff[90] notion, in putting pieces of animals into men. It is expressed, as in the vegetarian notion, in not putting pieces of animals into men. It is expressed in letting a man die as a dog dies, or in thinking it more pathetic that a dog should die than a man. Some are fussy about what happens to the bodies of animals, as if they were quite certain that a rabbit resented being cooked, or that an oyster demanded to be cremated. Some are ostentatiously indifferent to what happens to the bodies of men; and deny all dignity to the dead and all affectionate gesture to the living. But all these have obviously one thing in common; and that is that they regard the human and bestial body as common things. They think of them

[90] Serge Voronoff (1866–1951) was a Russian-born French physiologist who experimented with grafting animal glands in humans.

under a common generalization; or under conditions at best comparative. Among people who have reached this position, the *reason* for disapproving of cannibalism has already become very vague. It remains as a tradition and an instinct. Fortunately, thank God, though it is now very vague, it is still very strong. But though the number of earnest ethical pioneers who are likely to begin to eat boiled missionary is very small, the number of those among them who would explain their own real reason for not doing so is still smaller.

The real reason is that all such social sanities are now the traditions of old Catholic dogmas. Like many other Catholic dogmas, they are felt in some vague way even by heathens, so long as they are healthy heathens. But when it is a question of their not being merely felt but formulated, it will be found to be a formula of the Faith. In this case it is all those ideas that Modernists most dislike, about "special creation" and that Divine image that does not come merely by evolution, and the chasm between man and the other creatures. In short, it is those very doctrines with which men like Dean Inge are perpetually reproaching us, as things that forbid us a complete confidence in science or a complete unity with animals. It is these that stand between men and cannibalism — or possibly monkey-glands. They have the prejudice; and long may they retain it! We have the principle, and they are welcome to it when they want it.

If Euclid were demonstrating with diagrams for the first time, and used the argument of the *reductio ad absurdum,* he would now only produce the impression that his own argument was absurd. I am well aware that I expose myself to this peril by extending my opponent's argument to an extreme, which may be considered an extravagance. The question is, why is it an extravagance? I know that in this case it will be answered that the social feature of cannibalism is rare in our culture. So far as I know, there are no cannibal restaurants threatening to become fashionable in London like Chinese restaurants. Anthropophagy is not like Anthroposophy,[91] a subject of society lectures; and, varied as are the religions and moralities

[91] Anthroposophy was a form of mysticism derived from the teachings of the Austrian philosopher Rudolf Steiner (1861–1925).

among us, the cooking of missionaries is not yet a mission. But if anyone has so little of logic as to miss the meaning of an extreme example, I should have no difficulty in giving a much more practical and even pressing example. A few years ago, all sane people would have said that Adamitism was quite as mad as Anthropophagy. A banker walking down the streets with no clothes on would have been quite as nonsensical as a butcher selling man instead of mutton. Both would be the outbreak of a lunatic under the delusion that he was a savage. But we have seen the New Adamite or No Clothes Movement start quite seriously in Germany; start indeed with a seriousness of which only Germans are capable. Englishmen probably are still English enough to laugh at it and dislike it. But they laugh by instinct; and they only dislike by instinct. Most of them, with their present muddled moral philosophy, would probably have great difficulty in refuting the Prussian professor of nakedness, however heartily they might desire to kick him. For if we examine the current controversies, we shall find the same negative and defence-less condition as in the case of the theory of cannibalism. All the fashionable arguments used against Puritanism do in fact lead to Adamitism. I do not mean, of course, that they are not often practically healthy as against Puritanism; still less do I mean that there are no better arguments against Puritanism. But I mean that in pure logic the civilized man has laid open his guard; and is, as it were, naked against the inroads of nakedness. So long as he is content merely to argue that the body is beautiful or that what is natural is right, he has surrendered to the Adamite in theory, though it may be, please God, a long time before he surrenders in practice. Here again the modern theorist will have to defend his own sanity with a prejudice. It is the mediaeval theologian who can defend it with a reason. I need not go into that reason at length; it is enough to say that it is founded on the fall of Man, just as the other instinct against cannibalism is founded on the Divinity of Man. The Catholic argument can be put shortly by saying that there is nothing the matter with the human body; what is the matter is with the human soul.

In other words, if man were completely a god, it might be true that all aspects of his bodily being were godlike; just as if he were completely a beast, we could hardly blame him for any diet, however beastly. But we say that experience confirms our theory of his human complexity. It has nothing to do with the natural things themselves. If red roses mysteriously maddened men to commit murder, we should make rules to cover them up; but red roses would be quite as pure as white ones.

In most modern people there is a battle between the new opinions, which they do not follow out to their end, and the old traditions, which they do not trace back to their beginning. If they followed the new notions forward, it would lead them to Bedlam. If they followed the better instincts backward it would lead them to Rome. At the best they remain suspended between two logical alternatives, trying to tell themselves, as does Dean Inge, that they are merely avoiding two extremes. But there is this great difference in his case, that the question on which he is wrong is, in however perverted a form, a matter of science, whereas the matter in which he is right is by this time simply a matter of sentiment. I need not say that I do not use the word here in a contemptuous sense, for in these things there is a very close kinship between sentiment and sense. But the fact remains that all the people in his position can only go on being sensible. It is left for us to be also reasonable.

XXVI

SOME OF OUR ERRORS

The thoughtful reader, studying the literature of the enlightened and scientific when they advise us about ethics and religion, will be arrested by one phrase which really has a meaning. Nay, he will observe, with increasing interest and excitement, that it really contains a truth. Most of the phrases that are supposed to go along with it, and to be of the same sort, will be found to be not only untrue but almost unmeaning. When the Modernist says that we must free the human intellect from the mediaeval syllogism, it is as if he said we must free it from the multiplication-table. Some people can count or reason quicker than others; some people put in all the steps and are safe; some people leave out the steps and are still right; many leave out the steps and are consequently wrong. But the process of multiplication is the same, and the process of demonstration is the same. Men think in that way, except when they escape from it by ceasing to think. Or again, when we find in the same context the remark that some Christian doctrine which we do know is "only a form of" some Pagan cult that nobody really knows, we realize that the mathematician is treating the unknown quantity as the known. But when we find among these fallacies the remark I speak of, we shall be wise to pause upon it with greater patience. It is the remark, "We need a restatement of religion"; and though it has been said thirty thousand times, it is quite true.

It is also true that those who say it often mean the very opposite of what they say. As I have remarked elsewhere, they very often intend not to restate anything, but to state something else, introducing as many of the old words as possible. But this time not only the word religion, but also the word restatement, is becoming rather an old word. But anyhow the point is that they do not really mean that we should give freshness and a new aspect to religion by calling it roly-poly or rumptifoo. On the contrary, they mean that we should take something totally different and agree to call it religion. I mention, with some sadness, that I have said this before; because I have found it quite difficult to get them to see a fact of almost heart-breaking simplicity. It seems to strike them as being merely a fine shade of distinction; but it strikes me as a rather grotesque and staggering reversal. There would be the same fine shade of difference, if somebody of a sartorial sort came to me protesting that my aged father was waiting in rags on my door-step, and urgently needing a new hat and coat, and indeed a complete equipment; if he made the most animated preparations for the reclothing of my parent, and the whole episode ended by his introducing me to a total stranger begging for my father's old hat.

Now I do really believe that there is a need for the restatement of religious truth; but not the statement of something quite different, which I do not believe to be true. I believe there is a very urgent need for a verbal paraphrase of many of the fundamental doctrines; simply because people have ceased to understand them as they are traditionally stated. It does not follow from this that the traditional statement is not the true statement. It only means that the traditional statement now needs to be translated; although translation is seldom true. This is especially the case in connection with Catholic ideas; because they were originally stated in what some call a dead language and some an everlasting language. But anyhow, they were stated in a language that has since broken up into other languages, and mixed with other dialects, and produced a popular *patois* which is spirited, and often splendid, but necessarily less exact. Now I do think that the Catholic culture suffers very much from the popular misunderstanding of its original terminology. I do think that Catholics are themselves to blame, in many cases, for not realizing that their doctrines need to be stated afresh, and not left in language that is intrinsically correct but practically misleading. Those who call themselves liberal, commonly take for granted that the fault is with a dead language, as against a language that has developed. If they were really liberal, they could enlarge their minds to see that there is a case for the language having degenerated. But in either case, it is practically true that there are misunderstandings, and that we ought chiefly to desire to make people understand. And I think we have faults and follies of our own in this matter; and that it is not always the fault of our enemies that they misunderstand. There are cases in which we, more or less unconsciously, misinform them. We do not allow enough, in justifying the words that we speak, for the difference in the words that they hear.

And I propose to say a few words in this article upon what I may call Catholic criticisms of Catholic faults; or what are (in many cases) merely Catholic accidents and misunderstanding.

For instance, there is a sort of misunderstanding that is simply mistranslation. Probably we have never properly explained to them the real case for using Latin for something that must be immutable and universal. But as half of them are howling day and night for an international language, and accepting a journalese jibberish with plurals in "oj" because they can get no better, some glimmering of the old use of Latin by Erasmus or Bacon might reasonably be expected of them. Of the full defence of such a hieratic tongue I may say something later. But for the moment I am thinking of certain mistakes which arise very largely by our fault and not theirs. It is not the Church's Latin that is to blame; it is the English Catholic's English. It is not because we do not translate it into the vulgar tongue that we are wrong; it is because we do. Sometimes, I am sorry to say, we translate it into a very vulgar tongue. When we do translate things into English, they often only serve as a luminous argument for leaving them in Latin. Latin is Latin, and always says exactly what it means. But popular versions of Latin things often only serve to make them unpopular.

I will venture to take one example, about which I feel very strongly. Will somebody with better authority than I have announce in a voice of thunder, through a trumpet or with a salute of big guns, the vital and very much needed truth that "dulcis" is not the Latin for "sweet"? "Sweet" is not the English word for "dulcis"; any more than for "doux" or "dounce." It has a totally different connotation and atmosphere. "Dulce et decorum est pro patria mori" does not mean "it is sweet and decorous to die for our country." It means something untranslatable like everything that means anything; but something more like "It is a gracious thing and of good report to die for our country." When Roland[92] was dying in the mountains, having blown his horn and broken his sword, and thought of "la doulce France" and the men of his line, he did not sully his lips by saying "sweet France," but something like "beautiful and gracious France." In English the word "sweet" has been rendered hopelessly sticky by the accident of the word "sweets." But in any case it suggests something much more intense and even pungent in sweetness like the tabloids of saccharine that are of concentrated sugar. It is at once too strong and too weak a word. It has not the same savour as the same word in the Latin languages, which often means no more than the word "gentle" as it was used of "a perfect gentle knight." But English Catholicism, having in the great calamity of our history gone into exile in the sixteenth and seventeenth centuries (at the very moment when our modern language was being finally made) naturally had to seek for its own finest enthusiasms in foreign languages. It could not find a salutation to the Mass or the Blessed Virgin except in French or Italian or Spanish or some such tongue; and it translated these things back into a language with which the exile had lost touch and in which his taste was not quite firm and sure. It seemed to be thought necessary to use the word "sweet" in every single case of the kind; which produces not only something that did not sound English; but something which did not sound in the least as the Latin or French sounded. In a certain number of cases, of course, it is exactly the right word; just as it is from time to time in ordinary English poetry. Sometimes it is right because it is so obviously the natural and inevitable word that it would seem more affected not to use it than to use it; as in the song of Burns: "My love is like the melody that's sweetly played in tune."[93] Sometimes it is right because there is something to be a salt to its sweetness, as in Sir Philip Sidney's line: "Before the eyes of that sweet enemy France."[94] Similarly it is often exactly right in good Catholic translations or compositions in

[92] Roland was the most famous of Charlemagne's knights, and the hero of the *Chanson de Roland*, an epic poem of twelfth-century France.
[93] Burns' quotation is from "A Red, Red Rose".
[94] Sidney's quotation is from *Astrophel and Stella* (1590).

English. But this fixed notion that it must always be used wherever some such tender expression would be used in Romance literature is simply a blunder in translation; and a blunder that has had very bad effects in fields much more important than literature. I believe that this incongruous and inaccurate repetition of the word "sweet" has kept more Englishmen out of the Catholic Church than all the poison of the Borgias or all the poisonous lies of the people who have written about them.

Ours is at this moment the most rational of all religions. It is even, in a sense, the most rationalistic of all religions. Those who talk about it as merely or mainly emotional simply do not know what they are talking about. It is all the other religions, all the modern religions, that are merely emotional. This is as true of the emotional salvationism of the first Protestants as of the emotional intuitionalism of the last Modernists. We alone are left accepting the action of the reason and the will without any necessary assistance from the emotions. A convinced Catholic is easily the most hard-headed and logical person walking about the world today. But this old slander, of a slimy sentimentalism in all we say and do, is terribly perpetuated by this mere muddle about words. We are still supposed to have a silly sort of devotion, when we really have the most sensible sort, merely because we have taken a foreign phrase and translated it wrong; instead of either leaving it in Latin for those who can read Latin or trusting it in English to people who can write English. But if in this case we admit that the misunderstanding is more our fault than our opponents' fault, the fault which we confess is the very reverse of the fault of which the opponents complain. It has not arisen through the Catholic practice of saying prayers in Latin. On the contrary, it has arisen through the Protestant practice of always saying them in English. It has come through yielding merely weakly and mechanically to the Protestant pressure in the days when our tradition was completely out of fashion. In other words, it has come through doing exactly what they advised us to do, and not doing it well. Of course I do not mean that it is not a good thing to have good popular translation when it is done well. I think it is a very good thing indeed. But while I see what there is to be said for

the cult of the vernacular, the Protestant critic does not see what
there is to be said for the fixed form of the classic tongue. He does
not see that there is something to be said even for the general idea
that Catholic poetry should be in the vernacular like the Divine Comedy and Catholic worship in the fundamental language like the Mass.

It is a question between a dead language and a dying language.
Every living language is a dying language, even if it does not die.
Parts of it are perpetually perishing or changing their sense; there is
only one escape from that flux; and a language must die to be immortal. The style of the English Jacobean translation[95] is as noble
and simple a thing as any in the world; but even there the words degenerate. It is not their fault; but ours who misuse them; but they
are misused. No language could lift itself into a loftier or simpler
strain than that which begins, "Comfort ye, comfort ye my people";
but even then, when we pass on to "speak ye comfortably to Jerusalem," we stumble over a word we have vulgarized.

But the world plays havoc with all such words, whether they are
in the English Bible or the Latin Canon. There are many words of
Catholic usage which have in practice been thus misused. When an
outsider hears that a Catholic has refrained from something for fear
of "causing scandal," he instantly has an irritated impression that it
means a fear of setting all the silly old women in the town talking
gossip. Of course it means nothing of the kind. It does not mean
that in Greek. It does not mean that in Latin. It ought not to mean
that in English. It ought to mean what it says; the fear of tripping
somebody up, of putting a stumbling-block in the way of some struggling human being. If I encourage to carousals a man who must be
kept off drink, I am causing scandal. If I talk what might be a wholesome realism for some hearers, to a young and innocent person who is
certain to feel it as mere obscenity, I am causing scandal. I am doing
what for me is right, at the risk of making him do what for him is
wrong. To say that that is unjustifiable is manifest moral common
sense. But it is not conveyed in modern English by talking about
causing scandal. All that is conveyed in modern English is that the

---

[95] The Jacobean translation is the King James Version of the Bible, completed in 1611.

person so acting is disdaining idle chatter and irresponsible criticism; which is exactly what all the saints and martyrs have consistently lived and died by doing. And *that* is a good example of what I mean by translation; or, if the word be preferred, by restatement. But that does not mean turning round and abusing the old statement, which was really quite correctly stated. It only means restating exactly what the old statement states.

I could give many other examples of words which were right in their Latin use, but which have become obscured in their English misuse. I always feel it in the necessarily frequent phrase "offending" God; which had originally almost the awful meaning of wounding God. But the word has degenerated through its application to man, until the sound of it is quite petty and perverted. We say that Mr. Binks was quite offended or that Aunt Susan will take offence; and lose sight of the essential truth, and even dogma that (in that lower sense) God is the very last to take offence. But here again we should not abuse the Latin language; we should abuse our own vulgarization of the English language. Upon this one point, of the restatement of religious ideas, the reformers are right in everything except the one essential; which is knowing where to throw the blame.

XXVII

THE SLAVERY OF THE MIND

I have chosen the subject of the slavery of the mind because I believe many worthy people imagine I am myself a slave. The nature of my supposed slavery I need not name and do not propose specially to discuss. It is shared by every sane man when he looks up a train in Bradshaw.[96] That is, it consists in thinking a certain authority reliable; which is entirely reasonable. Indeed it would be rather difficult to travel in every train to find out where it went. It would be still more difficult to go to the destination in order to discover whether it was safe to begin the journey. Suppose a wild scare arose that Bradshaw was a conspiracy to produce railway accidents, a man might still believe the Guide to be a Guide and the scare to be only a scare; but he would know of the existence of the scare. What I mean by the slavery of the mind is that state in which men do not know of the alternative. It is something which clogs the imagination, like a drug or a mesmeric sleep, so that a person cannot possibly think of certain things at all. It is not the state in which he says, "I see what you mean; but I cannot think that because I sincerely think this" (which is simply rational): it is one in which he has never thought of the other view; and therefore does not even know that he has never thought of it. Though I am not discussing here my own religion, I think it only right to say that its authorities have never had this sort of narrowness. You may condemn their condemnations as oppressive; but not in this sense as obscurantist. St. Thomas Aquinas begins his inquiry by saying in effect, "Is there a God? it would seem not, for the following reasons"; and the most criticized of recent Encyclicals always stated a view before condemning it. The thing I mean is man's inability to state his opponent's view; and often his inability even to state his own.

Curiously enough, I find this sort of thing rather specially widespread in our age, which claims to possess a popular culture or

---

[96] Chesterton is referring to *Bradshaw's Monthly Railway Guide.*

enlightenment. There is everywhere the habit of assuming certain
things, in the sense of not even imagining the opposite things. For
instance, as history is taught, nearly everybody assumes that in all
important past conflicts, it was the right side that won. Everybody
assumes it; and nobody knows that he assumes it. The man has simply never seriously entertained the other notion. Say to him that we
should now all of us be better off if Charles Edward and the
Jacobites[97] had captured London instead of falling back from Derby,
and he will laugh. He will think it is what he calls a "paradox." Yet
nothing can be a more sober or solid fact than that, when the issue
was undecided, wise and thoughtful men were to be found on both
sides; and the Jacobite theory is not in any way disproved by the fact
that Cumberland[98] could outflank the clans at Drummossie. I am
not discussing whether it was right as a theory; I am only noting
that it is never allowed to occur to anybody as a thought. The things
that might have been are not even present to the imagination. If
somebody says that the world would now be better if Napoleon had
never fallen, but had established his Imperial dynasty, people have to
adjust their minds with a jerk. The very notion is new to them. Yet
it would have prevented the Prussian reaction; saved equality and
enlightenment without a mortal quarrel with religion; unified Europeans and perhaps avoided the Parliamentary corruption and the Fascist and Bolshevist revenges. But in this age of free-thinkers, men's
minds are not really free to think such a thought.

What I complain of is that those who accept the verdict of fate in
this way accept it without knowing why. By a quaint paradox,
those who thus assume that history always took the right turning
are generally the very people who do not believe there was any special
providence to guide it. The very rationalists who jeer at the trial by
combat, in the old feudal ordeal, do in fact accept a trial by combat as
deciding all human history. In the war of the North and South in
America, some of the Southern rebels wrote on their flags the rhyme,

[97] The Jacobites were partisans of the Stuart cause after the deposing of James II in
1688.
[98] William Augustus, Duke of Cumberland (1721–65), commanded the English
army that defeated the Scottish clans loyal to Prince Charles Edward.

"Conquer we must for our cause is just." The philosophy was faulty; and in that sense it served them right that their opponents copied and continued it in the form "Conquer they didn't; so their cause wasn't." But the latter logic is as bad as the former. I have just read a book called, "The American Heresy," by Mr. Christopher Hollis. It is a very brilliant and original book; but I know it will not be taken sufficiently seriously; because the reader will have to wrench his mind out of a rut even to imagine the South victorious; still more to imagine anybody saying that a small, limited and agricultural America would have been better for everybody—especially Americans.

I could give many other examples of what I mean by this imaginative bondage. It is to be found in the strange superstition of making sacred figures out of certain historical characters; who must not be moved from their stiff symbolic attitudes. Even their bad qualities are sacred. Much new light has lately been thrown on Queen Elizabeth and Mary Stuart. It is not only favourable to Mary but on the whole favourable to Elizabeth. It seems pretty certain that Mary did not plot to kill Darnley.[99] It seems highly probable that Elizabeth did not plot to kill Mary. But many people are quite as tenderly attached to the idea of a merciless Elizabeth as to that of a murderous Mary. That a man devoted to Protestantism should rejoice that Elizabeth succeeded, that a man devoted to Catholicism should wish that Mary had succeeded—all that would be perfectly natural and rational. But Elizabeth was not Protestantism; and it ought not to disturb anybody to discover that she was hardly a Protestant. It ought to be even less gratification to her supporters to insist that she was a tyrant. But there is a sort of waxwork history, that cannot be happy unless Elizabeth has an axe and Mary a dagger. This sense of fixed and sacred figures ought to belong to a religion; but a historical speculation is not a religion. To believe in Calvinism by faith alone is comprehensible. To believe in Cromwell by faith alone is incomprehensible. It is supremely incomprehensible that when Calvinists left off believing in Calvinism, they still insisted on believing in Cromwell. To a simple rationalist like myself, these prejudices are hard to understand.

[99] Henry Stuart, Lord Darnley (1545–67), was Mary Stuart's husband.

XXVIII

INGE VERSUS BARNES

None of us I hope ever wished to be unjust to Dean Inge: though in such fights the button will sometimes come off the foil. And a cruel injustice is being done to him, in the suggestion widely circulated that he agreed with Dr. Barnes. Such things should not be lightly said of any gentleman. It is in accordance with the current legend, at least, that the Gloomy Dean even when he comes to bless should remain to curse. But if there is one isolated human being whom he can be imagined as wanting to bless, one would think it would be his ally, Bishop Barnes of Birmingham. And yet the alliance only serves to soften the curse and not to secure the blessing. If we may use such popular terms of such dignified ecclesiastics, we might be tempted to say that the Dean has found it necessary to throw over the Bishop. An interesting review by the Dean of the Bishop's recent book of sermons contains, of course, a certain number of rather conventional compliments and a certan number of rather abrupt sneers, we might say snarls, at various other people including the greater part of Christendom. But on the two striking and outstanding matters on which Bishop Barnes was condemned by the Catholics, he is almost as strongly condemned by the Dean of St. Paul's. Dean Inge is far too intelligent and cultivated a man to pretend to have much patience with the nonsense about testing Transubstantiation either by chemical experiments or psychical research. He tries to break it to his Broad Church colleague as gently as possible that the latter has made himself a laughing stock. But allowing for such necessary politeness between partners, it could hardly be stated better or even more plainly. He curtly refers the Bishop to the responsible definition of the doctrine in Father Rickaby's book on metaphysics; and dryly observes that it will be found rather more subtle and plausible than the Bishop seems to be aware of. He also adds, with a grim candour which is rather attractive, that it is pretty disastrous to challenge Catholics about whether the Mass does them any spiritual good, since they would quite certainly unite in testifying that it does. After these frank and arresting admissions, it is a mere matter of routine, and almost of respectability, that the Dean should agree with the Bishop that all such sacramentalism is very deplorable; that the admittedly intelligent people he knows who say they have found Christ in the Mass and not in the Morning Service must be "natural idolators" and that it is "obvious" that the Blessed Sacrament has an affinity with the lower religions. Also with the lower classes. That, I fancy, is what the Dean really finds so disgusting about it.

The point is, however, that the Dean definitely snubs the Bishop on the one great point on which the newspapers have boomed and boosted him. And he does exactly the same thing, if in a lesser degree, on the second and lesser matter which was similarly boosted. I mean, of course, the matter of Evolution. The Dean, of course, believes in Evolution, as do a good many other people, Catholic and Protestant as well as agnostic. But though he believes in Evolution, he does not believe in Bishop Barnes's Evolution. He comments with admirable clarity and decision on the folly of identifying progress with evolution; or even mere complication with progress. Nothing could be better than the brief and brisk sentences in which he disposes altogether of that idealization of the scientific theory, which is in fact simply ignorance of it. In plain words, Bishop Barnes, for all his bluster, knows almost as little about Evolution as he does about Transubstantiation. The Dean of St. Paul's does not, of course, put this truth in such plain words; but he manages to make it pretty plain. His candour in this case also has to be balanced by general expressions of agreement with the Bishop, and somewhat heartier expressions of disagreement with everybody else, especially with the Bishop's enemies. The Dean alludes scornfully to the orthodox world, as if it necessarily repudiated certain biological theories; or as if it mattered very much if it did. The difference between the Broad Churchman and the Catholic Church is not that the former thinks Evolution true and the latter thinks it false. It is that the former thinks Evolution an explanation and the latter knows it is not an explanation. Hence the former thinks it all important; and the latter thinks it rather unimportant. Being unable to grasp this principle, the Dean has to fall back on quoting an old Victorian cant phrase; and saying that a new scientific discovery passes through three stages: that of being called absurd; of being called anti-scriptural; and of being discovered to be quite old and familiar. He might have added that it generally goes on to a fourth stage; that of being discovered to be quite untrue.

For that is the very simple fact which both Dean Inge and Bishop Barnes leave out; and which seems to be as utterly unknown to the more lucid rationalism of the one as to the cruder secularism of the other. Not only was the Archbishop of Canterbury right in suggesting that old gentlemen like himself had been familiar with Evolution all their lives; but he might have added that they were much more certain of it in the earlier part of their lives than they will be by the end of their lives. Those of them who have really read the most recent European inquiries and speculations know that Darwinism is every day becoming much less of a dogma and much more of a doubt. Those who have not read the speculations and the doubts simply go on repeating the dogma. While Dr. Barnes was preaching sermons carefully founded on the biology of fifty years ago, Mr. Belloc was proving conclusively before the whole world that Mr. H. G. Wells and Sir Arthur Keith were unacquainted with the biology of five years ago. In short, it is only just, as we have said, to insist on the difference between Dean Inge and Dr. Barnes; which is like the difference between Huxley and Haeckel.[100] Everybody would be better and happier if Dean Inge were known as Professor Inge; and if Dr. Barnes were not only a Professor but a Prussian Professor. Then he could be boomed along with other barbarians attacking Christianity, without having the ecclesiastical privilege of actually persecuting Christians. But there are heathens and heathens and there are persecutors and persecutors. The Dean is a pagan Roman of the Senate House. The Bishop is a pagan Teuton of the swamps and fens. The Dean dislikes the Christian tradition in the spirit of Diocletian and Julian. The Bishop dislikes it in the simpler spirit of a Danish pirate staring at the rigid mystery of a Roman-British Church. Even the common cause

---

[100] Ernst Haeckel (1834–1919) was a German scientist and champion of Darwinism against religious orthodoxy.

and broad brotherly maxim of *Christiani ad leones*[101] did not always, I fancy, reconcile the Roman and the Goth. These historical comparisons may seem fanciful; and indeed in one sense both parties are very much tied to their own historical period. They are both very Victorian; but even here there is a difference and a superiority. The superiority of the Dean is that he knows it and says so. He is man enough to boast of being Victorian and not to mind being called reactionary. Whereas the Bishop seems really to cherish the truly extraordinary notion that his notions are new and up-to-date.

Of course they have a philsophy in common; and it would be a cheap simplification to call it Materialism. Indeed, we should be almost as shallow in talking about Materialism as they are in talking about Magic. The truth is that the strange bigotry, which leads the Bishop to scream and rail at all sacramentalism as Magic, is in its inmost essence the very reverse of Materialism. Indeed it is nothing half so healthy as Materialism. The root of this prejudice is not so much a trust in matter as a sort of horror of matter. The man of this philosophy is always asking that worship shall be wholly spiritual, or even wholly intellectual; because he does really feel a disgust at the idea of spiritual things having a body and a solid form. It probably does really give him a mystical shudder to suppose that God can become as bread and wine; though I never understood why it should not give the same shudder to say that God could become flesh and blood. But whether or no these thinkers are logical in their philosophy, I think this is their philosophy. It has a very long history and an ancient name. It is not Materialist but Manichee.[102]

Indeed the Dean uttered an unconscious truth when he said the sacramentalists must be "natural idolators." He shrinks from it not only because it is idolatrous, but also because it is natural. He cannot bear to think how natural is the craving for the supernatural. He cannot tolerate the idea of it actually working through the elements of nature. Unconsciously, no doubt, but very stubbornly, that sort of intellectual does feel that our souls may belong to God, but our

[101] *Christiani ad leones* is Latin for "Christians to the lions".

[102] Manichee was Manichaeanism, a dualistic religion that originated with Mani in the third century A.D.

bodies only to the devil or the beast. That Manichean horror of matter is the only *intelligent* reason for any such sweeping refusal of supernatural and sacramental wonders. The rest is all cant and repetition and arguing in a circle; all the baseless dogmatism about science forbidding men to believe in miracles; as if *science* could forbid men to believe in something which science does not profess to investigate. Science is the study of the admitted laws of existence; it cannot prove a universal negative about whether those laws could ever be suspended by something admittedly above them. It is as if we were to say that a lawyer was so deeply learned in the American Constitution that he knew there could never be a revolution in America. Or it is as if a man were to say he was so close a student of the text of Hamlet that he was authorized to deny that an actor had dropped the skull and bolted when the theatre caught fire. The constitution follows a certain course, so long as it is there to follow it; the play follows a certain course, so long as it is being played; the visible order of nature follows a certain course if there is nothing behind it to stop it. But that fact throws no sort of light on whether there *is* anything behind it to stop it. That is a question of philosophy or metaphysics and not of material science. And out of respect for the intelligence of both these reverend gentlemen, and especially for the high intelligence of the Dean of St. Paul's, I much prefer to think that they are opposed to what they call Magic as consistent philosophers and not as inconsistent scientists. I prefer to think that they are thinking along the lines of great Gnostics[103] and Buddhists and other mystics of a dark but dignified historical tradition; rather than that they are blundering in plain logic in the interests of cheap popular science. I can even understand or imagine that thrill of repulsion that seizes them in the presence of the divine materialism of the Mass. But I still think they would be more consistent and complete, if they made it quite clear that they carried their principle to completion; and said, as the Moslem says about Christmas, "Far be it from him to have a Son," or the terrified disciples who cried, "Far be this from Thee," when God was going up to be crucified.

[103] Gnosticism, a dualistic heresy, flourished in the early Christian era.

XXIX

WHAT WE THINK ABOUT

I was looking the other day at a weekly paper of the sort that is supposed to provide popular culture; in this case rather especially what may be called popular science. In practice it largely provides what its supporters optimistically call Modern Thought and what we more commonly call Modernism. It is, however, a paper by no means unfair or exclusive of the opposite point of view; it has more than once permitted me to reply to these views; and in looking at the issue in question, my eye was arrested by my own name.

It occurred in an article on the religious doctrines of Mr. Arnold Bennett.[104] Indeed the prominence in the press of this name in this connection is one of the standing mysteries of modern journalism. I have not only a great admiration for the artistic genius, but in many ways a strong liking for the human personality of Mr. Arnold Bennett. I like his liveliness and contempt for contempt. I like his humanity and merciful curiosity about every thing human. I like that essential absence of snobbishness that enables him to sympathize even with snobs. But talking about the religious beliefs of Mr. Arnold Bennett seems to me exactly like talking about the fox-hunting adventures of Mr. Bernard Shaw or the favourite vintages of Mr. Pussyfoot Johnson or the celestial visions of Sir Arthur Keith or the monastic vows of Mr. Bertrand Russell. Mr. Arnold Bennett has never disguised, as it seems to me, the essential fact that he has not got any religious beliefs; as religious beliefs were understood in the English language as I learnt it. That he has a number of highly estimable moral sentiments and sympathies I do not for a moment doubt. But the matter of Mr. Arnold Bennett is, for the moment, a parenthesis. I mention it here merely because it was in the course of such an article that I found myself mentioned; and I confess I thought the reference a little odd. It will not surprise the reader to

[104] Arnold Bennett (1867–1931) was an English novelist, journalist and playwright.

learn that the writer found me less Modernist than Mr. Arnold Bennett. My religious beliefs did not present so pure and virgin and blameless a blank, but were defaced with definite statements about various things. But the writer professed to find something dubious or mysterious about my attitude; and what mystifies me is his mystification. He delicately implied that there was more in me than met the eye; that I had that within, which passed all these Papistical shows, but that it was hopeless to vivisect me and discover the secret. He said: "Mr. Chesterton does not mean to enlighten us; for all we know he is Modernist enough in his own thoughts."

Now it would be thought a little annoying if an atheist were to say of some harmless Protestant Christian like General Booth: "For all we know, he is atheist enough in his own thoughts." We might even venture to inquire how the atheist could possibly form any notion of what General Booth thought, in such complete contradiction to everything he said. Or I myself, on the other hand, might seem less than graceful, if I were to suggest that Mr. Arnold Bennett must be concealing his conversion out of cowardice; and were to express it in the form: "Mr. Bennett will never tell us the truth about it; for all we know he is Papist enough in his own thoughts." I might even be cross-examined about how I had come to form these suspicions about the secret thoughts of Mr. Arnold Bennett; as to whether I had hidden under his bed and heard him muttering Latin prayers in his dreams, or sent a private detective to verify the existence of his hair-shirt and his concealed relics. It might be hinted that, until I could produce some such *prima facie* case for my suspicions, it would be more polite to suppose that the opinions of Mr. Bennett were what he himself said they were. And if I were sensitive on such things, I might make a rather sharp request, that people who cannot possibly know anything about me except what I say, should for the sake of our general convenience believe what I say. On the subject of Modernism, at any rate, there has never been the least doubt or difficulty about what I say. For, as it happens, I had a strong intellectual contempt for Modernism, even before I really believed in Catholicism.

But I belong, as a biological product of evolution, to the order of the pachyderms. And I am not in the least moved by any annoyance in the matter; but only by a very strong mystification and curiosity about the real reason for this remarkable point of view. I know that the writer did not mean any harm; but I am much more interested in trying to understand what he did mean. And the truth is, I think, that there is hidden in this curious and cryptic phrase the secret of the whole modern controversy about Catholicism. What the man really meant was this: "Even poor old Chesterton must think; he can't have actually left off thinking altogether; there must be some form of cerebral function going forward to fill the empty hours of his misdirected and wasted life; and it is obvious that if a man begins to *think,* he can only think more or less in the direction of Modernism." The Modernists do really think that. That is the point. That is the joke.

Now what we have really got to hammer into the heads of all these people, somehow, is that a thinking man can think himself deeper and deeper into Catholicism, but not deeper and deeper into difficulties about Catholicism. We have got to make them see that conversion is the beginning of an active, fruitful, progressive and even adventurous life of the intellect. For *that* is the thing that they cannot at present bring themselves to believe. They honestly say to themselves: "What can he be thinking about, if he is not thinking about the Mistakes of Moses, as discovered by Mr. Miggles of Pudsey, or boldly defying all the terrors of the Inquisition which existed two hundred years ago in Spain?" We have got to explain somehow that the great mysteries like the Blessed Trinity or the Blessed Sacrament are the starting-points for trains of thought far more stimulating, subtle and even individual, compared with which all that sceptical scratching is as thin, shallow and dusty as a nasty piece of scandalmongering in a New England village. Thus, to accept the Logos as a truth is to be in the atmosphere of the absolute, not only with St. John the Evangelist, but with Plato and all the great mystics of the world. To accept the Logos as a "text" of an "Interpolation" or a "development" or a dead word in a dead document, only used to give in rapid succession about six different dates to that document, is to be altogether on a lower plane of human life; to be squabbling and scratching for a merely negative success; even if it really were a success. To exalt the

Mass is to enter into a magnificent world of metaphysical ideas, illuminating all the relations of matter and mind, of flesh and spirit, of the most impersonal abstractions as well as the most personal affections. To set out to belittle and minimize the Mass, by talking ephemeral back-chat about what it had in common with Mithras or the Mysteries, is to be in altogether a more petty and pedantic mood; not only lower than Catholicism but lower even than Mithraism.

As I have said before, it is very difficult to say how we can best set about these things. We and our critics have come to talk in two different languages; so that the very names by which we describe the things inside stand for totally different things in the absurd labels they have stuck upon the wall outside. Often if we said the great things we have to say, they would sound like the small things they accuse us of saying. A philosophical process can only begin at the right end; and they have got hold of everything by the wrong end. But I am myself disposed to think that we should begin by challenging one very common phrase or form of words; a thing that has become a catch-word and a caption; or in the ordinary popular phrase a headline. Because the journalists incessantly repeat it, and draw attention to it by repeating it, we may possibly draw attention by denying it.

When the journalist says for the thousandth time, "Living religion is not in dull and dusty dogmas, etc." we must stop him with a sort of shout and say, "There—you go wrong at the very start." If he would condescend to ask what the dogmas are, he would find out that it is precisely the dogmas that are living, that are inspiring, that are intellectually interesting. Zeal and charity and unction are admirable as flowers and fruit; but if you are really interested in the living principle you must be interested in the root or the seed. In other words, you must be intelligently interested in the statement with which the whole thing started; even if it is only to deny it. Even if the critic cannot come to agree with the Catholic, he can come to see that it is certain ideas about the cosmos that make him a Catholic. He can see that being Cosmic in that way, and Catholic in that way, is what makes him different from other people; and what makes him, at the very least, a not uninteresting figure in human history.

He will never get anywhere near it by sentimentalizing against Catholic sentiment or pontificating against Catholic pontiffs. He must get hold of the ideas as ideas; and he will find that the most interesting of all the ideas are those which the newspapers dismiss as dogmas.

For instance; the doctrine of the Dual Nature of Christ is in the most genuine sense interesting; it ought to be interesting to anybody who can understand it, long before he can believe it. It has what can be called with all reverence a sterioscopic interest; the interest of having the two eyes in the head that create an object; of having the two angles in the triangle that determine the third. The old Monophysite sect[105] declared that Christ had only the one divine nature. The new Monophysite sect declares that He has only the one human nature. But it is not a pun or a trick but a truth to say that the Monophysite is by nature monotonous. In either of his two forms, he is naturally on one note. The question of objective historical truth is another question, which I am not arguing here, though I am ready to argue it anywhere. I am talking about intellectual stimulation and the starting point of thought and imagination. And these, like all living things, breed from the conjunction of two, and not from one alone. Thus I read, with sympathy but a sympathy that hardly goes beyond sentiment, the studies of the modern Monophysites in the life of the limited and merely mortal Jesus of Nazareth. I respect their respect; I admire their admiration; I know that all they say about human greatness or religious genius is true as far as it goes. But it goes along one line; and cannot convince like the things that can converge. And then, after reading such a tribute to an ethical teacher in the manner of the Essenes,[106] perhaps I turn another page of the same or some similar book; and come upon some phrase used about a real though a pagan religion; perhaps some supposed parallel of what is called a Pagan Christ. I find it said, if only of Atys[107] or Adonis, "There was a conception that the god sacrificed himself to himself." The man who can read those words without a thrill is dead.

[105] The Monophysite sect was a heretical sect of the fifth century A.D.
[106] Essenes were members of a Jewish monastic and ascetic sect that existed in Palestine from the second century B.C. to the second century A.D.
[107] In ancient mythology, Atys was a god associated with the annual death and renewal of vegetation.

The thrill is deeper for us, of course, because it is concerned with a fact and not a fancy. In that sense we do not admit that there is any such parallel with the legends of the ancient pagans as is implied in the books of the modern pagans. And indeed we are surely entitled to call it mere common sense to say that there can be no complete parallel between what was admittedly a myth or mystery and what was admittedly a man. But the point here is that the truth hidden even in myths and mysteries is altogether lost if we are confined to the consideration of a man. In this sense there is an ironic and unconscious truth in the words of the modern pagan, who sang that "the heathen outface and outlive us," and that "our lives and our longings are twain." It is true of the modernists, but it is not true of us, who find simultaneously the realization of a longing and the record of a life. It is perfectly true that there were in many pagan myths the faint foreshadowing of the Christian mysteries; though even in saying so we admit that the foreshadowings were shadows. But, when all imaginative kinship has been explored or allowed for, it is not true that mythology ever rose to the heights of theology. It is not true that a thought so bold or so subtle as this one ever crossed the mind that created the centaurs and the fauns. In the wildest and most gigantic of the primitive epic fancies, there is no conception so colossal as the being who is both Zeus and Prometheus.

But I only advert to it here, not as arguing its truth against those who do not believe it, but only as insisting on its intense and intellectual interest for those who do believe it. I only wish to explain to those who are worried in this way, that a mind filled with the true conception of this Duality has plenty to think about along those lines and has no need to dig up dead gods to discredit the Everlasting Man. There is no necessity for me to be a Modernist in my own thoughts, or Monophysite in my own thoughts; because I think these views much duller and more trivial than my own. In the beautiful words of the love-song in *The Wallet of Kai Lung*, one of the few truly psychological love-songs of the world: "This insignificant and universally despised person would unhesitatingly prefer his thoughts to theirs."

Any number of other examples could of course be given. This person (if I may use once more the graceful Chinese locution) would very soon exhaust the excitement of discovering that Mary and Maia[108]

---

[108] Maia was the mother of Hermes in Greek mythology.

both begin with an M, or that the Mother of Christ and the Mother of Cupid[109] were both represented as women. But I know that I shall never exhaust the profundity of that unfathomable paradox which is defined so defiantly in the very title of the Mother of God. I know that there are not only far deeper, but far fresher and freer developments of thought and imagination, in that riddle of the perfectly human having once had a natural authority over the supernaturally divine, than in any sort of iconoclastic identification which assimilates all the sacred images by flattening all their faces. By the time that Christ is really made the same as Osiris, there can be very little left of either of them; but Christ, as conceived by the Catholic Church, is himself a complex and a combination, not of two unreal things, but of two real ones. In the same way an Ashtaroth[110] exactly like one of Raphael's Madonnas, or vice versa, would seem a somewhat featureless vision in any case; whereas there is something that is, in the most intellectual sense, unique about the conception of the Ηεοτοκος.[111] In short, in all this mere unification of traditions, true or false, there is something that may be quite simply described as dull. But the dogmas are not dull. Even what are called the fine doctrinal distinctions are not dull. They are like the finest operations of surgery; separating nerve from nerve, but giving life. It is easy enough to flatten out everything for miles round with dynamite, if our only object is to give death. But just as the physiologist is dealing with living tissues, so the theologian is dealing with living ideas; and if he draws a line between them it is naturally a very fine line. It is the custom, though by this time already a rather stale custom, to complain that the Greeks or Italians who disputed about the Trinity or the Sacrament were splitting hairs. I do not know that even splitting hairs is any drearier than bleaching hairs, in the vain attempt to match the golden hair of Freya[112] and the black hair of Cotytto.[113] The subdivision of a hair does at least tell us something of its

---

[109] The mother of Cupid was Venus in Roman mythology.

[110] In ancient Near Eastern mythology, Ashtaroth was a goddess of love and fertility.

[111] *Theotokos* is Greek for "God-bearer".

[112] Freya was the Norse goddess of love and beauty.

[113] Cotytto was a Greek fertility goddess.

structure; whereas its mere discoloration tells us nothing at all. Theology does introduce us to the structure of ideas; whereas theosophical syncretism merely washes all the colours out of the coloured fairy-tales of the world. But my only purpose in this place is to reassure the kind gentleman who was troubled about the secret malady of modernity that must be eating away my otherwise empty mind. I hasten earnestly to explain that I am quite well, thank you; and that I have plenty of things to think about without falling back on a Baconian madness of pagan parallels, or establishing the connection between the tale of the bull killed by Mithras and the tune the old cow died of.

XXX

THE OPTIMIST AS A SUICIDE

Freethinkers are occasionally thoughtful, though never free. In the modern world of the West, at any rate, they seem always to be tied to the treadmill of a materialist and monist cosmos. The universal sceptic, in Asia or in Antiquity, has probably been a bolder thinker, though very probably a more unhappy man. But what we have to deal with as scepticism is not scepticism; but a fixed faith in monism. The freethinker is not free to question monism. He is forbidden, for instance, in the only intelligible modern sense, to believe in a miracle. He is forbidden, in exactly the same sense in which he would say that we are forbidden to believe in a heresy. Both are forbidden by first principles and not by force. The Rationalist Press Association will not actually kidnap, gag or strangle Sir Arthur Keith if he admits the evidence for a cure at Lourdes. Neither will the Cardinal Archbishop of Westminster have me hanged, drawn and quartered if I announce that I am an agnostic tomorrow. But of both cases it is true to say that a man cannot root up his first principles without a terrible rending and revolutionizing of his very self. As a matter of fact, we are the freer of the two; as there is scarcely any evidence, natural or preternatural, that cannot be accepted as fitting into our system somewhere; whereas the materialist cannot fit the most minute miracle into his system anywhere. But let us leave that on one side as a separate question; and agree, if only for the sake of argument, that both the Catholic and the materialist are limited only by their fundamental conviction about the cosmic system; in both thought is in that sense forbidden and in that sense free. Consequently, when I see in some newspaper symposium, like that on Spiritualism, a leading materialist like Mr. John M. Robertson[114] discussing the evidence for Spiritualism, I feel exactly as I imagine him to feel when he hears a bishop in a mitre or a Jesuit in a cassock

[114] John Mackinnon Robertson (1856–1933) was a radical freethinker, politician and author of two histories of free thought.

discussing the evidence for materialism. I know that Mr. Roberston cannot accept the evidence without becoming somebody quite different from Mr. Roberston; which also is within the power of the grace of God. But I know quite well he is not a freethinker; except in the sense in which I am a freethinker. He has long ago come to a conclusion which controls all his other conclusions. He is not driven by scientific evidence to accept Materialism. He is forbidden by Materialism to accept scientific evidence.

But there is another way in which the freethinker is not only thoughtful, but useful. The man who rejects the Faith altogether is often very valuable as a critic of the man who rejects it piecemeal, or bit by bit, or by fits and starts. The man who picks out some part of Catholicism that happens to please him, or throws away some part that happens to puzzle him, does in fact produce, not only the queerest sort of result, but generally the very opposite result to what he intends. And his inconsistency can often be effectively exposed from the extreme negative as well as the extreme positive point of view. It has been said that when the half-gods go, the gods arrive; it might be said in amiable parody that when the no-goddites arrive, the half-goddites go; and I am not sure it is not a good riddance. Anyhow, even the atheist can illustrate how important it is to keep the Catholic system altogether, even if he rejects it altogether.

A curious and amusing instance comes from America; in connection with Mr. Clarence Darrow, the somewhat simple-minded sceptic of that land of simplicity. He seems to have been writing something about the impossibility of anybody having a soul; of which nothing need be said except that (as usual) it seems to be the sceptic who really thinks of the soul superstitiously, as a separate and secret animal with wings; who considers the soul quite apart from the self. But what interests me about him at the moment is this. One of his arguments against immortality is that people do not really believe in it. And one of his arguments for that is that if they did believe in certain happiness beyond the grave, they would all kill themselves. He says that nobody would endure the martyrdom of cancer, for instance, if he really believed (as he apparently assumes all Christians to believe) that in any case the mere fact of death would instantly introduce the soul to perfect felicity and the society of all its best friends. A Catholic will certainly know what answer he has to give. But Mr. Clarence Darrow does not really in the least know what question he has asked.

Now there we have the final flower and crown of all modern optimism and universalism and humanitarianism in religion. Sentimentalists talk about love till the world is sick of the most glorious of all human words; they assume that there can be nothing in the next world except the sort of Utopia of practical pleasure which they promise us (but do not give us) in this world. They declare that all will be forgiven, because there is nothing to forgive. They insist that "passing over" is only like going into the next room, they insist that it will not even be a waiting-room. They declare that it must immediately introduce us to a cushioned lounge with all conceivable comforts, without any reference to how we have got there. They are positive that there is no danger, no devil; even no death. All is hope, happiness and optimism. And, as the atheist very truly points out, the logical result of all that hope, happiness and optimism would be hundreds of people hanging from lamp-posts or thousands of people throwing themselves into wells or canals. We should find the rational result of the modern Religion of Joy and Love in one huge human stampede of suicide. Pessimism would have killed its thousands, but optimism its ten thousands.

Now, of course, as I say, a Catholic knows the answer; because he holds the complete philosophy which keeps a man sane; and not some single fragment of it, whether sad or glad, which may easily drive him mad. A Catholic does not kill himself because he does not take it for granted that he will deserve heaven in any case, or that it will not matter at all whether he deserves it at all. He does not profess to know exactly what danger he would run; but he does know what loyalty he would violate and what command or condition he would disregard. He actually thinks that a man might be fitter for heaven because he endured like a man; and that a hero could be a martyr to cancer as St. Lawrence or St. Cecilia were martyrs to cauldrons or gridirons. The faith in a future life, the hope of a future happiness, the belief that God is Love and that loyalty is eternal life, these things do not produce lunacy and anarchy, *if* they are taken along with the other Catholic doctrines about duty and vigilance and watchfulness against the powers of hell. They might produce lunacy and anarchy, if they were taken alone. And the Modernists, that is, the optimists and the sentimentalists, did want us to take them alone. Of course, the same would be true, if somebody took the other doctrines of duty and discipline alone. It would produce another dark age of Puritans rapidly blackening into Pessimists. Indeed, the extremes meet, when they are both ends clipped off what should be a complete thing. Our parable ends poetically with two gibbets side by side; one for the suicidal pessimist and the other for the suicidal opitimist.

The point is that in this passage the American sceptic is answering the Modernist; but he is not answering the Catholic. The Catholic has an extremely simple and sensible reason for not cutting his throat in order to fly instantly into Paradise. But he might really raise a question for those who talk as if Paradise were invariably and instantly populated with people who had cut their throats. And this is only one example out of a long list of historical examples; in which those who tried to make the Faith more simple invariably made it less sane. The Moslems imagined that they were merely being sensible when they cut down the creed to a mere belief in one God; but in the world of practical psychology they really cut it down to one Fate. The actual effect on ordinary men was simply fatalism; like that of the Turk who will not take his wound to a hospital because he is resigned to Kismet or the will of Allah. The Puritans thought they were simplifying things by appealing to what they called the plain words of Scripture; but as a fact they were complicating things by bringing in half a hundred cranky sects and crazy suggestions. And the modern universalist and humanitarian thought they were simplifying things when they interpreted the great truth that God is Love, as meaning that there can be no war with the demons or no danger to the soul. But in fact they were inventing even darker riddles with even wilder answers; and Mr. Clarence Darrow has suggested one of them. He will be gratified to receive the thanks of all Catholics for doing so.

XXXI

THE OUTLINE OF THE FALL

I have remarked on the curious rearguard action of bluff that is being fought to cover the retreat of the Darwinians. An example of the same thing has appeared in connection with a much more famous name; indeed, with two famous names. Mr. H. G. Wells has replied to Mr. Belloc, who wrote a criticism of the "Outline of History," chiefly to protest against a certain tone of arbitrary generalization and sham knowledge of the unknown. A typical case was that in which Mr. Wells said of the men who drew reindeers in caves: "There seems no scope in such a life for speculation or philosophy," and Mr. Belloc not unnaturally answered: "Why on earth not?" But the details of the various works in question do not concern me immediately here; they mostly depend on that habit of talking as if every cave-drawing had its date obligingly inscribed on it; or any stone hatchet might bear the inscription 400,000 B.C. or possible, B.O.H., or Before the Outline of History. At the moment the only point of contact is that which affects continuation of our previous criticism, touching the present state of Darwinism. And what strikes me is that even Mr. Wells, often a sufficiently warm controversialist, is relatively and really cold in the matter; and his defence of Darwin is much more of an apology than an apologia. Indeed, like so many other modern apologies, it almost amounts to pleading that Darwin was not a Darwinian.

The Victorian evolutionists devoted themselves to declaring how great Darwin's thesis was. The new evolutionists seem to devote themselves to explaining how small it was. They really seem to plead, as in the old anecdote, that it gave birth to a theory, but a very little one. Some of Mr. Wells's words may surely, without unfairness, be called apologetic. He does not, like the professor previously mentioned, try to get over the word "origin" by talking about "the cause of the origin." So he concentrates on the word "species," as if evolution had not only applied to a sub-division. He

adds that Darwin did not at the beginning even apply it to man. What
in the world would the Victorian Darwinians have said had they heard
it urged in defence of Darwinism that it was not applied to man? Are
we to understand that only the first book of Darwin is divinely inspired? Again, Mr. Wells says that natural selection is common sense.
And doubtless, if it only means that things fitted for survival do survive, it is common sense. We may also add that it is common knowledge. Has it come to this, that Darwin is defended because he only
discovered what was common knowledge? The real question, of
course, is that stated by Mr. Belloc; when he said that nobody needs
to be told that in a flood fish live and cattle die. The question is, How
soon do cattle turn into fish? That would be an example of the true
Darwinian theory; and it is now merely minimized, represented as only
one element of evolution and without even the elements of an explanation. We fancy there is a healthy prejudice behind it all. Mr. Wells
indignantly repudiates the slander uttered by Mr. Belloc, who called
him a patriot. But it is true; the deep English national pride has
much to do with this devotion. And rather than deprive England of
her Darwin, they have deprived Darwin of his discovery.

When a man is as great a genius as Mr. Wells, I admit it sounds
provocative to call him provincial. But if he wants to know why
anybody does it, it will be enough to point silently to the headline of
one of his pages, which runs: "Where is the Garden of Eden?" To
come down to a thing like that, and to think it telling, when talking
to an intelligent Catholic about the Fall, that *is* provinciality; proud
and priceless provinciality. The French peasants of whom Mr. Wells
speaks are not in that sense provincial. As Mr. Wells says, they do
not know anything about Darwin and Evolution. They do not
know and they do not care. That is where they are much better philosophers than Mr. Wells. They hold the philosophy of the Fall, in
the form of a simple story which may be historic or symbolic, but
anyhow cannot be more important than what it symbolizes. In comparison with that truth, it does not matter twopence whether any
evolutionary theory is true or not. Whether or no the garden was an
allegory, the truth itself can be very well allegorized as a garden.
And the point of it is that Man, whatever else he is, is certainly *not*

merely one of the plants of the garden that has plucked its roots out of the soil and walked about with them like legs, or on the principle of a double dahlia has grown duplicate eyes and ears. He is something else, something strange and solitary; and more like the statue that was once the god of the garden; but the statue has fallen from its pedestal and lies broken among the plants and weeds. This conception has nothing to do with materialism as it refers to materials. The image might be made of wood; the wood might have come from the garden; the sculptor presumably might, and probably did, allow for the growth and grain of the wood in what he carved and expressed. But my fable fixes the two truths of the true scripture. The first is that the wood was graven or stamped with an image, deliberately, and from the outside; in this case the image of God. The second is that this image has been damaged and defaced, so that it is now both better and worse than the mere plants in the garden, which are perfect according to their own plan. There is room for any amount of speculation about the history of the tree before it was turned into an image; there is room for any amount of doubt and mystery about what really happened when it was turned into an image; there is room for any amount of hope and imagination about what it will look like when it is really mended and made into the perfect statue we have never seen. But it has the two fixed points, that man was uplifted at the first and fell; and to answer it by saying, "Where is the Garden of Eden?" is like answering a philosophical Buddhist by saying, "When were you last a donkey?"

The Fall is a view of life. It is not only the only enlightening, but the only encouraging view of life. It holds, as against the only real alternative philosophies, those of the Buddhist or the Pessimist or the Promethean, that we have misused a good world, and not merely been entrapped into a bad one. It refers evil back to the wrong use of the will, and thus declares that it can eventually be righted by the right use of the will. Every other creed except that one is some form of surrender to fate. A man who holds this view of life will find it giving light on a thousand things; on which mere evolutionary ethics have not a word to say. For instance, on the colossal contrast between the completeness of man's machines and the continued corruption of his motives; on the fact that no social progress really seems to leave self behind; on the fact that the first and not the last men of any school or revolution are generally the best and purest; as William Penn was better than a Quaker millionaire or Washington better than an American oil magnate; on that proverb that says: "The price of liberty is eternal vigilance,"[115] which is only what the theologians say of every other virtue, and is itself only a way of stating the truth of original sin; on those extremes of good and evil by which man exceeds all the animals by the measure of heaven and hell; on that sublime sense of loss that is in the very sound of all great poetry, and nowhere more than in the poetry of pagans and sceptics: "We look before and after, and pine for what is not";[116] which cries against all prigs and progressives out of the very depths and abysses of the broken heart of man, that happiness is not only a hope, but also in some strange manner a memory; and that we are all kings in exile.

Now to people who feel that this view of life is more real, more radical, more universal than the cheap simplifications opposed to it, it comes with quite a shock of bathos to realize that anybody let alone a man like Mr. Wells, supposes that it all depends on some detail about the site of a garden in Mesopotamia, like that identified by General Gordon. It is hard to find any parallel to such an incongruity; for there is no real similarity between our muddled mortal affairs and events that were divine if they were mysterious, and scriptures that are sacred even if they are symbolical. But some shadow of a comparison could be made out of the modern myths. I mean the sort of myths that men like Mr. Wells generally do believe in; such as the Myth of Magna Carta or the Myth of the Mayflower. Now many historians will maintain that Magna Carta was really nothing to speak of; that it was largely a piece of feudal privilege. But suppose one of the historians who holds this view began to argue with us excitedly about the fabulous nature of our ordinary fancy picture of Magna Carta. Suppose he produced maps and documents to prove that Magna Carta was not signed at Runnymede,

[115] This quotation is from a speech delivered in 1790 by John Philpot Curran (1750–1817), Irish lawyer, orator and patriot.

[116] The quotation is from Shelley's "To a Skylark".

but somewhere else; as I believe some scholars do maintain. Suppose he criticized the false heraldry and fancy-dress costumes of the ordinary sort of waxwork historical picture of the event. We should think he was rather unduly excited about a detail of mediaeval history. But with what a shock of astonishment should we realize at last that the man actually thought that all modern attempts at democracy must be abandoned, that all representative government must be wrong, that all Parliaments would have to be dissolved and all political rights destroyed, if once it were admitted that King John did not sign that special document in that little island in the Thames! What should we think of him, if he really thought we had no reasons for liking law or liberty, except the authenticity of that beloved royal signature? That is very much how I feel when I find that Mr. Wells really imagines that the luminous and profound philosophy of the Fall only means that Eden was somewhere in Mesopotamia. Now the only explanation of a great man like Mr. Wells having a small prejudice, like this about the snake, is that he does come of a religious tradition that regarded the text of Hebrew Scripture as the only authority and had forgotten all about the great mediaeval metaphysic and the discussion of fundamental ideas.

The man who does that is provincial; and there is no harm in saying so even when he is one of the greatest men of letters and a glory to the English name.

XXXII

THE IDOLS OF SCOTLAND

The thing that strikes me most in current controversy is that our opponents are talking almost entirely in terms of the past, and that an entirely dead past; whereas we are making some sort of attempt, whether it be considered impertinent or eccentric or meddlesome or paradoxical, to deal with the practical conditions of the present. An amusing comedy on these lines seems to have arisen on the subject of Scottish Nationalism or the notion of Home Rule for North Britain. A worthy Presbyterian has warned his fellow countrymen that the movement is tainted by the presence of Roman Catholics, and especially by that of Mr. Compton Mackenzie;[117] and that no little degree of the deadly peril is indicated by the fact that Mr. Cunninghame Grahame[118] is interested in a book by Mr. Belloc; in which the hideous sentiment is uttered that the Reformation was the shipwreck of Christendom. Personally I should have thought it was obvious to anybody on any side, in one solid and objective sense, that it was the shipwreck of Christendom. I should imagine that it would be obvious to anybody, for instance, who desires or even discusses the Reunion of Christendom. There certainly was a united vessel or vehicle and it certainly did break up into different parts. Some people may think the ship was a rotten old-fashioned three-decker that was bound to break up; and that the people were lucky who got away from it in boats. But it is certain that it did break up and that the boats were not the same as the original ship. A man might as well resent our saying that the rise of the feudal kingdoms and the modern nationalities was part of the decline and fall of the Roman Empire. This is only one of the marks of such bigotry; but it is worth noting at the outset. One of the peculiarities of this sort of

[117] Compton Mackenzie (1883–1972) was an English novelist best known for *Sinister Street*.

[118] Robert Cunninghame Graham (1852–1936) was a Scottish travel writer famed for his books on Latin America. Chesterton mistakenly adds an "e" to the last name.

bigot is that he cannot distinguish between provocative statements and plain inevitable statements. If I say that the Reformation was a relapse into barbarism, a return to all that was worst in the Dark Ages without anything of what was best in them, an idolatry of dead Hebrew documents full of visions and symbols without any Daniel to interpret the dreams, a stampede of brutal luxury and pride with a vulgar howl of hot-gospelling for an excuse, a riot of thieves and looters with a few foaming and gibbering lunatics carried in front of it like live mascots for luck; the return of the Manichee, the dirty ape of the ascetic, conspiring with the devil to destroy the world — if I were to say all this I should think that these remarks about Protestantism certainly had a slightly provocative flavour. But if I were to say, with Mr. Belloc, that Protestantism was the shipwreck of Christendom, I should regard it as an ordinary historical statement, like saying that the American War of Independence was a split in the British Empire. The bigot cannot see the difference between these two types of statement, whether made by us or by himself.

The next interesting thing to note about the protest is that the Protestant goes on to say that Mr. Compton Mackenzie and his friends are going to ruin Scotland by removing the stern teaching of John Knox, which has apparently created the Scottish character. This seems a little hard on the Scottish character. I cannot quite bring myself to believe that the character of Scott or of Stevenson, the character of Burns or Barrie,[119] are exact and unaltered reproductions of the stern teaching of John Knox. But before we come to any such comparisons, it is worth remarking, on the face of the thing that a rather more living world, a life more in touch with modern conditions, a grasp of the actual problems of the present and the immediate future, is rather more indicated by saying the words "Compton Mackenzie" than by saying the words "John Knox." Many very modern young men have recently joined the same religion as Mr. Compton Mackenzie. No such modern young men, that I ever heard of, have ever exhibited the smallest desire to go back to the religion of John Knox. As a matter of plain fact, there is hardly one modern Scotsman in a thousand who has the smallest sympathy with the real

---

[119] James Barrie (1860–1937) was the Scottish author of *Peter Pan*.

religion of John Knox. He may vaguely respect John Knox as a Scottish hero, on the supposition (quite startlingly false) that he was a Scottish patriot. As a matter of fact, the patriotic party in Scotland was the wicked Papistical party; Knox and his Presbyterians were all for helping the pressure of England and Elizabeth. They would have justified themselves by saying that they had the one, true and only right religion. The question is, who is left even in Scotland who believes that it was the one, true and only right religion? I repeat, about one in a thousand; perhaps only a few splendidly fanatical old Wee Frees[120] in the Highlands. Anybody who knows anything of the Scottish Presbyterian Churches, during the last fifty years, knows that the prevailing doctrine taught in them has *not* been the severe Calvinism of the eighteenth and seventeenth centuries, still less the wild Calvinism of the sixteenth. It has been a mild hash of Hegelian philosophy and Higher Criticism, all borrowed from Germany and carefully learnt by Scotch students in German Universities. And anybody who has noticed what the modern Scottish character is really like, knows that it does not by this time (thank heaven) bear the smallest resemblance to the sternness of John Knox. It is rather sentimental than otherwise, though its sentiment finds expression in more than one brilliant and admirable man of genius. Modern Scotland is not even remotely represented by John Knox. It is represented much more accurately, and much more honourably, by Sir Harry Lauder[121] and Sir James Barrie.

This dull habit of invoking dead things, in a world in which we are surrounded by more and more interesting living things, is the second mark of the sort of bigot I am describing. It would be an extremely interesting business to write a real, respectful and sympathetic history of the remarkable episode of Scottish Puritanism; insisting on its integrity and its intellectual vigour while it lasted. But any sincere study of it must conclude with the statement that it did not last. One of the most brilliant and distinguished of Scottish professors, at Edinburgh University, himself of an origin wholly Puritan and of sympathies

[120] Wee Frees was a group within the Free Church of Scotland that rejected the merger in 1900 that joined their church with the United Presbyterian Church.
[121] Harry Lauder (1870–1950) was a Scottish balladeer.

the very reverse of Catholic, used to me the true and forcible expression about the old Scottish Sabbatarianism, "It covered all Scotland; and then one morning, it had suddenly vanished everywhere like the snow." And though the story might be told truly from either standpoint, or from many others, it is but natural that we should draw our own moral from it. And the moral is, of course, one which we find running through the whole of our history.

The birth and death of every heresy has been essentially the same. A morbid or unbalanced Catholic takes one idea out of the thousandfold throng of Catholic ideas; and announces that he cares for that Catholic idea more than for Catholicism. He takes it away with him into a wilderness, where the idea becomes an image and the image an idol. Then, after a century or two, he suddenly wakes up and discovers that the idol is an idol; and, shortly after that, that the wilderness is a wilderness. If he is a wise man, he calls himself a fool. If he is a fool, he calls himself an evolutionary progressive who has outgrown the worship of idols; and he looks round him at the wilderness, spreading bare and desolate on every side and says, in the beautiful words of Mr. H. G. Wells: "I see no limit to it at all."

That is what happened to the Calvinistic Scotsman; and the chief comfort in the prospect is that the Scotsman is not generally a fool, even when he has ceased to be a Calvinist. But he very often becomes an atheist; and the fact that so many of the hard destructive sceptics, from Hume downwards, came from Scotland, was the early and significant evidence of the discovery of the idol and the wilderness. But in any case, that is the compact parable of what occurred. The Calvinist was a Catholic whose imagination had been in some way caught and overpowered by the one isolated theological truth of the power and knowledge of God; and he offered to it human sacrifice, not only of every human sentiment, but of every other divine quality. Something in that bare idea of all-seeing, all-searching and pitiless power intoxicated and exalted certain men for a certain period, as certain men are intoxicated by a storm of wind or some terrible stage tragedy. The more moderate Protestants, the Anglicans and to a large extent the Lutherans, had something of the same queer feeling about the King. Hence came the Cavalier doctrine of Divine Right—and the court chaplains of Prussia. Nothing is more intriguing and challenging to the imagination than the necessity of trying to understand how men in the sixteenth and early seventeenth centuries felt a sort of abstract altruistic joy in the mere might and triumph of the Prince; in the mere autocracy of the earthly ruler. The Calvinists, to do them justice, felt it only about the heavenly ruler. In that sense the Scots can look proudly back on their Calvinism. But they cannot look proudly forward to Calvinism. They really know, as well as anybody else, that this isolated religious idea can no longer be kept separate from all the other religious ideas to which it belongs. The Calvinism of the Puritan is as dead as the Divine Right of the Cavaliers; men can no longer worship the idol, whether it is Presbyterianism or Erastianism.[122] They can only worship the wilderness; which is atheism—or, as the more polite say, pantheism.

Whether it be called a Catholic tendency or no, all the movements of all the sects of late have been in the direction of trying to put together again those separate pieces that were pulled apart in the sixteenth century. The main feature of our time has been the fact that one person after another has recovered one piece after another, and added it to the new scheme by borrowing it from the old. There is one sufficient proof that there has indeed been a shipwreck. And that is that Robinson Crusoe has, ever since, been continually going back to get things from the wreck.

[122] Erastianism called for state supremacy over the church in ecclesiastical affairs, as in England.

XXXIII

IF THEY HAD BELIEVED

One of the things our enemies do not know is the real case for their own side. It is always for me a great matter of pride that the proudest, the most genuine and the most unanswerable boast, that the Protestants of England could ever make, was made for them by a Catholic. Very few of the Protestants, of his time at any rate, would have had the historical enlargement or enlightenment to make it. For it was said by Newman, when that great master of English was surveying the glorious triumphs of our tongue from Bacon and Milton, to Swift and Burke, and he reminded us firmly that, though we convert England to the true faith a thousand times over, "English literature will always *have been* Protestant."

That generous piece of candour might well be represented as even too generous; but I think it is very wise for us to be too generous. It is not entirely, or at least not exclusively true. The name of Chaucer is alone enough to show that English literature was English a long time before it was Protestant. Even a Protestant, if he were also English, could ask for nobody more entirely English than Chaucer. He was, in the essential national temper, very much more English than Milton. As a matter of fact, the argument is no stronger for Chaucer than it is for Shakspere. But in the case of Shakspere the argument is long and complicated, as conducted by partisans; though sufficiently simple and direct for people with a sense of reality. I believe that recent discoveries, as recorded in a book by a French lady, have very strongly confirmed the theory that Shakspere died a Catholic. But I need no books and no discoveries to prove to me that he had lived a Catholic, or more probably, like the rest of us, tried unsuccessfully to live a Catholic; that he thought like a Catholic and felt like a Cathlolic and saw every question as a Catholic sees it. The proofs of this would be matter for a separate essay; if indeed so practical an impression can be proved at all. It is quite self-evident to me that he was a certain real and recognizable

Renaissance type of Catholic; like Cervantes; like Ronsard.[123] But if I were asked offhand for a short explanation, I could only say that I know he was a Catholic from the passages which are now used to prove he was an agnostic.

But that is another and much more subtle question, which is not the question I proposed to myself in starting this essay. In starting it, I proposed to grant the whole sound and solid truth of Newman's admission; that there has indeed arisen out of the disunion of Europe a great and glorious English Protestant literature; and to make some further speculations upon the point. And I think that nothing could make clearer to the modern English, the one supreme thing that they don't know (which is what our religion really is and why we think it real) than to put this rather interesting historical question. What difference would it have made to the great masters of English literature, if they had been Catholics?

Of course, the question cannot be strictly and scientifically answered; because nobody knows what difference would be made to anybody by any change in the circumstances of his life. But taking the matter broadly, as a question of ideas or even of doctrines it is worth asking as a matter of religious history. How far did the great Protestant writers depend on Protestantism?

I have no intention of discussing it adequately here; and indeed this is not so much an essay as an essay to suggest an essay. It is, in fact, a delicate indication, to people more learned than myself, that I am in possession of a very good title and subject for an essay. But at least it will be safe to say that the common or conventional impression among English people on this point is wildly wrong. It is wrong because it imagines that purely Protestant ideas were in some vague way the same as liberal and emancipated ideas. And it is wrong in a more special sense, because it is founded on the utterly false history, which supposes that the Renaissance was the same as the Reformation. It would be very difficult to say what English literature owes to the Reformation as distinct from the Renaissance. There is the splendid sincerity that inspired the plain English of Bunyan;

[123] Pierre de Ronsard (1524–85) was a French lyric poet.

but even Bunyan was a sort of exception that proved the rule. He was a Puritan; but he was emphatically not a Puritan of the Puritans. He was a man actually suspected by his fellow Puritans, because he was not so much a Puritan as a Christian. It was remarked at the time, and it has often been remarked since, that his theory is not very sectarian by the standard of seventeenth century sects. Among the Calvinists he was so much of a moderate, that thousands must have read his great book without thinking about Calvinism at all. And if we take the great scenes in his great book, the battle with Apollyon, the Mission of Greatheart, the death of Valiant-for-the-Truth, when all the trumpets sounded on the other side — there is really no reason whatever why they should not have been written by a Catholic. I do not affirm that they *would* have been written by a Catholic, if the course of history had left the common people Catholics; for that is a question which nobody can possibly answer one way or the other. But I am speaking strictly of doctrines in their relation to ideas and images; and there is no possible reason why a Catholic should be prevented by his Catholicism from writing such a story of the pilgrimage of Man and the fight to attain to God.

Milton in one way is an even stronger case; since he had much more in him of Shakspere and the Catholic Renaissance. And I really cannot think of any deep difference that it would have made to his poetry, as poetry, if he had followed other members of his family in the old faith; I do not see that he need have been much altered, except possibly by being a much jollier man. Many will not realize this, because they insist on regarding artistic and intellectual freedom as something that was closed to the Catholic countries and open only to the Protestant. But all history is in flat contradiction to this view. The tide of culture in the seventeenth century flowed from France to England, not from England to France. Milton might have been as central as Molière and still remained a Catholic man in a Catholic atmosphere. Descartes the Catholic was more truly than Bacon the Protestant, the *philosopher* of rationalist science. The experiments, the new forms, the great names in criticism and philosophy, appeared during the last two or three centuries quite as much in the Catholic countries as in the Protestant, if not rather more.

England could have produced a great English literature, as France produced a great French literature, without any change in the ancient European religion.

The real test case, to be considered in some such essay, would be a case like that of Cowper.[124] There you do most emphatically have the Protestant theology; and there you do most emphatically have the English poetry. But the two have precious little to do with each other; until the coming of that dark hour when the theology destroyed the poetry. Poor Cowper's Calvinism drove him mad; and only his poetry managed for some time to keep him sane. But there was nothing whatever either in the poetry or the sanity that could have prevented him from being a Catholic. On the contrary, he was exactly the sort of man who would have been very happy as a Catholic. He was the sort of man to have been devoted to the memory of St. Francis, if he had ever heard of him; and there was nothing to prevent the one any more than the other from keeping pet birds or stroking wild hares out of the woods. It was the brutal blow of Calvin, two centuries before, that broke the heart of that natural saint; and it is not the least of his crimes.

After the time of Cowper, there does indeed begin to appear another type of difficulty; but it is not the presence but rather the absence of Protestant theology. There were elements even in Burns and Byron, there were still more elements in Shelley and Swinburne, which would doubtless have been at issue with their Catholic tradition, if they had had it. But it would not have been a revolt against Catholicism half so much as it was a revolt against Protestantism. In so far as they tended to mere scepticism, they could have found their way to it more quickly from reading Rabelais and Montaigne in a Catholic country than from reading Shakspere and Milton in a Protestant one. As soon as the Revolution has begun, in a sense as soon as the Romantic Movement has begun, the positive Puritan theology is left behind even more completely than the mediaeval theology. Indeed the Romantics did develop a faint and hazy sympathy, if not with mediaeval theology, at least with mediaeval religion. It is true that

[124] William Cowper (1731–1800) was an English poet whose best-known serious poem is *The Task* (1785). He also wrote many hymns.

Byron or Hugo probably preferred an abbey to be a ruined abbey; but they would not have visited a Baptist chapel even for the pleasure of seeing it ruined. It is true that Scott advised us to see mediaeval Melrose[125] by moonlight; with the delicate implication that the mediaeval religion was moonshine. But he would not in any case have wanted to see Exeter Hall[126] by gaslight; and he would have thought its theology not moonshine but gas. The tributes which he occasionally forces himself to make to the official Puritanism of his own country are, it will be generally agreed, the most sullen and insincere words to be found in his works. On the negative side, therefore, the conclusion is altogether negative. It is very difficult to find, at least after the doubtful case of Bunyan and the deadly case of Cowper, anything that can be called a purely literary inspiration coming from the purely Protestant doctrines. There is plenty of inspiration coming more or less indirectly from Paganism; but after the first excitement, hardly any from Protestantism.

If this is true on the negative side, it is even truer on the positive side. I take it that the imaginative magnificence of Milton's epic, in such matters as the War in Heaven, would have been much more convincing, if it had been modelled more on the profound mediaeval mysteries about the nature of angels and archangels, and less on the merely fanciful Greek myths about giants and gods. *Paradise Lost* is an immortal poem; but it has just failed to be an immortal religious poem. Those are most happy in reading Milton who can read him as they would read Hesiod. It is doubtful whether those seeking spiritual satisfaction now read him even as naturally as they would read Crashaw.[127] I suppose nobody will dispute that the pageantry of Scott might have taken on a tenfold splendour if he could have understood the emblems of an everlasting faith as sympathetically as he did the emblems of a dead feudalism. For him it was the habit that made

[125] Melrose Abbey appears in Sir Walter Scott's poem *The Lay of the Last Minstrel* (1805).

[126] Exeter Hall was a meeting and concert hall that opened in London in 1831. It became the headquarters of the Young Men's Christian Association, from which the name derived its Evangelical connotations.

[127] Richard Crashaw (c. 1612–49) was an English poet and convert to Catholicism.

the monk; but the habit would have been quite as picturesque if there had been a real monk inside it; let alone a real mind inside the monk, like the mind of St. Dominic or St. Hugh of Lincoln.[128] "English literature will always have been Protestant"; but it might have been Catholic; without ceasing to be English literature, and perhaps succeeding in producing a deeper literature and a happier England.

[128] St. Hugh of Lincoln (1140–1200) was a Carthusian monk who became bishop of Lincoln. He was known especially for his defense of the poor and the Jews.

XXXIV

PEACE AND THE PAPACY

There is a famous saying which to some has seemed lacking in reverence, though in fact it is a support of one important part of religion: "If God had not existed, it would have been necessary to invent Him." It is not at all unlike some of the daring questions with which St. Thomas Aquinas begins his great defence of the faith. Some of the modern critics of his faith, especially the Protestant critics of it, have fallen into an amusing error, chiefly through ignorance of Latin and of the old use of the word *divus,* and have accused Catholics of describing the Pope as God. Catholics, I need not say, are about as likely to call the Pope God as to call a grasshopper the Pope. But there is a sense in which they do recognize an eternal correspondence between the position of the King of Kings in the universe and of his Viceroy in the world, like the correspondence between a real thing and its shadow; a similarity something like the damaged and defective similarity between God and the image of God. And among the coincidences of this comparison may be classed the case of this epigram. The world will more and more find itself in a position in which even politicians and practical men will find themselves saying, "If the Pope had not existed, it would be necessary to invent him."

It is not at all impossible that they may really try to invent him. The truth is that multitudes of them would already accept the Pope if he were not called the Pope. I firmly believe that it would be quite possible, in this and many other matters, to play a sort of pious practical joke on large numbers of heretics and heathens. I fancy it would be quite feasible to describe in accurate but abstract terms the general idea of an office or obligation, which would exactly correspond to the position of the Papacy in history, and which would be accepted on ethical and social ground by numbers of Protestants and free-thinkers; until they discovered with a reaction of rage and astonishment that they had been entrapped into accepting the international arbitration of the Pope. Suppose somebody were to advance the old idea as if it were a new idea; suppose he were to say: "I propose that there be erected in some central city in the more civilized part of our civilization the seat of a permanent official to represent peace and the basis of agreement among all the surrounding nations; let him be by the nature of his post set apart from them all and yet sworn to consider the rights and wrongs of all; let him be put there as a judge to expound an ethical law and system of social relations; let him be of a certain type and training different from that which encourages the ordinary ambitions of military glory or even the ordinary attachments of tribal tradition; let him be protected by a special sentiment from the pressure of kings and princes; let him be sworn in a special manner to the consideration of men as men." There are not a few already, and there will soon be many more, who would be perfectly capable of proposing such an ideal international institution on their own account; there are also many who would really, in their innocence, suppose that it had never been attempted before.

It is true that as yet large numbers of such social reformers would shrink from the idea of the institution being an individual. But even that prejudice is weakening under the wear and tear of real political experience. We may be attached, as many of us are, to the democratic ideal; but most of us have already realized that direct democracy, the only true democracy which satisfies a true democrat, is a thing applicable to some things and not others; and not at all to a question such as this. The actual speaking voice of a vast international civilization, or of a vast international religion, will not in any case be the actual articulate distinguishable voices or cries of all the millions of the faithful. It is not the people who would be the heirs of a dethroned Pope; it is some synod or bench of bishops. It is not an alternative between monarchy and democracy, but an alternative between monarchy and oligarchy. And, being myself one of the democratic idealists, I have not the faintest hesitation in my choice between the two latter forms of privilege. A monarch is a man; but an oligarchy is not men; it is a few men forming a group small enough to be insolent and large enough to be irresponsible. A man in the position of a Pope, unless he is literally mad, must be responsible. But aristocrats can always throw the responsibility on each other; and yet create a common and corporate society from which is shut out the very vision of the rest of the world. These are conclusions to which many people in the world are coming; and many who would still be much astonished and horrified to find where those conclusions lead. But the point here is that even if our civilization does not rediscover the need of a Papacy, it is extremely likely that sooner or later it will try to supply the need of something like a Papacy; even if it tries to do it on its own account. That will be indeed an ironical situation. The modern world will have set up a new Anti-Pope, even if, as in Monsignor Benson's romance, the Anti-Pope has rather the character of an Antichrist.

The point is that men will attempt to put some sort of moral power out of the reach of material powers. It is the weakness of many worthy and well-meaning attempts at international justice just now, that the international council can hardly help being merely a microcosm or model of the world outside it, with all its little things and big things, including the things that are much too big. Suppose that in the international interchanges of the future some power, say Sweden, is felt to be disproportionate or problematical. If Sweden is powerful in Europe, she will be powerful in the council of Europe. If Sweden is too powerful in Europe, she will be too powerful in the council of Europe. And because she is the very thing that is irresistible, she is the very thing to be resisted; or at any rate to be restrained. I do not see how Europe can ever escape from that logical dilemma, except by discovering again an authority that is purely moral and is the recognized custodian of a morality. It may very reasonably be said that even those dedicated to that duty may not always practise what they profess. But the other rulers of the world are not even bound to profess it.

Again and again in history, especially in mediaeval history, the Papacy has intervened in the interests of peace and humanity; just as the greatest saints have thrown themselves between the swords and daggers of contending factions. But if there had been no papacy and no saints and no Catholic Church at all, the world left to itself would certainly not have substituted social abstractions for theological creeds. As a whole, humanity has been far from humanitarian. If the world had been left to itself, let us say in the age of feudalism, all the decisions would have been rigidly and ruthlessly on the lines of feudalism. There was only one institution in that world that had existed before feudalism. There was only one institution which could possibly carry on some faint memory of the Republic and the Roman Law. If the world had been left to itself in the time of the Renaissance and the Italian statecraft of the Prince, it would have been arranged entirely in the current fashion of the glorification of princes. There was only one institution that could at any moment be moved to repeat, "Put not your trust in princes."[129] Had it been absent, the only result would have been that the famous settlement of *cujus regio ejus religio*[130] would have been all *regio* with precious little *religio*. And so, of course, our own day has its unconscious dogmas and its universal prejudices; and it needs a special, a sacred and what seems to many an inhuman separation to stand above them or to see beyond.

I know that this ideal has been abused like any other; I only say that even those who most denounce the reality will probably begin again to search for the ideal. But I do not, in fact, propose that any such spiritual tribunal should act like a legal tribunal or be given powers of practical interference with normal and national government. I am quite sure, for one thing, that it would never accept any such material entanglement. Nor do I, for that matter, desire that any of the secular tribunals now set up in the interests of international peace should thus have the power to interfere with nationality and local liberty. I would much rather give such power to a pope than to politicians and diplomatists of the sort to whom the world is giving it. But I do not want to give it to anybody and the authority in question does not want to accept it from anybody. The thing of which I speak is purely moral and cannot exist without a certain moral loyalty; it is a thing of atmosphere and even in a sense of affection. There is no space to describe here the manner in which such a general popular attachment grows up; but there is no doubt whatever that it did once grow up round such a religious centre of our civilization; and that it is not likely to

129 The quotation is from Psalms 146:3.

130 The phrase *cujus regio ejus religio* is Latin for "whom the region, his the religion."

grow up again except for something which aims at a higher standard of humility and charity than the ordinary standard of the world. Men cannot have an affection for other people's emperors, or even for other people's politicians; they have sometimes been known to cool in affection even for their own politicians. I see no prospect of any such positive nucleus of amity except in some positive enthusiasm for something that moves the deepest parts of man's moral nature; something which can unite us not (as the prigs say) by being entirely international, but by being universally human. Men cannot agree about nothing any more than they can disagree about nothing. And anything wide enough to make such an agreement must itself be wider than the world.

XXXV

THE SPIRIT OF CHRISTMAS

I have rather rashly undertaken to write of the Spirit of Christmas; and it presents a preliminary difficulty about which I must be candid. People are very curious nowadays in their way of talking about "the spirit" of a thing. There is, for example, a particular sort of prig who is always lecturing us about having the spirit of true Christianity, apart from all names and forms. As far as I can make out, he means the very opposite of what he says. He means that we are to go on using the names "Christian" and "Christianity," and so on, for something in which it is quite specially the spirit that is not Christian; something that is a sort of combination of the baseless optimism of an American atheist with the pacificism of a mild Hindoo. In the same way, we read a great deal about the Spirit of Christmas in modern journalism or commercialism; but it is really a reversal of the same kind. So far from preserving the essentials without the externals, it is rather preserving the externals where there cannot be the essentials. It means taking two mere material substances, like holly and mistletoe, and spreading them all over huge and homeless cosmopolitan hotels or round the Doric columns of impersonal clubs full of jaded and cynical old gentlemen; or in any other place where the actual spirit of Christmas is least likely to be. But there is also another way in which modern commercial complexity eats out the heart of the thing, while actually leaving the painted shell of it. And that is the much too elaborate system of dependence on buying and selling, and therefore on bustle and hustle; and the actual neglect of the new things that might be done by the old Christmas.

Normally, if anything were normal nowadays, it would seem a truism to say that Christmas has been a family festival. But it is now possible (as I have had the good or bad luck to discover) to earn a reputation for paradox simply by going on saying that truisms are true. In this case, of course, the reason, the only reasonable reason, was religious. It was concerned with a happy family because it was consecrated to the Holy Family. But it is perfectly true that many men saw the fact without specially feeling the reason. When we say the root was religious, we do not mean that Sam Weller was concentrated on theological values when he told the Fat Boy[131] to "put a bit on Christmas," into some object, probably edible. We do not mean that the Fat Boy had gone into a trance of mystical contemplation like a monk seeing a vision. We do not even mean that Bob Cratchit defended punch by saying he was only looking on the wine when it was yellow, or that Tiny Tim quoted Timothy. We only mean that they, including their author, would have confessed humbly and heartily that there was someone historically quite anterior to Mr. Scrooge, who might be called the Founder of the Feast. But in any case, whatever the reason, all would have agreed about the result. Mr. Wardle's feast centred in Mr. Wardle's family; and none the less because the romantic shadows of Mr. Winkle and Mr. Snodgrass[132] threatened to break it up for the formation of other families.

The Christmas season is domestic; and for that reason most people now prepare for it by struggling in tramcars, standing in queues, rushing away in trains, crowding despairingly into tea-shops, and wondering when or whether they will ever get home. I do not know whether some of them disappear for ever in the toy department or simply lie down and die in the tea-rooms; but by the look of them, it is quite likely. Just before the great festival of the home the whole population seems to have become homeless. It is the supreme triumph of industrial civilization that, in the huge cities which seem to have far too many houses, there is a hopeless shortage of housing. For a long time past great numbers of our poor have become practically nomadic. We even confess the fact; for we talk of some of them as Street Arabs. But this domestic institution, in its present ironical phase, has gone beyond such normal abnormality. The feast of the family turns the rich as well as the poor into vagabonds. They are so scattered over the bewildering labyrinth of our traffic and our trade, that they sometimes cannot even reach the tea-shop; it would be

[131] Sam Weller and Fat Boy are characters in Dickens' *The Pickwick Papers.*
[132] Mr. Wardle, Mr. Winkle and Mr. Snodgrass are also characters in Dickens' *The Pickwick Papers.*

indelicate, of course, to mention the tavern. They have a difficulty in crowding into their hotels, let alone separating to reach their houses. I mean quite the reverse of irreverence when I say that their only point of resemblance to the archetypal Christmas family is that there is no room for them at the inn.

Now Christmas is built upon a beautiful and intentional paradox; that the birth of the homeless should be celebrated in every home. But the other sort of paradox is not intentional and is certainly not beautiful. It is bad enough that we cannot altogether disentangle the tragedy of poverty. It is bad enough that the birth of the homeless, celebrated at hearth and altar, should sometimes synchronize with the death of the homeless in workhouses and slums. But we need not rejoice in this universal restlessness brought upon rich and poor alike; and it seems to me that in this matter we need a reform of the modern Christmas.

I will now emit another brilliant flash of paradox by remarking that Christmas occurs in the winter. That is, it is not only a feast dedicated to domesticity, but it is one deliberately placed under the conditions in which it is most uncomfortable to rush about and most natural to stop at home. But under the complicated conditions of modern conventions and conveniences, there arises this more practical and much more unpleasant sort of paradox. People have to rush about for a few weeks, if it is only to stay at home for a few hours. Now the old and healthy idea of such winter festivals was this: that people being shut in and besieged by the weather were driven back on their own resources; or, in other words, had a chance of showing whether there was anything in them. It is not certain that the reputation of our most fashionable modern pleasure-seekers would survive the test. Some dreadful exposures would be made of some such brilliant society favourites, if they were cut off from the power of machinery and money. They were quite used to having everything done for them; and even when they go to the very latest American dances, it seems to be mostly the negro musicians who dance. But anyhow, on the average of healthy humanity I believe the cutting off of all these mechanical connections would have a thoroughly enlivening and awakening effect. At present they are always accused of merely amusing themselves; but they are doing nothing so noble or worthy of their human dignity. Most of them by this time cannot amuse themselves; they are too used to being amused.

Christmas might be creative. We are told, even by those who praise it most, that it is chiefly valuable for keeping up ancient customs or old-fashioned games. It is indeed valuable for both those admirable purposes. But in the sense of which I am now speaking it might once more be possible to turn the truth the other way round. It is not so much old things as new things that a real Christmas might create. It might, for instance, create new games, if people were really driven to invent their own games. Most of the very old games began with the use of ordinary tools or furniture. So the very terms of tennis were founded on the framework of the old inn court-yard. So, it is said, the stumps in cricket were originally only the three legs of the milking-stool. Now we might invent new things of this kind, if we remembered who is the mother of invention. How pleasing it would be to start a game in which we scored so much for hitting the umbrella-stand or the dinner-wagon, or even the host and hostess; of course, with a missile of some soft material. Children who are lucky enough to be left alone in the nursery invent not only whole games, but whole dramas and life-stories of their own; they invent secret languages; they create imaginary families; they laboriously conduct family magazines. That is the sort of creative spirit that we want in the modern world; want both in the sense of desiring and in the sense of lacking it. If Christmas could become more domestic, instead of less, I believe there would be a vast increase in the real Christmas spirit—the spirit of the Child. But in indulging this dream we must once more invert the current convention into the form of a paradox. It is true in a sense that Christmas is the time at which the doors should be open. But I would have the doors shut at Christmas, or at least just before Christmas; and then the world shall see what we can do.

I cannot but remember, with something of a smile, that on an earlier and more controversial page of this book I have mentioned a lady who shuddered at the thought of the things perpetrated by my co-religionists behind closed doors. But my memory of it is mellowed by distance and the present subject, and I feel quite the reverse of controversial. I hope that lady, and all of her way of thinking, may also have the wisdom to close their doors; and discover that only when all the doors are closed the best thing will be found inside. If they are Puritans, whose religion is only based on the Bible, let it for once indeed be a Family Bible. If they are Pagans, who can accept nothing but the winter feast, let it at least be a family feast. The discordance or discomfort complained of by modern critics, in the family reunion, is not due to that mystical focal fire having been left burning, but to its having been left to go cold. It is because cold fragments of a once living thing are clumsily lumped together; it is no argument against making the thing alive. Christmas toys are incongruously dangled before heavy and heathen uncles who wish they were playing golf. But that does not alter the fact that they might become much brighter and more intelligent if they knew how to play with toys; and they are horrible bores about golf. Their dullness is only the last deadly product of the mechanical progress of organized and professional sports, in that rigid world of routine outside the home. When they were children, behind closed doors in the home, it is probable that nearly every one of them had day-dreams and unwritten dramas that belonged to them as much as Hamlet belonged to Shakspere or Pickwick to Dickens. How much more thrilling it would be if Uncle Henry, instead of describing in detail all the strokes with which he ought to have got out of the bunker, were to say frankly that he had been on a voyage to the end of the world and had just caught the Great Sea-Serpent. How much more truly intellectual would be the conversation of Uncle William if, instead of telling us the point to which he had reduced his handicap, he could still say with conviction that he was King of the Kangaroo Islands, or Chief of the Rango Dango Redskins. These things, projected from within, were in almost all human spirits; and it is not normal that the inspiration of them should be so utterly crushed by the things without. Let it not be supposed for a moment that I also am among the tyrants of the earth, who would impose my own tastes, or force all the other children to play my own games. I have no disrespect for the game of golf; it is an admirable game. I have played it; or rather, I have played at it, which is generally regarded as the very opposite. By all means let the golfers golf and even the organizers organize, if their only conception of an organ is something like a barrel-organ. Let them play golf day after day; let them play golf for three hundred and sixty-four days, and nights as well, with balls dipped in luminous paint, to be pursued in the dark. But let there be one night when things grow luminous from within: and one day when men seek for all that is buried in themselves; and discover, where she is indeed hidden, behind locked gates and shuttered windows, and doors thrice barred and bolted, the spirit of liberty.

THE END

THE WELL AND THE SHALLOWS

1935

INTRODUCTORY NOTE

I was monstrously attracted by a suggestion that these essays should bear the general title of "Joking Apart." It seemed to me a simple and sensible way of saying that the reader of these pages must not look for many jokes, certainly not merely for jokes, because these are controversial essays, covering all subjects on which a controversialist is challenged, and not particular subjects chosen as they are chosen by a essayist. It is an awful revelation of the world of unreason into which we have wandered, that people more practical than I are convinced that if I say that this is apart from joking, everyone will think it is a joke. To my simple mind it seems very much as if I wanted to call a book, "Away from Jericho," and everybody assumed that I had accepted a very general recommendation to go to Jericho. Many essays could be written on this strange modern sensibility to mere verbal allusion, or the introduction of certain words, even to repudiate them. But the only point here involved is that these essays are all under the conditions of controversy, which involve the absolute necessity of disgusting those with whom we disagree on any subject, and boring those who are indifferent to that subject. I have had, if I may say so, a very happy and lucky literary life; and have often felt rather the indulgence than the impatience of critics; and it is in a perfectly amiable spirit that I note that it has involved a certain transition or change. Up to a certain point, I was charitably chaffed for saying what I could not possibly mean; and I was then rather more sharply criticised, when it was discovered that I did really mean it. Now anybody driven to the defence of what he does really mean must cover all the strategic field of the fight, and must fight at many points which he would not have chosen in fancy, but only in relation to fact. He cannot hope to deal only with heresies that amuse him; he must, in common fairness, deal seriously with heresies that bore him. He must settle down to stating his real reasons for contradicting real statements, which are not made by him as statements, and not chosen by him as subjects. All this seems to me, with my mild rationalistic mind, excellently summarised in the words, "Joking Apart."

Anyhow, this is why I have opened this series with an essay called "An Apology for Buffoons," because it is in some sense, I will not say a swan-song (that ornithological metaphor would not occur to me in relation to myself), but at least a sort of summary of my more frivolous mode of writing, and all that I still think may be fairly advanced for it. Unfortunately, a man fighting what he honestly believes to be false can hardly preserve the glorious immunity of a buffoon. He is forced to be serious, and even those who despise him most are driven desperately to take him seriously. But there is one other reason for adding this preliminary note, in connection with the preliminary essay. Since I wrote it, I have come to appreciate much more warmly the admirable work of Mr. T. S. Eliot; and I should like to offer an apology to him for some errors that occurred accidentally in the article itself. It was not he, but another critic, with whom I confused him, who made the particular point against alliteration; and the quotation from him was made from memory; and I have not been able to trace it so as to reproduce the exact order of words. The inaccuracy, if any, does not affect the argument; but the article which I have already planned to put in the same magazine, called "Apology to T. S. Eliot" would have gone far beyond any such verbal point. It would be adding impudence to injury to dedicate a book to an author merely on the claim of having misquoted him; but I should be proud to dedicate this book to T. S. Eliot, and the return of true logic and a luminous tradition to the world.

AN APOLOGY FOR BUFFOONS

There was a time when I appeared in the *Mercury*, covered with blushes, to acknowledge a friendly criticism which asked if my journalism held enough of autobiography; and I attempted with great embarrassment to give thanks for the criticism—and the compliment. My blush has faded; my sense of decency has departed; and I appear now with the shameless purpose of being, not merely autobiographical, but grotesquely egotistical. In a spirit of brazen contradiction, I even propose to be egotistical in disproving the charge of egotism. Nay, in a yet wilder illogicality, I claim to be egotistical in the interests of other people. It is a contradiction in terms; but as the higher mathematics, the higher morality, the higher religion and the rest now entirely consist of contradictions in terms, I go on with a ghastly calm. And I do it because I cannot think of any other way of drawing attention to a real problem of literature, and especially of popular literature (if I may dare to dream of that contradiction also) except this particular line of argument, which inevitably involves the mention of my own case—let us hope along with more amusing ones.

It is commonly alleged of writers that they resent mild criticisms as infamous personal imputations, taking them as seriously as slanders. Without affectation, I fancy my own case to be rather different and even opposite. Most of the adverse criticisms written about me strike me as quite true. Where I am in invincible ignorance, I suppose, is in a proper sense of the importance of the things thus rightly reproved. For instance, a very sympathetic reviewer said that I used too much alliteration; and quoted Mr. T. S. Eliot* as saying that such a style maddened him to the point of unendurance; and a similar criticism of my English was made, I think, by another American writer, Mr. Cuthbert Wright. Now I think, on fair consideration, that it is perfectly true that I do use a great deal too much alliteration. The only question on which these gentlemen and I would probably differ is a question of degree; a question of the exact importance or

* See apology in Introduction.

necessity of avoiding alliteration. For I do strongly maintain that it
is a question of avoiding alliteration — and even that phrase does not
avoid it! If an English writer does not avoid it, he is perpetually
dragged into it when speaking rapidly or writing a great deal, by the
whole trend and current of the English speech; perhaps that is why
the Anglo-Saxon poetry even down to Piers Plowman[1] (which I enjoy hugely) was all alliteration. Anyhow, the tendency in popular
and unconscious speech is quite obvious, in phrases and proverbs and
rhymes and catchwords and a thousand things. Time and tide, wind
and water, fire and flood, waste not, want not, bag and baggage,
spick and span, black and blue, deaf and dumb, the devil and the
deep sea, when the wine is in the wit is out, in for a penny, in for a
pound, a pig in a poke, a bee in a bonnet, a bat in a belfry, and so on
through a myriad fantastic changes of popular imagery. What elaborate art, what sleepless cunning even, must these more refined
writers employ to dodge this rush of coincidences; and run between
the drops of this deluge! It must be a terrible strain on the presence
of mind to be always ready with a synonym. I can imagine Mr. T. S.
Eliot just stopping himself in time, and saying with a refined cough,
"Waste not, *require* not." I like to think of Mr. Cuthbert Wright, in
some headlong moment of American hustle, still having the self-
control to cry, "Time and Fluctuation wait for no man!" I can imagine his delicate accent when speaking of a pig in a receptacle or of
bats in the campanile. It is a little difficult perhaps to image the latter
critic apparently confining himself to the isolated statement, "Mr.
Smith is spick," while his mind hovered in momentary hesitation
about how to vary the corresponding truth that Mr. Smith is span.
But it is quite easy to conceive an advanced modern artist of this
school, looking for some sharp and graphic variation in the old colour scheme of black and blue. Indeed, we might almost invent a sort
of colour test, like that which somebody suggested about red grass
and green sky as a test of different schools of painting. We might

[1] "Pier's Plowman", an Anglo-Saxon poem attributed to William Langland, expressed in a complex allegory the author's faith in man's need for Christian truth and
charity. Although long and irregularly constructed, the poem is considered a
magnificent statement of the mind and faith of the late fourteenth century.

suggest that Decadents[2] beat people black and yellow, Futurists[3] beat them black and orange, Neo-Victorians beat them black and magenta; but all recoil from the vulgar alliteration of beating them black and blue.

Nor indeed is the reference to these new and varied styles irrelevant. Some of the more bizarre modern methods seem to me to make it rather difficult to have any fixed criticism at all, either of their style or mine. Take, for instance, the case of Mr. T. S. Eliot himself. I recently saw a poem of his praised very highly and doubtless very rightly; though to some extent (it seemed) because it was a poem of profound "disillusionment and melancholy." But the passage specially quoted for commendation ran, if I remember right:

"the smell of steak in passages."

That quotation[4] is enough to indicate the difficulty I mean. For even style of this severe and classic sort is after all to some extent a matter of taste. It is not a subject for these extreme controversial passions. If I were to say that the style of that line maddened me to the point of unendurance, I should be greatly exaggerating its effect on the emotions. I should not like everything to be written in that style; I should not like to wander for ever in passages stuffy with steak (there we go again!) but I cannot think these questions of style are quite so important as these pure stylists suppose. We must be moderate in our reactions; as in that verse specially headed "The Author's Moderation" in the Bab Ballad[5] about Pasha Bailey Ben — another great poem written in a tone of melancholy disillusion.

[2] Decadents were adherents of a French literary movement of the 1880s and 1890s. They rejected moral and religious restraints, emphasized the bizarre and unusual, and exalted sexual aberration. The poet Paul Verlaine was the most prominent figure associated with the group.

[3] Futurism, whose major proponent was the Italian Filippo Marinetti (1876–1944), was an avant-garde artistic and literary movement that arose just before World War I. It celebrated dynamism, violence and the machine age.

[4] Eliot's quotation is from "Preludes I".

[5] W. S. Gilbert published the "Bab Ballads" in two volumes of humorous verse in 1869 and 1873.

> To say that Bailey oped his eyes
> Would feebly paint his great surprise;
> To say it almost made him die
> Would be to paint it much too high.

I may be allowed to open my eyes for a moment at some of the literary models thus commended to me; but I shall soon close them again in healthful slumber. And when the more refined critic implies that my own manner of writing almost makes him die, I think he over-estimates my power over life and death.

But I have begun with this personal example of alliteration; because a question like that of alliteration is not so simple as it looks; and the answer to it applies to much more important things than my own journalistic habits. Alliteration is an example of a thing much easier to condemn in theory than in practice. There are, of course, many famous examples in which an exaggerated alliteration seems quite wrong. And yet those are exactly the examples which it would be most difficult for anybody to put right. Byron (a splendid example of the sort of writer who does not bother much about avoiding anything) did not hesitate to say of his hero at Quatre Bras that he "rushed into the field and foremost fighting fell."[6] That is so extreme that we might well suppose it described the end of the life and adventures of Peter Piper. But I will trouble anybody to alter one word in the line so as to make it better; or even so as to make it sense. Byron used those words because they were the right words; and you cannot alter them without deliberately choosing the wrong words. This is more often the case in connection with alliteration than many people imagine. I do not mean to claim any such exalted company when I say that, on this particular point of conduct, I agree with Byron. But Byron does not stand alone; Coleridge, a person of some culture, could burst out boisterously and without stopping for breath:[7]

> The fair breeze blew, the white foam flew,
> The furrow followed free.

[6] Byron's quotation is from "The Eve of Waterloo".
[7] The Coleridge quotation is from "The Rime of the Ancient Mariner".

and I do not see that he could have done anything else. I do not think anybody could interfere with that foaming spate of f's, if the verse that followed was really "to follow free."

There is a problem behind all this which is also illustrated in other ways. It is illustrated in the other much controverted question of puns. I know all about the judgments regularly cited as if from dusty law-books in the matter. I know all about the story that Dr. Johnson said, "The man who would make a pun would pick a pocket." How unlucky that the lexicographer and guardian of our language, in the very act of purging himself of puns, should have plunged so shamelessly deep into the mire of alliteration! His example, in that very instance, would alone be enough to prove the first part of my case, even when it is brought forward against the second. Johnson spluttered out all those p's because he was an Englishman with a sense of the spirit and vigour of the English language; and not a timid prig who had to mind his p's and q's by using them in exact alternation with a pattern. But if it came to the old joke of invoking authorities, it would be equally easy to invoke even greater authorities on the side of the pun. Also there is something that is more important to my purpose here. It would not only be easy to quote the puns of the poets; it would be easy to quote the very bad puns of the very good poets. But the question I wish to ask is wider and more essential than all this hotch-potch of snobbery and legalism and A Hundred Familiar Quotations, which goes to make up the modern invocation of authorities. I wish to point out that there is a general attitude of mind, which is defensible; or rather two attitudes of mind, which are both defensible. It is a question of style; but there are here two different styles; because there are two different motives. If one is now criticising the other, I do not merely wish to retort the criticism; but rather to proclaim liberty for both.

It might be roughly suggested thus. It is not merely a question of a man who makes a pun; we might almost ask what is to happen to a man who meets a pun. Is he to cut it dead; is he always to pass by on the other side; is he to disown such disreputable company, as of course our refined stylists would do? I am presupposing that he is not out hunting for puns or similar monsters; I presuppose that he is walking down the street on some legitimate business of his own. But if the grotesque animal actually comes to meet him, if it stands obviously in his path, I think it is natural for him to take it in his stride. At least it is natural to one sort of man engaged in one sort of business; and it is the man and the business that I am here concerned to defend. This is quite a different sort of question from the elaborate construction of such fireworks as a form of art for art's sake; though many men of genius, Hood[8] for example, have occupied themselves even with that. But I am not talking about that. When I was a Pauline, an assistant master received a testimonial on leaving the school for a fellowship at Peterhouse. A solemn upper master made on this occasion the first and last joke of his life by observing in a deep voice, "We are robbing Paul to pay Peter." An old schoolfellow of mine, now a journalist but cynical even at that early age, declared that the older master must have engineered the whole career of the younger, and made him a teacher at that particular school and then a don at that particular College, solely in order to enjoy one moment of supreme triumph in making that single pun. It is not in the sense of such a triumph of engineering that I am here apologising for the pun. I am not speaking of the man whose life's purpose, or even whose purpose, is to make a pun; but of the man who is ready to make puns to serve his purpose. And there is a whole atmosphere and appetite involved here; which we may call if we like the spirit of the demagogue or of the buffoon or of the popular minstrel or of the orator; but which cannot be understood merely in terms of style as style, any more than of art for art's sake.

In any case, things of this sort do exist; coincidences or combinations like alliteration or punning; repetitions or conjunctions that have in prose something of the effect of rhyme in poetry. The only question is how to deal with them when they offer themselves very obviously; as they often do. There are, I think, in a general view, three different ways of dealing with them. First, a man may reject them consciously; as the stylist of the serious school of Mr. Wright does when he speaks of "wind and H_2O," or instinctively writes,

---

[8] Thomas Hood (1799–1845) and his son, also named Thomas (1835–74), were both known for their humorous writings. Chesterton probably means Hood the younger.

"In for a penny, in for a Treasury note of the value of twenty shillings." I do not say that these examples are taken from the text; but it is quite a mistake to suppose that such fastidiousness is not a real literary problem. I remember a critic pointing out, even in a master of such direct and telling English as Mr. A. E. Housman, a case in which the poet had obviously written, "The chestnut cast her flambeaux,"[9] simply and solely to avoid writing, "The chestnut cast her candles" — which is twenty times better in every possible way. Second, he can accept them consciously, as I very often do; largely because it is not worth the trouble to reject them. I said a moment ago, "disown disreputable company," because I do not propose to search in a dictionary for an unnatural alternative to "disown". Third, he may accept them unconsciously; and that is a great deal more dangerous than anything else, and a great deal more common than most people imagine. Nobody has yet made an adequate study of the effect of mere phonetics in confusing logic and misleading philosophers. And the worst of that sort of danger is that it is deep and subtle. To decorate an argument with puns and verbal tricks may be a superficial folly. But it is better than the sort of folly that is not superficial.

I am almost certain that many moderns suffer from what may be called the disease of the suppressed pun. I mean that, in men who would disdain to make anything so vulgar as a joke out of a verbal coincidence, there is a subconscious movement of the mind to meet the sound of the word. Thus those who would denounce creeds (a Latin word for anything that anybody believes) are seldom or never, you will notice, moved to describe them by any milder name; they must have a word that sounds like a portmanteau of "crank" and "crabbed" and "greed." They cannot really let themselves go in reviling doctrine. It must be in reviling dogma. They would never sink so low as to make a positive pun about it, as might some poor Popish buffoon like Erasmus or Crashaw.[10] They would not say of the Dominicans,[11] "The dogs of God are always dogmatic." But

[9] Housman's quotation is from *Last Poems* (1922).

[10] See footnote 127, page 323, above.

[11] This reference to Dominicans is a play on the Latin words *Domini* (the Lord's) and *canes* (dogs).

they are in fact affected all the time by a vague verbal association between a dogma and a mad dog. It is the accidental sound of the word that makes them use it so incessantly, and so monotonously, in preference to all other terms, even terms of abuse. On re-reading the end of Stevenson's not consciously unsympathetic sketch of the Trappists, in the *Travels with a Donkey*,[12] I could swear that he was involuntarily influenced by the suggestion that Trappists are caught in a trap. He cries out, like one who has escaped, that he thanks heaven he is free to hope, to wander and to love. The logic of it would suggest that somebody had been trying to capture and imprison him; a notion which would certainly have surprised the monks very much. He seems to forget that they also were all free to wander, to love, to do anything they liked, including going into a monastery; and that they had gone into the monastery exactly as he had gone into the mountains. Suppose some burgess of Balham, contemplating the wanderer in the Cevennes, had said, "Thank heaven, I am free to dine properly, sit in an armchair and sleep in a bed." Stevenson might have replied that he also was free to do these things, but preferred to do something else. But he never saw the parallel between the journey to the mountain and the journey to the monastery. The terror of old words and traditional associations choked him like a nursery nightmare. And I believe he quailed inwardly at the terrible pun of La Trappe.

Now I for one greatly prefer the sort of frivolity that is thrown to the surface like froth to the sort of frivolity that festers under the surface like slime. To pelt an enemy with a foolish pun or so will never do him any grave injustice; the firework is obviously a firework and not a deadly fire. It may be playing to the gallery; but even the gallery knows it is only playing. But to associate an enemy always with certain ugly-sounding words, and never with their logical synonyms that sound a little better, is in a very real sense to poison our own minds. And that is the case with the man who is subconsciously moved by the sound of words, without realising that the very assonance is a sort of pun. He must describe a Socialist as a Bolshevist; because the word Boshie has a vague savour of Boshy. He must refer to a Liberal as a Radical, because there is a hard sound about Rads as there is

[12] *Travels with a Donkey* is Robert Louis Stevenson's account of his trip in 1878 through the Cevennes Mountains of southern France.

about Cads. It is a sound heard in many English names for foreigners, from the time that we first talked about Rapparees[13] to the time when we began, more faintly, to talk about Yankees. The criticism of these foreigners is not in question; but the point is this. If a man can say about a Yankee what he would hardly say about an American, or even about a Northern American, then he is allowing this shadow of a pun, or sound of a word, to spoil his sense of justice and reality. He is obscurely confusing the word Yank with the word Swank. If he can speak of a Froggy more scornfully than he could really speak of a Frenchman, then he is being verbally affected by the word frog, as was the other man by the word dog. I do not think it matters how much we play about with these puns or rhymes or resemblances, or echoes of sound, so long as we are obviously doing it on the surface for the sake of the sound. Exactly when this sort of style becomes dangerous to the sense is when it is concealed, as these more sensitive stylists would conceal it. It is so that class-consciousness is worse than ever when it is class subconsciousness. It is so that the professed impartiality of certain academic historians stinks with their buried prejudice.

Compared with this, I do think there is something sporting about conscious buffoonery. As it is embarrassing to use the egotistic example, I will take the example of a very much more distinguished person, who is in this respect of the same type or temper as I; I mean Mr. Bernard Shaw. There used to be at one time a great fashion of arguing about Shaw and Shakespeare, and, by the way, that must surely have been an artificial trick of alliteration. Yet it would be dangerous to suggest to Shaw that he copied Shakespeare, and there are difficulties even in telling Shakespeare he copied Shaw. Anyhow, one of the few things in which there is a real resemblance between Shaw and Shakespeare is this; that they both seem so very often to make jokes that are not worth making. When Polonius says he was Julius Caesar; whom Brutus killed in the Capitol; and Hamlet is made to answer, "It was a brute part of him, to kill so capital a calf there," I do not imagine that Shakespeare, any more than anybody else, thought that the two puns were the most perfect and pointed specimens of wit. But he did think it vital to the story that Hamlet should make a flippant remark of some sort at that

[13] Rapparees were Irish freebooters of the seventeenth century.

moment; and he thought it a very probable sort of flippant remark for him to make. There are any number of flippancies in Shaw's plays that are no better than this, and serve no other purpose than this. But the point is that flippancies of this sort are only used by a very serious person; and Mr. Bernard Shaw is a very serious person. He wants to say something. He has something to say. If ever the perfect stylistic critics should find themselves in such a peculiar position, they will discover the nature of these temptations to flippancy.

It is not an idle contradiction to say that Mr. Shaw is flippant because he is serious. A man like Mr. Shaw has the deliberate intention of getting people to listen to what he has to say; and therefore he must be amusing. A man who is only amusing himself need not be amusing. Generally, when he is a perfect and polished stylist, he is not. And there is a good deal of misunderstanding about the relative moral attitude of the two types; especially in connection with the old morality of modesty. Most persons, listening to these loud flippancies, would say that Mr. Bernard Shaw is egotistical. Mr. Bernard Shaw himself would emphatically and violently assert that he is egotistical; and I should emphatically and violently assert that he is not. It is not the first time we have somewhat tartly disagreed. And perhaps I could not more effectively perform the just and necessary public duty of annoying Mr. Shaw than by saying (as I do say) that in this matter he really inherits an unconscious tradition of Christian humility. The preaching friar puts his sermon into popular language, the missionary fills his sermon with anecdotes and even jokes, because he is thinking of his mission and not of himself. It does not matter that Mr. Shaw's sentences so often begin with the pronoun "I." The Apostles' Creed begins with the pronoun "I"; but it goes on to rather more important nouns and names.

Father Ronald Knox,[14] in his satire on Modernism, has described the courteous vagueness of the Oxford manner which

[14] Monsignor Ronald Knox (1888–1957) was one of the most famous Anglican converts to Catholicism in twentieth-century England. He served as Catholic chaplain at Oxford University from 1926 to 1939, produced a fresh translation of the Vulgate Bible, authored detective stories and became one of England's most articulate Catholic apologists.

. . . . tempering pious zeal
Corrected, "I believe" to "One does feel."

And though I have much of such courtesy to be thankful for, both
in conversation and criticism, I must do justice to the more dogmatic type, where I feel it to be right. And I will say firmly that it is
the author who says, "One does feel," who is really an egoist; and
the author who says, "I believe," who is not an egoist. We all know
what is meant by a truly beautiful essay; and how it is generally written in the light or delicate tone of, "One does feel." I am perfectly
well aware that all my articles are articles, and that none of my articles are essays. An essay is often written in a really graceful and exquisitely balanced style, which I doubt if I could imitate, though I
might try. Anyhow, it generally deals with experiences of a certain
unprovocative sort in a certain unattached fashion; it begins with
something like . . .

> "The pond in my garden shows, under the change of morning, an ap-
> prehension of the moving air, hardly to be called a wave; and so little
> clouding its lucidity as to seem rather vacuity in motion. Here at least is
> nothing to stain the bright negation of water; none of those suburban
> gold-fish that look like carrots and do but nose after their tails in a circle
> of frustration, to give some sulky gardener cause to cry 'stinking fish'.
> The mind is altogether carried away upon the faint curve of wind over
> water; the movement is something less solid than anything that we can
> call liquid; the smoke of my light Virginian cigarette does not mount
> more unsubstantially towards the sky. Nor indeed inaptly: it needs
> some such haven of patriarchal mildness to accent sharply the tang of
> mild tobacco; alone perhaps, of all the attributes of Raleigh's red-haired
> mistress, rightly to be called virginal."

I think I might learn to do it some day; though not by a commercial correspondence course; but the truth is that I am very much occupied. I confess to thinking that the things which occupy me are
more important; but I am disposed to deny that the thing I think
important is myself. And in justice not only to myself but to Mr.
Shaw and Mr. Belloc and Mr. Mencken and many another man in
the same line of business, I am moved to protest that the other literary method, the method of, "One does feel," is much more really

arrogant than ours. The man in Mr. Shaw's play remarks that who says artist says duellist. Perhaps, nevertheless, Mr. Shaw is too much of a duellist to be quite an artist. But anyhow, I will affirm, on the same model that who says essayist says egoist. I am sorry if it is an alliteration, almost a rhyme and something approaching to a pun. Like a great many such things, it is also a fact.

Even in the fancy example I have given, and in a hundred far better and more beautiful extracts from the real essayists, the point could be shown. If I go out of my way to tell the reader that I smoke Virginian cigarettes, it can only be because I assume the reader to be interested in me. Nobody can be interested in Virginian cigarettes. But if I shout at the reader that I believe in the Virginian cause in the American Civil War, as does the author of *The American Heresy*,[15] if I thunder as he does that all America is now a ruin and an anarchy because in that great battle the good cause went down—then I am not an egoist. I am only a dogmatist; which seems to be much more generally disliked. The fact that I believe in God may be, in all modesty, of some human interest; because any man believing in God may affect any other man believing in God. But the fact that I do not believe in gold-fish, as ornaments in a garden pond, cannot be of the slightest interest to anybody on earth, unless I assume that some people are interested in anything whatever that is connected with me. And that is exactly what the true elegant essayist does assume. I do not say he is wrong; I do not deny that he also in another way represents humanity and uses a sort of artistic fiction or symbol in order to do so. I only say that, if it comes to a quarrel about being conceited, he is far the more conceited of the two. The one sort of man deals with big things noisily and the other with small things quietly. But there is much more of the note of superiority in the man who always treats of things smaller than himself than the man who always treats of things greater than himself. The latter at least must be very small if he does not feel that they are greater.

Now the next two steps bring us to the climax of the matter. First, this dogmatist is always something of a demagogue. Second, this

[15] Chesterton is referring to Christopher Hollis (1902–77), English author, Conservative politician and convert to Catholicism.

demagogue is always something of a buffoon. I am very far from denying that he becomes too much of a demagogue and too much of a buffoon. But he does not do so because he prefers superficial things, but
rather because he is concerned with fundamental things. If I may illustrate my meaning by one of those deplorable verbalisms over which we
are all lamenting, I would say that it is exactly because he is concerned
with fundamentals that he is tempted to tickle the groundlings. He is
interested in primary facts; and one of those primary facts is the people.
He may make jokes and play to the gallery; but there is something more
than a joke for him in the phrase which calls the gallery the gods.

I also am a tub-thumper; and I exaggerated my meaning a moment ago, in the necessity of defending myself, of defending Mr.
Shaw and (most exciting of all) of defending Mr. Shaw against Mr.
Shaw. I do not really mean, of course, that the essayist is an egoist in
any selfish sense. Nobody in the world, I imagine, gets more good
than I do out of good essays like those of Mr. Max Beerbohm or Mr.
E. V. Lucas or Mr. Robert Lynd.[16] I only ask, in all seriousness, that
they should understand the necessities of our sort of self-assertion as
well as recognising the existence of their own. And I do ask them to
believe that when we try to make our sermons and speeches more or
less amusing, it is for the very simple and even modest reason that
we do not see why the audience should listen unless it is more or less
amused. Our mode of speech is conditioned by the fact that it really
is what some have fancifully supposed the function of speech to be;
something addressed by somebody to somebody else. It has of necessity all the vices and vulgarities attaching to a speech that really is a
speech and not a soliloquy.

I have come to the conclusion that this last point is too plain to
be understood. Some of the simplest things of human history are
now quite invisible to minds that have grown accustomed to sub-
division or specialism. Thus the idea of the vow, one of the first facts
about our social foundation, is not disputed or denied; it is simply

[16] Max Beerbohm (1872–1956) was an English satirist and caricaturist. Edward
Verrall Lucas (1868–1938) was an English essayist and biographer of Charles Lamb.
Robert Lynd (1879–1949) was an English journalist best known for his essays that
appeared regularly in the *New Statesman* from 1913 to 1945.

nibbled out of existence by people who do not know that it exists. It is so with the gesture of the sacrifice, without which man is hardly human; and it is so with the gesture of the speaker or the singer dealing directly with the people. I found a case of this confusion in connection with this point, after I had tried to suggest it in an article in the *Mercury* called, "The True Case Against Cliques." A critic in the American *Bookman* immediately assumed that it was only the old and conventional case against cliques. He got it into his head that I had merely been grumbling about log-rolling; and he said that Aristophanes and Euripides had their cliques and backers like anybody else. It seems to me that American criticism, so far from being merely crude, is rather too traditional. It has a curious conservative way with it and labels things in the manner of a museum; indeed I found in the same number a very Victorian article called, "Science and Religion," in which these two forces were studied under the representative figures of Charles Darwin and Mr. Moody.[17] Many things have been written about Science and Religion; but I should not feel myself overwhelmed by the onward rush of a new world which had never considered any science later than Darwin or any religion better than Moody and Sankey.[18] Many things have also been written against log-rolling and literary clannishness; but I did not write anything against them or indeed anything about them. What I was trying, I fear rather clumsily, to express was that there is now an entirely new danger in the clique; because it is not merely a clique. It has taken on the character of an interpreter; by hypothesis the interpreter of something unintelligible; and its existence encourages the artist to be unintelligible, when it is his whole function to be intelligible. The artist is the man who is more and not less intelligible than other men; it is the mass of men whose feelings remain relatively incomprehensible, even to themselves.

Aristophanes undoubtedly had his faction and in that sense his clique. But I gravely doubt whether his audience needed anybody to explain to them that when the dead man said, "May I come to life if I do," it was a joke and a parody of the phrase, "May I die if I do." In other words, the

[17] Dwight L. Moody (1837–99) was an American revivalist.
[18] Ira D. Sankey (1840–1908) was a hymn writer and Dwight Moody's music director.

jokes of Aristophanes, like the jokes of Bernard Shaw, were good jokes; but they were obvious jokes. There was not normally any question of a new and secretive sense of humour, which only a certain school of aesthetes or critics could understand. The buffoonery of Bernard Shaw is in this respect like the buffoonery of Aristophanes; or if it be difficult to make sure of the conditions in the time of Aristophanes, the element of obviousness is equally obvious in the best jokes of Molière or the best jokes of Dickens. The whole case for buffoons is that jokes ought to be obvious. We may even say that they are not really jokes unless they are obvious. There are, of course, special conditions for the thing called irony; in which it is the joke that somebody does not see the joke. But even there that person is not the audience; or if he is, the irony has failed. But in any case there is here a joke that the critics cannot apparently see; and a joke which is also something of a tragedy. There is under the surface of all this conspiratorial culture, a fantastic notion of new and even disparate psychologies breaking up the brotherhood of the common human mind; incommunicable or at least without communication between one and another. As Mr. Wells imagined man evolving into two animals, we are really called on to imagine mind breaking up not so much into cliques as into species. The buffoon may make bad jokes; I myself, who am a very minor buffoon to be mentioned with Mr. Shaw, let alone Aristophanes, do regularly and as a matter of business make a multitude of bad jokes. I do it for reasons connected with the duties of demagogy, and I am not defending it here, but rather something much more important. Buffoons may make bad jokes; but it is quite another thing that a man should make a joke and another man *really* not know that it is a joke at all. The first man may think it a good joke and the second a bad joke; that is normal and has always been; in the case above-mentioned my critic and I can embrace in agreeing that it is a bad joke. But if aberration and mystery be so deliberately cultivated that the jest of one school is not a jest at all but only a riddle to another, we are at the beginning of a schism more perilous than any in the past. We are suffering Taste to tear men asunder as they have never been torn asunder by religion or revolution or the wars of the world. In other times there were other and nobler examples of this direct relation between the maker and mankind. The orator could make a mob feel like an army of heroes; the prophet or preacher could isolate every soul in a crowd and make each feel immortal. To make what is now called a popular speech it is indeed necessary to make it only too like what is called an after-dinner speech; to keep our connection with the normal life only by a thin thread of flippancy. But at least the connection is kept; and something remains of what is really the archetypal relation implied in the very existence of the arts. It is not altogether our fault if a chasm has opened in the community of beliefs and social traditions, which can only be spanned by the far halloo of the buffoon.

MY SIX CONVERSIONS

I. The Religion of Fossils

At least six times during the last few years, I have found myself in a situation in which I should certainly have become a Catholic, if I had not been restrained from that rash step by the fortunate accident that I was one already. The point is not merely personal but has some representative interest, because our critics constantly expect the convert to suffer some sort of reaction, ending in disappointment and perhaps desertion. As a rule, the most that they will concede to us is that we have found peace by the surrender of reason; which generally means in practice that we pass the rest of our lives in interminable controversies with a perpetual appeal to logic. But, as a fact, it is in a rather peculiar sense, the other way about. The strongest sort of confirmation often comes to the convert after he has received enough to establish conviction. In these articles I propose to discuss some examples of this singular sort of post-conversion conversion. I mean that things have happened, since I was received into the Church, which would in any case have rendered impossible any intellectual position outside the Church, and especially the position in which I originally found myself. One occasion was the Parliamentary settlement of the controversy on the Prayer-Book — or Prayer-Books.[19] Another was the Lambeth decision, or indecision, about Birth-Control. But I will take first the example of the latest turn of political events in Europe. I take it first because it is both typical and topical; that is, it gives perhaps the clearest and simplest example of the sort of thing I mean, and it is a thing of which the facts are fresh and familiar to everybody, even those who live only from day to day with the assistance of the daily Press; that very synthetic substitute for daily bread. But in order to explain what I think has really happened, rather more lucidly than the daily Press explains it, it is

[19] Chesterton is referring to the controversy surrounding the revised *Book of Common Prayer* of 1928.

necessary to say a preliminary word about the Protestant Reformation and the sense in which its consequences, rather than itself, continue to bewilder and mislead Christendom.

Men of the type or school of Bishop Barnes or Dean Inge[20] are, as we know, very fond of appealing to the discoveries of science; generally the not very recent discoveries of nineteenth-century science. They delight in dealing with what my grandfather would have called the Testimony of the Rocks; the geological record of natural development; and they often treat fossils and similar traces as if they were sacred hieroglyphics, by which some priesthood had symbolised the secret of the universe. And yet it is doubtful, it is more than doubtful, whether one of the Broad Church ecclesiastics would be soothed and flattered if I addressed him personally as an Old Fossil. Nor indeed should I dream of indulging in this playful form of social address; since there are truths, or half-truths, that cannot be coarsely stated without giving rise to misunderstanding even about their true meaning.

In one sense these liberal theologians are interested in fossils. They continue to demonstrate the Darwinian theory from the geological record, by means of all the fossils that ought to be found in it. They will even explain luminously why the geological evidence does not apparently exist; and they seem to think that this is quite as convincing as if it did exist. But I doubt whether they have really thought profoundly and delicately about what a fossil is, or there would be no danger of their resenting so innocent and inoffensive a comparison. For a fossil is really a very curious thing. A fossil is not a dead animal, or a decayed organism, or in essence even an antiquated object. The whole point of a fossil is that it is the *form* of an animal or organism, from which all its own animal or organic substance has entirely disappeared; but which has kept its shape, because it has been filled up by some totally different substance by some process of distillation or secretion, so that we might almost say, as in the medieval metaphysics, that its substance has vanished and only its accidents remain. And that is perhaps

[20] Ernest William Barnes (1874–1953) was an Anglican bishop of Birmingham; William Inge (1860–1954) was dean of St. Paul's Anglican cathedral, London, from 1911 to 1934.

the very nearest figure of speech we can find for the truth about the New Religions, which were started only three or four hundred years ago. They are Fossils.

It is easy to see the sense in which they are now dying. But in a much deeper sense, they have long been dead. The extraordinary thing about them was that they really died almost as soon as they were born. And this was due to a fact not always emphasised, but which always strikes me as the most outstanding fact of the mysterious business; the incredible clumsiness of the Reformers. The real Protestant theologians were such very bad theologians. They had an amazing opportunity; the old Church had been swept out of their way, along with many things that were really unpopular, and some things that were deservedly unpopular. One would suppose it was easy enough to set up something that would at least look a little more popular. When they tried to do it, they made every mistake that they could make. They waged an insane war against everything in the old faith that is most normal and sympathetic to human nature; such as prayers for the dead or the gracious image of a Mother of Men. They hardened and fixed themselves upon fads which anybody could see would pass like fashions. Luther lashed himself into a sort of general fury, which obviously could not last; Calvin was logical, but used his logic for a scheme which humanity manifestly would not long find endurable. Perhaps the most successful were those who really had no ideas to offer at all; like the founders of the Anglican Church. They at least did not exasperate human nature; but even they showed the same blindness, in binding themselves instantly to the Divine Right of Kings, which was almost immediately to break down.

For this reason, there is really no historical doubt about what Protestantism did; it died. It did not die because the Protestants were wrong; Mahomet, for instance, was a far shrewder person, and his heresy has not died. The creed of the Protestants died, not because they were wrong, but because they were wrong-headed. They did not really think what they were doing; and this was chiefly because the real driving force behind them was the impatient insolence and avarice of new nobles and rebellious princes. But, anyhow, the theological and theoretical part of their work withered with extraordinary rapidity; and the void that was left was almost as rapidly filled with other things. What those things were is clear enough in many cases, including cases much more apparently harmless; but it is clearest of all in what is confronting us to-day; the Race Religion of the Germans.

Needless to say, there was no such nonsense talked in Luther's time, or for long after his time; and, least of all, to do him justice, by Luther. Germans were turbulent and a little barbaric, as he was himself; but it is only fair to him to say that he was a Christian, in the sense that he believed that nothing could be done except in the strength of Christ. A superbly typical story reaches me from Germany; that some of the Nazis started out to sing the great reformers's famous hymn, "A strong fortress is our God" (which sounds quite promisingly militaristic), but found themselves unable to articulate the very words at the beginning of the next verse, which ran, "Of ourselves we can do nothing." Luther did, in his own mad way, believe in humility; but modern Germany believes simply, solely and entirely in pride. That is an example of what I mean by a void being filled up, not only by another substance, but actually by an antagonistic substance.

Luther was subject to irrational convulsions of rage, in one of which he tore out the Epistle of St. James from the Bible, because St. James exalts the importance of good works. But I shudder to imagine into what sort of epileptic convulsion he would have fallen if anybody had told him to tear out the Epistles of St. Paul, because St. Paul was not an Aryan. Luther, if possible, rather exaggerated the weakness of humanity, but at least it was the weakness of all humanity. John Knox achieved that queer Puritan paradox, of combining the same concentrated invocation of Christ with an inhuman horror and loathing for all the signs and forms and traditions generally characteristic of Christians. He combined, in the way that puzzles us so much, the adoration of the Cross with the abomination of the Crucifix. But at least John Knox would have exploded like dynamite, if anybody had asked him to adore the Swastika. All this new Nordic nonsense would seem to have nothing whatever to do with Protestant theology; or rather to be completely contrary to it. No one is more sincerely glad than we are to know that some of the German Protestants are still most consistent and courageous Christians; and that a definite number of the Lutherans still have some sort of remote connection with Luther. But, taking the development simply as an historical development, as a part of the science and philosophy of history, it is obvious by this time that the hollow places that were once filled with the foaming fanaticism of the first Reformation doctrines are now filled with a foaming fanaticism of a totally different kind. Those who are rebelling like Luther are rebelling against Luther.

The main moral of this is so large and simple and striking, that it will soon be impossible to conceal it from the world. It is the simple fact that the moment men began to contradict the Church with their own private judgment, everything they did was incredibly ill-judged; that those who broke away from the Church's basis almost immediately broke down on their own basis; that those who tried to stand apart from Authority could not in fact stand at all. Islam stood by being stagnant; it is not unfair to say it stood up by lying down. But Protestantism could not stand in the staggering rush of the West; it could only maintain itself by ceasing to be itself, and announcing its readiness to turn into anything else.

II. When the World Turned Back

For the first forty years of my life, practically no man in the world, and certainly no man of the world, had any doubt whatever about what Matthew Arnold called, "the way the world is going." A man did not necessarily agree with Matthew Arnold, who seemed to think that he must necessarily go the way the world was going. Some regretted ages that were gone; some again were prepared to go farther than others, some to go faster than others; some almost passionately desired to go slow. But all agreed that it was, in the vulgar phrase, going it; and still going strong. It was, very broadly, the demand for freedom and fraternity flowing from the French Revolution and the American Revolution, making towards an ideal of democracy. Elements were indeed mixed in it, which logically had very little to do with each other. There was a tendency to materialism, to monism or to scepticism, which I rejected long before I was a Catholic. There was an element of equal justice, and the dignity of all citizens, which I accepted long after I was a Catholic; and which I accept still. But I assumed, like everybody else, that the main movement was still moving; and would presumably go on moving. There were three ways in which it could be recognised by a Catholic, or a man of increasingly Catholic sympathies. (1) He could say that this was the way the world was going; and so much the worse for the world. He could say the world would certainly go further and fare worse. (2) He could say, with considerable truth, that no such movement that was purely secular really touched the question that was purely spiritual. To take a simple example, the most ideal Republicans could not somehow get out of the human habit of dying; and generally of wondering whether dying meant being completely dead. Democracy could not satisfy all desires, even if it could purge itself enough to satisfy all democratic desires. (3) He could look forward, with some historical justification, to a time when any temporal quarrel between the Church and the Republic should end in a real and reasonable reconciliation of the truths in both; as St. Thomas reconciled the philosophy of Aristotle with the religion of Augustine.

Something like this has largely been done, in recent Papal pronouncements; but the point is here that whether or no the Church could close this particular quarrel with the world, every one was certain that a quarrel with democracy *was* a quarrel with the world. In short, a Catholic might reject the present progress; or say his creed was independent of the present progress; or say his creed would find a place for the present progress. But everybody believed that the progress of the present would be the progress of the future.

Then came the astounding judgments; the strange signs of Apocalypse. First the Great War; then the paradox of Fascism in Italy; then the parody of Fascism in Germany. Now these things have left in the minds of all thinking men (as the Rationalist Press Association would say) an enormous overturn or reversal of thought, which has nothing whatever to do with thinking any of these movements right or wrong. It is very vital to realise that the change is something more fundamental than agreement or disagreement with the factions concerned. A man may think the war waged by the Allies justifiable, as I did and do; he may think that the stroke of Mussolini had considerable justification, or even that the stroke of Hitler achieved many things that were just. Or he may think exactly the opposite, and regard the whole militant epoch as a relapse into blood and barbarism, from the first recruit of Kitchener's Army[21] to the last ruffian dripping with the blood of Dollfuss.[22] But there is a changed landscape at the back of all these fighting figures; and it is a landscape like an earthquake. What a man knows, now, is that the whole march of mankind can turn and tramp backwards in its tracks; that progress can start progressing, or feeling as if it were progressing, in precisely the contrary course from that which has been called progress for centuries. It can not only lose but fling away all that its fathers fought for and valued most; it can not only restore but restore exclusively all that its grandfathers

[21] Horatio Herbert Kitchener (1850–1916) was an English field marshal and secretary of state for war in World War I. At the outbreak of the war, his appeals raised thousands of patriotic volunteers.

[22] Engelbert Dollfuss (1892–1934), an Austrian statesman, was the leader of the Christian Socialist party and became chancellor in 1932. In 1933 he suspended parliamentary government, crushed the socialists. In 1934 he was murdered by the Nazis.

were forced to abandon, or felt themselves unable to defend. The whole world is moving again; but it is moving the other way.

To-day *this* is the way the world is going, if there is any such thing. But in fact there is no such thing. A Catholic perhaps should have seen it from the first; but many a Catholic has only seen it in a flash at the last. There is no way the world is going. There never was. The world is not going anywhere, in the sense of the old optimist progressives, or even of the old pessimist reactionaries. It is not going to the Brave New World which Mr. Aldous Huxley described with detestation, any more than to the New Utopia which Mr. H. G. Wells described with delight. The world is what the saints and the prophets saw it was; it is not merely getting better or merely getting worse; there is one thing that the world does; it wobbles. Left to itself, it does not get anywhere; though if helped by real reformers of the right religion and philosophy, it may get better in many respects, and sometimes for considerable periods. But in itself it is not a progress; it is not even a process; it is the fashion of this world that passeth away. Life in itself is not a ladder; it is a see-saw.

Now that is fundamentally what the Church has always said; and for about four hundred years has been more and more despised for saying. The Church never said that wrongs could not or should not be righted; or that commonwealths could not or should not be made happier; or that it was not worth while to help them in secular and material things; or that it is not a good thing if manners become milder, or comforts more common, or cruelties more rare. But she did say that we must not count on the certainty even of comforts becoming more common or cruelties more rare; as if this were an inevitable social trend towards a sinless humanity; instead of being as it was a mood of man, and perhaps a better mood, possibly to be followed by a worse one. We must not hate humanity, or despise humanity, or refuse to help humanity; but we must not trust humanity; in the sense of trusting a trend in human nature which cannot turn back to bad things. "Put not your trust in princes; nor in any child of man."[23] That is the precise point of this very practical

[23] The quotation is from Psalms 146:3.

sort of politics. Be a Royalist if you like (and there is a vast amount to be said, and a vast amount being said, just now, for more personal and responsible rule); try a Monarchy if you think it will be better; but do not trust a Monarchy, in the sense of expecting that a monarch will be anything but a man. Be a Democrat if you like (and I shall always think it the most generous and the most fundamentally Christian ideal in politics); express your sense of human dignity in manhood suffrage or any other form of equality; but put not your trust in manhood suffrage or in any child of man. There is one little defect about Man, the image of God, the wonder of the world and the paragon of animals; that he is not to be trusted. If you identify him with some ideal, which you choose to think is his inmost nature or his only goal, the day will come when he will suddenly seem to you a traitor.

He seems a traitor to-day to all that world of liberal and enlightened opinion, which had made up its mind about the way the world was going, in the path of progress and of peace; the world of Wells and Webb[24] and the Pacifists of America and the social reformers of Cambridge. Most of them are reduced to muttering, like the villain in the old melodrama, "a time will come." But it is in a very different tone from that in which they were crying quite lately, like the man in the comic song, "Now we shan't be long!" The most hopeful of them admit that we shall probably be very long, in reversing all that the reaction in Europe has done already. If, that is, it is ever reversed; and these people really have nothing except a purely mystical faith to suggest that it ever will be reversed. I am really more hopeful in being what they would call more hopeless; for I suspect that pretty nearly everything is eventually reversed. But it was exactly because they would not see this, that they were startled when their own reform or revolution was reversed before their own eyes. The point here, however, is that if there is something stable and not subject to reversal, it is not like anything that they imagine. Its habitation is not in the future or necessarily in any development of ideas peculiar to the present; we are not at the beginning of any endless

[24] Sidney Webb (1859–1947) was a prominent figure in the founding of the Fabian Society and in the development of socialist thought in England.

and expanding dawn, but only of the ordinary daily dawns each followed by its own darkness; and the Faith, as Mr. Belloc said, "is the only beacon in this night, if beacon there be."

In the heart of Christendom, in the head of the Church, in the centre of the civilisation called Catholic, there and in no movement and in no future, is found that crystallisation of commonsense and true traditions and rational reforms, for which the modern man mistakenly looked to the whole trend of the modern age. From this will come the reminders that mercy is being neglected or memory cast away, and not from the men who happen to make the next batch of rulers on this restless and distracted earth. That is the fact that we have all found at last; and that is why I have put it first. It is not the first in order, but it is the first in importance, of the facts I have discovered after I had discovered the truth; and if I had still been out in the darkness, it would in this dark hour have brought me to the door.

III. The Surrender upon Sex

I have explained that these are sketches of six separate occasions, on which I should have become a Catholic, if I had not been the one and only kind of human being who cannot become a Catholic. The excitement of conversion is still open to the atheist and the diabolist; and everybody can be converted except the convert. In my first outline, I mentioned that one of the crises, which would in any case have driven me the way I had gone already, was the shilly-shallying and sham liberality of the famous Lambeth Report on what is quaintly called Birth Control. It is in fact, of course, a scheme for preventing birth in order to escape control. But this particular case was only the culmination of a long process of compromise and cowardice about the problem of sex; the final surrender after a continuous retreat.

There is one historical human fact which now seems to me so plain and solid, that I think that even if I were to lose the Faith, I could not lose sight of the fact. It has rather the character of a fact of chemistry or geology; though from another side it is mysterious enough, like many other manifest and unmistakable facts. It is this: that at the moment when Religion lost touch with Rome, it changed instantly and internally, from top to bottom, in its very substance and the stuff of which it was made. It changed in substance; it did not necessarily change in form or features or externals. It might do the same things; but it could not be the same thing. It might go on saying the same things; but it was not the same thing that was saying them. At the very beginning, indeed, the situation was almost exactly like that. Henry VIII was a Catholic in everything except that he was not a Catholic. He observed everything down to the last bead and candle; he accepted everything down to the last deduction from a definition; he accepted everything except Rome. And in that instant of refusal, his religion became a different religion; a different sort of religion; a different sort of thing. In that instant it began to change; and it has not stopped changing yet. We are all somewhat wearily aware that some Modern Churchmen call such continuous change progress; as when we remark that a corpse crawling with worms has an increased vitality; or that a snow-man, slowly turning into a puddle, is purifying itself of its accretions. But I am not concerned with this argument here. The point is that a dead man may look like a sleeping man a moment after he is dead; but decomposition has actually begun. The point is that the snow-man may in theory be made in the real image of man. Michelangelo made a statue in snow; and it might quite easily have been an exact replica of one of his statues in marble; but it was not in marble. Most probably the snow-man has begun to melt almost as soon as it is made. But even if the frost holds, it is still a stuff capable of melting when the frost goes. It seemed to many that Protestantism would long continue to be, in the popular phrase, a perfect frost. But that does not alter the difference between ice and marble; and marble does not melt.

The same sort of progressives are always telling us to have a trust in the Future. As a fact, the one thing that a progressive cannot possibly have is a trust in the Future. He cannot have a trust in his own Future; let alone in his own Futurism. If he sets no limit to change, it may change all his own progressive views as much as his conservative views. It was so with the Church first founded by Henry VIII; who was, in almost everything commonly cursed as Popery, rather more Popish than the Pope. He thought he might trust it to go on being orthodox; to go on being sacramentalist; to go on being sacerdotalist; to go on being ritualist, and the rest. There was only one little weakness. It could not trust itself to go on being itself. Nothing else, except the Faith, can trust itself to go on being itself.

Now touching this truth in relation to Sex, I may be permitted to introduce a trivial journalistic anecdote. A few years before the War, some of my fellow-journalists, Socialists as well as Tories, were questioning me about what I really meant by Democracy; and especially if I really thought there was anything in Rousseau's ideal of the General Will. I said I thought (and I think I still think) that there can be such a thing, but it must be much more solid and unanimous than a mere majority, such as rules in party politics. I applied the old phrase of the Man in the Street, by saying that if I looked out of the window at a strange man walking past my house, I could bet heavily on his thinking some things, but not the common controversial things. The Liberals might have a huge majority, but he need not be a Liberal; statistics might prove England to be preponderantly Conservative, but I would not bet a button that he would be Conservative. But (I said) I should bet that he believes in wearing clothes. And my Socialist questioners did not question this; they, too, accepted clothes as so universal an agreement of common sense and civilisation, that we might attribute the tradition to a total stranger, unless he were a lunatic. Such a little while ago! To-day, when I see the stranger walking down the street, I should not bet that he believes even in clothes. The country is dotted with Nudist Colonies; the bookstalls are littered with Nudist magazines; the papers swarm with polite little paragraphs, praising the browness and braveness of the special sort of anarchical asses here in question. At any given moment, there may be a General Will; but it is an uncommonly weak and wavering sort of will, without the Faith to support it.

As in that one matter of modesty, or the mere externals of sex, so in all the deeper matters of sex, the modern will has been amazingly weak and wavering. And I suppose it is because the Church has known from the first this weakness which we have all discovered at last, that about certain sexual matters She has been very decisive and dogmatic; as many good people have quite honestly thought, too decisive and dogmatic. Now a Catholic is a person who has plucked up courage to face the incredible and inconceivable idea that something else may be wiser than he is. And the most striking and outstanding illustration is perhaps to be found in the Catholic view of marriage as compared with the modern theory of divorce; not, it must be noted, the *very* modern theory of divorce, which is the mere negation of marriage; but even more the slightly less modern and more moderate theory of divorce, which was generally accepted even when I was a boy. This is the very vital point or test of the question; for it explains the Church's rejection of the moderate as well as the immoderate theory. It illustrates the very fact I am pointing out, that Divorce has already turned into something totally different from what was intended, even by those who first proposed it. Already we must think ourselves back into a different world of thought, in order to understand how anybody ever thought it was compatible with Victorian virtue; and many very virtuous Victorians did. But they only tolerated this social solution as an exception; and many other modern social solutions they would not have tolerated at all. My own parents were not even orthodox Puritans or High Church people; they were Universalists more akin to Unitarians. But they would have regarded Birth-Prevention exactly as they would have regarded Infanticide. Yet about Divorce such liberal Protestants did hold an intermediate view, which was substantially this. They thought the normal necessity and duty of all married people was to remain faithful to their marriage; that this could be demanded of them, like common honesty or any other virtue. But they thought that in some very extreme and extraordinary cases a divorce was allowable. Now, putting aside our own mystical and sacramental doctrine, this was not, on the face of it, an unreasonable position. It certainly was not meant to be an anarchical position. But the Catholic Church, standing almost alone, declared that it would in fact lead to an anarchical position; and the Catholic Church was right.

Any man with eyes in his head, whatever the ideas in his head, who looks at the world as it is to-day, must know that the whole social substance of marriage has changed; just as the whole social substance of Christianity changed with the divorce of Henry VIII. As in the other case, the externals remained for a time and some of them remain still. Some divorced persons, who can be married quite legally by a registrar, go on complaining bitterly that they cannot be married by a priest. They regard a church as a peculiarly suitable place in which to make and break the same vow at the same moment. And the Bishop of London, who was supposed to sympathise with the more sacramental party, recently submitted to such a demand on the ground that it was a special case. As if every human being's case were not a special case. That decision was one of the occasions on which I should have done a bolt, if I had delayed it so long. But the general social atmosphere is much the most important matter. Numbers of normal people are getting married, thinking already that they may be divorced. The instant that idea enters, the whole conception of the old Protestant compromise vanishes. The sincere and innocent Victorian would never have married a woman reflecting that he could divorce her. He would as soon have married a woman reflecting that he could murder her. These things were not supposed to be among the daydreams of the honeymoon. The psychological substance of the whole thing has altered; the marble has turned to ice; and the ice has melted with most amazing rapidity. The Church was right to refuse even the exception. The world has admitted the exception; and the exception has become the rule.

As I have said, the weak and inconclusive pronouncement upon Birth-Prevention was only the culmination of this long intellectual corruption. I need not discuss the particular problem again at this point; beyond saying that the same truth applies as in the case of Divorce. People propose an easy way out of certain human responsibilities and difficulties; including a way out of the responsibility and difficulty of doing economic justice and achieving better payment for the poor. But these people propose this easy method, in the hope that some people will only use it to a moderate extent; whereas it is much more probable that an indefinite number will use it to an indefinite extent. It is odd that they do not see this; because the writers and thinkers among them are no longer by any means optimistic about human nature, like Rousseau; but much more pessimistic about human nature than we are. Considering mankind as described, for instance, by Mr. Aldous Huxley, it is hard to see what answer he could possibly give, except the answer which we give, if the question were put thus: "On the one side, there is an easy way out of the difficulty by avoiding childbirth; on the other side, there is a very difficult way out of the difficulty, by reconstructing the whole social system and toiling and perhaps fighting for the better system. Which way are the men you describe more likely to take?" But my concern is not with open and direct opponents like Mr. Huxley; but with all to whom I might once have looked to defend the country of the Christian altars. They ought surely to know that the foe now on the frontiers offers no terms of compromise; but threatens a complete destruction. And they have sold the pass.

IV. The Prayer-Book Problem

One of the events which would have made me a Catholic, if I had not already been a Catholic, was the curious affair of the New Prayer-Book. It revealed to me a reality I had not hitherto realised. There really was a Church of England; or rather there really was an England which largely imagined that it possessed and controlled a Church. But this Church was not the Church I thought I had belonged to; the keen, cultivated and sincere group of men who claimed to be Catholic. It was a much vaster and vaguer background of men; who did not believe in anything in particular, but who claimed to be Protestant. But the vital point was that, whether they claimed to be Protestants or clamorously bragged of being atheists, they all seemed to have this fixed idea; that they owned the Church of England; and could turn it into a Mormon temple if they liked. I could not, in any case, have gone on being owned in that way.

But in order to understand all that was involved, it is necessary to say a word about the Anglican Prayer-Book itself. The Book of Common Prayer is the masterpiece of Protestantism. It is more so than the work of Milton. It is the one positive possession and attraction; the one magnet and talisman for people even outside the Anglican Church, as are the great Gothic cathedrals for people outside the Catholic Church. I can speak, I think, for many other converts, when I say that the only thing that can produce any sort of nostalgia or romantic regret, any shadow of homesickness in one who has in truth come home, is the rhythm of Cranmer's prose. All the other supposed superiorities of any sort of Protestantism are quite fictitious. Tell a Catholic convert that he has lost his liberty, and he will laugh. A distinguished literary lady wrote recently that I had entered the most restricted of all Christian communions, and I was monstrously amused. A Catholic has fifty times more feeling of being free than a man caught in the net of the nervous compromises of Anglicanism; just as a man considering all England feels more free than a man obeying the Whips of one particular party. He has the range of two thousand years full of twelve-hundred thousand controversies, thrashed out by thinker against thinker, school against school, guild against guild, nation against nation, with no limit except the fundamental logical fact that the things were worth arguing, because they could be ultimately solved and settled. As for Reason, our monopoly is practically admitted in the modern world. Except for one or two dingy old atheists in Fleet Street[25] (for whom I have great sympathy), nothing except Rome now defends the reliability of Reason. Much stronger is the appeal of unreason; or of that beauty which perhaps is beyond reason. The English Litany, the music and the magic of the great sixteenth-century style—*that* does call a man backwards like the song of the sirens; as Virgil and the poets might have called to a Pagan who had entered the Early Church. Only, being a Romanist and therefore a Rationalist, he does not go back; he naturally does not forget everything else, because his opponents four hundred years ago had a stylistic knack which they have now entirely lost. For the Anglicans cannot do the trick now, any more than anybody else. Modern prayers, and theirs perhaps more than any, seem to be perfectly incapable of avoiding journalese. And the Prayer-Book prose seems to follow them like a derisive echo. Lambeth or Convocation will publish a prayer saying something like, "Guide us, O Lord, to the solution of our social problems"; and the great organ of old will groan in the background. . . . "All who are desolate and oppressed." The first Anglicans asked for peace and happiness, truth and justice; but nothing can stop the latest Anglicans, and many others, from the horrid habit of asking for improvement in international relations.

But *why* has the old Protestant Prayer-Book a power like that of great poetry upon the spirit and the heart? The reason is much deeper than the mere avoidance of journalese. It might be put in a sentence; it has style; it has tradition; it has religion; it was written by apostate Catholics. It is strong, not in so far as it is the first Protestant book, but in so far as it was the last Catholic book. As it happens, this can be proved in the most practical manner from the actual details of the prose. The most moving passages in the old Anglican Prayer-Book are exactly those that are least like the atmosphere of the

[25] Fleet Street was the locus of the newspaper publishing industry in London.

Anglicans. They are moving, or indeed thrilling, precisely because they say the things which Protestants have long left off saying; and which only Catholics still say. Anybody who knows anything of literature knows when a style lifts itself to its loftiest efforts; and in these cases it is always to say strongly what we still endeavour to say, however weakly; but which nobody else ever endeavours to say at all. Let anyone recall for himself the very finest passages in the Book of Common Prayer, and he will soon see that they are concerned specially with spiritual thoughts and themes that now seem strange and terrible; but anyhow, the reverse of common; ". . . in the hour of death and in the day of Judgment." Who talks about the hour of death? Who talks about the Day of Judgment? Only a litter of shabby little priests from the Italian Mission. Not certainly the popular and eloquent Dean of Bumblebury, who is so Broad and yet so High. Certainly not the charming and fashionable Vicar of St. Ethelbald's, who is so High and yet so Broad. Still less the clergyman helping in the same parish, who is frankly Low. It is the same on every page, where that spirit inspires that style. "Suffer us not, for any pains of death, to fall from Thee." . . . "Ah, that's what gets you" (or words to that effect), as Lord Peter Wimsey truly said of this phrase, in the detective tale of Miss Dorothy Sayers;[26] who, like Lord Peter, knows a good deal about other things besides poisons; and understands her hero's historical traditions very well. But did you ever hear the curate fresh from the cricket-field, or the vicar smiling under the Union Jacks of the Conservative Rally, dwell upon that penultimate peril; or the danger of falling from God amid the pains of death? Very morbid. Just like those Dago devotional books. So very *Roman*.

I do not think the old Anglo-Catholics who were my friends, or the many who are still my friends, would deny that there has been a modern vulgarisation of religion, largely through the spread of this official optimism. But though they themselves are often quite free from the vulgar form of it, they could hardly deny that it is largely official and very widely spread. Yet it came as a great shock to me

[26] Dorothy Sayers (1893–1957) was an English author of detective stories (featuring Lord Peter Wimsey), a playwright and a translator of Dante.

to discover how official and widespread it was. I had exaggerated the importance of an intelligent minority, because it was important to me. But the public and the world without were given up to Arian and Pelagian[27] demagogues like Dean Inge and Dr. Barnes; and a sort of negative Protestantism could still sweep the field. It swept the whole field in the matter of the Prayer-Book. The proposal of an amended Prayer-Book, or rather two alternative Prayer-Books, was not decided for the Church by the Church; or by the communicants; or by the congregation. It was settled by a mob of politicians, atheists, agnostics, dissenters, Parsees; avowed enemies of that Church or of any Church, who happened to have M.P. after their names. If the whole thing had any historic motto, or deserved anything higher than a headline, what was written across all that Anglican story was not *Ecclesia Anglicana,* or *Via Media,*[28] or anything of the sort; it was *Cujus Regio Ejus Religio;*[29] or rendering unto Caesar the things that are God's.

I add one incident to contrast Style, among men who had been Catholics for fourteen-hundred years, with that among men who have been Protestants for four-hundred years. A Protestant organisation presented all the atheists, etc., who had voted Protestant, with a big black Bible or Prayer-Book, or both, decorated outside with a picture of the Houses of Parliament. *In hoc signo vinces.*[30] It would be very idolatrous to put a cross or crucifix outside a book; but a picture of Parliament where the Party Funds are kept, and the peerages sold——. That is the temple where dwell the gods of Israel. . . . We know the world progresses, and education is certainly extended, and there are fewer illiterates; and I suppose it is all right. But those four

[27] Arianism and Pelagianism were both early Christian heresies. Arianism, which flourished in the early fourth century, viewed Christ as a lesser being than God the Father. Pelagianism, which arose in the late fourth century, rejected the doctrine of original sin and contended that the human will is capable of good without the aid of divine grace.

[28] *Via media* was the Anglican "middle way" between the Catholicism of Rome and the Calvinism of Geneva.

[29] See footnote 130, page 328, above.

[30] *In hoc signo vinces* is Latin for "In this sign you shall conquer", the words the Emperor Constantine saw, along with a cross, in the sky before the battle of Milvian Bridge in 312.

strong centuries of Protestant England begin with a Book of Common-Prayer, in which, even amid the treachery and panic of Cranmer, and in the very moment of men rending themselves from Rome and Christendom, they could lift in such sublime language so authentic a cry of Christian men: "By Thy precious death and burial; by Thy glorious resurrection and ascension; and by the coming of the Holy Ghost." Those centuries begin with that speech of men still by instinct and habit of mind Catholic; and the Protestant civilization evolves and the education spreads, and widens in wealth and power and towns and colleges; until at last the ripe and final fruit of its culture is produced, in the form of a fat black book of a cushiony sort, with a real photo-view, a view of one of the Sights, nicely tucked in to its neat back padded binding or frame. . . . A Present from Ramsgate . . . anyhow, four-hundred years march from Rome.

V. The Collapse of Materialism

Some little time ago Dr. David Forsyth delivered to the Section of Psychiatry (Royal Society of Medicine) an address which was certainly a psychological curiosity; of considerable interest to psychologists, pathologists, alienists and all other students of the mental breakdown in the modern world. It was a perfect and compact illustration of the very common combination of a superiority complex with arrested development, and inhibitions on almost all forms of intelligent curiosity. But I mention it here, not because of its narrowness, but of its direct negation of all that is really new in scientific discovery. It is no news to us that a materialist can be bigoted; but we do not always come upon so startling an example of his being antiquated.

It is not worth while to take any particular notice of all the diseased stuff about sadism and masochism being the sources of religion. We may note in passing, with a rather dreary amusement, that this sort of writer can never sustain a connected train of thought; and that he gets even these dismal technical terms hopelessly entangled; for he declares that Islam stands for sadism and Christendom for masochism, having just argued that the Christian persecution of heretics was typically sadistic. But all this judgment of great human events, good or bad, in terms of some obscure streak of lunacy, is itself an amusement for lunatics. It is exactly as if a man were to argue: "There is a special sort of madman who thinks he is made of glass; I will call this disease Vitreosity; and I will then show that anybody anywhere, who for any reason had anything to do with glass was a victim of vitreosity. The desert-merchants who were said to have invented glass, the medieval craftsmen who so successfully coloured glass, the early astronomers who first fitted telescopes with lenses of glass, all showed Vitreosity in various stages of that disease; it is akin to subconscious *libido* because Peeping Tom looked through a window, which may have been made of glass; it is the root impulse of alcoholism, because people drink out of glasses; and Prince Albert and Queen Victoria were obviously stricken with raving and uncontrolled

Vitreosity; because they built the Crystal Palace."[31] The slight defect in this theory (which is quite as scientific as Dr. Forsyth's) is that in order to theorise, it is sometimes useful to think. It is obvious that all these people had a thousand other reasons for doing all they did, besides being mad on glass; and it is equally obvious that the great religions, true or false, had a thousand reasons for doing all they did, without being mad on masochism or sadism.

Only, as I say, we may well emerge from this slime and consider the real case of Dr. Forsyth, and his strange ignorance of the very elements of modern thought, and even rather specially of modern science. Now on the larger matter, his thesis was essentially this; that science and religion, so far from being reconciled or even reconcilable, were divided by the vital contradiction that science belongs to what he called "reality-thinking," or we call objective truth; while religion belonged to what he called "pleasure-thinking," or what most people call imagination. I need not mention the hundred obvious objections to this crude division; as, for instance, that religion has not confined itself to imagining pleasurable things, but has often been blamed by people like Dr. Forsyth for imagining unpleasant ones; or that it is arguing in a circle to prove at the end that religion is inconsistent with science merely by assuming at the beginning that it is inconsistent with truth. I am only concerned here to insist, not merely that the view is the reverse of the truth, but that the view is actually the very reverse of the modern view.

If there are two staring and outstanding facts about science and religion at this particular moment, they are these. First, that science is claiming much less than it did to show us a solid and objective reality. And second, that religion is claiming much *more* than it did (at least for centuries past) that its miracles and marvels of mystical experience can be proved to exist as a solid and objective reality. On the one side, the Atom has entirely lost the objective solidity it had for the nineteenth-century materialists. On the other side, the Ascension is accepted as a case of Levitation by many who would not accept it as an Ascension. On the one hand, the science of physics has

[31] The Crystal Palace was a vast building erected in London in 1851 to house the first international exhibition of the products and machines of the industrial age.

almost become a science of metaphysics. For it is not merely, as is often said, that the Atom has become an abstract mathematical formula; it is almost as true to say that it has become a mere algebraic symbol. For the new physicists tell us frankly that what they describe is *not* the objective reality of the thing they observe; that they are not examining an object as the nineteenth century materialists thought they were examining an object. Some of them tell us that they are only observing certain disturbances or distortions, actually created by their own attempt to observe. Eddington[32] is more agnostic about the material world than Huxley ever was about the spiritual world. A very unfortunate moment at which to say that science deals directly with reality and objective truth.

On the other hand, on the other plane, the plane of historical and practical argument, it is the very moment at which religion really is appealing to reality and objective truth. The Church throws down the unanswered challenge of Lourdes; the Spiritualists positively claim to prove their new religion by experiments, like a thesis in chemistry or electricity; and a vast number of independent intellectuals, who are neither Catholics nor Spiritualists, have begun to show an entirely new interest in the logical, or even the legal case for some of the great historic miracles. For instance, there have been two or three books following on the line of the brilliant but strictly scientific book called *Who Moved the Stone*; and the tendency of the most detached writers is to admit more and more that the evidence for such events has been underrated. The youngest school of Catholic apologists, such as Father Knox and Mr. Christopher Hollis and Mr. Arnold Lunn,[33] attack almost entirely with the weapons of proof and practical evidence; and it is no longer pretended that they always have the worst of it. A very unfortunate moment at which to say that religion deals only with pleasant fancies and imaginations.

Dr. Forsyth's antiquated style of thought interests me here, however, only as drawing attention to the familiar modern facts of which he seems never to have heard. And most relevant here is the fact of that

[32] Sir Arthur Stanley Eddington (1882–1944) was an English astronomer and popularizer of modern theories of physics. He became director of the Royal Observatory in Greenwich in 1914.

[33] Arnold Lunn (1886–1974) was an English writer and convert to Catholicism.

extraordinary scientific change in the attitude to facts. It has its place in this series, because it is one of the great changes which had not developed in any full and public fashion, even by the time that I finally sought admission to the Church; and, at the much earlier time when I had already begun to think about it, all the popular science that a layman heard of was dominated by the now dead materialism of Haeckel.[34] It is, therefore, true to say that this huge revolution in the philosophy of physical science was one of the world events which came after my conversion; but would have hugely hastened it, if it had come before my conversion. Only the exact nature of the effect, of this scientific revolution upon personal religion, is often misstated and widely misunderstood.

It is not, as some seem to fancy, that we think there is anything particularly Christian about electrons, any more than there is anything essentially atheistic about atoms. It is not that we propose to base our philosophy on their physics; any more than to base our ancient theology on their most recent biology. We are not "going to the country" with a set of slogans or party-cries, like *Electrons for the Elect,* or *For Priest and Proton.* The catastrophic importance for Catholics, of this collapse of materialism, is simply the fact that the most confident cosmic statements of science can collapse. If fifty years hence the electron is as entirely exploded as the atom, it will not affect us; for we have never founded our philosophy on the electron any more than on the atom. But the materialists did found *their* philosophy on the atom. And it is quite likely that some spiritual fad or other is at this moment being founded on the electron. To a man of my generation, the importance of the change does not consist in its destroying the dogma (which was after all a detail, though a very dogmatic dogma), "Matter consists of indivisible atoms." But it does consist in its destroying the accepted, universal and proclaimed and popularised dogma: "You must accept the conclusions of science." Scores and hundreds of times I have heard, through my youth and early manhood, the repetition of that ultimatum: "You must accept the conclusions of science." And it is that notion or experience that has now been concluded; or rather excluded. Whatever else is questionable, there is henceforth

[34] Ernst Haeckel (1834–1919) was a German scientist and champion of Darwinism against religious orthodoxy.

no question of anybody "accepting" the conclusions of science. The new scientists themselves do not ask us to accept the conclusions of science. The new scientists themselves do not accept the conclusions of the new science. To do them justice, they deny vigorously that science has concluded; or that it has, in that sense, any conclusion. The finest intellects among them repeat, again and again, that science is inconclusive.

Which is all very well, and all very wise, and all very true to the gradual adjustment of truths on their own plane. But meanwhile — there is such a thing as human life. The Victorian agnostics waited hopefully for science to give them a working certainty about life. The new physicist philosophers are in no way different, except that they wait hopelessly instead of hopefully. For they know very well the real meaning of relatively right to being relatively wrong. And meanwhile, as I say, there is such a thing as wanting a working rule as to whether we should pay our debts or murder our enemies. We would not wait for a nineteenth-century enlightenment that might come. We certainly will not wait for a twentieth-century enlightenment that cannot come. If we want a guide to life, it seems that we must look elsewhere.

VI. The Case of Spain

The point of the recent political story in Spain has never been put clearly in the English papers; perhaps not quite clearly even in the Catholic papers. It is a very striking example of how the world has really moved, since my own most important change of conviction occurred. There is a paradox in every story of conversion; which is perhaps the reason why the records of it are never ideally satisfactory. It is in its very nature the extinction of egoism; and yet every account of it must sound egoistic. It means, at least in the case of the Religion in question, a recognition of reality which has nothing to do with relativity. It is as if a man said, "This inn really exists, even if I have never found it"; or, "My home is actually in this village; and would be there, if I had never reached it." It is the recognition that the truth is true, apart from the truth-seeker; and yet the description must be the autobiography of a truth-seeker; generally a rather depressing sort of person. It will therefore sound egotistical, if I preface these remarks by saying that I was for a long time a Liberal in the sense of belonging to the Liberal Party. I am still a Liberal; it is only the Liberal Party that has disappeared. I understood its ideal to be that of equal citizenship and personal freedom; and they are my own political ideals to this day. The point here, however, is that I worked for a long time with the practical organization of Liberalism; I wrote for a great part of my life for the old *Daily News*; and I knew of course that it identified political liberty, rightly or wrongly, with representative government. Then came the breach, on which I need not insist; except by saying that I became quite convinced of two facts. First, that representative government had ceased to be representative. Second, that Parliament was in fact gravely menaced by political corruption. Politicians did not represent the populace, even the most noisy and vulgar of the populace. Politicians did not deserve the dignified name of demagogues. They deserved no name except perhaps the name of bagmen; they were travelling for private firms. If they represented anything, it was vested interests, vulgar but not even popular.

For this reason, when the Fascists' revolt appeared in Italy, I could not be entirely hostile to it; for I knew the hypocritical plutocracy against which it rebelled. But neither could I be entirely friendly to it; for I believed in the civic equality in which the politicians pretended to believe. For the present purpose, the problem can be put very briefly. The whole of the real case for Fascism can be put in two words never printed in our newspapers: *secret societies*. The whole case against Fascism could be put in one word now never used and almost forgotten: *legitimacy*. For the first, the Fascist was justified in smashing the politicians; for their contract with the people was secretly contradicted by their secret contracts with gangs and conspiracies. For the second, Fascism could never be quite satisfactory; for it did not rest on authority but only on power; which is the weakest thing in the world. The Fascists said in effect, "We may not be the majority, but we are the most vigorous and intelligent minority." Which is simply challenging any other intelligent minority to show that it is more vigorous. It may well end in the very anarchy it attempted to avoid. Compared with this, despotism and democracy are *legitimate*. I mean there is no doubt about who is the King's eldest son or about who has most votes in the most mechanical election. But a mere competition of intelligent minorities is a rather dreadful prospect. That, it seems to me, is a fair statement of the case for and against the Fascist movement. And now I should like to apply it to the curious case of Spain; and note how Liberalism met the issue.

For weeks and months on end my old organ the *Daily News* (now the *News-Chronicle*) had warned the public of all these doubtful and dangerous implications of Fascism. It had reviled Fascism for its vices; and rather more virulently for its virtues. But anyhow it had furiously denounced the notion of a minority imposing its will by mere violence, by weapons or military training, in contempt of the constitutional democracy in which the people expressed its will through Parliament. I think there is a great deal to be said for that view; especially in England, where Parliament is really normal and national as it never was in Italy or Germany. I could write much for and much against the Liberal theory as enunciated in the *News-Chronicle*. And then, suddenly, the whole case was thrown over, and turned upside down, in face of the simple situation in Spain.

First it must be remembered that the Church is always in advance of the world. That is why it is said to be behind the times. It discussed everything so long ago that people have forgotten the discussion. St. Thomas was an internationalist before all our internationists; St. Joan was a nationalist almost before there were nations; Blessed Robert Bellarmine[35] said all there is to be said for democracy before any ordinary worldling dared to be a democrat; and (what is to the purpose here) the Christian social reform was in full activity *before* any of these quarrels of Fascists and Bolshevists appeared. The Popular Party was working out the ideas of Leo XIII[36] before a single Blackshirt had been seen in Italy. The same popular ideals had been moving in Spain; with the result that they had really become popular. There were other complications, of course; the Court had never been quite popular; the Dictatorship had not, I think, been imaginative about the curious problem of Catalonia;[37] but all this did not effect the profound and popular Catholic change. The Pope particularly insisted that he had no objection to the Republic as such; there was no opposition to anything but to certain inhuman ideals, by which men would lose humanity in losing personal liberty and property. Well, in the perfectly fair and open intellectual interchange, in which all Liberals are supposed to believe, the Catholic ideals won. At an entirely peaceful and legal election, exactly like any English election, a vast majority voted in various degrees for the traditional truths, which had been normal to the Nation for much more than a thousand years. Spain spoke; if indeed elections do speak; and declared constitutionally against Communism, against Atheism, against the negation that starved normality in our time. Nobody said that this majority had been achieved by military violence. Nobody pretended that an armed minority had imposed it on the State. If the Liberal theory of Parliamentary majorities was just,

---

[35] Robert Bellarmine (1542–1621) was an Italian cardinal known for his polemics against Protestantism and for his defense of the temporal power of the pope.

[36] The Popular Party, or *Partito Popolare*, was an Italian Catholic political party founded in 1919. Pope Leo XIII reigned from 1878 to 1903. His encyclical *Rerum novarum* (1891) supported the rights of labor, called for a just wage and defended trade unions.

[37] Catalonia is a region in the northeastern corner of Spain that was involved in a long and constant struggle with its neighbors to maintain political and cultural autonomy.

this was just. If the Parliamentary system was a popular system, this was popular. And then the Socialists suddenly jumped up and did exactly everything that the Fascists have been blamed for doing. They used bombs and guns and instruments of violence to prevent the fulfilment of the will of the people, or at least of the will of the Parliament. Having lost the game by the rules of democracy, they tried to win it after all entirely by the rules of war; in this case of Civil War. They tried to overthrow a pacific Parliament by a militarist *coup d'état*. In short, they behaved exactly like Mussolini; or rather they did the very worst that has ever been attributed to Mussolini; and without a rag of his theoretical excuse.

And what did Liberalism say? What did my dear old friends of liberty and peaceful citizenship say? Naturally, I assumed on opening the paper that it would rally to the defence of Parliament and peaceful representative government and rebuke the attempt to make a minority dominant by mere military violence. Judge of my astonishment, when I found Liberals lamenting aloud over the unfortunate failure of these Socialistic Fascists to reverse the result of a General Election. I had been a Liberal in the old Liberal days; we were not unacquainted with Tory and unionist victories at the polls; we had often gone contentedly into Opposition. It had never been suggested that when Balfour or Baldwin[38] constitutionally became Prime Ministers, all the Nonconformists should go out with guns and bayonets to reverse the popular vote; or the Leader of the Opposition begin to throw dynamite at the elected Leader of the House. The only inference was that Liberalism was only opposed to militarists when they were Fascists; and entirely approved of Fascists so long as they were Socialists.

Now that is a small and purely political point. But to me it was very awakening. It showed me quite clearly the fundamental truth of the modern world. And that is this: there are no Fascists; there are no Socialists; there are no Liberals; there are no Parliamentarians. There is the one supremely inspiring and irritating institution in the

[38] Arthur James, Earl of Balfour (1848–1930), British prime minister from 1902 to 1905, authored books on religion and philosophy. Stanley Baldwin (1867–1947) was a three-time Conservative British prime minister between the two world wars.

world; and there are its enemies. Its enemies are ready to be for violence or against violence, for liberty or against liberty, for representation or against representation; and even for peace or against peace. It gave me an entirely new certainty, even in the practical and political sense, that I had chosen well.

VII. The Well and the Shallows

In numberless novels and newspaper articles, we have all read about a process which is still apparently regarded as novel or new; though it has been described in almost exactly the same terms for nearly a hundred years; and in slightly different terms for hundreds of years before that. I mean what is called the growth of doubt or the disturbance of faith; and the only point about it which is pertinent here is this; that it is always described as a revolt of the deeper parts of the mind against something that is comparatively superficial. We need not deny that modern doubt, like ancient doubt, does ask deep questions; we only deny that, as compared with our own philosophy, it gives any deeper answers. And it is a general rule, touching what is called modern thought, that while the questions are often really deep, the answers are often decidedly shallow. And it is perhaps even more important to remark that, while the questions are in a sense eternal, the answers are in every sense ephemeral. The world is still asking the questions that were asked by Job. The world will not long be contented with the answers that are given by Joad.[39]

The chances of the Book of Joad being as permanent as the Book of Job are limited by certain perfectly practical calculations. Mr. Joad is an able and sincere man; and nobody doubts that his opinions are the product of his own mind; but they are very unmistakably the product of his own age. In this case it would be more correct to say, of his own generation. For the sceptics throughout the ages inherit nothing except a negation. Their positive policy or ideal varies, not only from century to century, but even from father to son. A free-thinker like Bradlaugh,[40] coming out of the individualistic nineteenth century and the mercantile spirit of the Midlands, was careful to explain that he was an Individualist. A free-thinker of the next generation, like Mr. Joseph McCabe,[41]

---

[39] Cyril Edwin Mitchinson Joad (1891–1953) was an English philosopher, author and teacher. A pacifist (he was a conscientious objector during World War I) and agnostic, he championed unpopular causes and wrote popular philosophical works; the *Book of Joad* is probably a reference to one or all of them. He won fame as a regular guest on the BBC radio program "Brain Trust".

[40] Charles Bradlaugh (1833–91) was an English journalist, politician and freethinker.

[41] Joseph McCabe (1867–1955) was the English founder of the Rationalist Press Association.

THE WELL AND THE SHALLOWS

was careful to explain that he was a Socialist. A free-thinker wanting to make a splash to-day would almost certainly insist that he was not a Socialist; which has come to mean something as mild as Mr. Ramsay Mac-Donald.[42] For those who can believe in each of these social moves in turn, as they happen to turn up, the matter may be irrelevant. But some of us will simply draw the moral which determines the whole question of this issue between the traditions of truth and doubt. Those who leave the tradition of truth do not escape into something which we call Freedom. They only escape into something else, which we call Fashion.

That is really the crux of the controversy between the two views of history and philosophy. If it were true that by leaving the temple we walked out into a world of truths, the question would be answered; but it is not true. By leaving the temple, we walk out into a world of idols; and the idols of the marketplace are more perishable and passing than the gods of the temple we have left. If we wished to test rationally the case of rationalism, we should follow the career of the sceptic and ask how far he remained sceptical about the idols or ideals of the world into which he went. There are very few sceptics in history who cannot be proved to have been instantly swallowed by some swollen convention or some hungry humbug of the hour, so that all their utterances about contemporary things now look to us almost pathetically contemporary. The little group of Atheists, who still run their paper in Fleet Street and frequently honour me with hearty but somewhat hasty denunciation, began their agitation in the old Victorian days, and selected for themselves a terrible appropriate title. They did not call themselves Atheists, they called themselves Secularists. Never was a more bitter and blighting confession made in the form of a boast. For the word "secular" does not mean anything so sensible as "worldly." It does not even mean anything so spirited as "irreligious." To be secular simply means to be of the age; that is, of the age which is passing; of the age which, in their case, is already passed. There is one tolerably correct translation of the Latin word which they have chosen as their motto. There

[42] James Ramsay MacDonald (1866–1937), leader of the Labour party in Britain from 1911 to 1914, was a pacifist by conviction and opposed England's participation in World War I. He lost leadership of the Labour party in 1914 and his seat in the House of Commons in 1918, though he regained both in 1922.

is one adequate equivalent of the word "secular"; and it is the word "dated."

In the essays in this series, I have considered some of the effects of this continuous process of time and change, as it has affected the world, even after I myself ceased to look to its changes for essential guidance. I have noted that the changes, which continue to occur, point more and more to the truth of the unchanging philosophy which stands apart from them. I could add, of course, a long list of other examples of exactly the same truth. I could point, for instance, to the collapse of Prohibition; not so much in narrow sense of Prohibition as in the general sense of Prohibitionism. For what failed with the American experiment was not merely a particular chemical experiment with some alleged chemical constituent, which they chose to call alcohol. It was a whole attitude towards all the complex uses and abuses of human things. The great outstanding principle of the modern materialistic world has been Prohibition; even Prohibition in the abstract. Where we say that a social element is dangerous or doubtful, that it must be watched, that it may on due occasion be restrained, the thing that was called the Modern Mind always cried aloud with a voice of thunder that it must be forbidden. The Prohibitionist declares that there must be no wine; the Pacifist that there must be no war; the Communist that there must be no private property; the Secularist that there must be no religious worship. The failure of Prohibition in the one country in which it was a favourite, in which it was a popular idea in so far as anything so inhuman can be popular, was the collapse of the whole conception of wiping out entirely the temptations of man and the trials of mortal life. After that, it is tacitly agreed that there is no such simple way out of moral problems; it is almost admitted that they must be referred to the moral sense. We were actually driven back on the desperate and tragic duty of our fathers, of deciding for ourselves whether we were drinking too much, or whether we were fighting in a just quarrel, or whether we were only defending our own lawful property, or getting other people's property by lawless usury. Such a demand was naturally a great strain on the Modern Mind. For the Modern Mind is not at all accustomed to making up its mind.

It finds the task almost as unfamiliar as working its own farm or practising its own craft; or doing a hundred other things, that human beings had done from the foundations of the world. In short, it would not accept the Catholic doctrine that human life is a battle; it only wanted to have it announced, from time to time in the newspapers, that it was a victory.

There are, I say, a number of other more general defeats of the attack on the Faith, on each of which it would be easy to write a long essay; the longer as the essential truth in the matter was more subtle and more universal. But I will close this series with the examples which I have given, because I think they suffice to show the general trend of the truth which I desire to suggest. The simplest summary of my meaning is to throw my mind back to all the things that seemed in my youth to be the rivals or reasonable alternatives to my religious conviction, and consider whether they could still play even the part which they did. The answer is that not one of them could now even remotely resemble a rival; or be even reasonable as an alternative. There was a time when men of my sympathies felt even tragically the quarrel between the Republic and the Church; the apparent misunderstanding between political equality and mystical authority. It is a commonplace to-day that the world has reacted much more against equality than against authority. But that in itself would not have disposed of the democratic ideals of any sincere democrat. It is the thing called democracy that has itself disappointed the democrat. However much I might hate the Fascists, heartily as I do indeed despise the Hitlerites, that would never restore the mere abstract faith in the Republicans. If I lost my religion to-morrow, I could not again believe that the mere fact of turning Kamchatka from a Monarchy to a Republic would solve all its social sins. I have seen too many Republicans, with their greasy platform promises and their guzzling secret societies. I can remember when being a Socialist was a real inspiration to youth; but anybody who thinks it could be an inspiration to the more elderly phase of maturity, has only to look at the more elderly Socialists. In short, the point I mentioned at the beginning of this article is the point of the whole matter; that while the questions are deep and tragic enough, the recent answers have not really been revolutionary, but only superficial. I could not abandon the faith, without falling back on something more shallow than the faith. I could not cease to be a Catholic, except by becoming something more narrow than a Catholic. A man must narrow his mind in order to lose the universal philosophy; everything that has happened up to this very day has confirmed this conviction; and whatever happens tomorrow will confirm it anew. We have come out of the shallows and the dry places to the one deep well; and the Truth is at the bottom of it.

THE RETURN TO RELIGION

In the days when Huxley and Herbert Spencer and the Victorian agnostics were trumpeting as a final truth the famous hypothesis of Darwin, it seemed to thousands of simple people almost impossible that religion should survive. It is all the more ironic that it has not only survived them all, but it is a perfect example (perhaps the only real example) of what they called the Survival of the Fittest.

It so happens that it does really and truly fit in with the theory offered by Darwin; which was something totally different from most of the theories accepted by Darwinians. This real original theory of Darwin has since very largely broken down in the general field of biology and botany; but it does actually apply to this particular argument in the field of religious history. The recent re-emergence of our religion is a survival of the fittest as Darwin meant it, and not as popular Darwinism meant it; so far as it meant anything. Among the innumerable muddles, which mere materialistic fashion made out of the famous theory, there was in many quarters a queer idea that the Struggle for Existence was of necessity an actual struggle between the candidates for survival; literally a cut-throat competition. There was a vague idea that the strongest creature violently crushed the others. And the notion that this was the one method of improvement came everywhere as good news to bad men; to bad rulers, to bad employers, to swindlers and sweaters and the rest. The brisk owner of a bucket-shop compared himself modestly to a mammoth, trampling down other mammoths in the primeval jungle. The business man destroyed other business men, under the extraordinary delusion that the eohippic horse had devoured other eohippic horses. The rich man suddenly discovered that it was not only convenient but cosmic to starve or pillage the poor, because pterodactyls may have used their little hands to tear each other's eyes. Science, that nameless being, declared that the weakest must go to the wall; especially in Wall Street. There was a rapid decline and degradation in the sense of responsibility in the rich, from the merely rationalistic eighteenth century to the purely scientific nineteenth. The great

Jefferson,[43] when he reluctantly legalised slavery, said he trembled for his country, knowing that God is just. The profiteer of later times, when he legalised usury or financial trickery, was satisfied with himself; knowing that Nature is unjust.

But, however that may be (and of course the moral malady has survived scientific mistake) the people who talked thus of cannibal horses and competitive oysters, did not understand what Darwin's thesis was. If later biologists have condemned it, it should not be condemned without being understood, widely as it has been accepted without being understood. The point of Darwinism was not that a bird with a longer beak (let us say) thrust it into other birds, and had the advantage of a duellist with a longer sword. The point of Darwinism was that the bird with the longer beak could reach worms (let us say) at the bottom of a deeper hole; that the birds who could not do so would die; and he alone would remain to found a race of long-beaked birds. Darwinism suggested that if this happened a vast number of times, in a vast series of ages, it might account for the difference between the beaks of a sparrow and a stork. But the point was that the fittest did not need to *struggle* against the unfit. The surviver had nothing to do except to survive, when the others could not survive. He survived because he alone had the features and organs necessary for survival. And, whatever be the truth about mammoths or monkeys, that is the exact truth about the present survival of religion. It is surviving because nothing else can survive.

Religion has returned; because all the various forms of scepticism that tried to take its place, and do its work, have by this time tied themselves into such knots that they cannot do anything. That chain of causation of which they were fond of talking seems really to have served them after the fashion of the proverbial rope; and when modern discussion gave them rope enough, they quite rapidly hanged themselves. For there is not a single one of the fashionable forms of scientific scepticism, or determinism, that does not end in stark paralysis, touching the practical conduct of human life. Take any three of the normal and necessary ideas on which civilisation and

[43] This reference is to a passage in Jefferson's *Notes on the State of Virginia*. Jefferson did not "legalize" slavery in Virginia; it had never been illegal.

even society depend. First, let us say, a scientific man of the old normal nineteenth-century sort would remark, "We can at least have common sense, in its proper meaning of a sense of reality common to all; we can have common morals, for without them we cannot even have a community; a man must in the ordinary sense obey the law; and especially the moral law." Then the newer sceptic, who is progressive and has gone further and fared worse, will immediately say, "Why should you worship the taboo of your particular tribe? Why should you accept prejudices that are the product of a blind herd instinct? Why is there any authority in the unanimity of a flock of frightened sheep?" Suppose the normal man falls back on the deeper argument: "I am not terrorised by the tribe; I do keep my independent judgment; I have a conscience and a light of justice within, which judges the world." And the stronger sceptic will answer: "If the light in your body be darkness — and it is darkness because it is only in your body — what are your judgments but the incurable twist and bias of your particular heredity and accidental environment? What can we know about judgments, except that they must all be equally unjust? For they are all equally conditioned by defects and individual ignorances, all of them different and none of them distinguishable; for there exists no single man so sane and separate as to be able to distinguish them justly. Why should your conscience be any more reliable than your rotting teeth or your quite special defect of eyesight? God bless us all, one would think you believed in God!" Then perhaps the normal person will get annoyed and say rather snappishly, "At least I suppose we are men of science; there is science to appeal to and she will always answer; the evidential and experimental discovery of real things." And the other sceptic will answer, if he has any sense of humour: "Why certainly. Sir Arthur Eddington[44] is Science; and he will tell you that science cannot destroy religion, or even defend the multiplication table. Sir Bertram Windle[45] was Science; and he would tell you that the scientific mind is completely satisfied in the Roman Catholic Church. For that

[44] See footnote 32, page 379, above.

[45] Bertram Windle (1858–1929) was an English Catholic anthropologist and physician who sought in his writings to demonstrate that there was no conflict between science and Church teachings.

matter, Sir Oliver Lodge[46] was Science; and he reached by purely experimental and evidential methods to a solid belief in ghosts. But I admit that there are men of science who cannot get to a solid belief in anything; even in science; even in themselves. There is the crystalographer of Cambridge who sites in the *Spectator* the lucid sentence: 'We know that most of what we know is probably untrue.' Does that help you on a bit, in founding your sane and solid society?"

We have of course seen just lately the most dramatic exit of great material scientists from the camp of Materialism. It was Eddington I think, who used the phrase that the universe seems to be more like a great thought[47] than a great machine: and Dr. Whitney as reported, has declared that there is no rational description of the ultimate cosmic motion except the Will of God. But it is the perishing of the other things, at least as much as the persistence of the one thing, that has left us at last face to face with the ancient religion of our fathers. The thing once called free thought has come finally to threaten everything that is free. It denies personal freedom in denying free will and the human power of choice. It threatens civic freedom with a plague of hygienic and psychological quackeries; spreading over the land such a network of pseudo-scientific nonsense as free citizens have never yet endured in history. It is quite likely to reverse religious freedom, in the name of some barbarous nostrum or other, such as constitutes the crude and ill-cultured creed of Russia. It is perfectly capable of imposing silence and impotence from without. But there is no doubt whatever that it imposes silence and impotence from within. The whole trend of it, which began as a drive and has ended in drift, is towards some form of the theory that a man cannot help himself; that a man cannot mend himself; above all, that a man cannot free himself. In all its novels and most of its newspaper articles it takes for granted that men are stamped and fixed in certain types of abnormality of anarchical weakness; that they are pinned and labelled in a museum of morality or immorality; or of that sort of unmorality which is more priggish than the one and more

[46] Sir Oliver Lodge (1851–1940) was an English physicist who attempted to reconcile science and religion.
[47] Chesterton could be referring to Mary Watson Whitney (1847–1920), an American astronomer who published observations on the positions of comets and asteroids and on variable stars.

hoggish than the other. We are practically told that we might as well ask a fossil to reform itself. We are told that we are asking a stuffed bird to repent. We are all dead, and the only comfort is that we are all classified. For by this philosophy, which is the same as that of the blackest of Puritan heresies, we all died before we were born. But as it is Kismet without Allah, so also it is Calvinism without God.

The agnostics will be gratified to learn that it is entirely due to their own energy and enterprise, to their own activity in pursuing their own antics, that the world has at last tired of their antics and told them so. We have done very little against them; *non nobis, Domine*;[48] the glory of their final overthrow is all their own. We have done far less than we should have done, to explain all that balance of subtlety and sanity which is meant by a Christian civilisation. Our thanks are due to those who have so generously helped us by giving a glimpse of what might be meant by a Pagan civilisation. And what is lost in that society is not so much religion as reason; the ordinary common daylight of intellectual instinct that has guided the children of men. A world in which men know that most of what they know is probably untrue cannot be dignified with the name of a sceptical world; it is simply an impotent and abject world, not attacking anything, but accepting everything while trusting nothing; accepting even its own incapacity to attack; accepting its own lack of authority to accept; doubting its very right to doubt. We are grateful for this public experiment and demonstration; it has taught us much. We did not believe that rationalists were so utterly mad until they made it quite clear to us. We did not ourselves think that the mere denial of our dogmas could end in such dehumanised and demented anarchy. It might have taken the world a long time to understand that what it had been taught to dismiss as mediaeval theology was often mere common sense, or *communis sententia*, was a mediaeval conception. But it took the world very little time to understand that the talk on the other side was most uncommon nonsense. It was nonsense that could not be made the basis of any common system, such as has been founded upon common sense.

[48] *Non nobis, Domine* is Latin for "Not to us, O Lord (but to Thy name be the glory)," from Psalms.

To take one example out of many; the whole question of Marriage has been turned into a question of Mood. The enemies of marriage did not have the patience to remain in their relatively strong position; that marriage could not be proved to be sacramental, and that some exceptions must be treated as exceptions, so long as it was merely social. They could not be content to say that it is not a sacrament but a contract, and that exceptional legal action might break a contract. They brought objections against it that would be quite as facile and quite as futile, if brought against any other contract. They said that a man is never in the same mood for ten minutes together; that he must not be asked to admire in a red daybreak what he admired in a yellow sunset; that no man can say he will even be the same man by the next month or the next minute; that new and nameless tortures may afflict him if his wife wears a different hat; or that he may plunge her into hell by putting on a pair of socks that does not harmonise with somebody else's carpet. It is quite obvious that this sort of sensitive insanity applies as much to any other human relation as to this relation. A man cannot choose a profession; because, long before he has qualified as an architect, he may have mystically changed into an aviator, or be convulsed in rapid succession by the emotions of a ticket-collector, a trombone-player and a professional harpooner of whales. A man dare not buy a house for fear a fatal stranger with the wrong sort of socks should come into it; or for fear his own mind should be utterly changed in the matter of carpets or cornices. A man may suddenly decline to do any business with his own business partner; because he also, like the cruel husband, wears the wrong necktie. And I saw a serious printed appeal for sympathy for a wife, who deserted her family because her psychology was incompatible with an orange necktie. This is only one application, as I say; but it exactly illustrates how the sceptical principle is now applied; and how scepticism has recently changed from apparent sense to quite self-evident nonsense. The heresies not only decay but destroy themselves; in any case they perish without a blow.

For the reply, not merely of religion but of reason and the rooted sanity of mankind is obvious enough. "If you feel like that, why certainly you will not found families; or found anything else. You will not build houses; you will not make partnerships; you will not in any fashion do the business of the world. You will never plant a tree, lest you wish next week you had planted it somewhere else; you will never put a potato into a pot or stew, because it will be too late to take it out again; your whole mood is stricken and riddled with cowardice and sterility; your whole way of attacking any problem is to think of excuses for not attacking it at all. Very well; so be it; the Lord be with you. You may be respected for being sincere; you may be pitied for being sensitive; you may retain some of the corrective qualities which make it useful on occasion to be sceptical. But if you are too sceptical to do these things, you must stand out of the way of those who can do them; you must hand over the world to those who believe that the world is workable; to those who believe that men can make houses, make partnerships, make appointments, make promises—and keep them. And if it is necessary in order to keep a promise or boil a potato or behave like a human being, to believe in God making Man, in God being made Man, or in God made Man coming in the clouds in glory —well, then you must at least give a chance to these credulous fanatics who can believe the one and who can do the other." That is what I mean by the spiritual Survival of the Fittest. That is why the old phrase, which is probably a mistake in natural history, is a truth in supernatural history. The organic thing called religion has in fact the organs that take hold on life. It can feed where the fastidious doubter finds no food; it can reproduce where the solitary sceptic boasts of being barren. It may be accepting a miracle to believe in free will; but it is accepting madness, sooner or later, to disbelieve in it. It may be a wild risk to make a vow; but it is a quiet, crawling and inevitable ruin to refuse to make a vow. It may be incredible that one creed is the truth and the others are relatively false; but it is not only incredible, but also intolerable, that there is no truth either in or out of creeds, and all are equally false. For nobody can ever set anything right, if everybody is equally wrong. The intense interest of the moment is that the Man of Science, the hero of the modern world and the latest of the great servants of humanity, has suddenly and dramatically refused to have anything more to do with this dreary business of nibbling negation, and blind scratching and scraping away of the very foundations of the mastery of man. For the work of the sceptic for the past hundred years has indeed been very like the fruitless fury of some primeval monster; eyeless, mindless, and merely destructive and devouring; a giant worm wasting away a world that he could not even see; a benighted and bestial life, unconscious of its own cause and of its own consequences. But Man has taken to himself again his own weapons; will and worship and reason and the vision of the plan in things; and we are once more in the morning of the world.

THE REACTION OF THE INTELLECTUALS

I have been asked if I think there is a reaction against the tendencies called "ultra-modern" and in favour of many things blasted by the term, "Victorian" and "virtuous" and "respectable," and other wild and wicked words. I answer that there is a reaction, and I am glad of it; but it is a reaction of a very peculiar kind. It is not what I expected. It is not even particularly what I wanted. But anything is a relief from the desolate dullness and staleness of the Bright Young Thing.

First, it will clear the human mind (and save the advanced mind from many disappointments) if we realise that there always *can* be a reaction, right or wrong, against anything, good or bad. Life is far too complex not to leave some desirable or defensible things behind with every movement it makes. We have reactions in favour of things much more remote than Victorianism. I always remember a confident and contemptuous phrase in one of Macaulay's[49] speeches for the Reform Bill, which abolished Rotten Boroughs.[50] "There has been no reaction. There will be no reaction. I no more expect a reaction in favour of Gatton and Old Sarum than a reaction in favour of Odin and Thor." I will not discuss whether there is a reaction in favour of Gatton and Old Sarum; there most certainly is a reaction against Reform Bills and Representative Government. But what amuses me is that, even while Macaulay said the words, there was beginning a most unmistakable reaction in favour of Odin and Thor. Carlyle already had pen in hand and his Northern genius was slowly turning into Nordic insanity. He was already telling us to go back to the stark Scandinavian beginnings. A little while afterwards Nietzsche took the next step by throwing over Christian ethics as well as theology, and invoking the old gods of violence and war. And it ended with a great German General (who had led through

[49] Thomas Babington Macaulay (1800–1859) authored a multivolume history of England, and was Great Britain's most famous historian in the nineteenth century.
[50] The Reform Bill of 1832 broadened the franchise for parliamentary elections. Rotten boroughs were sparsley populated voting districts that held equal representation with more populous districts.

the Great War and might have had enough of it) actually filling Germany with pagan propaganda and a publicity campaign in favour of Odin and Thor. So much for reactions in general. The most modern art finds the Ancient Greeks too modern and goes back to the Ancient Egyptians. We revive Primitive Art and may revive Prehistoric Art. We may paint on rock with red ochre, for all I know, or discover special qualities in stone hatchets and flint arrows.

There is a reaction; but that would not alone prove that the reaction is right. I think it is right; because it is a reaction in favour of civilisation; and against the destruction of civilisation. But with that word "civilisation" we come to the rather curious quality which this particular reaction shows. It is not, as I myself might have hoped or expected, a revolt of plain, old-fashioned people against the sophisticated. It is a revolt of the sophisticated. It is, at any rate, a revolt of the highly civilised; perhaps of the over-civilised. But if they are over-civilised, they are still highly intelligent. That is why they are kicking the Bright Young Thing down the street.

I will take one particular case which is rather a parable. Some time ago all the fine old English critics, Constant Readers and Conservative people generally, were in a ferment of fury and mockery against the impudent innovations of "the Sitwells";[51] that is, the three poets of that family. They were a proof that being modern means going mad. They were the very latest and loudest anarchists, destroying both rhyme and reason. I will not discuss their merits here. When Miss Sitwell accused the Dawn of "creaking," there were discussions as to her meaning. Her foes said it was random nonsense, like describing the sun as sneezing or the grass as blowing its nose. Her friends said it was a bold and novel way of suggesting something harsh and reluctant about the cold morning light. But everybody agreed that it was the very latest and newest experiment, whether in liberty or in lunacy. The Sitwells were accused of beating the big drum, or blowing their own trumpet; but it was agreed that their drums and trumpets were the newest musical instruments of the queerest shape; and that they used the newest methods of shrieking for what they wanted. But what did they want?

[51] The Sitwells were Edith (1887–1964), Osbert (1892–1969) and Sacheverell (1897–1969).

Now, what the Sitwells want is Victorianism. What they do definitely desire, demand and incessantly describe, is a reaction to Victorian habits; to Victorian manners; and even to Victorian morals. As certainly as Shelley wanted a lot of wind and light and the rise of the pure pagan republic, as surely as Walt Whitman wanted democratic breadth and a sort of bodily brotherhood among men out-of-doors, so certainly what the Sitwells want is Victorian flower-beds and hothouses, Victorian coloured patchwork and curios under glass; and, in no small degree, Victorian etiquette, dance and dignity. This may be a fad but it is a fact; and it is a fact that vividly illustrates the real revolt against recent moral, or immoral, tendencies. The Victorian revolt is not a revolt of Victorians. It is a revolt of Post-Victorians or rather of Post-Post-Victorians. They are going back to something remote, as much as the Pre-Raphaelites[52] in going back to the Middle Ages. In both cases the reason is the same; because the modern ages have become too unbearably stupid for intelligent people. But the more modern case is the more acute case of this revolt against modernity among the moderns. To understand it, we must take a more general view of the singular situation in the world to-day.

Those specially called the Moderns, who are now most of them Ancients, conceived of human history as a progress in the sense of a procession. That is, they said that some slower people might bring up the rear but all were moving onward. They also supposed that certain bold sprits, whom they called the Pioneers of Progress, went on in front and made a path for mankind. I have a great admiration for Walt Whitman; but it cannot be denied that he did exclaim, in a moment of weakness, "Pioneers, O Pioneers!" It was characteristic of all that world; first, that it relied upon a metaphor; and second, that it got the metaphor quite wrong. Whitman seems to associate his intellectual pioneers with the practical pioneers of the American Civil War. But a pioneer is not a person who leads the army, or

[52] The Pre-Raphaelite Brotherhood, a movement to infuse art with morality, flourished in mid-nineteenth-century England. Its members, most prominent of whom were William Holman Hunt, John Everett Millais and Dante Gabriel Rossetti, contended that the degeneration of Western art had begun in the Renaissance with Raphael.

decides where it shall go. The pioneers in front are as much under orders as any camp-followers in the rear. If Sherman had thrown out pioneers to clear his road to Atlanta; and if the pioneers had seen a futuristic vision and gone off to found the future city of Oklahoma, Sherman would have been very much surprised; nay, vexed. And the moral is that the marching column of mankind must have some kind of notion of where it wants to go, before it can decide whether a pioneer is a useful pioneer or not.

Now, at this moment, the marching column of mankind is in an extraordinary position. For one thing, it is not marching. But it is marking time; because it still has the general notion that it ought to march. It may seem quaint to recur to Macaulay as well as Whitman; but it is better described in Macaulay's poem of Horatius than in Whitman's poem about the Pioneers; though to many, I fear, Whitman is now as distant as Macaulay. But it is really true that the exact and very extraordinary position of the procession at this moment is expressed with precision in the familiar lines.[53]

> "And those behind cried 'Forward!'
> And those before cried 'Back'!"

The camp-followers may be charging; but the pioneers are retreating. In other words, it is exactly the sort of bold and enquiring spirits, who were always said to be in advance of the age, who are now most doubtful about the desirability of advancing. It is exactly those who are content to follow tradition or convention or familiar fashions who are still following (as they suppose, at least) the tradition of progress, the convention of movement and the hundred fashions, familiar to the nineteenth-century, of appealing to the hope of change. Men are progressive because they are a little behind the times. They are reactionary because they are a little in advance of the times. It sounds like a paradox; but it is really a very practical and even inevitable state of things, given certain conditions. Those behind will still cry "Forward!"; and only those far in front will cry "Back!"; when the vanguard of the army has come suddenly to the edge of a precipice.

[53] The quotation is from Macaulay's *Lays of Ancient Rome* (1842).

In short, I maintain that it is the Intellectuals (for want of a more intellectual term) who have now suddenly discovered the dangers of mere novelty, of mere anarchy, of mere negation. It is not all the Intellectuals, of course; and certainly not those who modestly gave themselves that name in the middle of the nineteenth-century. For these, by the ironic operation of their own favourite argument, are now old and venerable and established and respected; and, therefore, of no importance whatever. Men like Bertrand Russell, and H. G. Wells, are left behind by the advance; and are, therefore, under the illusion that it is still advancing. The particular state of mind I mean (which is not always a very pretty state of mind at present) is peculiar to a section of the younger Intellectuals. And, whatever it is, it is not a positive faith in the promise of the future or the tendencies of the present. If we take any typical contemporary poetry of the sort that is sensitive and critical, say the poems of Mr. Osbert Sitwell, it is quite obvious that they are *not* merely in revolt against the nineteenth-century; though the progressive theory was bound up with the nineteenth-century. They are in revolt against the twentieth-century; and potentially more in revolt against the twenty-first.

But the point is that it is because they are so very Modern that they have rebelled against Modernism. It is because they have themselves seen all the new tricks, and in many cases played all the new tricks, that they have realised before anybody else that the whole bag of tricks may soon be played out. Mr. Humbert Wolfe[54] may be justified in beginning every line with a small letter; indeed, in that he is classical rather than revolutionary; for the old Latin texts were always printed so. But he is far too intelligent a man not to see that those who would prove themselves progressive, by abandoning all capital letters, can only prove themselves still more progressive by abandoning all small letters; and that this sort of destructive reform can only end in a blank page. So this kind of destructive progress ends in a blank wall. Mr. Sitwell may think himself right, in this or that case, in attaching a musical adjective to an entirely visual or pictorial

---

[54] Humbert Wolfe (1885–1940) was a popular British satiric poet and critic.

substantive. But he can see, as well as anybody else, that if a hundred howling imitators come in and claim the right to attach any adjective to any substantive, it is not so much a question of literature being lawless as of its ceasing to be anything at all. And we see more and more, every day, this curious sort of new alarm spreading among the most intelligent of the new schools; which is almost unintelligible to many of the old schools; and especially to that very old school which supposes that the young have no business to be anything but reckless and revolutionary.

I will take the case of two of the most acute and individual among contemporary writers, one probably younger than the other, at least in fashion and fame; one American and the other English, and the inheritor of a name already famous for a very English style. I will take the cases of Mr. T. S. Eliot and Mr. Aldous Huxley. They are different enough, of course; but they exactly express two different ways of recoiling from the recent riot and vulgarity of the merely "modern" world. Mr. Eliot, who began like a child of his age with the recognised stark and jagged experiments in free verse, has come to have something like a suspicion of every sort of freedom. He had come to stand for an almost cloistered refinement, full of the virginal traditions of old religion and repudiating not only the demagogy of to-day, but even the democracy of yesterday. There are passages in the works of Mr. Aldous Huxley which few will call cloistered, which few, perhaps, will call virginal. But he is none the less a representative of the same reaction against recent vulgarity and vice. Only he reacts more in the manner of Swift; showing the ugly their own ugliness; even pelting the filthy with samples of their own filth. But he is, if not on the side of the angels, at least horribly bored with the devils. Anyone who will read his admirable account of Hollywood, which he calls, "The City of Dreadful Joy," will find it more dreadful than joyful. There is a fight against the recent licence; but what is fighting it is a sort of fierce fastidiousness.

I am not imagining this reaction because I want it; for, indeed, it is not especially the reaction that I want. I should have hoped for a popular revolt against perversions and pedantries of vice, which have never, in fact, been popular. I should have liked the ordinary, old-fashioned, obstinate people, who still stick to the notion of some connection between themselves and their own babies, to rise and bash in the heads of the inhuman prigs whose ideal is a sort of prophetic infanticide. I should like a howling rabble of really respectable people (and the rabble is still really respectable) to burn down the houses where Luxury takes on its true Latin sense of Luxuria. I should like the normal people, who live on beef and beer, to make war on the hypocritical cranks who take their vegetarianism in the form of vegetable cocktails less wholesome than the fruit of the vine. I should prefer the Intellectuals to be slaughtered by what may be called the Moral; and the mob is still very moral. But the great point is that they should be slaughtered; if not by the clubs of the crowd, then by the rapier of the more intellectual Intellectual. God moves in a mysterious way and does not disdain the stangest or the humblest instruments; and we must not be ashamed of finding ourselves, if necessary, on the side of the cultivated and the clever.

Or again, it might have been that picturesque paradox; a revolt of the old against the young. It might have been a rebellion of oppressed parents breaking the yoke of servile obedience now laid on them by their tyrannical sons and daughters. It might have been the heavy father breaking out of the coal-cellar with the original big stick, or the maiden aunt emerging from the bedroom armed with the poker; and the joyous spectacle of their smashing the gramophones and the saxophones and the ukuleles, hurling away the cocktails, wrecking the racing cars and generally showing that there is life in the old dog yet. But, as a fact, it does not seem to be coming through the fury of the father or the grandfather but rather with the slowly maturing disgust of the great-grandson with the manifest idiocy of the grandson.

It is not coming by the big stick or the cudgels of the populace; but by something which I have compared to a rapier; and might compare to a razor. Some young men of the school of Mr. Aldous Huxley have, indeed, a touch of pessimism that is only too suggestive of a razor; at once the symbol of elegance and of suicide. And yet there is a broader sense in which this is, perhaps, rather too true. When the Victorians rebuked little boys for playing with razors or rapiers, or such acute instruments and arguments ensued, the elders often used a proverbial expression here very relevant: "If you get so sharp as that, you will cut yourself." The minority of the most intelligent, in the younger generation, has really become very sharp; and it has really discovered the peril of cutting itself. Men like Mr. Huxley and Mr. Eliot have the sense to see that the half-truths of the sceptic are not only edged tools, but double-edged tools. They cut the ground from under rationalism as well as from under religion; they can be used to wound democracy as easily as despotism; in the last resort they can inoculate the mind with doubts about doubt itself. More and more the really clever young man will find that he has grown sharp enough to cut himself; and, if he does not try something beyond scepticism, he will grow sceptical enough to cut his throat.

Lastly, why do I think this small minority of rather fastidious and over-refined persons will finally have an effect? I answer, with a profound sigh, because of the great social institution which we call Snobbery. As soon as the quite brainless mob of Bright Young Things discovers that it is really being *despised*, as a mob of dull old things (though it were only by two well-educated minor poets) there will be a panic. The mass of the immoralists never believed in immorality or in anything else. They never really thought that wrong was right, because they never really thought at all. They merely believed what they were told; that being lawless was the latest thing. If once they hear that there is something later still, even later than the latest, they will rush for it and roll in the mud in front of it, though it were a Hermit out of the desert like St. Anthony. If it is a humorous, but slightly superior young man, who regards all their vulgar and raucous games as *vieux jeu*, and will only condescend to talk about Humanism and St. Thomas Aquinas, they will grovel before him. I know them. They play the goat; but they none the less do it like sheep. For they are sheep that have not a shepherd, and the shepherd named Pan is dead.

LEVITY—OR LEVITATION

I do not see why a man should not sometimes have a holiday, even while he is doing his work, and write about something merely because it amuses him. I know I should be doing my duty as a Distributist, doing it dismally with the pen when others are already doing it more nobly with the plough. But, for once in a way, I am going to write merely for fun; and about something only because it is funny. And the funniest thing I can find for miles round is in a paper called *Psychic News*, a past issue of which was adorned with a portrait of me, accompanied with the extraordinary and rather mysterious caption, "G.K.C., the Catholic who goes up in the air." Believing as I do in miracles, I have never claimed levitation as a power particularly likely to be manifested in my own case. But though not at present drawn irresistibly towards levitation, I am much tempted to levity. The charges are rather vague, except that they all seem to be equally unfortunate in relation to the facts of the case. The writer seemed to take it for granted that an article quite plainly signed by somebody else must really have been written by me, and written by me from no other motive but a fanatical Catholicism, although the man who really wrote is not a Catholic at all and said nothing whatever to suggest in any way that he was. He, however, is supremely capable of looking after himself, and the mere facts about this absurd muddle I have dealt with elsewhere. At the moment I only wish to wallow in sheer shameless enjoyment of the way in which the *Psychic News* attacks the Catholic Church and attacks me. I admit that this is mere self-indulgence on my part. I know that numbers of judicious friends will tell me that I ought not to take any notice of such an article. But nothing that can be called human is uninteresting, and this involves, to begin with, one puzzle which always interests me very much. And that is why people who fly into a rage with the Catholic Church always use an extraordinary diction, or verbal style, in which all sorts of incommensurate things are jumbled up together, so that the very order of the words is a joke. "Spiritualism depends only on the evidence which people receive in their own homes. It does not require priests. Neither do enquirers have to buy rosaries or beads, or crucifixes, or pay for candles or masses." It must be a dreadful moment of indecision for the enquirers, when they have to make up their minds whether they will buy rosaries or beads. But the last term is the best; and here the order of words is especially significant. Apparently the first object of a Catholic is to get a candle. If once he can get hold of a candle, and walk about everywhere clasping his candle, he is all right. But if he cannot get a candle, he has the alternative of purchasing a mass; an instrument that is a sort of substitute for a candle.

Now I did not, as it happens, launch any grand persecuting personal spiritual attack on Spiritualism, as this writer imaginatively described. But if I did, as of course I might, I do think I could make a better job of attacking Spiritualism than he does of attacking Catholicism. I should not talk as if a Spiritualist hung suspended between the two divine dogmas of the Sacredness of Tambourines and the Return of the Dead. I should not talk as if men chose between a planchette and a Ouija-board. I should not talk about "tables or furniture," or imply that a trumpet was the same sort of thing as a séance. But I never read an attack on Catholicism without finding this ignorant gabble of terms all topsy-turvy. There is always some such medley of misused words, in which mitres, misereres, nones, albs, croziers, virgins and viaticums tumble over each other without the wildest hope that anybody could possibly know what any of them mean. That is the first curiosity about this kind of writing. We can now go back to the only sentence in the paragraph in which anything like a meaning is apparent. It is that passage in which, we are told, Spiritualism does without a priesthood.

It does not require priests. It only requires a spiritual aristocracy really much more exclusive and privileged than priests; seeing they have direct access to new revelations, and their superiority is in their personal spiritual structure; they are abnormal as priests are not necessarily abnormal. But, however that may be, the paper in question reveals some remarkable impressions about spiritual functions and degrees. There is an astonishing caption under a picture of St. Joan of Arc; saying that she did not care whether she was a saint or a witch, because "she had a job to do and did it." How refreshing this language is. How full of the fifteenth century! Joan was just all out to get that job. She reckoned she could hold down that job. Gee! Joan wasn't the sort of skirt to bother about whether it came from God or the Devil, when there was a good job to hold down. The paper informs us that its religion is entirely founded on facts; but it seems possible to manufacture a good deal of abstract vulgarity without employing them. It were vain, I suppose, to point out the historical fact that Joan debated desperately for days and days to prove she was not a witch, long after it was obvious that her job, as a job, was either done or done for. But might not the suggestion, that it does not matter whether one is a witch or a saint, explain something of the distrust that some of us feel about Spiritualism?

As I am writing this for fun, I would not say very much about the central mystery of my own religion, or the laboriously offensive terms in which the writer asks me to "prove" Transubstantiation, as he apparently claims to "prove" Spiritualism. To him I am content to say one thing. Suppose the Church had tried to give such proofs, and with such results. Suppose Pope after Pope, and Priest after Priest, had stood up at the altar rails promising on the spot to prove Transubstantiation. And suppose Pope after Pope, and Priest after Priest, had been exposed as proving it by a faked apparatus in the Communion Table, by hidden wires in the cross and candles, and all the apparatus of fraud. Suppose, while many priests were doubtless honest men and perhaps honest dupes, it was a plain, palpable historical fact that the miracle had again and again been a mere conjuring trick, and the most famous Catholic saints had been caught and exposed doing the trick. If *that* had happened, I venture to say that the Eucharistic Congress would not now be so much respected by the whole civilised world; or by everybody except the hooligans of Portadown[55] and journalists of the *Psychic News*.

[55] Portadown is a municipal borough in northern Ireland known for its linen and cotton goods industry.

THE CASE FOR HERMITS

Anyone who has ever protected a little boy from being bullied at school, or a little girl from some childish persecution at a party, or any natural person from any minor nuisance, knows that the being thus badgered tends to cry out, in a simple but singular English idiom, "Let me alone!" It is seldom that the child of nature breaks into the cry, "Let me enjoy the fraternal solidarity of a more socially organised group-life." It is rare even for the protest to leap to the lips in the form, "Let me run around with some crowd that has got dough enough to hit the high spots." Not one of these positive modern ideals presents itself to that untutored mind; but only the ideal of being "let alone." It is rather interesting that so spontaneous, instinctive, almost animal an ejaculation contains the word *alone*.

There are now a great many boys and girls, both old and young, who are really in that state of mind; not only through being teased, but also through being petted. Most of them will fiercely deny it, since it contradicts the conventions of their new generation; just as a child kept up too late at night will more and more indignantly deny the desire to go to bed. Indeed I am always expecting to hear that a scientific campaign has been opened against Sleep. Sooner or later the Prohibitionists will turn their attention to the old tribal traditional superstition of Sleep; and they will say that the sluggard is merely encouraged by the cowardice of the moderate sleeper. There will be tables of statistics, showing how many hours of output are lost by miners, smelters, plumbers, plasterers, and every trade in which (it will be noted) men have contracted the habit of sleep; tables showing the shortage of aconite, alum, apples, beef, beetroot, bootlaces, etc., and other statistics carefully demonstrating that work of this kind can only rarely be performed by sleep-walkers. There will be all the scientific facts, except one scientific fact. And that is the fact that if men do not have Sleep, they go mad. It is also a fact that if men do not have solitude, they go mad. You can see that, by the way they go on, when the poor miserable devils only have Society.

The incident of Miss Fitzpatrick, the lady who really liked to be alone, challenges all recent fashions, which are all for Society without Solitude. We must Get Together; as the gunman said when he ran his machine-gun into two other machine-guns and killed all the children caught between them. And we know that this sociability and communal organisation has already produced in fashionable society all that sweetness and light, all that courtesy and charity, all that True Christianity of pardon and patience, which we see in the modern organisers of gangs or "group-life." In contrast with this happy mood now pervading our literature and conversation, it is customary to point to hermits and solitaries as if they were savages and man-haters.

But it is not true. It is not true in history or human fact. The line that ran, "Turn, gentle hermit of the Vale," was truer to the real tradition about the real hermits. They were doubtless, from a modern standpoint, lunatics; but they were nice lunatics. Twenty touches could illustrate what I mean; for instance, the fact that they could make pets of the wild aminals that came naturally to them. But many of them really had charity—even to human beings. They felt more kindly about men than men in the Forum or the Mart felt about each other. Doubtless there have been merely sulky solitaries; unquestionably there have been sham cynics and *cabotins*,[56] like Diogenes. But he and his sort are very careful not to be *really* solitary; careful to hang about the market-place like any demagogue. Diogenes was a tub-thumper, as well as a tub-dweller. And that sort of professional sulks remains; but it is sulks without solitude. We all know there are geniuses who must go out into polite society in order to be impolite. We all know there are hostesses who collect lions and find they have got bears. I fear there was a touch of that in the social legend of Thomas Carlyle and perhaps of Tennyson. But these men must have a society in which to be unsociable. The hermits, especially the saints, had a solitude in which to be sociable.

St. Jerome lived with a real lion; a good way to avoid being lionised. But he was very sociable with the lion. In his time, as in ours, sociability of the conventional sort had become social suffocation. In the decline of the Roman Empire, people got together in amphitheatres and public festivals, just as they now get together in trams and

56 *Cabotins* is French for "bad actors".

tubes. And there were the same feelings of mutual love and tenderness, between two men trying to get a seat in the Colosseum, as there are now between two men trying to get the one remaining seat on a Tooting tram. Consequently, in that last Roman phase, all the most amiable people rushed away into the desert, to find what is called a hermitage; but might almost be called a holiday. The man was a hermit because he was more of a human being; not less. It was not merely that he felt he could get on better with a lion than with the sort of men who would throw him to the lions. It was also that he actually liked men better when they let him alone. Now nobody expects anybody, except a very exceptional person, to become a complete solitary. But there is a strong case for more Solitude; especially now that there is really no Solitude.

The reason why even the normal human being should be half a hermit is that it is the only way in which his mind can have a half-holiday. It is the only way to get any fun even out of the facts of life; yes, even if the facts are games and dances and operas. It bears most resemblance to the unpacking of luggage. It has been said that we live on a railway station; many of us live in a luggage van; or wander about the world with luggage that we never unpack at all. For the best things that happen to us are those we get out of what has already happened. If men were honest with themselves, they would agree that actual social engagements, even with those they love, often seem strange brief, breathless, thwarted or inconclusive. Mere society is a way of turning friends into acquaintances. The real profit is not in meeting our friends, but in having met them. Now when people merely plunge from crush to crush, and from crowd to crowd, they never discover the positive joy of life. They are like men always hungry, because their food never digests; also, like those men, they are cross. There is surely something the matter with modern life when all the literature of the young is so cross. That is something of the secret of the saints who went into the desert. It is in society that men quarrel with their friends; it is in solitude that they forgive them. And before the society-man criticises the saint, let him remember that the man in the desert often had a soul that was like a honey-pot of human kindness, though no man came near to taste it; and the man in the modern salon, in his intellectual hospitality, generally serves out wormwood for wine.

In conclusion, I will take one very modern and even topical case. I do not believe in Communism, certainly not in compulsory Communism. And it is typical of this acrid age that what we all discuss is compulsory Communism. I often sympathise with Communists, which is quite a different thing; but even these I respect rather as bold or honest or logical than as particularly genial or kindly. Nobody will claim that modern Communism is a specially sweet-tempered or amiable thing. But if you will look up the legends of the earliest Hermits, you will find a very charming anecdote, about two monks who really were Communists. And one of them tried to explain to the other how it was that quarrels arose about private property. So he thumped down a stone and observed theatrically, "This stone is mine." The other, slightly wondering at his taste, said, "All right; take it." Then the teacher of economics became quite vexed and said, "No, no; you mustn't say that. You must say it is yours; and then we can fight." So the second hermit said it was his; whereupon the first hermit mechanically gave it up; and the whole lesson in Business Methods seems to have broken down. Now you may agree or disagree with the Communist ideal, of cutting oneself off from commerce, which those two ascetics followed. But is there not something to suggest that they were rather nicer people than the Communists we now meet in Society? Somehow as if Solitude improved the temper?

KILLING THE NERVE

It is now generally agreed, with great cheerfulness and good temper, that one of the chief features of the state of Peace we now enjoy is the killing of a considerable number of harmless human beings. We are not wild and reckless and pugnacious in such things, even as these Latins. Relatively, we seem almost reconciled to the general notion of killing; so long as we can feel a real assurance that it is aimless and purposeless and fruitless. If an old woman is knocked down dead in the quiet village street where she played as a child, if a gutter-boy is not quite quick enough in getting out of the gutter and suffers the death penalty for his negligence, we all agree that it is very regrettable. But it does not withdraw the attention of some of us from quite exclusive concentration upon the horrors of war, because nobody could confuse an old woman crossing the road with an old-world romance in any way connected with adventure or valour; and the boy has not ventured into the road (thank God) under any delusion that he is sacrificing himself for his native land. If death strikes down suddenly somebody who does not expect to die, and is not deceived by any nonsense about being faithful unto death . . . O death, where is thy sting? If a tramp is taken to a pauper's grave unstained by any hopes or dreams of war or revolution, or any vision of justice victorious . . . O grave, where is thy victory? It is obvious that death is a very different thing when it is the product of such peaceful surroundings. The modern version of Killing No Murder is that only militarism is murder; and there is nothing wrong with killing when it is not military.

But I have here introduced the word killing in a lighter sense; even lighter than that in which some progressives take the killing in the streets. For there are other things, though they are things less vivid and less sacred, which are killed in the streets. Even as it is we use the world "kill" in a more metaphorical sense. For instance we talk of colours killing each other. And, as one example out of many, it may be noted that we do live in a scheme of social life in which colours kill each other. That is, we live in a world which gives us a vast exhibition of that vividness which is symbolised by colour, but which is wholly without that concerted unity of rule or tradition which is symbolised by harmony in colour. The illuminated advertisements of a big city like London, which is now in this respect almost indistinguishable from New York, exhibit exactly that contradiction between colour and design. The design, even in the sense of the purpose, is patchy and personal and not only vulgar but essentially venal. The colour is often the best and most beautiful experience given to the senses of man, if only man were in a position to make the best of it. The psychological effect produced by random commercial illumination is something which is to the real possibilities of colour what a drunken slumber is to the divine gift of wine. Or rather, it should be compared to that habit, which springs up so easily in Prohibitionist or semi-Prohibitionist countries, of trying to get the best out of the divine gift of wine by preceding it with excessive quantities of whisky, following it by equally excessive quantities of beer, or possibly beginning the whole banquet with liqueurs and ending it with cocktails. In short, Prohibitionists get drunk because they have never been taught to drink; and commercial advertising wastes its artistic materials, even when it possesses them, because it has never been taught to colour or even to enjoy colours. Colours are being killed; and they are being killed by being worked to death. The nerve is being killed; and it is being killed by being overstimulated and therefore stunted and stunned.

When I was a child, I had a toy-theatre, illuminated in those days by candles (to which perhaps the psychoanalyst will trace my subsequent downfall into ecclesiastical crypts and cloisters) and in the ordinary way I was quite content with this type of illumination, the candles seeming to my barbarous mind to be themselves like a forest of fairy trees, with flames for flowers. There were also yet more rich and rare delights, which were sufficiently rare to those not sufficiently rich. It was sometimes possible to purchase a sort of dark red powder, which when ignited burst into a rich red light. Fire was wonderful enough—but red fire! But then I was only a dull Victorian infant somewhere between five and seven; and I only used red fire rarely; when it was effective. Living under such limitations, my immature brain perceived that it was more suitable to some things than to others; as, for instance, to a goblin coming up through a trap-door out of the cavern of the King of the Copper Mines, or to the final conflagration that made a crimson halo round the dark mill and castle of the execrable Mad Miller. I should not even then have used red fire in a scene showing the shepherd (doubtless a prince in disguise) piping to his lambs in the pale green meadows of spring; or in a scene in which glassy gauzes of green and blue waved in the manner of waves round the cold weeds and fishes at the entrance to Davy Jones's Locker. Science and progress and practical education and knowledge of the world are necessary before people can make blunders like that. Therefore, that red fire of the nursery still glows in my memory as in inward imaginative revelation, in spite of years, in spite of time, in spite even of passing through the streets of modern London.

In the London streets to-day, in what Mr. Cuthbert Baines has so vividly called, "the floodlit, bloodlit street," the rare effect of red fire is wholly wasted and ruined, by the loss of its rarity and by the loss of its suitability. The child who has been made too familiar with all that redhot lettering will probably never have the romance that I remember in my childhood; and it is perhaps strictly true to say that he will never see red fire in his life. First, of course, because he has seen too much of it. For this is not the decorative process of using red in a scheme of colour; it is simply the dull process of painting the town red. But second, also, because the toy-theatre showed him little pictures of large things; and the town signs show him large pictures of little things. He will very soon discover that the ideas associated with these signs, the motives of the men who put them up, the mood of the men who accept them are things connected entirely with dreary money-grubbing or shoddy luxury. He will be unable to get any great vista or vision out of a glimpse; he will know nothing but a glaring wilderness of proclamations that have emphasis without significance; and will grow up without any poetical associations with a colour he has only seen used to sell a cosmetic or a quack medicine.

THE CASE OF CLAUDEL

I have heard a story, which I have never verified either by history or topography, otherwise known as being on the spot, to the effect that the French Academy accepted the accident of the absence of Molière from its records with a magnificent gesture. It may have been only a tradition about something that somebody planned to do; it may even have been only a tale of somebody about what ought to be done; but it is exactly the sort of tradition that would represent the nation; and it is exactly the sort of thing that Frenchmen would or could have done. The French Academy, founded by Richelieu for the establishment of classical literature in the country, naturally passed over a wandering play-actor and playwright like Molière; just as Oxford and Cambridge would have passed over a wandering play-actor and playwright like Shakespeare. But here the story, even if it is only a story, stikes the note that only the French can strike. For it was said tht the French Academy erected in its inner courts a special statue of Molière, with the inscription "Rien ne manque à sa gloire; il manque à la notre"[57] . . . and if you want to know what is the difference between the atmosphere of France and England, both of them very jolly atmospheres in their way, you have only to imagine anybody making, or even anybody suggesting, a public apology of that sort of Shakespeare. Can you imagine a huge statue of Shakespeare in Balliol Quad, inscribed with the statement, "Shakespeare never went to Balliol." Can you conceive even Cambridge rearing a colossal monument to Dickens, to celebrate the fact that he never had a University education — or indeed any other education? If that story about Molière is true, or even if it is a true parable or fable, there is an obvious moral to the fable. The English rather ignore defeats; the French rather exaggerate defeats; but the French do sometimes have the talent of snatching victories out of defeats.

A little while ago, to my great regret, the French Academy suffered a very serious defeat. It was when it preferred a clever writer of

[57] Chesterton's translation of this French quotation is: "Nothing is wanting to his glory; but he is wanting to ours."

rather decadent verse to Paul Claudel;[58] but nobody supposes, I hope, that it was M. Claudel who was defeated. If we are to talk about anybody really great being defeated, let us say that Richelieu was defeated. A man of the first rank of French Letters, which the great Cardinal loved, and the Catholic culture which he also loved, with all his diplomatic and even unscrupulous encouragement of those who hated it, has been met with a sort of mute resistance; presumably by those who hated more than the most unscrupulous Cardinal could ever do. Without presuming to pronounce upon the literary comparison, it is enough to say that even if the Academy were right, it would here prove itself entirely academic. It would be proved in the fact that nobody in the literary world has heard of Claudel's rival; and everybody in the literary world has heard of Claudel. He is recognised as standing for something quite literally from China to Peru; at least from Japan to Washington. It looks as if the Academy has made one of its rather rare mistakes; and without the obvious excuses which applied to the case of Molière. And it looks as if there might some day be another statue, with another inscription: "Nothing is wanting to his glory; but he is wanting to ours."

There is no space here even to suggest the sumptuous wealth of images and ideas in the work of Paul Claudel. It is only important to note the fact, as a fact of history rather than of literature, that it is on his side, and not on the other side, that the wealth of ideas can now be found. It might very well happen, at one time it probably did happen, that the historic culture he represents had dwindled down to narrow channels and rare and isolated notes; like the last pipe of the pastoral poets that sounded from the eighteenth-century clerics imitating the innocence of the Georgics;[59] or that Irish harp of which a single string snapped whenever a heart had broken for liberty. But to-day it is exactly the other way. It is the rationalistic tradition of the nineteenth century that has narrowed into monotony and repetition. It is the artist who is an atheist who has taken refuge in a garden, to escape from the cry of all the ancient Christian civilization for the ploughing of all the

[58] Paul Claudel (1868–1955) was a French Catholic poet, playwright and diplomat.
[59] The *Georgics* is Virgil's long poem on agriculture, beekeeping and livestock-raising.

fields of the earth. It is the musical instrument of the modernist that has broken all its strings but one, like the lute in the agnostic picture of Hope; and continues to strike the same few chords of truth remaining to it, but drearily and all on one note. Nobody denies, and certainly I do not deny, that the truths of the emancipated epoch are still true, even when thus isolated and irrelevant; just as the spiritual truths were still true, even when repeated mechanically by the court chaplains or stale preachers of the eighteenth century. But in the matter of fullness, of richness, and of variety, the whole advantage is now with the ancient cause. The thoughts that throng in a sort of hubbub, in a work like *The Satin Slipper*,[60] are like a crowd of living men bursting the barriers of a deserted fortress. It is Claudel or the same type of man who is now storming the Bastille; a prison with all the harshness and inhumanity of a prison, except that it now contains fewer and fewer prisoners. An empty prison may be almost more depressing than a full prison; and such an empty prison is the tradition of academic scepticism to-day. Prejudice, the very spirit of a prison, alone shuts out the new generation from the full realization of the greater fruitfulness promised by the revival of Christendom. In one sense we may agree with all the old and weary jounalists who say that the age is to be the age of Youth; but its most youthful manifestation is in something that renews its youth like the eagle.

[60] *The Satin Slipper* is a play written by Claudel in the 1920s and set in the sixteenth century.

THE HIGHER NIHILISM

Mr. Middleton Murry[61] has written a generous, a stimulating and rather a strange book. It is called *The Necessity of Communism*: and my own first feelings about it may be expressed by saying that I have much more sympathy with the Communism than with the Necessity. I cannot but feel that Mr. Middleton Murry is caught in a sort of net of necessity; that his spirited and active mind is actually hampered by his queer religion of destiny. The reader trips over it, as if it were barbed wire, when striding through what is otherwise an open field of freedom and fairmindedness. To take one example; no Catholic could possibly ask for a more just or even generous judgment on the Middle Ages, and their relation to the Reformation, than that given in Mr. Murry's chapter called "The Pattern of History"; and yet it ends with a twist of phrase so abrupt and perverse that I almost cried out aloud at the inconsequence. "In England the Church was expropriated, by men who had not as individuals the faintest ethical superiority over those they expropriated, but who had the impersonal justification of being instruments of economic destiny." Now, with all respect, I do not know in the least what the last words of that sentence mean. What is "impersonal justification"? How can anything except a person be justified, and how can he be justified except by another person judging him to be just? What are "instruments of economic destiny" or any other destiny? Instruments mean tools chosen by some person for some purpose. Who is Destiny; and in what sense can he have a purpose? It always seems to me that all this sort of thing is not even metaphysics, far less metabiology, but simply metaphor. It is all the more difficult to deal with, because the ideas for which it stands are delivered quite dogmatically as dogmas. Mr. Middleton Murry tells us at the very beginning that a man must be a complete materialist; that it is mere shilly-shallying to be only a behaviourist. But he does not give a man like me any reason for being either; and I have not the smallest intention

---

[61] John Middleton Murry (1889–1957) was an English literary critic and editor.

of being either. He says that any reversion to the past is "forbidden," and I can only say "By whom?" It would be a mere wanton veto on all art and action to forbid us to take materials from the past. But as a fact it is impossible for anybody to avoid using the past. In reality, it is impossible to use anything except the past. And why is it any more forbidden to me to say that the Catholic Church is a thing of the future and the present, as well as the past, than it is to Mr. Murry to say that Karl Marx fulfilled the purpose of the Hebrew Prophets or that Jesus of Nazareth became the supreme type of disinterestedness? But in logic there is no need even to go back to Jesus or the Jewish prophets. Karl Marx is as much a part of the past as King John Sobieski;[62] and the Russian Revolution is as past as the Roman Empire. The book is full of violent affirmations of this sort, entirely unsupported by arguments of any sort. Nevertheless, there is an argument running through the book; and a very curious and interesting one it is.

The writer starts, as he starts with so many unexplained things, with the very dangerous word, "disinterested." It is dangerous because a mere touch will make it mean "uninterested"; in the sense of the Buddhist and the pessimist. We all know it has a sane sense, as meaning sincerely unselfish, self-sacrificing for a faith, and so on. But Mr. Murry does not mean merely giving up our pleasures for the sake of our ideals. In some places, he really seems to mean giving up our ideals, or some of our ideals, for a sort of super-ideal which has sometimes precious little to say for itself, except that it is Destiny. There really is a wild cry from Asia in his classic speech; an altruism that is almost nihilism; a sacrifice that is nearly suicide. We are to give up liberty; we are to give up everything. This passionate paradox is undoubtedly sincere; and yet it conceals another paradox which it will be well to watch and suspect. Morally, it is all very heroic; but intellectually, it actually contains too much caution; it is more cautious than wise. It has behind its position two alternative lines of retreat. For the logical reader will at once perceive that, by thus rising into wild renunciation, the controversialist really has it

[62] King John III Sobieski ruled Poland from 1674 to 1696 and was a key figure in driving the Turks from the gates of Vienna in 1683.

both ways. Wherever Communism can be made attractive, he will make it attractive. Wherever Communism is quite obviously repulsive, he will say it proves the selfless hardihood of Communists who embrace so repulsive a thing. When it is human, it is in sympathy with all humanity; when it is inhuman, it calls for a superhuman sympathy. When it is good it is good; and when it is bad, they are very good to swallow it. This form of Necessity might be found in that proverb from the mouldering past: "Heads I win, tails you lose."

What Mr. Middleton Murry wants, of course, is real religion; and in parts of this book he seems to be growing desperate, or almost going mad, under the limitations of his unreal religion. He has got authority in the wrong place and asceticism in the wrong place. He is more limited by the idea of Destiny than we are by the idea of Deity. And he wants man to sacrifice civilisation as monks sacrifice luxury. He seems almost satisfied with it as a giant gesture of renunciation; there is really uncommonly little in this book about what will be the practical advantages of Communism when established. Reading between the lines, we almost find the meaning to be merely this: that he and the rest of us have come to breaking point; and this is the obvious point at which to break. There are other aspects of the book, with many of which I warmly agree, but I will conclude by saying that my fundamental objection to his Communism is that it consents to be the heir of Capitalism. His unfortunate necessitarianism narrows the possibilities of politics; and is content to say that industrialism has turned the world into One Man, who is aching in all his limbs. No doubt; and so would you and I, if we were all unnaturally tied to each other neck and heels, that we might make up together the monstrous and tottering figure of a pantomime ogre. But I do not want the ogre; I only want to cut him up. I am more revolutionary than Mr. Middleton Murry. I do not believe the unnatural monster will ache any the less, because he calls himself a Communist. I am more sceptical than Mr. Middleton Murry. I deny the pantomime myth of the One Man; and I should like to break him up again into men.

THE ASCETIC AT LARGE

My note on the Communism of Mr. Middleton Murry reads to me as rather too hasty and hostile; because I had no space to mention some strong and substantial parts of the book; notably those expressing contempt for the respectable sort of Socialist who will not call himself a Communist. The study of 'parasitic' Parliamentary Labour is masterly, and my own sympathies would be all with a man like Mr. Maxton as compared with a man like Mr. Thomas.[63] But the sequel is still puzzling; for in the last short note there is no practical programme except a Minimum Wage for all, which is said to obviate the need of expropriation of land and property. I suppose this means that employers would be taxed till they were too poor to employ; and then the State would employ. But what State—and, my God, what statesmen! Why, presumably (if *nothing* is needed but a new wage raised by a new tax) just the jolly statesmen the world produces at present, the parasitic Parliamentarians turned into omnipotent bureaucrats. I should refuse it, of course; first, because it preserves the wage-system; second because the worst wage-system is one with only one employer, who may be an omnipresent enemy; and third because, in the purely practical statement, there is no provision for any change in the type of tyrant. But this is unfair to the unpractical part; which of course is the better part. Mr. Murry does demand a terrific change of heart, though his scheme hardly ensures it. We may well struggle on as Distributists, when Communism seems so steep even to Communists; and they must endure the same abnormal austerity in order to be abnormal, that we endure to be normal.

In theory, or this part of his theory at least, Mr. Middleton Murry is an ascetic who wishes to transfer asceticism from the individual life, where it may be noble and beautiful, to the whole social and historical life, where it becomes simply vandalism or barbaric destruction.

[63] James Maxton (1885–1946) was a Scottish socialist who chaired the Independent Labour party in the late 1920s and again in the late 1930s. James Henry Thomas (1874–1949) was an English trade union leader who held cabinet positions under Ramsay MacDonald's Labour ministries.

In this he is undoubtedly at one with the Puritan or the Prohibitionist or the more mechanical sort of Pacifist; in short he is entirely at one with that sort of modern world which he most justly detests. Broadly considered, the fact that bulks biggest in the modern industrial world is this: that its moral movements are much *more* utterly and ruthlessly repressive than the past forms of mysticism or fanaticism that commonly affected only the few. Mediaeval men endured frightful fasts; but none of them would have dreamed of seriously proposing that nobody anywhere should ever have wine any more. And Prohibition, which was accepted by a huge modern industrial civilisation, did seriously propose that nobody should ever have wine any more. Cranks who dislike tobacco would utterly destroy all tobacco; I doubt whether they would even allow it medically as a sedative. Some Pagan sages and some Christian saints have been vegetarians, but nobody in the ancient world would ever have prophesied that flocks and herds would utterly vanish from the earth. But in the Utopia of the true vegetarian, I suppose they would utterly vanish from the earth. The more pedantic Pacifist has the same view of fighting, even for justice, and disarmament is as universal as conscription. For both conscription and disarmament are very modern notions. And modern notions of the sort are not only negative but nihilist; they always demand the absolute annihilation or "total prohibition" of something.

Now I am as adamant against Mr. Murry in this notion of mutilating our whole culture in a frenzy of moral renunciation. I admit that a saint may cut off his hand and enter heaven, and have a higher place there than the rest of us. But a plea for the amputation of the hands of all human beings, the vision of a Handless Humanity as the next evolutionary stage after that of the tailless ape, leaves me cold, however much it is commended as a splendid corporate self-sacrifice. These things are an allegory, in more ways than one. We may say indeed that the inhuman industrial era did really abolish the Hand, since it did abolish the Handicraft. I admit that monks have their own reasons for shaving their heads or nuns for cutting off their hair; but my advice to humanity outside such ecstasies would be to remain calm and keep its hair on. That a man should surrender his luxury is one thing; that mankind should surrender its liberty to deal with the problem of luxury is quite another. It is one thing to impoverish oneself; it is quite another responsibility to impoverish a whole cultural system of its culture. I might or might not be the better for giving up wine; I am absolutely certain that the world would not be better for giving up wine. Mr. Middleton Murry may be moved by a noble impulse to give up private property, but I do not for one single moment believe that humanity would be happier for giving up private property.

As a matter of fact, it is exactly this sort of sweeping destruction that has made it unhappy. The modern Capitalist world, which we unite to curse, actually came out of that notion of utterly abandoning the old for the promise of the new. Men said about the business of scarring English hills with rails or rolling English villages in smoke, exactly what Mr. Murry is now saying about sacrificing ancient faith or freedom and taxing moderate property out of existence. They said, as he does, that it was sad, that it was hard, that it called for a heroic sacrifice; but that we must not be sentimentalists clinging to the past, but must look to the brighter and broader future. And the brighter future was the epoch of Mr. Carnegie and Mr. Ford. Capitalism was actually founded by urging a new realism against an old romanticism. The answer is that it was not necessary for a whole society to give up beauty; and it is not necessary for a whole society to give up liberty. And if we look back at history, we shall see that these sweeping social renunciations have done nothing but harm. Over all America lies like an incubus the cold corpse of Puritanism, *because* one fervid generation thought that man must say farewell for ever to priests as well as play-actors, to sacraments as well as feasts. In short, men were asked to sacrifice everything for Calvinism as they are now asked to sacrifice everything for Communism. But though man may sacrifice anything, Everyman must not sacrifice everything. Individual men must sacrifice their own liberties, but only to restore liberty. And it is a grand irony that, while the cultured Communist (with all respect to him) is rending everybody else's garments and scattering ashes on other people's heads, away in many quiet places, on the hills of Lanark or deep in my own Buckingham beech-woods, priests and friars who have themselves renounced private property are rebuilding the farms and families of Distributism.

THE BACKWARD BOLSHIE

After all, the Bolshevist is really a Victorian. His is a nineteenth-century dream, even if it be a twentieth-century reality. It is notably so in the aspect which now makes the dream a nightmare; I mean the mad optimism about the advantages of machinery. What was offered to us as a Five Years Hence Plan ought really to have been called a Fifty Years Ago Plan. For they are only trying to do with Russia exactly what the Victorians did actually do with England; turn it into the workshop of the world and fill it with dirty tools and dismal mechanics. Marx was much more of a Victorian than Morris.[64] He may not have been technically a subject of Queen Victoria, though it is quite likely that he was. By geographical extraction I suppose he was a German—like Queen Victoria's husband and more remotely, Queen Victoria herself. By real or racial extraction he was a Jew; like Queen Victoria's favourite Prime Minister[65] and a good many other persons unnecessary to mention. But the late Victorian period was the very period at which the Jews, and especially the German Jews, were at the very top of their power and influence. From the time when they forced the Egyptian War[66] to the time when they forced the South African War,[67] they were imperial and immune. Certainly much more so than they are now; for the Jews are now being jumped on very unjustly in Germany itself, and old Victorians like Mr. Belloc and myself, who began in the days of Jewish omnipotence by attacking the Jews, will now probably die defending them. Anyhow, Karl Marx did not differ from any number of Victorian Jews in type or externals. He lived mostly in England, and launched his world religion from something more British than the British Empire: the British Museum. The Beard which moves Mr. Wells to impatience was simply

[64] William Morris (1834–96) was an English poet, novelist, artist and prominent advocate of socialism.

[65] Victoria's favorite prime minister was Benjamin Disraeli.

[66] Chesterton is referring to the British war against Egypt in 1882, a conflict prompted by the need to protect European investments.

[67] Chesterton is referring to the Boer War, 1899–1902.

the beard of Victorian romance; the beard of Tennyson and Longfellow and Trollope. And though his plan has been very imperfectly
applied in the one place in the world where he would have said it
could not be applied at all (for this true Victorian saw the great commercial cities of Western Europe as the only possible battlefields of
the future) it has all the character of a new and rather barbaric people
imitating something that is already stale, not to say stinking, for
civilised people. It was exactly like the very Victorian incident of the
industrialising of japan. That is, it was and is something essentially
behind the times. The Japanese wear billycock hats presumably
under the impression that we admire billycock hats. But, whatever
just vengeance may fall upon our hats, this is to do an injustice to
our heads. Now, as a matter of fact, our heads have in many ways
advanced a little, since the days when our own Five Year Plan filled
England with filth and smoke. Some rather deeper questions have
arisen; questions about the individual, about the purpose of life,
about religion in history, and so on. Philosophy, even Thomist
philosophy, is heard again in Paris and Oxford.

Now Marx had no more philosophy than Macaulay. The Marxians therefore have no more philosophy than the Manchester
School.[68] It was enough for Macaulay to rejoice in the mere excitement of extension, in the hope that "the roofs and chimneys of a
new Manchester may rise in the wilds of Connemara." Similarly, it
is enough for the Moscow Marxians to hope that the roofs and
chimneys of a new Manchester may rise in the wilds of Siberia. It is
true that the original Manchester men desired competition while the
Marxians desire combination; or the Combine of all Combines. But
the competition ended in a Combine and the Combine has not really
ended in a Communist State. For it seems clear that grades of un-
equal wages do exist in Bolshevist Russia, and the Bolshevist rulers
can only explain that it is a temporary necessity at this political stage
and that true, pure, perfect Communism will come in the future. It
might be the Labour Party, mightn't it?

[68] The Manchester School in mid-nineteenth-century England was a school of
political economy associated with John Bright and Richard Cobden; it advocated
free trade and government nonintervention in the economy.

But to carry competition to any lengths, because it is the fashion, or to carry combination to any lengths because it is the fashion, is not a Philosophy. A philosophy begins with Being; with the end and value of a living thing; and it is manifest that a materialism that only considers economic ethics, cannot cover the question at all. If the problem of happiness were so solved by economic comfort, the classes who are now comfortable would be happy, which is absurd. This humourless hammering on one note is like the worst Victorian fads; Temperance or Feminism. It is especially like that very old-fashioned Feminism that hated to be feminine. I am told that in Russia men and women dress roughly alike. But, mark you, that does not mean that men wear flowers in their hair or trail about in those noble pontifical robes with which tradition clothed every woman like a queen. It means that women dress like men; not that men dress like women. Now that is sheer stark, stale, dead Victorianism. That is the only original Woman's Rights Woman, who deliberately made herself hideous with bloomers and goggles. By the following reigns, even the Suffragettes had learned better than that; but while the Suffragettes are things of the past for us, they are still far in the rosy future for the backward and belated Bolshevist. He is still plodding through that foggy factory twilight that was supposed to be the enlightened daylight of the nineteenth century; and it is truer now than in the time of the Czars to say that Russia is the most backward of the nations.

THE LAST TURN

The only difficulty about the evident reawakening of Catholicism in modern England, is that conversion calls on a man to stretch his mind, as a man awakening from a sleep may stretch his arms and legs. It calls on the imagination to stretch itself, for instance, over a wider area than England, and a longer period than English history. And, for certain rather curious reasons, the stretching of the mind generally stops short of anything like a complete comprehension of any great historical or philosophical process. This is what Bernard Shaw meant when he said that the world will never really progress, until every man lives for three hundred years. I remember remarking at the time that there was a sort of truth symbolised in this; and that, most certainly, if Bernard Shaw had lived for three hundred years he would be a Catholic.

This preliminary point can be quite sufficiently proved even from this particular case. Three hundred years would mean that he would remember, as part of the positive poetry of childhood, the first phase of the Reformation. The first phase of the Reformation in England was the Divine Right of Kings. It was a romantic enthusiasm for Royalty itself, and the duty of an utterly prostrate passive obedience to it. This was the first effect of the New Religion; but before the child was barely a boy it would be overthrown by another New Religion. The Calvinist killed the sacred King, who had been sacred enough to kill the Church; and darkened the land with a creed of total Depravity and the Scottish Sabbath. By the time Mr. Shaw was a growing lad of only a hundred years old, the world would have rebelled against this tyranny in turn. The Scottish Mr. Hume would soon be preparing to burst up the Scottish Sabbath. The ingenious Mr. Rousseau would be denying total Depravity and asserting total Innocence, Naturalness and Niceness. Out of this, as he grew to maturity, nearing a century and a half, there would grow gradually the most pleasant and plausible, the most happy, healthy and exhilarating of all the purely human visions: the vision of Liberty. Let men be only free from their feudal chains and theological gags; let them speak as they like, write as they like, buy and sell as they like, trade and travel and enquire as they like; and the race will waken from the nightmare of ages into the broad brotherhood of reason and justice. About the time when Mr. Shaw's first grey hair appeared, in the year 1832, when he was barely two hundred, there was much talk about a Reform Bill in England; but I do not think Mr. Shaw would have been taken in, even then. Already, for a long time, men had been buying and selling as they liked, and trading and travelling as they liked. And already the result stood up solid and enormous, in the thing called Capitalism: that is the dispossession of the populace of all forms of real productive property; all instruments of production in the hands of the few; all the millions merely the servants of the few, working for a wage, always an insecure wage, generally a mean and inhuman wage. It was when this process had gone even further that the real historical Mr. Bernard Shaw was born; with the natural consequence that Mr. Bernard Shaw has devoted his life to making war on Capitalism. He has done so because the special evil of his own lifetime was Capitalism. But shall we not guess that he would have done it rather differently, if he had already spent two or three lifetimes warring against Divine Right, and then against the Calvinism that attacked Divine Right, and then against the Rousseauan prostration before Liberty, which destroyed Calvinism—and produced Capitalism. Would he not conclude that the whole State had been staggering about in a most extraordinary and irrational manner, ever since he was first born under the Elizabethan Settlement? Would it not be obvious that the mind of man had been filled with nothing but frantic exaggerations, crude simplifications, provincial panaceas and quack medicines and sheer raving monomania, ever since it had broken away from the central civilisation and the philosophy which the Saints had handed down from the Ancients? Would it not interest him to find that, all the time, there had been written in the open books of Aquinas or Bellarmine or Suarez,[69] a perfectly reasonable apportionment of the authority of princes, the claims of peoples, the possibilities of democracy, the use and abuse of property, and the right function of freedom?

[69] Francisco Suarez (1548–1617) was a Spanish Jesuit and neoscholastic theologian.

Three hundred years felt with their full weight, really measured out in time and experience, endured as a man actually endures the passsage of his days, would prove the whole Protestant story to have been the most preposterous and disproportionate detour, or straggling a chapter of accidents, that ever set out in the wrong direction and came back to the same place. For we have in a hundred ways come back to the same place; even to the detail of an exaggerated reaction, like that of the *Action Française*,[70] renewing the absolute appeal to The King. And nothing is more amusing than to note the way in which those who regard themselves as the most advanced leaders, of the most modern groups, are already rearing and bucking against the whole tendency of liberal and humanitarian progress, which the last revolutionary leaders marked out for them. Nobody is less in the spirit of Walt Whitman than Wyndham Lewis[71] or T. S. Eliot; nobody less a real heir of H. G. Wells than Aldous Huxley; nobody less disposed to follow the humanitarian paths of Mr. Nevinson the adventurous journalist, than his son Mr. Nevinson[72] the Futurist painter. All these of the most recent school of rebels are rebelling against rebellion; that is, against the Revolution and all its heritage of liberty, equality and fraternity. Mr. Eliot, though an American, is an avowed Royalist. Mr. Nevinson has become a quite ferocious Kiplingite Imperialist. Mr. Wyndham Lewis seems to prefer a Dictatorship, in so far as he may be said to prefer anything. All this last turn of the twisting road of progress is pointing back towards what we have called for a hundred years reaction. It is apparent in the Fascists; in the Hitlerites; and even in the open anti-democracy of the Bolshevists.

[70] Action Française was a French monarchist group that flourished in the 1920s and 1930s under the leadership of the poet and journalist Charles Maurras (1868–1952).

[71] Percy Wyndham Lewis (1884–1957) was an English novelist, critic and painter involved in avant-garde artistic movements.

[72] Henry Woodd Nevinson (1856–1941) was an English journalist and war correspondent during the Boer War and campaigns in the Balkans and Dardanelles. In 1904 he exposed the Portuguese slave trade in Angola. His son, Christopher Nevinson (1889–1946), achieved fame as a Futurist painter and an official war artist; his war pictures were exhibited in London in 1916.

Now the great danger of the moment is that young men will go on being content with these revolts against revolt, these reactions against reactions; so that we have nothing but an everlasting seesaw of the Old Young and the New Young; the last always content with its fleeting triumph over the last but one. And the only way to avoid that result is to teach men to stretch their minds and inhabit a larger period of time. It is to insist, not that we now feel inclined to stress this or stress that, in mere fashion or mere fatigue, but that there really does exist somewhere a reasonable plan of the proportions of things, which, at least in its general outline, is true all the time. The moment men, so intelligent as those I have named, begin to realise that this permanent plan is necessary, they will certainly realise that the only existing plan, that has any plausible claim to look like it, is the plan of the Catholic Faith. For the present, they seem to be quite content to continue the old squabble of fathers and sons; even if the fathers are very young fathers, or the sons actually appeal to the grandfathers against them. But this merely modern squabble is after all local and therefore provincial; it can never satisfy the thirst of thinking people for the reality of things. Nevertheless, as I stated at the beginning, the great difficulty is whether a man can stretch his mind, or (as the moderns would say) can broaden his mind, enough to see the need for an eternal Church.

And yet surely this is only the last lap in the long race in which the ancient truth, so heavily handicapped, has one by one outdistanced all the runners who prided themselves on their youth or their advance positions. If a man could have learned it by a process of elimination, merely by living through the last three hundred years, he would learn the same lesson even more clearly by living through the next three hundred years. By that time it will be more apparent than ever that these jerks of novelty do not create either a progress or an equilibrium. The very newest of the intellectuals have already learnt not to trust to mere progress, in the sense of a process of change; they already know that they have sometimes more in common with some antique authority than with some merely modern rebellion. Some of them would set up dictators to enforce obedience; it is hard if we may not obey willingly, when they would have men obey even unwillingly. They would set up violent authority in the hands of individuals; they can hardly complain if we recognise merely moral authority in a merely mystical office. For that mystical office contains all the liberties and all the philosophies, and judges only upon their right balance and proportion; and every other thing that the moderns call a movement is only securing for a monomania the brief life of a sect.

THE NEW LUTHER

It seems that there is some movement or other, of a religious sort; which, being founded by a Lutheran of German race and American origin, naturally connects itself with the name of Oxford. Some people say it is called the Oxford Group Movement. Other people seem to be somewhat needlessly alarmed, lest it be identified by historians with the Oxford Movement. I would suggest, in a friendly spirit, that it should be called the Oxford Street Movement. Oxford Street does actually contain the name of the University town, which seems to be all that is required; and at the same time, it is a long way from Oxford. I think the atmosphere there would be more congruous and comfortable; and somehow I feel that Mr. Gordon Selfridge,[73] being in the neighbourhood, would be more really sympathetic and spiritually helpful than the Master of Balliol.

When I had made some such idle jest I received a letter of remonstrance against what I had written of the Buchman Group Movement.[74] The letter was written in a pained and almost pathetic tone, expressing regret that I should depreciate anything that brought men back to the reality of religion; and I ought at least to assure the writer that I am not insensible to any such plea. In this as in many things, however, religion is treated in a curious manner, as distinct from politics or ethics or economics. Nobody says that because all political parties may be presumed to contain many well-wishers to the public good, therefore we must not resist Communism or attack Capitalism, or express our trust or distrust of Fascism. The roads which lead to different social solutions are recognised as divergent. It is only the paths to hell and heaven of which it is enough to say

[73] Gordon Selfridge (1858–1947) was an American businessman who moved to England in 1906 and opened a popular department store in London.
[74] The Buchman Group Movement, better known as Moral Re-armament (the name it took in 1938), was founded in the 1920s by the American Frank Buchman (1878–1961). It was a nondenominational religious movement that sought to change the world order by persuading individuals to confess their sins and follow God's guidance. These confessions took place at "house parties".

that they are paved with good intentions. Let me say at once that I do sympathise with any sinners who seek such an outlet; even with the rather exclusive and arrogant spiritual aristocracy which writes over its gates, "For Sinners Only." I sympathise with them, not so much as I sympathise with the ignorant fishermen bawling hymns in any dingy old chapel in any Devonshire fishing village; not quite so much as I sympathise with a company of Holy Rollers rolling on the ground in the neighbourhood of Dayton, Tennessee,[75] to avert the curse of Evolution; and not half so much as I sympathise with Moslem fakirs howling in the desert and shaking their splendid spears and dying on the British bayonets. But I do sympathise with all these people; since they are all seeking God. And I am sufficiently orthodox to know that, in some mystical way beyond our measurement, it is true that seeking is finding.

But if my correspondent, or anybody else, wishes to know why I rather prefer the followers of the Mad Mullah to the followers of Herr Buchman, he will find it perfectly summed up in an interview and article which appeared in the *News-Chronicle* and was headed in huge letters with the words, "Vision of a New Reformation: Group Leader's Hope from Germany." He will find it exquisitely and exactly concentrated, as in the crystallization of a gem, in these words; read them; re-read them; ponder them. They contain the whole substance of the subject. "These Groupers think on a large scale. The Canadians, for instance, have not only booked the Chateau Frontenac for a house-party of 3,000 at Quebec next year, but have already chartered a C.P.R. liner to bring their contingent to England for the next Oxford house-party."

That, you will observe, is thinking largely. To rude, rustic, Distributist minds, it would not appear that it is thinking at all. There have been any number of sectarians and Puritan fanatics who have very genuinely thought; some who have thought and thought until they went mad. But I should say that the sanity and solidity of the Group Movement was quite safe from any such danger as that. Note that it is not a question of whether religion may think too

[75] Dayton, Tennessee, was the site of the Scopes trial of evolutionary theory, in 1925.

much about pomp and grandeur. It is a question of whether religion is to boast of having pomp without thinking at all. There is a real case to be made out both for and against the most Pagan phase of the Papacy, which filled Rome with trophies that might have stood for the triumphs of Trajan or Augustus. But it does need some thought to build even a Pagan temple or erect even an Imperialistic monument. The dome which Michelangelo made the culmination of St. Peter's is not only a large dome. It is a dome made by a man who was thinking largely. Nay, it might have been less large if it had been larger. Lift it a little higher in the air and the curve is constricted; spread it a little wider and the curve is flattened. That is what is meant by thinking; and especially by thinking largely. At any rate, it is a rather different operation from buying up somebody else's steamboat, or securing all the beds in somebody else's hotel.

Finally, what shall we say in the light (or twilight) of all this, of the magnificent claim made in such large letters that they would cover a whole paragraph of this essay; the "Vision of a New Reformation: Group Leader's Hope from Germany?" We may say this to begin with; that here, as in every single thing I have read about the Group Movement, as in every page and paragraph of the book called *For Sinners Only*, there is an extraordinary ambiguity. What is meant by a New Reformation? What is it that is to be reformed? Is it just possible that it is the Reformation that is to be reformed? And, for those who have a pedantic fancy for looking at the structure of the words they write or speak, into what form is it to be reformed? Can it be into the old original form? Certainly in all this there is no trace or outline of any new form. Or does it mean by a New Reformation, a repetition of the Reformation? Does it mean an extension of the Reformation? Does it mean that we are to look for somebody who shall be more Lutheran than Luther? I suppose the real doctrine of the great Reformer might possibly be pushed further than he pushed it. It is very difficult to imagine any doctrine that could make man more base, describe human nature as more desperately impotent, blacken the reason and the will of man with a more utterly bottomless and hopeless despair than did the real doctrine of Luther. But it may be that there are depths below the depths and that it is possible to damn the dignity of Adam more completely than Luther damned it. Is that what is meant by a New Reformation? That is the only Reformation that would bear the remotest resemblance to the old Reformation. But that is just the difficulty; and that is just the point. I cannot accuse the Buchmanites of repeating the Lutheran pessimism. I cannot accuse them of revolting against the Lutheran pessimism. The very language they use is so loose and vague and journalistic, that it might mean either that the New Reformation is to restore Luther or reverse Luther. All they are sure about is that it will come from Germany, like Luther — or like Hitler. There is a certain intellectual courage, which some would call impudence, about saying at this moment that the Vision of a New Reformation is of necessity a Hope from Germany. It is amusing to read it at the very moment when even the Pro-Germans have begun to think that Germany is hopeless. Anyhow, the religious leader in question is welcome, so far as I am concerned, to any New Reformation which puts the Swastika above the Cross and teaches men first to be very arrogant Germans before it allows them to be very apologetic Christians. All that may be a reformation in the sense of a new form; but it seems to me, on the side of religious thought, to be the very essence of formlessness.

BABIES AND DISTRIBUTISM

I hope it is not a secret arrogance to say that I do not think I am exceptionally arrogant; or if I were, my religion would prevent me from being proud of my pride. Nevertheless, for those of such a philosophy, there is a very terrible temptation to intellectual pride, in the welter of wordy and worthless philosophies that surround us today. Yet there are not many things that move me to anything like a personal contempt. I do not feel any contempt for an atheist, who is often a man limited and constrained by his own logic to a very sad simplification. I do not feel any contempt for a Bolshevist, who is a man driven to the same negative simplification by a revolt against very positive wrongs. But there is one type of person for whom I feel what I can only call contempt. And that is the popular propagandist of what he or she absurdly describes as Birth-Control.

I despise Birth-Control first because it is a weak and wobbly and cowardly word. It is also an entirely meaningless word; and is used so as to curry favour even with those who would at first recoil from its real meaning. The proceeding these quack doctors recommend does not *control* any birth. It only makes sure that there shall never be any birth to control. It cannot, for instance, determine sex, or even make any selection in the style of the pseudo-science of Eugenics. Normal people can only act so as to produce birth; and these people can only act so as to prevent birth. But these people know perfectly well that they dare not write the plain word Birth-Prevention, in any one of the hundred places where they write the hypocritical word Birth-Control. They know as well as I do that the very word Birth-Prevention would strike a chill into the public, the instant it was blazoned on headlines, or proclaimed on platforms, or scattered in advertisements like any other quack medicine. They dare not call it by its name, because its name is very bad advertising. Therefore they use a conventional and unmeaning word, which may make the quack medicine sound more innocuous.

Second, I despise Birth-Control because it is a weak and wobbly and cowardly thing. It is not even a step along the muddy road they call Eugenics; it is a flat refusal to take the first and most obvious step along the road of Eugenics. Once grant that their philosophy is right, and their course of action is obvious; and they dare not take it; they dare not even declare it. If there is no authority in things which Christendom has called moral, because their origins were mystical, then they are clearly free to ignore all difference between animals and men; and treat men as we treat animals. They need not palter with the stale and timid compromise and convention called Birth-Control. Nobody applies it to the cat. The obvious course for Eugenists is to act towards babies as they act towards kittens. Let all the babies be born; and then let us drown those we do not like. I cannot see any objection to it; except the moral or mystical sort of objection that we advance against Birth-Prevention. And that would be real and even reasonable Eugenics; for we could then select the best, or at least the healthiest, and sacrifice what are called the unfit. By the weak compromise of Birth-Prevention, we are very probably sacrificing the fit and only producing the unfit. The births we prevent may be the births of the best and most beautiful children; those we allow, the weakest or worst. Indeed, it is probable; for the habit discourages the early parentage of young and vigorous people; and lets them put off the experience to later years, mostly from mercenary motives. Until I see a real pioneer and progressive leader coming out with a good, bold, scientific programme for drowning babies, I will not join the movement.

But there is a third reason for my contempt, much deeper and therefore much more difficult to express; in which is rooted all my reasons for being anything I am or attempt to be; and above all, for being a Distributist. Perhaps the nearest to a description of it is to say this: that my contempt boils over into bad behaviour when I hear the common suggestion that a birth is avoided because people want to be "free" to go to the cinema or buy a gramophone or a loudspeaker. What makes me want to walk over such people like doormats is that they use the word "free." By every act of that sort they chain themselves to the most servile and mechanical system yet tolerated by men. The cinema is a machine for unrolling certain regular patterns called pictures; expressing the most vulgar millionaires' notion of the taste of the most vulgar millions. The gramophone is a machine for recording such tunes as certain shops and other organisations choose to sell. The wireless is better; but even that is marked by the modern mark of all three; the impotence of the receptive party. The amateur cannot challenge the actor; the householder will find it vain to go and shout into the gramophone; the mob cannot pelt the modern speaker, especially when he is a loud-speaker. It is all a central mechanism giving out to men exactly what their masters think they should have.

Now a child is the very sign and sacrament of personal freedom. He is a fresh free will added to the wills of the world; he is something that his parents have freely chosen to produce and which they freely agree to protect. They can feel that any amusement he gives (which is often considerable) really comes from him and from them, and from nobody else. He has been born without the intervention of any master or lord. He is a creation and a contribution; he is their own creative contribution to creation. He is also a much more beautiful, wonderful, amusing and astonishing thing than any of the stale stories or jingling jazz tunes turned out by the machines. When men no longer feel that he is so, they have lost the appreciation of primary things, and therefore all sense of proportion about the world. People who prefer the mechanical pleasures, to such a miracle, are jaded and enslaved. They are preferring the very dregs of life to the first fountains of life. They are preferring the last, crooked, indirect, borrowed repeated and exhausted things of our dying Capitalist civilisation, to the reality which is the only rejuvenation of all civilisation. It is they who are hugging the chains of their old slavery; it is the child who is ready for the new world.

THREE FOES OF THE FAMILY

It was certainly a very brilliant lightning-flash of irony by which Mr. Aldous Huxley lit up the whole loathsome landscape of his satirical Utopia, of synthetic humanity and manufactured men and women, by the old romantic quotation of "Brave New World". The quotation comes, of course, from that supreme moment of the magic of youth, nourished by the magic of old age, when Miranda[76] the marvellous becomes Miranda the marvelling, at the unique wonder of first love. To use it for the very motto of a system which, having lost all innocence, would necessarily lose all wonder, was a touch of very withering wit. And yet it will be well to remember that, in comparison with some other worlds, where the same work is done more weakly and quite as wickedly, the Utopia of the extremists really has something of the intellectual integrity which belongs to extremes, even of madness. In that sense the two ironical adjectives are not merely ironical. The horrible human, or inhuman, hive described in Mr. Huxley's romance is certainly a base world, and a filthy world, and a fundamentally unhappy world. But it is in one sense a new world; and it is in one sense a brave world. At least a certain amount of bravery, as well as brutality, would have to be shown before anything of the sort could be established in the world of fact. It would need some courage, and even some self-sacrifice, to establish anything so utterly disgusting as that.

But the same work is being done in other worlds that are not particularly new, and not in the least brave. These are people of another sort, much more common and conventional, who are not only working to create such a paradise of cowardice, but who actually try to work for it through a conspiracy of cowards. The attitude of these people towards the Family and the tradition of its Christian virtues is the attitude of men willing to wound and yet afraid to strike; or ready to sap and mine so long as they are not called upon to fire or fight in the open. And those who do this cover much more than half, or nearly two-thirds, of the people who write in the most

[76] Miranda is a character in Shakespeare's *The Tempest*.

respectable and conventional Capitalist newpapers. It cannot be too often repeated that what destroyed the Family in the modern world was Capitalism. No doubt it might have been Communism, if Communism had ever had a chance, outside that semi-Mongolian wilderness where it actually flourishes. But, so far as we are concerned, what has broken up households, and encourages divorces, and treated the old domestic virtues with more and more open contempt, is the epoch and power of Capitalism. It is Capitalism that has forced a moral feud and a commercial competition between the sexes; that has destroyed the influence of the parent in favour of the influence of the employer; that has driven men from their homes to look for jobs; that has forced them to live near their factories or their firms instead of near their families; and, above all, that has encouraged, for commercial reasons, a parade of publicity and garish novelty, which is in its nature the death of all that was called dignity and modesty by our mothers and fathers. It is not the Bolshevist but the Boss, the publicity man, the salesman and the commercial advertiser who have, like a rush and riot of barbarians, thrown down and trampled under foot the ancient Roman statue of Verecundia.[77] But because the thing is done by men of this sort, of course it is done in their own muggy and muddle-headed way; by all the irresponsible tricks of their foul Suggestion and their filthy Psychology. It is done, for instance, by perpetually guying the old Victorian virtues or limitations which, as they are no longer there, are not likely to retaliate. It is done more by pictures than by printed words; because printed words are supposed to make some sense and a man may be answerable for printing them. Stiff and hideous effigies of women in crinolines or bonnets are paraded, as if *that* could possibly be all there was to see when Maud[78] came into the garden, and was saluted by such a song. Fortunately, Maud's friends, who would have challenged the pressman and photographer to a duel, are all dead; and these satirists of Victorianism are very careful to find out that all their enemies are dead. Some of their bold caricaturists have been known to charge an old-fashioned bathing-machine as courageously

[77] The statue depicts Modesty.
[78] *Maud* is a poetic monodrama published by Tennyson in 1855.

as if it were a machine-gun. It is convenient thus courageously to attack bathing-machines, because there are no bathing-machines to attack. Then they balance these things by photographs of the Modern Girl at various stages of the nudist movement; and trust that anything so obviously vulgar is bound to be popular. For the rest, the Modern Girl is floated on a sea of sentimental sloppiness; a continuous gush about her frankness and freshness, the pefect naturalness of her painting her face or the unprecedented courage of her having no children. The whole is diluted with a dreary hypocrisy about comradeship, far more sentimental than the old-fashioned sentiment. When I see the family sinking in these swamps of amorphous amorous futility, I feel inclined to say, "Give me the Communists." Better Bolshevist battles and the Brave New World than the ancient house of man rotted away silently by such worms of secret sensuality and individual appetite. "The coward does it with a kiss; the brave man with a sword."[79]

But there is, curiously enough, a third thing of the kind, which I am really inclined to think that I dislike even more than the other two. It is not the Communist attacking the family or the Capitalist betraying the family; it is the vast and very astonishing vision of the Hitlerite defending the family. Hitler's way of defending the independence of the family is to make every family dependent on him and his semi-Socialist State; and to preserve the authority of parents by authoritatively telling all the parents what to do. His notion of keeping sacred the dignity of domestic life is to issue peremptory orders that the grandfather is to get up at five in the morning and do dumb-bell exercises, or the grandmother to march twenty miles to a camp to procure a Swastika flag. In other words, he appears to interfere with family life more even than the Bolshevists do; and to do it in the name of the sacredness of the family. It is not much more encouraging than the other two social manifestations; but at least it is more entertaining.

[79] The quotation is from Oscar Wilde's *The Ballad of Reading Gaol* (1898).

THE DON AND THE CAVALIER

Mr. Christopher Hollis has written an excellent book on John Dryden. It is an instructive book; it is also an amusing book; but not so amusing as some of the reviews of it. And it concerns me here, at the moment mainly in relation to the general position to-day of the school of academic critics, who have upheld for so long a time the historical theory which is often called Parliamentarism and is in fact Plutocracy. It is of some moment to the Distributist movement because it was the official defence of this policy which made possible the dispossession of the populace. Now about the present position of that official criticism there are several rather curious things to note. The first is its *tone*; which is quite queer in its difference from the tone used in my youth, when historians were as simple as Macaulay; I might almost say when scholars were as ignorant as Macaulay. For a man can be very learned and very ignorant; and Macaulay achieved the combination to the admiration of heaven and earth. Macaulay would make short work, or imagine that he could make short work, of any young man who played at being a Jacobite;[80] he was impatient with him as with a crank; but he was *honestly* impatient; his impatience was a sort of innocence. The critics on the same side to-day have lost their innocence. They know perfectly well that they have been defeated in battle after battle upon the big facts; and they have a curious carefulness in dealing only with very small facts. Anybody who said thirty years ago that Charles the First was not in fact a tyrant, dethroned by an indignant democracy, could really be treated as a sort of Mr. Dick,[81] with a weakness for weeping over King Charles's Head. The modern critic does not really dare to-day to appear as the executioner (even though the critic, like the executioner, can wear a mask and remain nameless); he has not now the nerve to shake King Charles's Head at the people and shout confidently, "Behold the Head of a Traitor." So he becomes more fussy and particular than ever over the ancient, profound, pressing and

[80] A Jacobite was a partisan of the Stuart cause after the deposing of James II in 1688.
[81] Mr. Dick is a character in Charles Dickens' *David Copperfield*, written in 1849-1850.

all-important question: "Out of which window in Whitehall did Charles the First step to have his head cut off?" And that, as Disraeli very truly observed, is one of the two or three quite infallible ways of becoming a bore.

And the new professor of the old history is rather a bore; but what is much worse, he is a nervous bore. He not only drawls, but he also stammers. And his tone, as I have said, has achieved a most peculiar accent of acrid timidity. I read one criticism of Mr. Hollis's book, in a highly learned and authoritative weekly; and it largely left me wondering whether the critic who wrote it had read that particular passage in it, in which Mr. Hollis, contrasting the methods of Dryden and Pope, quotes the whole of the latter poet's famous satire upon Addison. Whether or no it was like Addison, it was exactly like the critic.[82]

> "Willing to wound and yet afraid to strike,
> Just hint a doubt and hesitate dislike;
> Damn with faint praise, assent with civil leer,
> And without sneering teach the rest to sneer."

Again, over and above this unmistakable tone, there is the change in the method which I have compared to the change from laughing at Mr. Dick over King Charles's Head to quarrelling about which windowsill had the honour to be bestridden by King Charles's legs. There was an excellent example in this review, of the method of avoiding battle on the main issue and picking a quarrel about a trifle. Mr. Hollis made the general remark, which is a true and valuable remark, that it is rather a disadvantage of revolutions that they often have to be followed by new and rigid repressions, set up by the revolutionists themselves. He gives the example that William of Orange's government censored a sort of controversy which under the last Stuarts was much more free. The critic then suggested that the whole book and its author were historically unreliable, upon some verbal interpretation of William of Orange's government; because the censorship was removed later; I think in 1695. The point of general interest is that there was a new censorship; and the critic's

---

[82] The quotation is from Pope's "Epistle to Dr. Arbuthnot" (1735).

way of proving that there was not a censorship is to say that there was a censorship, that lasted for about eight years. Now Mr. Hollis's general philosophy may be right or wrong; but Mr. Hollis's general remark was perfectly philosophical and a quite reasonable comment on this and many other cases of the same truth. The critic's correction, if his correction is correct, is not of the slightest philosophical or rational interest to anybody; it has no relation to the point that was really raised; it only says that somebody did something, but did not do it all the time. That is what I mean by the one side being concerned with triviality and the other side with truth. Mr. Hollis's suggestion is of some intelligent importance to us, who are living among real revolutions; Bolshevist revolutions or Hitlerite revolutions. It is not necessarily a complete condemnation of revolutions. It is simply a note on the natural history of revolutionists. But his history really is natural history, and the academic and pedantic history has become utterly unnatural.

There is a saying that a great silence broods over the great battlefields. There is certainly a very astounding silence over the great recent defeats of the Orangemen's theory of history. Mr. Hollis begins his book by noting the picturesque coincidence that Dryden sat fishing in the river upon which Mary Stuart had looked out from the Tower of Fotheringay.[83] The storming and taking of that Tower, with all its secrets, was a struggle that once made an amazing noise, that has now been followed by a more amazing stillness. Hardly anything is said about its sensational termination; simply because the main part of the old accepted case against the Catholic Queen has completely broken down. Considering how frightfully important it was that the Casket Letters[84] were all certainly genuine, it is very funny to find how unimportant it is that they are most of them probably forgeries. The war was so fierce and ruthless while they thought they were winning it; it is so very quiet and casual and gentlemanly, now that they know they are losing it. That

[83] Mary Stuart was imprisoned in Fotheringay castle in 1586, tried for her role in a plot to assassinate Elizabeth, and executed in 1587.

[84] The Casket Letters, purportedly written by Mary Stuart, implicated her in the murder of her husband, Lord Darnley.

intellectual interlude at least is over; England is returning to her own past, and could hardly march under a better battle-sign than what Macaulay himself had the magnanimity to call "the towering crest of Dryden."

I also came upon another critique of the book on Dryden; and one which goes far beyond the sort of negative hostility in the critics which I have criticised. That was, after all, only the confession that the Whig and Puritan school of history is fighting the rearguard action of a retreat, and that it mostly consists of rather futile sniping. Instead of the old uproarious cannonade of Macaulay, we do now in practice only "hear the distant and random gun that the foe is sullenly firing." But the later criticism involved something more universal and significant than that. It really did represent the amazing, mystifying and in some ways almost exciting muddle, in what calls itself the Modern Mind. I say exciting, because when a mystification becomes as mad as that, it has almost the character of a mystery story; it is as if the modern man must have had a knock on the head, and we were all detectives trying to find out who really did it. How did it really happen that the cultivated, sometimes even the classical critic of this particular period, suffers from a heavy blow from some blunt instrument, so that he thinks and writes in the following fashion?

The critic in question said in these words, or almost these words: "We have no reason to doubt the sincerity of Dryden's conversion to Roman Catholicism; but, after all, in the case of so great a man as Dryden, does the question matter very much?" That is the Modern Mind. This is the forest primeval, the murmuring pines and the hemlocks. This is the Jungle. This is the thickest of all thickets and the thorniest of all earthly briar-patches; and though I was born and bred in that briar-patch, like Brer Rabbit, I found it difficult to discover a path out of it; and I did not know how we are really to make a path through it.

Of course we can always begin by using the primitive implement of reason; and try to let in a little light merely by letting in a little logic. So far as I understand the argument as an argument, it is this. If John Dryden had been born half-witted, or if he had been a dunce and a dull fellow entirely insignificant in the intellectual and social life of his time — *then* it would have been frightfully and sensationally important to know whether he was or was not sincere, with a soul-searching sincerity, in his intellectual acceptance of the complete Catholic philosophy. But as he was not a dunce but a poet, as he was not a half-wit but a wit, as he was not a mindless person but a very great mind, then it must be a matter of indifference whether such an intellect can accept such an intellectual philosophy. Dryden was so great a thinker that it does not matter what he thought; he was almost certainly in search of the truth, but he was so capable of searching for it that nobody can take any interest in whether he found it; and it is only in the case of a small man that we could take a great interest in the great truth that he thought he found. How, I ask you, do people get their minds into a tangle like that? How could a man be sincere in his Catholicism, and yet think himself superior to his Catholicism? How could his greatness be detached from anything so great as a belief in a universal order of life, death and eternity; if he really had the greatness and really had the belief? It might make some sense if Dryden was not sincere; but it is practically admitted that he was sincere. It might make some sense if Dryden was small; but it is actually based on the view that he was great.

While the world has been talking about removing Victorian taboos, I have been resolved from the first to remove that one Victorian taboo; which really was a senseless and strangling taboo; the taboo on the *topic* of real religion, and its real and inevitable place in practical life. Most of the things the Moderns call Victorian taboos are about as Victorian as the Ten Commandments or the maxims of Confucius. But this really was Victorian, in the sense of having arisen recently in a vulgar, commercial and cowardly social system. It is not the notion that it is right or wrong to be a Moslem; it is the notion that it cannot really matter even to a Moslem that he is a Moslem. What is totally intolerable is the idea that everybody must pretend, for the sake of peace and decorum, that moral inspiration only comes from secular things like Distributism, and cannot possibly come from spiritual things like Catholicism. That is the fixed idea like a fossil that lies under all the labyrinthine wrappings or coil of contradictory conventions, in the minds of the reviewer whose words I quote.

It has nothing to do with what he would call being religious; or forcing religion upon him or anybody else. No Catholic thinks he is a good Catholic; or he would by that thought become a bad Catholic. I for one am not even tempted to any illusion in that matter; I fear that very often, when I have got up early to go to Mass, I have said with a groan, *Tantum religio potuit suadere malorum*, which, I may explain to the Moslem, is not a quotation from the Mass. But the critic here in question does not say, in the grand Lucretian manner, "Religion alone can persuade men to such evils." He says, "Religion alone cannot really have persuaded anybody to anything." He stands for a stupid interlude of intellectual history, in which men would not recognise religion either as a friend or an enemy, which supposed that a great man must be great, not merely in spite of it, but even without reference to it. That intellectual interlude was never very intellectual; and anyhow, it is over.

THE CHURCH AND AGORAPHOBIA

The erection of a great cathedral in a great city, and especially in a great port, that is a city that is also a wide gate of the world, recalls certain truths that are curiously forgotten, or sometimes still more astonishingly contradicted or reversed. Before we come to count the million mistakes and misunderstandings which separate men from the Catholic Church, there is one enormous and elementary mistake, which has to do with this question of scale and position in the world. To put it shortly; the man who fears to enter the Church commonly fancies that what he feels is a sort of claustrophobia. As a fact, what he really feels, is rather a sort of agoraphobia. Some silly little historical accidents, almost entirely peculiar to the particular way in which Catholicism survived in England, have given many Englishmen an extraordinary notion that it is a sort of hole and corner affair. These honest Protestants, like the imaginary nuns in the impossible romances, walk about in perpetual fear of being "walled up." For them the typical Catholic act is not going into a great thing like a church, but into a small thing like a confessional box. And to their nightmare fancy a confessional box is a sort of mantrap; and presents in its very appearance some combination of a coffin and a cage. The same notion is reinforced by the use of the words "cells," which in a Protestant community means prison-cells, and not monastic cells. The same is suggested by the word "crypt," about which there must obviously be something cryptic. These and many other tags of tradition have preserved in this country the custom of talking as if the danger of being a Catholic was the danger of being buried in a deep dark hole. And yet even the tradition was, not only a legend, but very nearly a pretence. Even the man who said these things knew in his heart, or at least had a vague knowledge at the back of his mind, that his fear was really a fear of something larger than himself and his tribal traditions; that he was really, as it was sometimes stated from both points of view, leaving a national for an international church. As I have said, it was not claustrophobia, the fear of the crypt or the cell; it was agoraphobia, or the fear of the

451

forum, of the market-place, of the open spaces and the colossal public buildings. To the really insular and individualistic type of sectarian, even the fear of the Church was also partly a fear of the world. It can be seen in the terror which some of the English Tories, in the old times, felt towards the cosmopolitan culture of the Jesuits; who honestly seemed to them a sort of universal anarchists. It can be seen in the exaggerated revulsion from the very varied experiments, failures and successes of the Baroque. Of nearly all the non-Catholic types of our time we can truly say, that any such type must broaden his mind to become a Catholic. He must grow more used than he is at present to the long avenues and the large spaces. This is really what is meant by the Puritans who say that the Church is Pagan; that it does open a very long avenue, which is the only avenue left connecting us with Pagan antiquity. That is largely what is meant by insisting that the Church covers all sorts of dubious or disreputable people; all the motley mobs of tramps and pedlars and beggars, who do make up the life of an open market-place. *Quicquid agunt homines*;[85] which even Matthew Arnold wisely saw was the true motto of the practical life of the Roman Catholic Church.

Now a great deal has been said by Protestants, naturally enough, and not a little even by Catholics, about the danger of displaying before the world a pomp and triumph that may easily be called worldly. Undoubtedly some harm was done, and some misunderstandings did arise, when the Popes of the Renaissance filled Rome with trophies that might have marked the triumphs of the Caesars, and permitted the slander that the father of Christian man had usurped the title of King of Kings and forgotten his own actual title of Servant of Servants. But, taking human nature as a whole, the method is justified; because it is some sort of proclamation of the profound truth mentioned above; that the Faith belongs to the heights and the open spaces, and the circle of the whole world, and is *not* the one thing which its enemies go on desperately calling it; a conspiracy. There could not be a better way of suggesting the very reverse of that suggestion, than by the continual use in public buildings of

---

[85] *Quicquid agunt homines* is Latin for "Whatever men do."

what is large in design and hospitable in gesture. Art, and especially architecture, can here express actualities that are at once too large and too elusive to be expressed in words. St. Mark's Cathedral at Venice is in some ways a very curious building, and to some northern eyes does not look like a cathedral at all; but it does look like a thing coloured with the sunrise and the sunset, in touch with the very ends of the earth; open like a harbour and full of popular poetry like a fairy-palace. That is, it does express the first essential fact that Catholicism is not a narrow thing; that it knows more than the world knows about the potentialites and creative possibilites of the world, and that it will outlast all the worldly and temporary expressions of the same culture. Christianity has gone northward and established richer ports in colder seas; it has been changed and chilled for a time by colder heresies; but the same principle still stands for its expansion and exaltation; that which is expressed in the expansion and exaltation of great buildings; in the breadth of great gates declaring the brotherhood of men or the lifting of great domes pointing the way of their destiny. To-day another such building is being reared in what Mr. Belloc's fantasy once called a Harbour in the North; and its scope and scale would indeed be idle things; if they did not remind us of the two essential truths; first, that even within the world the boundaries of the Faith are being enlarged; and second, and much more important, that the Faith itself enlarges the world; which would be a small thing without it.

The dome of sky above Dublin was clear with the awful clarity of a burning-glass, and such a glaring gap or rent in the grey skies of Ireland was itself a portent, with some savour of a miracle. But though it was very rare in the Dublin climate, it was curiously representative of the Dublin mentality. It was none the less Irish weather because it is almost unknown in Ireland. It corresponded to the Irish brilliancy of intercourse; to the continual blend of lucidity and levity. And it was all the more Irish because there was, as there always is, in the intensity of summer, a faint thrill of thunder. It was as if the very light were lightning, and shone between two storms.

And I, who love both countries, but my own best and with most anxiety, could not help saying to myself, "This is always the real Dublin daylight. And the moment I return home, I shall find myself in the London fog."

The difference is indescribable; but that is the nearest description. There is more hatred in Dublin; and yet there is a harder sense of the obligation of justice. There is even more slander in Dublin; and yet in some strange way there is more truth. What there is in London is something that is not so much falsehood as falsification; and not so much falsification as simply fog. After a week in Ireland, the newspaper politics of England seem to be like a vast vapour, inhabited only by phantoms. There is no question of hating men or slandering men; for they are not the same men for ten weeks together; and they are never the real men at all. I will take two examples; the two men who happened to be the heads of the two Parliamentary systems of the two countries at that moment. I will not take the case of Jim Thomas; because it is beneath the seriousness of this subject. Jim Thomas is a joke; and I am sorry to say that the joke is against us. He is not a person in the same historical world as de Valera,[86] even as seen by those who hate de Valera, of whom there are probably more in Ireland than in England. But I will take the relatively dignified figure of Mr. Thomas's revered leader; and

[86] Eamon de Valera (1882–1975) led a party of insurgents in the 1916 Irish national uprising. He was the president of Sinn Fein (1918–26) and of the provisional Irish government (1918–22). He led the opposition to the Anglo-Irish treaty (1921) and was imprisoned by the Irish Free State in 1923.

point out as respectfully as possible that he is a ghost. He is an apparition. He is not really there. At least the figure that is recognised is not really there. Londoners live in a fog of journalism, out of which there looms from time to time a figure, who strikes certain spectral attitudes, and then vanishes in the fog and is forgotten. Not many years ago we saw start out of the mist, like the pale face of a fiend, the face of a traitor. He was reeling and ragged as if torn by patriot mobs; a golf-club was broken in his hand; as if it had been broken across his head, when he was expelled for treason from his club of fashionable golfers. He had been detected in a dastardly effort to escape to Stockholm and make a treacherous peace, and was only frustrated by the gallantry of our British tars. He was the wildest ruffian of the I.L.P.[87] and wore a red tie, which had certainly been sent to him secretly from Moscow. Well, this person, after throwing himself into a few bodily postures expressive of moral baseness and political perfidy, vanished in the fog and was never seen again. This was the infamous James Ramsay MacDonald, of atrocious memory. Only, as it happens there has been a slight lapse in the memory. The crowd waiting in the fog, however, has had other diversions. There even burst upon it just recently a beautiful and ennobling vision: a stately and handsome presence, clad almost entirely in Union Jacks, with a few patches of tartan, and wearing the ancient Civic Crown; *ob cives servatos*: the Saviour of the State. For this being was indeed that noble statesman who became the head of the National Government, sacrificing Party to Patriotism, and triumphantly routing the traitor Henderson.[88] This was the heroic James Ramsay MacDonald, of immortal memory, so long as he is remembered. There had once been another person called Henderson who had been a Patriot; when the other person called MacDonald was a Traitor; but neither of these persons could possibly be remembered. Perhaps it is quite right that they should none of them be remembered; for none of them ever really existed at all. There never

[87] The I.L.P. was the Independent Labour party, a socialist organization established in Great Britain in 1893 under the leadership of Keir Hardy.

[88] Arthur Henderson (1863–1935) was a British labor leader and politician who at the outbreak of World War I was instrumental in influencing most of the Labour party to support the government's war policy.

was any traitor named MacDonald who betrayed his country to its enemies, any more than there ever was any patriot called MacDonald who preferred his country to his party. All these shadows in the shadow-pantomime of London politics have no reference to the respectable, rather vain, very serious, self-respecting "Scotsman on the make" who has risen in the profession of politics rather less scandalously than most. That is what I mean by the London fog, and that is what I mean by the Dublin daylight.

In Dublin there are men who would kill de Valera; and there are men who would die for de Valera. But there are no men who do not know the main facts for or against him. That he is not a native Irishman, in the normal sense; that he came from America, is admitted as much by his friends as his foes. It had to be, in Ireland; for there the family is everything; and a man could not even announce himself as Mr. Brown, without provoking the most sweeping generalisations about the Browns. That he helped the guerilla war which some would call the murder of English soldiers is, of course, a matter of pride and not of apology; but at least it is not a matter of mystification. That he was anti-clerical, in the sense that the bishops and priests mostly opposed his irreconcilable indignation, is known to everybody; even to the clerics or clericals who may afterwards come to support him. There is nobody in Dublin who does not know the *story* of de Valera; and there is next to nobody in London who does know the *story* of MacDonald. That is what I mean by the London Fog.

THE HISTORIC MOMENT*

The Eucharistic Congress in Dublin has one aspect which most Englishmen will almost certainly miss altogether. It is not the Irish
aspect. The English have thought too much of Ireland, even when
they thought too little for Ireland; or thought only against Ireland.
When debaters are informed that they must not debate on politics or
religion, the more spirited and intelligent naturally retort that there
is nothing else to debate about. And yet there is a third thing, which
is not identical with the debate about politics and religion in Ireland,
which has filled all the debating-clubs of England. That third thing
is History; and it sums up the whole problem to say that the average
Englishman will hardly know what is meant by mentioning it.

The average Englishman once had a hearty and even heroic hatred
of the Roman Catholic religion; it has long since turned into something much milder and more tolerant. It has slowly broadened
down, if not from precedent to precedent, at least from prejudice to
prejudice. At worst a morbid and malignant curiosity has been replaced by a more Christian condition of ignorance. But the point is
that the religious hostility has been softened; and that the special political hostility has been softened too. The average Englishman once
had a passionate patriotic distrust of the political Irish; he regarded
their hope of national self-expression as a mere mad mutinous breaking up of his own Empire. That also has since turned into something
much milder and more tolerant. The average Englishman probably
does not understand the Irish any better, if so well, as in the time of
Gladstone and Parnell;[89] but he is much less disposed to punish them
for being different. The Englishman no longer execrates Mr. Gladstone; he is not very likely to attend the anniversary celebration of
the Boyne;[90] and is the less anxious to incure the curse of Cromwell,
because he has lately begun rather to curse the Puritans himself.

* Written at the Eucharist Congress in Dublin.
[89] Charles Stewart Parnell (1846–91) was a proponent of home rule for Ireland; in
the 1880s he convinced Gladstone to support the measure.
[90] Boyne was a battle in Ireland in 1690 in which the army of King William III
defeated the forces supporting the deposed James II.

But there is one thought that will hardly cross his mind. And that is—how very small a part of History is that which divides us from Gladstone, or from William of Orange, or even from Oliver Cromwell.

Ages before Englishmen had any notion of being Protestants, ages before Irishmen had any need to be Nationalists, there moved across the world the great searchlights of Rome; the omnipresence of those historic and hieratic things now enthroned on their two thousand years. What corresponds to the Congress is the Council; that ancient assembly of Christendom which shifted so swiftly from Athens to Spain, or from Arabia to Gaul. Any man whose mind has been magnified by History, the greatest of all the works of the imagination, can feel the futility of allowing lesser and later quarrels entirely to obliterate the memory of that marching capital; the winged and Flying City. Wherever was that presence there was Rome; Rome was set up in the sands of the African desert; Rome in the rocky plains about Toledo. And but a few years ago, Rome was in Australia, a raw and remote colony under the Southern Cross; and to-day Rome is in Ireland, the most ancient of the Celtic cultural countries of the West. That presence was already old when Ireland civilised stood up and taught England barbarous; or rather taught something still too barbarous to be called England. It was already old when England converted Germany; when St. Boniface[91] went forth from among our own people, to baptize the barbarians of the Rhine. It is this sense of the grandeur of the great distances of human history, and the huge changes they have made between nation and nation, that is the true manner of assuaging and healing the tribal quarrels of men.

It is Ancient History that will unite the nations. It is certainly not Modern History; which has only managed to divide them. It is, least of all, Future History, of which nobody knows anything at all; which is described in a series of Utopias discarded in turn by the Utopians. The best hope for the relations of England and Ireland is that they should both acknowledge the human authority of history; and the fact which is a fact, whether we call it Europe or Christendom.

[91] St. Boniface (680–755) was an English missionary to the pagan Germanic tribes.

The difficulty of the English is to understand that they come out of the old religion. The difficulty of the Irish is to understand that they come out of the old civilisation. Ireland was Roman in religion but never Roman in rule. England was always Roman in rule and suddenly ceased to be Roman in religion. The essential for both is to find something deep and distant enough to be shared without the exasperation of recent political memories.

To say that new things like wireless and aviation have united nations is simply false. England and Ireland are only two out of many now much more divided. It is not new but old things that unify mankind; it is at the back of history that we rediscover humanity; it is quite strictly, in Genesis or the beginnings that we find the brotherhood of men; even if some controversy continues about which was Abel or Cain.

MARY AND THE CONVERT

I was brought up in a part of the Protestant world which can best be described by saying that it referred to the Blessed Virgin as the Madonna. Sometimes it referred to her as *a* Madonna; from a general memory of Italian pictures. It was not a bigoted or uneducated world; it did not regard all Madonnas as idols or all Italians as Dagoes. But it had selected this expression, by the English instinct for compromise, so as to avoid both reverence and irreverence. It was, when we came to think about it, a very curious expression. It amounted to saying that a Protestant must not call Mary "Our Lady," but he may call her "My Lady." This would seem, in the abstract, to indicate an even more intimate and mystical familiarity than the Catholic devotion. But I need not say that it was not so. It was not untouched by that queer Victorian evasion; of translating dangerous or improper words into foreign languages. But it was also not untouched by a certain sincere though vague respect for the part that Madonnas had played, in the actual cultural and artistic history of our civilisation. Certainly the ordinary reasonably reverent Englishman would never have intended to be disrespectful to that tradition in that aspect; even when he was much less liberal, travelled and well-read than were my own parents. Certainly, on the other hand, he was entirely unaware that he was saying "My Lady"; and if you had pointed out to him that, in fact, he was generally saying "a My Lady," or "the My Lady," he would have agreed that it was rather odd.

I do not forget, and indeed it would be a very thankless thing in me to forget, that I was lucky in this relative reasonableness and moderation of my own family and friends; and that there is a whole Protestant world that would consider such moderation a very poor-spirited sort of Protestantism. That strange mania against Mariolatry; that mad vigilance that watches for the first faint signs of the cult of Mary as for the spots of a plague; that apparently presumes her to be perpetually and secretly encroaching upon the prerogatives of Christ; that logically infers from a mere glimpse of the blue robe the presence of the Scarlet Woman—all that I have never felt or known or understood, even as a child; nor did those who had the care of my childhood. They knew nothing to speak of about the Catholic Church; they certainly did not know that anybody connected with them was ever likely to belong to it; but they did know that noble and beautiful ideas had been presented to the world under the form of this sacred figure, as under that of the Greek gods or heroes. But, while putting aside all pretence that this Protestant atmosphere was actively an anti-Catholic atmosphere, I may still say that my personal case was a little curious.

I have here rashly undertaken to write on a subject at once intimate and daring; a subject which ought indeed, by its own majesty, to make it impossible to be egotistical; but which does also make it impossible to be anything but personal. "Mary and the Convert" is the most personal of topics, because conversion is something more personal and less corporate than communion; and involves isolated feelings as an introduction to collective feelings. But also because the cult of Mary is in a rather peculiar sense a personal cult; over and above that greater sense that must always attach to the worship of a personal God. God is God, Maker of all things visible and invisible; the Mother of God is in a rather special sense connected with things visible; since she is of this earth, and through her bodily being God was revealed to the senses. In the presence of God, we must remember what is invisible, even in the sense of what is merely intellectual; the abstractions and the absolute laws of thought; the love of truth, and the respect for right reason and honourable logic in things, which God himself has respected. For, as St. Thomas Aquinas insists, God himself does not contradict the law of contradiction. But Our Lady, reminding us especially of God Incarnate, does in some degree gather up and embody all those elements of the heart and the higher instincts, which are the legitimate short cuts to the love of God. Dealing with those personal feelings, even in this rude and curt outline, is therefore very far from easy. I hope I shall not be misunderstood if the example I take is merely personal; since it is this particular part of religion that really cannot be impersonal. It may be an accident, or a highly unmerited favour of heaven, but anyhow it is a fact; that I always had a curious longing for the remains of this particular tradition, even in a world where it was regarded as a legend. I was not only haunted by the idea while still stuck in the ordinary stage of schoolboy scepticism; I was affected by it before that, before I had shed the ordinary nursery religion in which the Mother of God had no fit or adequate place. I found not long ago, scrawled in very bad handwriting, screeds of an exceedingly bad imitation of Swinburne, which was, nevertheless, apparently addressed to what I should have called a picture of the Madonna. And I can distinctly remember reciting the lines of the "Hymn To Proserpine," out of pleasure in their roll and resonance; but deliberately directing them away from Swinburne's intention, and supposing them addressed to the new Christian Queen of life, rather than to the fallen Pagan queen of death.

> "But I turn to her still; having seen she shall surely abide in the end;
> Goddess and maiden and queen, be near me now and befriend."

And I had obscurely, from that time onwards, the very vague but slowly clarifying idea of defending all that Constantine had set up, just as Swinburne's Pagan had defended all he had thrown down.

It may still be noted that the unconverted world, Puritan or Pagan, but perhaps especially when it is Puritan, has a very strange notion of the collective unity of Catholic things or thoughts. Its exponents, even when not in any rabid sense enemies, give the most curious lists of things which they think make up the Catholic life; an odd assortment of objects, such as candles, rosaries, incense (they are always intensely impressed with the enormous importance and necessity of incense), vestments, pointed windows, and then all sorts of essentials or unessentials thrown in in any sort of order; fasts, relics, penances or the Pope. But even in their bewilderment, they do bear witness to a need which is not so nonsensical as their attempts to fulfil it; the need of somehow summing up "all that sort of thing," which does really describe Catholicism and nothing else except Catholicism. It should of course be described from within, by the definition and development of its theological first principles; but that is not the sort of need I am talking about. I mean that men need an image, single, coloured and clear in outline, an image to be called up instantly in the imagination, when what is Catholic is to be distinguished from what claims to be Christian or even what in one sense is Christian. Now I can scarcely remember a time when the image of Our Lady did not stand up in my mind quite definitely, at the mention or the thought of all these things. I was quite distant from these things, and then doubtful about these things; and then disputing with the world for them, and with myself against them; for that is the condition before conversion. But whether the figure was distant, or was dark and mysterious, or was a scandal to my contemporaries, or was a challenge to myself—I never doubted that this figure was the figure of the Faith; that she embodied, as a complete human being still only human, all that this Thing had to say to humanity. The instant I remembered the Catholic Church, I remembered her; when I tried to forget the Catholic Church, I tried to forget her; when I finally saw what was nobler than my fate, the freest and the hardest of all my acts of freedom, it was in front of a gilded and very gaudy little image of her in the port of Brindisi, that I promised the thing that I would do, if I returned to my own land.

A CENTURY OF EMANCIPATION

When we really wish to know how the world is going, it is no bad test to take some tag or current phrase of the press and reverse it, substituting the precise contrary, and see whether it makes more sense that way. It generally does; such a mass of outworn conventions has our daily commentary become. An excellent example occurred recently concerning the prospects of Protestantism and Catholicism. The editor of the *Sunday Express*, once better known as a sympathetic critic of letters, summed up the matter by saying that he had no prejudice against Catholicism or Anglo-Catholicism, that he had every respect for them, but that England (evidently including himself) was solidly Protestant. This is a very neat and convenient statement of the exact opposite of the truth. I have most friendly feelings to the gentleman in question; and it is without the least animosity to him that I say that what is sincere and alive and active in him is Anti-Catholicism and nothing else. What is really working in the world to-day is Anti-Catholicism and nothing else. It certainly is not Protestantism; not half so much as it is Pelagianism. And if the religion of modern England is to be called Protestant, there is at least one other adjective which cannot conceivably be applied to it. Whatever else it is, it is not solid Protestantism. There might perhaps be a case for calling it liquid Protestantism.

Now this marks the chief change of the century since Catholic Emancipation.[92] The political circumstances of the final Tory surrender to Emancipation were, of course, complex. Emancipation seemed to some a sort of mongrel and monster; produced by two opposites; the survival of the Old Religion and the principles of the French Revolution. But in such things there are complex harmonies as well as contradictions. In some ways the ultimate quarrel of Rome with the French Revolution was rather like the recent quarrel of Rome with the French Royalists. It was resistance to a pagan extreme; but there had been not a little Catholic sympathy before the

[92] By a parliamentary act of 1829, Catholics in Great Britain gained full political and civil rights.

thing reached that extreme. There had been countless liberal clerics in the first movements of the reform; Pius IX[93] had begun by being the reverse of reactionary; and the atmosphere was such that the gigantic protagonist of Catholic Emancipation himself, the great Daniel O'Connell,[94] could combine passionate Ultramontanism with the largest political Liberalism without any division in the simplicity of his mind or the general humanity of his ideals. Those who hated him both as a Radical and a Roman Catholic would have seen no inconsistency in those two hated things. The truth to seize about all that earlier situation is that the bigotry was on the other side; in one sense the theology was on the other side. We cannot see it clearly in the statesmen; for they were either freethinkers or opportunists. Wellington[95] met his Waterloo; but he was a good soldier and therefore retreated when it was futile to stand. But if we look at the mass of the people, we find a real religious resistance—because there was a real religion. That resistance is now only found in America where just such a Democrat[96] as Daniel O'Connell is still threatened with political exclusion solely for being a Catholic. In some points the Americans are a hundred years behind the times.

But this sort of purely political exclusiveness will not be the chief problem of the future. Whatever be the relation of Rome to the new world, her authority will not be transferred to Dayton, Tennessee. The political effects of the political emancipation are relatively simple and in a sense the easiest part of the speculation. Everybody knows that Catholic Emancipation has never led, and will never lead, to the direct political disasters that some foretold. The Duke of Norfolk was never actually caught in the act of imitating Guy

[93] Pius IX, who reigned from 1846 to 1878, is one of the most famous of modern popes. He proclaimed the dogma of the Immaculate Conception, issued the Syllabus of Errors and called the First Vatican Council, which declared papal infallibility in matters of faith and doctrine.

[94] Daniel O'Connell (1755–1847) was an Irish political leader.

[95] The Duke of Wellington, prime minister in 1829, opposed Catholic emancipation, but, for fear of civil war in Ireland, he pushed the bill through Parliament.

[96] In 1928 Al Smith was defeated in his bid for the presidency, in part because of opposition to his Catholicism.

Fawkes;[97] and Lord Russell of Killowen[98] seldom if ever invited a Spanish Armada to these shores. Outside certain local Puritan fevers, chiefly in America, there is no reason to suppose that the world will be so unreasonable as to repent having elected Catholic Mayors or sent out Catholic Ambassadors. The cant about a foreign allegiance is still heard; but that is because a cant can long outlive a cause. Men who are wide awake are well aware that the Catholic internationalism, which bids men respect their national governments, is considerably less dangerous than the financial internationalism which may make a man betray his country, or the revolutionary internationalism which may make him destroy it. It is, of course, possible that, under the pressure of Catholic conversions, the world may return to older and rougher types of persecution; but it is not immediately probable. But when we turn from the political to the spiritual prospect, we find a change which is exactly represented by the reversal of the journalistic maxim mentioned above. We must realise what England has become, under all titles and terminology, if we would make a guess about what she is next destined to be.

If we want to measure the distance between the date of emancipation and the day in which we live, between Catholic Emancipation and its consequences after a century, we shall find this newspaper quotation very important. If we want to describe the conditions a hundred years ago in this country, we could not do it better than by saying that *then* England was solidly Protestant; or the Protestantism of England was solid. And we shall still better understand the modern change, if we ask what is meant by that solidarity. It had a very definite meaning, which has now so completely disappeared that even those who most frequently invoke it are least able to imagine it. There is nothing like that sort of solid confidence to-day. It meant this: that the types and ranks of society really and sincerely interested in religion did really and sincerely believe that Protestant religion had been proved superior to

[97] Henry Fitzalan-Howard, Duke of Norfolk (1847–1917) was an English Catholic prominent in public life. Guy Fawkes was a participant in the alleged Catholic plot of 1605 to blow up the House of Parliament.

[98] Charles Russell, Baron Russell of Killowen (1832–1900), was Lord Chief Justice of England from 1894 to 1900.

Catholic religion. It was strongest in the middle class, especially the wealthier middle class; but that middle class had been steadily growing stronger and wealthier, as was natural in a specially mercantile and capitalist community. It covered a multitude of healthy, hardheaded and even clear-headed professional and commercial men; I say "even clear-headed" because, though the English had the name of not being logical, they were far more logical in those days than they are now. If they sat longer over their wine, they argued longer over their politics; they did not live on hurried cocktails and hurried headlines. Their mercantile politics might be narrow; but the number of them who could expound some connected thesis, such as Free Trade, was very large. And as their politics consisted of certain definite theories, right or wrong, so their religion consisted of certain definite doctrines, true or false. If you had asked any such Protestant why he was a Protestant, or what he meant by being a Protestant, he would have instantly stated or explained those doctrines; just as a Free Trader would explain Free Trade. There were Englishmen, of course, for whom the whole business was vaguer or more indifferent; but they did not make the tone of that solid mercantile England. The populace made the Pope a guy, just as they made Guy Fawkes a guy; but the poor were at the best treated like children and left, like children, to make a guy or a game of anything. A great part of the higher aristocracy had been quite sceptical and pagan throughout the eighteenth century, or even from the seventeenth century; but the same tact and informal secrecy, which keeps such a class together, kept it from any public insult to the Protestant religion of England. And that religion was a religion; it was Protestant, and it was national; that is, it was the religion of the nomal citizen.

Now if you had asked an educated English Protestant in 1828 why Protestantism was right, or why Popery was wrong, he would not have had the smallest difficulty in answering. Of course the first thing to be emphasised would have been what has since been the first thing to be doubted or denied. It was the literal inspiration and inerrancy of the Hebrew Scriptures, and sometimes even of the English translation of those Scriptures. It was the view that still lingers in provincial corners and is called Fundamentalism.

At the beginning of the nineteenth century, practically all Protestantism was Fundamentalism. But it is a great mistake to suppose that the true Protestant of history had nothing better to do for men than to throw a Bible at their heads. What he valued was the theological Scheme of Salvation supposed to be set forth in that work; as the Free Trader valued Adam Smith as the instrument of a theory. Of that theological theory there were two main versions; one, universal in Scotland and very prevalent in England, that God chose some to receive the benefits of redemption and rejected others even in the act of creating them; the other, that men could accept God but only by accepting this theological scheme of salvation, and that their good works had no effect on the result. This was the great doctrine of Faith independent of Works, which was so universally recognised as the chief mark and test of Protestantism that we might almost say that it was the whole of Protestantism, except indeed where Protestantism took the very fiercest form of Calvinism. It is not a question of making points against Protestantism; this was the chief point that could be made for Protestantism. It was especially the popular point; the most persuasive point, the most sympathetic point. From this idea of instantaneous individualist acceptance of the Atonement, by a pure act of faith, came the whole system of appeals on which this form of Christianity relied. That was why it was so easy, so personal, so emotional; that was why the *whole* of Christian's burden fell off at the foot of the Cross. There were no degrees of sin or details of penance; because works were not in question at all. That is why they needed no Confessor or Sacrament of Penance; because there was nothing *they* could do to diminish sins either hopeless or already abolished or ignored. That was why it was wicked to pray for the dead; for the dead could not be anything but instantly beatified by dogmatic faith alone, or lost for lack of it. That was why there could be no progress of further enlightenment in the life to come; or, in other words, no Purgatory. And *that* was what was meant by being a Protestant; disapproving of prayers for the dead, disapproving of progress after death; disapproving of any religion that relied on good works. That was the great Protestant religion of Western Europe, of which we would speak as respectfully as we would of the virility and equality of Islam; and a hundred years ago it was normal and national. It was, in the newspaper phrase, solid.

To-day, as a national and normal thing, it has utterly vanished. Not one man in ninety really disapproves of praying for the dead. The War, in killing many million men, killed that pedantry and perversity. Not one man in ninety is either a Calvinist or an upholder of Faith against Works. Not one man in ninety thinks he will go to hell if he does not instantly accept the theological theory of redemption; perhaps it would be better if he did. Not one man in ninety believes the Bible infallible, as real Protestants believed it infallible. Of all that wonderful system of religious thought, thundered against Rome in so many sermons, argued against Rome in so many pamphlets, thrown out scornfully against Rome in so many Exeter Hall[99] meetings and Parliamentary debates, nothing remains. Of all that, as it affects the forward movement of the educated classes, and the future of the world, nothing remains.

But there is something that remains. Anti-Catholicism remains; though it is no longer Protestantism, any more than it is Albigensianism or Donatism.[100] And that is the factor we must grasp and estimate, if we are to estimate the outlook to-day. Protestantism is now only a name; but it is a name that can be used to cover any or every "ism" except Catholicism. It is now a vessel or receptacle into which can be poured all the thousand things that for a thousand reasons react against Rome; but it can only be full of these things because it is now hollow; because it is itself empty. Every sort of negation, every sort of new religion, every sort of moral revolt or intellectual irritation, that can make a man resist the claim of the Catholic Faith, is here gathered into a heap and covered with a convenient but quite antiquated label. When the journalists say that

[99] Exeter Hall was a meeting and concert hall that opened in London in 1831. It became the headquarters for the Young Men's Christian Association, from which the name derived its evangelical connotations.

[100] Albigensianism was a form of Manichaean dualism that arose in southern France in the late twelfth century. In 1208 Pope Innocent III called for a crusade to stamp out the heresy; the orthodox forces prevailed by the 1220s. Donatism was a Christian heresy of the fourth and fifth centuries that contended that an unworthy priest could not perform valid sacraments.

there is solid Protestantism, all they mean is that there is a pretty heavy reluctance or resistance in the matter of any return of the English to their ancient religion; and this, up to a point, may be quite true. But the heap is a hotch-potch; the resistance is not a rational resistance, in the sense of having a clear and commonly accepted reason; and in so far as it has a prevailing colour, it is quite the contrary colour to that which prevailed in Protestantism. It is even more against Calvinism than against Catholicism; it is even more insistent on works than were the Catholics; it would make a future life far less final and more purely progressive than did the Catholic doctrine of Purgatory; it would make the Bible far less important than it is to a Catholic. On every single point on which the Protestant attacked the Pope, he would now say that the modern spirit was a mere exaggeration of the Popish errors. In so far as there is such a vague modern spirit, common to all these things, a spirit that may be called either liberality or laxity, it never was at any time the spirit of Protestantism. It came from the Revolution and the Romantic Movement, indirectly perhaps from the Renaissance of men like Rabelais and Montaigne; and ultimately much more from men like More and Erasmus than from men like Calvin and Knox. When the Protestant orators in the present crisis repeat rather monotonously, "We will not lose the freedom we gained four hundred years ago," they show how little they share the religion they defend. Men gained no freedom four hundred years ago; there was no particular freedom about creating the Scottish Sabbath or preaching nothing but Predestination or even yielding to the Tudor Terror or the Cromwellian Terror.[101] But it is arguable that they gained freedom a hundred years ago, as Catholics gained it a hundred years ago. It is tenable that such freedom was the expanding effect of the American and French Revolutions and the democratic idealism which came with the nineteenth century and seems in some danger of declining with the twentieth. Above all, it is arguable that they have a certain kind of freedom *now*; not because they are Protestants,

[101] The Tudor terror was Queen Elizabeth's persecution of English Catholics in the late sixteenth century. The Cromwellian terror was Oliver Cromwell's invasion of Ireland, from 1649 to 1652.

for they are not; but because they are anything they like and nothing if they like that better; because they are theists, theosophists,[102] materialists, monists or mystics on their own. How much such freedom is worth, or how much chance it has of bearing any fruit in anything positive or creative, is another matter; but in order to anticipate the next phase, it is necessary to realise that this phase is one of negative liberty, not to say anarchy. Whatever it is, it is not Protestantism; and whatever it is, it is not solid.

This is the truth symbolised in the remark on the Prayer-Book Debate; that a crowd of Free-Thinkers and Nonconformists and people of any opinions dictated the affairs of the Church of England. I am very proud of the fact that Catholics abstained from doing so and avoided a very obvious piece of bad taste. But the fact itself contains fine shades that have hardly been noticed. It is not sufficiently realised that even a congregation at the City Temple, or a crowd hearing a Dean or Canon in St. Paul's Cathedral, is often in fact almost as mixed and dubious in religion as the members of the House of Commons. Many Nonconformists are not conforming to Nonconformity; and a churchman often means only a man who never goes to chapel. Such differences exist in the same sect or even in the same man. If we would grasp the modern problem, we must simply take at random some fairly typical Englishman and note how little he really *is* anything. He has, let us say, been brought up a Congregationalist and drifted away; he is by normal and rather negative habit an Anglican; he has become by unanswered doubts and vague popular science an Agnostic; he has often wondered if there is anything in being a Theosophist; he has attended one or two séances and might be persuaded to be a Spiritualist. *That* is the man we have got to deal with; and not some rigid Protestant labelled Methodist or even some rigid Atheist labelled Materialist. It is the man whom we have to set out to convert, after a hundred years of relative political liberty have left the old Protestant England far behind us and the new Catholic England still far away.

It is only fair to say, of course, that events have falsified almost

[102] Theosophy, a syncretistic faith that combined elements from Christianity and various Asian religions, was founded in New York City in 1875 by Helena Blavatsky.

as much the prophecies of those who promoted Catholic Emancipation as of those who resisted it. Many Liberals hardly disguised the idea that to emancipate Catholicism would be to extinguish Catholicism. Many thought they were tolerating a dying superstition; some thought they were killing it. It is the other superstition that has been killed. But there are always new superstitions; or, to put it more moderately, new religions. And a general estimate of the chances will see them chiefly affected, I think, by the presence of these new religions side by side with that very ancient thing called Agnosticism. The real interest of the speculation is in the question of which of the two will turn out to be the really formidable opponent of the Faith in the future.

We know what is really meant by saying that the Church is merely conservative and the modern world progressive. It means that the Church is always continuous and the heresies always contradictory. We have already noted it in the case of Protestantism; and the men who now completely contradict Protestantism, even in order to contradict Catholicism. But one effect of this contrast between continuity and bewildering variety is that the Church is generally seen in the light of the last heresy. The Church is supposed to consist chiefly of the things of which that heresy happens to disapprove. So much of the Protestant tradition still remains that a great many people suppose that the chief marks of Catholicity are those which stood out as stains in the eyes of the last school of critics. Romanism is supposed to be made up of Popery and Purgatory and the Confessional, with the queerest things thrown in, such as incense and rosaries and the images of saints. But these were often the things most important to Protestants, not most important to Catholics; and not most important to the other opponents of Catholics. A Mahommedan would not connect Rome with Purgatory, because he himself believes in Purgatory; a Buddhist would not connect her with images, because he himself has images; an old pagan would not have been horrified at incense, because he used it himself. In the same way the new religions will not attack the old religion for the old reasons. A Christian Scientist will not assume that all stories of miraculous healing must have been frauds.

A Spiritualist will not assume that all supernatural messages received through men must be impossible. It will be an entirely new list of charges or challenges that will come from the new mystics, who have imitated so many of the old marvels. In so far as the new religions become the leaders of the opposition, a new class of controversies will arise; with the faith-healers, for instance, upon the mystery of matter; with the psychic investigators upon the influences of evil. All this will bring us further and further from the special Protestant problems; and a hundred years hence the Church may look to her enemies something utterly different from what she looked like a hundred years ago. She will look different because she will be the same.

But if no new religion becomes important enough to be the main issue, the immediate change will be much simpler. The two centuries will probably have completed the full transition from Protestantism to Paganism. The Church will be facing once more her first and her most formidable enemy; a thing more attractive because more human than any of the heresies. This condition that can only be called Paganism is not easily defined and has often been misrepresented. In one aspect, it may be called practical materialism without the narrowness of theoretical materialism. The Pagan looks for his pleasures to the natural forces of this world; but he does not insist so strictly upon dry negations about the other; he has commonly admitted a vague borderland of the unknown, providing him with possibilities of inspiration or of awe which are forbidden to the cheap modern atheist with his clockwork cosmos. The worshippers of the Unknown God could at least build an altar, though they could not inscribe it with a name. But I fancy that men who have once been Christians, or whose fathers have been Christians, will not be long in discovering, or rather rediscovering, the profound defect that destroyed Paganism and filled centuries with a horror of its final phase. The natural forces, when they are turned into gods, betray mankind by something that is in the very nature of nature-worship. We can already see men becoming unhealthy by the worship of health; becoming hateful by the worship of love; becoming paradoxically solemn and overstrained even by the idolatry of sport; and in some cases strangely morbid and infected with horrors by the perversion of a just sympathy with animals. Unless all these things are subject to a more centralised and well-balanced conception of the universe, the local god becomes too vivid, we might say too visible, and strikes his worshippers with madness. The pantheist is always too near to the polytheist and the polytheist to the idolator; the idolator to the man offering human sacrifice. There is nothing in Paganism to check its own exaggerations; and for that reason the world will probably find again, as it found before, the necessity of a universal moral philosophy supported by an authority that can define. In any case, that quarrel between Paganism and Catholicism will again be one raising issues very unfamiliar to many even now; and issues that would have very much mystified the men who debated a hundred years ago the issue of Catholic Emancipation.

In any case, this emergence of new issues will reveal more and more one of the advantages of an old religion. Whole aspects of Catholic doctrine and tradition, hidden by historical accident and the special quarrels of recent times, will be revealed to the world when it begins to address new questions to the Church. This is a point that has not been sufficiently stressed in the relations between Protestantism and Catholicism. Very often a Protestant was not only a man merely protesting, but a man merely protesting against a particular thing. He sometimes thought that thing was Rome; but it was really only one of the thousand aspects of Rome. When new aspects appear under new searchlights, he will be not so much defeated as simply outside the affair. A Baptist disapproves of baptising babies; a Presbyterian disapproves of bishops; a Prohibitionist disapproves of beer, and so on. But a Presbyterian, as such, has nothing very special to say about the Subconscious Mind. A Baptist as such has nothing special to say to a Behaviourist as such. But a Catholic may have a great deal to say to these people. For the Catholic commentary on life has gone on so much longer, it has covered so many different social conditions, has dealt so carefully with countless fine shades of metaphysics or casuistry, that it really has a relation to almost any class of speculation that may arise. Thus, in the matter of psychoanalysis and the study of the subconscious, the Church will probably be found sooner or later defending certain essentials about Will and Conscience against a welter of wild impersonality. Catholics remembering Catholicism will have a right and reason to do this. But Calvinists who have half forgotten Calvinism have no particular reason to do it.

There is, for instance, one influence that grows stronger every day, never mentioned in the newspapers, not even intelligible to people in the newspaper frame of mind. It is the return of the Thomist Philosophy; which is the philosophy of commonsense, as compared with the paradoxes of Kant and Hegel and the Pragmatists. The Roman religion will be, in the exact sense, the only Rationalistic religion. The other religions will not be Rationalist but Relativist; declaring that the reason is itself relative and unreliable; declaring that Being is only Becoming or that all time is only a time of transition; saying in mathematics that two and two make five in the fixed stars, saying in metaphysics and in morals that there is a good beyond good and evil. Instead of the materialist who said that the soul did not exist, we shall have the new mystic who says that the body does not exist. Amid all these things the return of the Scholastic will simply be the return of the sane man. There will perhaps be belated and benighted modernists, lingering from the nineteenth century, who will repeat the jaded journalistic catchword that the Schoolman only cared to ask how many angels could stand on the point of a needle. But it will be difficult to make even that fancy appear very fantastic, in a world where men deny that it hurts a man to stick the point of the needle in his leg. If there are angels, they have presumably some intellectual relation to place and space; and if there are no angels, there are still men and presumably sane men. But to say that there is no pain, or no matter, or no evil, or no difference between man and beast, or indeed between anything and anything else—this is a desperate effort to destroy all experience and sense of reality; and men will weary of it more and more, when it has ceased to be the latest fashion; and will look once more for something that will give form to such a chaos and keep the proportions of the mind of man. Millions of men are already at least wondering whether this solution is not to be found in the Catholic order and philosophy. Above all, the Church has regained that unique position in the world in a fair field and under the very reverse of favour; having had for a hundred years no more than the common right of speaking and publishing and voting in popular assemblies; and as her Master affirmed his divinity by becoming a man among men, she has become for a season a sect among sects, to emerge at the end as something separate or supreme.

TRADE TERMS

It is grimly significant that the Organ of Empire[103] has already begun to call its Imperial policy by the cheerful name of "The Empire Merger." The sort of combine, which all free peoples have punished as a conspiracy, is now so fashionable that it is considered quite a compliment to apply this commercial term instead of a political title. Courtiers in the future, instead of saying "Your Majesty" will say "Your Monopoly"; especially when addresing Moritz IV, of the historic House of Mond,[104] by that time Emperor of the World State. But indeed we rather doubt whether there will be even so much dignity as this in such a despotism as that. The man who prefers to say, "Imperial Merger" rather than Imperial Protection or Imperial Free Trade, is already in this curious modern mood, which actually thinks mercantile terms higher than moral or social ones. The whole system of a great nation will be remodelled on the habits of a big business. The national envoy in Paris, instead of being called, "His Excellency the British Ambassador," will be called "Our Mr. Honey-bubble," and he will travel with samples and be proud of being called a commercial traveller. The monopolist newspapers never weary of telling us that the world ought to have outgrown the stilted and pompous language of the old Protocols and Ultimatums, and all the formal statements of the treaties which have so often been denounced as Secret Diplomacy. Doubtless the great statesmen of the great states, the heirs of Richelieu and Canning,[105] will correspond in a brighter and brisker English, running "Yrs. rcd. and conts: noted," when indeed it is necessary to put the arrangements into writing at all. After all, it will be even more business-like to make the international arrangements in a husky and confidential voice, in the intervals of observing "What's yours?" and "Say

[103] The Organ of Empire was Lord Beaverbrook's *Daily Express*.

[104] Chesterton is alluding to Alfred Moritz Mond (1868–1930), an English financier and magnate in the chemical industry; he advocated industrial consolidation.

[105] George Canning (1770–1827) was a British foreign secretary in the 1820s and briefly, in 1827, prime minister.

when." That is the great advantage of the New Diplomacy over the old Secret Diplomacy. The old was so very secret as to write down all its secrets in laborious documents and send them round to about fifty people in Government offices. The New Diplomacy need never be written down at all; indeed, it is better not.

We are prepared, of course, to be told that all this ugly and undignified school of manners is very practical, and that the old stately or stilted school of manners was very unpractical. After all, the old theory of dignity did only trivial and incidental things, such as creating the Roman Empire, creating the French Monarchy and the French Revolution, founding the American Republic and establishing by personal adventure that very Empire, which our hustlers and hucksters can only help by impersonal advertisement. These are slight achievements compared with that of insuring that the same bad ginger-beer shall be sold everywhere, to the exclusion and extinction of good ginger-beer, or that over some thousand square miles of God's green earth nobody shall have anything but one kind of hat or one kind of house. But though these arguments are undoubtedly cogent and persuasive, and bear a certain appearance of practicality and realism, we are disposed to supplement them by a suggestion or reminder; the hint of something which even thinkers so lucid seem to have overlooked. Nowadays, it is considered very horrible to mention it; and it is indeed very horrible to test it or experience it. Nevertheless, it is a thing that may be tested or experienced; and, even to be avoided, had much better be mentioned.

Authority ruling men must be respected; it must even be loved. Men must in the last resort love it; for the simple reason that men must in the last resort die for it. No community or constitution can survive and retain its identity at all, that has not in the minds of its subjects enough of an ideal identity, to appear to them in certain extremes of peril as the vision of something to be saved. It is on that ideal, inhering in the reality, that every state will depend when there is a struggle of life and death. Men must feel something more about England than that she is commercial, something more about France than that Frenchmen are practical and careful about money, something more about America than that she happens at the moment to be monstrously rich,* before any healthy and humorous human being will kill some-body else or be killed himself, and go out from the sunlight and the sane loves of this world, for the sake of any such abstraction. It will be found, therefore, that the practical theory fails at the most practical mo-ment. It is useful while there is question of whether the commonwealth shall continue to be rich, or continue to be imperial, or continue to be monopolist. It is useless when there is question of whether the com-monwealth shall continue to be. The materialistic state, cemented only with money as with mud, will fall apart under the blow of any people who have love or loyalty to their leaders or their cause; for the simple reason that those who care most for money care more for life. One may like or dislike the Fascism of Italy, the fiery nationalism of the Poles, the deep Catholicism of the Irish; but there is no doubt that their ideals can be idealised. They are conceptions for which real men can be worked up into a real rapture of sacrifice. The images under which they are presented to the world, and especially the world of their worshippers, the golden or the silver eagle, the breastplate of St. Patrick, the Roman salute, are things that do in fact lift up the heart, and were made by the mind so that they should uplift the heart. In short there is in them poetry; and that poetry is the most practical thing in the world.

Now if the new Imperialists insist on talking of everything in terms of the counter and the commercial room, if they insist on call-ing Imperial Preference a Merger, as Lord Beaverbrook[106] did, if they insist on comparing a General Election to a Company Flota-tion, as Mr. Amery[107] did, they will make men familiar indeed with their government, and in a sense at home with it, but no more capable of loving it than of loving any unlucky investment. The time will come when its existence will depend on its power on the imagination; and it will be dignity or death. Nor will that dignity come solely from an Imperial Isolation; which seems merely to mean, "How we may think in continents without thinking of the Continents."

* But easier to die for, now she is poor.

[106] William Max Aitken, Lord Beaverbrook (1879–1964), was a Canadian-born English newspaper magnate and politician.

[107] Leopold Charles Maurice Stennet Amery (1873–1955) was an English journalist and prominent figure in the Conservative party in the 1920s.

FROZEN FREE THOUGHT

I believe I am in possession of a piece of news which, as we say in Fleet Street, has a certain news-value. It is hardly fitted to be flashed along the telegraph wires or blazoned on the big posters; it does not definitely involve an individual, but rather generally a school; it is an historical event; something that has happened and has hardly been noticed among the many changes of the day. The substance of the news is this. The sort of man we once knew as a Secularist has become a religious maniac.

Of course he is not actually mad, in the medical sense; nor, for that matter, is he religious in the religious sense, or perhaps in any sense. Yet the words I have used, to cover very varying stages of the malady in a fairly loose group, are the only words that convey the sharpness and importance of the incident. I mean that the *tone* of the old Fleet Street atheism, which I knew and loved of old, has entirely altered. It has come to resemble almost exactly the tone of the Seventh Day Adventists or the Millennial Dawnists,[108] or all those queerly prosaic and even prim fanatics who wander about handing out pamphlets, crowded with texts and vivid with italics, in which a new heaven and a new earth can be made out of a neglected cloud in the Book of Daniel or an unusually Little Horn in the Apocalypse. Perhaps the shortest way of distinguishing between the two literary styles is to record that the first was readable and the second is unreadable. The old atheist arguments, inherited from Bradlaugh and Foote, were always crude and therefore a little heavy, even for any agnostic with some background of history and philosophy. But they were at least as clear as they were crude; and we should all of us have agreed that a paper like the *Freethinker* was easy to read; even if some of us would have added that it was easy to answer. The *Freethinker* as it is to-day is not easy to read. I know, because I have just been reading it. Its editor has kindly sent me a copy, containing what appears from the frequent mention of my name to be an attack on myself;

[108] The Millennial Dawnists were Jehovah's Witnesses.

and when I am thus personally addressed I think it only polite to answer. If it is now not so easy to answer, it is simply because it is now not so easy to understand. It seems to be about a book I wrote on Victorian Literature[109] several years before the War; but the Freethinkers of Fleet Street, ever on the alert for fresh developments, have pounced upon it already. I have read the critique over patiently several times, and am still somewhat puzzled by what the critic can possibly mean by some of his allusions and complaints. I remember that in that very able book *The Flight from Reason*, Mr. Arnold Lunn narrates a similar experience with the same paper. He prints the whole of the Freethinker's criticism on him, and, naturally not being able to make head or tail of it, simply leaves it to the reader in despair. It was something about how anybody, who thinks there is good historical evidence for the Resurrection, is logically bound to believe the story of Aladdin in the *Arabian Nights*. I have no idea why. But what I would first emphasise, before trying to explain my critic's remarks to myself and him, is the curious character of this change in the Secularist Press, from a tone that was crude to a tone that is really crazy.

We might take a working parallel; fortunately outside the sphere of religion. I can imagine a jolly old Radical working man talking in the old mutinous manly fashion against the King or the House of Lords, saying with surly geniality and some repetition; "What we want with a King? Why should 'e 'ave a golden crown on 'is 'ead and me only my old boko? What's 'e blasted well doing in Buckingham Palace —— " and so on. Now I like that sort of man. I like him very much. I know what he means. I think there is, in the last resort, a lot to be said for it. It is not in the style of the *De Monarchia*;[110] it hardly appreciates the subtleties of Mr. Charles Maurras. But it has truths behind it; the equality of men and something that is right in republican simplicity. But suppose that man, who begins by saying he is as good as the King, broods and eventually goes mad saying that he *is* the King. Suppose his grievance

[109] Chesterton is referring to *The Victorian Age in Literature* (1912).
[110] *De Monarchia* was Dante's defense, written between 1309 and 1312, of the Holy Roman Emperor's supremacy over the pope in temporal affairs.

becomes a personal grievance about his great-grandfather, and he goes about boring people with plans and pedigrees to prove his Plantagenet blood. We know the whole atmosphere will alter; but chiefly in clarity. Everybody knew what the grumbler meant; nobody will listen to what the lunatic means. That is very like the difference between the Old Secularist and the New Secularist or the Millennial Dawnist.

Take some puzzles out of this page about me. "Chesterton uses his talents tyrannously in the service of the most reactionary of all Churches," — to which he didn't belong at the time. And how do you use talents tyrannously? I wish I knew. "He has nothing but the crudest insults for the great intellectuals." Well, there is the book; anybody can see what I really said about Mill, about Meredith,[111] about Matthew Arnold, about Huxley, even supposing that nobody is an intellectual unless he is an agnostic. To say I had "nothing" but crude insult for them is — well, something that could be described still more crudely. Swinburne, it seems "is accused of composing a learned and sympathetic and indecent parody on the Litany of the Blessed Virgin." And the critic adds mysteriously, "an ironical suggestion in a Protestant country." I do not know what the word "accused" means here. If the critic has read Swinburne he knows that an early verse in *Dolores* is a parody of the Litany of the Virgin. It is hardly an accusation to call it learned and sympathetic; by which I meant artistically sympathetic in an archaic Gothic mode; as were the profane Pre-Raphaelites as well as the pious ones. Whether such a thing is indecent may be discussed; but the critic is quite wrong in fancying that only Papists thought it indecent. The indecency of *Dolores* was denounced, more harshly than I dreamed of doing it, by the first Freethinker in English public life; the late John Morley.[112]

Finally, here is one wonderful example of how the *Freethinker* gets hold of the wrong end of the stick, even when I actually offer him the right end. He writes the amazing sentence, "Even the great authors of the nineteenth century do not escape his Romish censure,

[111] George Meredith (1828–1909) was an English poet and novelist, best known for the novel *The Egoist* (1879).

[112] John Morley (1838–1923) was an English statesman, biographer, historian and editor.

and are dubbed, spitefully, 'lame giants'." It is not very spiteful to call an author a giant; but anyone consulting the book will see that the men I called "lame giants" were not "the great authors of the nineteenth century," but specially the English authors of the Victorian time; whom I compared unfavourably with the franker and bolder Freethinkers of France and the Continent. Thus I praised Renan as a more logical sceptic than Tennyson, who was a lame sceptic, hampered by respectability and provincial religion. You would think a Freethinker would recognise that as an obvious concession to Freethinkers. But the new Freethinker does not *read* a book. He looks through it feverishly for texts to be twisted in favour of a prejudice, like the religious maniac with the Bible.

To take another instance. I wrote an article, which appeared in the *London Mercury* and was called "The End of the Moderns," in which I tried to describe a certain quality in works like *Brave New World*, and in much of the cult of D. H. Lawrence; a quality (not necessarily a bad quality) of being near the end of its tether, or having nearly run through its resources: of having stretched something very nearly as far as it will go. It was a psychological and literary note upon certain literary psychologists of recent years; it had nothing directly to do with religion, still less with irreligion; it had nothing in the world to do with any attack on atheism. Now the Freethinker reads through all this stuff about Lawrence and Aldous Huxley, all terribly modern to him, of course; but the point is that he cannot believe that any article I write can be anything except an attack on atheism; and especially on his own antediluvian sort of atheism. That anybody should want to write an article about modern authors, and their psychological, sociological and ethical difficulties, he cannot conceive. Therefore he runs his eye through my article, until it brightens suddenly at the sight of the word "blasphemy". At last he has found something that he understands; something that he knows all about. Blasphemy brings back Bradlaugh and the brave days of old; and, by a pardonable optical illusion, I appear to him in the form of Lord Randolph Churchill[113] in

---

[113] Lord Randolph Churchill (1849–95) led the fight to prevent Charles Bradlaugh from taking his seat in Parliament, unless Bradlaugh, a noted freethinker, agreed to swear his oath of office on the Bible.

the '80s, moving the expulsion of the Senior Member for Northampton. I am, after all, making my unscrupulous Attack on Atheism, though (for some dark reasons best known to myself) I prefer to stick it into the middle of an article stuffed with all sorts of strange nonsense about literature and a man named Lawrence.

Why, and in what connection, as a matter of fact, did I use the sacred word "balasphemy?" The point was this; I wished to give the reader a rough working example, to begin with, of what I meant by saying that a literary process or argument could be doomed to an early exhaustion; could be of a kind that was fated to come to a finish. And I gave the example of the purely literary and artistic effect of blasphemy. I was careful to state, in so many words, that I was only talking of the literary and artistic effect. I said the particular shock or thrill, given by breaking the silence about a sanctity, cannot be repeated indefinitely, when the sanctity is no longer there. I never said a word about whether it would be a good thing, on general social grounds, that the sanctity should be no longer there. I was not discussing that question, but another question about short-lived literary effects, of which blasphemy happens to be a good working example. But the monomaniac solemnity of the Free-thinker leads him to come blundering out with a very heavy club, against the blasphemer who has blasphemed the sanctity of blasphemy. He labours a ludicrous comparison, according to which saying, "there is no sense in blasphemy when there is nothing sacred to blaspheme" is no more sensible than saying "there is no sense in sanitation when there are no enemies of sanitation to attack." What has become of the reasoning power of atheists, I cannot think. This comparison is obviously rubbish; because sanitation is supposed to be useful whether it is opposed or no; and all I said was blasphemy was not startling or thrilling unless there was something to which it was opposed. Whether secularism would be a good thing, when once established and unopposed, as sanitation is supposed to be a good thing when established and unopposed, was a question which I simply did not raise in that particular article at all. I only said that such a settled secular state could not enjoy eternally the artistic excitement of blasphemy; and this the secularist, after beating wildly about the bush is eventually forced to admit. "What Mr. Chesterton ought to have said is that the defiance of God, the criticism of God, or ridiculing God, can only exist so long as men believe in God. That is quite true." That is also, as it happens, exactly what Mr. Chesterton said, and all that Mr. Chesterton said; and Mr. Chesterton is very much gratified to learn that it is also what he ought to have said. But Mr. Chesterton also said a lot more, on literary and psychological matters of the moment, in which he happens to be interested; and he is now mildly interested in the fact that *The Freethinker* is not in the least interested in them. The atheist is not interested in anything except attacks on atheism, so he insists that I am attacking atheism, even when I explain elaborately that I am doing something else. He therefore blames me for saying what he himself declares to be true; or for not proving what I had never set out to prove.

But the queerest thing of all is this. I was not then attacking atheism, and I was actually defending rationalism. I was doing the poor old Freethinker's job for him; and defending the Reason that he ought to defend. I was defending it against the more modern mysticism of D. H. Lawrence, who said that we should rebel *against* reason: and rely entirely upon instinct and emotion. And *this*, I pointed out, was an instance of something which, like blasphemy in literature, may be stimulating at the very start, but cannot run very long. An attempt really to conduct life, without constant reference to reason, would quite certainly break down. That was my point about all these modern social suggestions; that they would break down. For the rest, he repeats at intervals with hissing emphasis that I am a Roman Catholic; he is so much out of touch with the twentieth century that he really seems to imagine that a Roman Catholic is now at an intellectual disadvantage among other Christians. But I want to know why the Roman Catholic is left to do the work of the Rationalist; and attack the really recent upheaval of Unreason in the world, and why the Rationalist actually attacks him for attacking it.

SHOCKING THE MODERNISTS

How do we manage to stagger on blinded by the blaze of wit and starry brilliancy, that is showered upon us like everlasting fireworks every day in the daily papers? The writers in those papers who so often remind us, with never-failing freshness, that things that were once rare luxuries are now multiplied and minutely and exactly imitated everywhere, surely will not fail to apply this same striking truth to the intellectual world. They will doubtless point out that those perfect and pointed epigrams, which were once heard only from exceptional individuals, like Voltaire and Talleyrand, are now invented by the hundred in every column of every newspaper, and it is hardly possible to find a single dull sentence wedged between the witty repartees and immortal jests, which can now, like everything else of any value, be produced in any quantity by mass production.

However this may be, there can be no doubt that our journalism, and the world it describes, has reached an acute sensibility to wit and verbal brilliance, which has never been known before; and is so vividly alert and alive to any such ringing and rapier-like logical fencing as to cry "a hit! a palpable hit!" in circumstancs in which it is only too likely that our duller forefathers would have remained deaf or indifferent. I once read a paragraph in a daily paper, about a notable outburst among the most advanced intellects in the Church of England, which bears witness to the promptitude with which such triumphs are appreciated. Under the two headlines of "Youth Finds Church a Bore," and "A Girl Tells Clergy," the paragraph, or rather series of paragraphs was arranged in a suitably sensational way as follows:—

"Youth finds church a bore — and stays away from it.

This contention, put forward by a girl of eighteen from the platform at Girton College, Cambridge, yesterday, made the elderly delegates to the Modern Churchman's Conference sit up sharply in their seats.

The speaker was the attractive daughter of a Portsmouth naval chaplain.

Her most telling passage was this: 'I don't think public worship has any attraction whatsoever for the young. Religion is supposed to express God through truth and beauty, we are told, but in this age of specialisation people turn to science, art and philosophy to satisfy those needs'."

I wonder what her least telling passage was.

Of course the fun really begins with the astounding and staggering effect produced by the original thunderbolt of thought "Youth Finds Church a Bore," on all those admittedly elderly delegates who were sufficiently ancient to be described as Modern Churchmen. Dr. Major[114] leapt to his feet with a howl; Dean Inge bounced up to the ceiling like a ball. Dr. Rashdall[115] uttered one piercing shriek and fainted; for not one of these venerable doctors, in all their long experience of the Modernist Movement, had ever heard one human being articulate with human lips the star-staggering blasphemy that youth finds church a bore. Not one of them had ever heard so much as a rumour of young people yawning during a sermon; to none had any voice dared to to whisper that little boys have been known to catch flies or dig penknives into pews during Divine service; not one of them had ever in his life heard a baby begin to squeal in church; none had ever listened to the hideous slander that youths and maidens in church had been known to look at each other instead of keeping their eyes fixed rigidly on the lectern (for nobody in the church of a Modern Churchman would condescend to look at the altar); none of them ever knew before that there had ever been any friction between the fits and moods of youth and the routine of religion. Never, until the attractive daughter of a Portsmouth naval chaplain made this stupendous discovery in modern psychology, had they even thought of the possibility that a long religious service might be rather a bore to a boy.

But yet, even about that discovery, it seems as if there might be more to be said. Some of the elderly Modern Churchmen have been schoolmasters. It seems just possible that some of them had discovered

---

[114] Henry Major (1871–1961) was one of the foremost Anglican modernist theologians. He founded the magazine *Modern Churchman* in 1911 and edited it until 1955.

[115] Hastings Rashdall (1858–1924) was an English philosopher, theologian and historian, known especially for his writings on medieval universities.

that the Sixth Book of the Aeneid can be a bore to a boy. But in those cases it was not invariably assumed that the boy was right and the poet was wrong. It was not taken for granted that the boredom of the boy in itself proves that Virgil is a bad poet; still less did anyone ever propose that a simplified and modernised version of Virgil must be substituted for the old one. Nobody proposed that passages from Kipling about the British Empire should be substituted for the more austere salutations of Virgil to the Roman Empire, because such education would be more modern, compact and convenient to a truly National Church. Nobody proposed that a really smart and snappy up-to-date description of the Derby, taken from an evening paper, should be regarded as a complete substitute for that thundering line in which the very earth shakes with the horsehoofs of the charioteers. And, if I may venture to hint a disagreement with the Prophetess of Girton College, Cambridge, I think it will be found that the same argument applies even to the substitutes that she herself proposes. She says that people turn to science, art and philosophy. Will she swear by the Oath of Nelson, or whatever oath binds the daughter of a Portsmouth naval chaplain, that no science student ever shirks or plays truant in a science school? It will be vain for her to swear any such thing in the case of an art school; for I have been to an art school myself, and I can assure her that there were quite as many art students who found application to art a bore as there could possibly be divinity students who found divinity a bore. As for young philosophers, I have known a good many of them; at an age when nearly all of them were much more fond of philosophising than of learning philosophy. And I might hint that there are other young agitators, of the sort that seem to agitate so strangely the Modern Churchmen and the modern newspapers, who seem to have a certain spirited and spontaneous preference for saying things rather than for thinking what they are saying. Is it really necessary that we should toil through all this tiresome repetition about the perfectly obvious difficulty of getting young people to work when they naturally want to play, before we even begin to discuss the mature problem of the relation of doctrine to the mind? It is perfectly natural that the boy should find the church a bore. But why are we bound to treat what is natural as something actually superior to what is supernatural; as something which is not even merely supernatual, but is in the exact sense super-supernatural?

A GRAMMAR OF KNIGHTHOOD

I think it very likely that many have never even heard of *The Broadstone of Honour*, the manual of chivalry written by Kenelm Digby[116] early in the nineteenth century; unless they remember one contemptuous reference to it in Macaulay's Essays. The reference is not much of a criticism on *The Broadstone of Honour*, but it is a very damaging criticism of Macaulay's Essays. It illustrates, not only his spirited superficiality, but that considerable element of ignorance that went along with his remarkable reputation for omniscience. Just as his celebrated sneer at Spenser shows that he had not read Spenser, so his less famous sneer at Kenelm Digby shows that he had not read Kenelm Digby. He set himself to belittle certain old tales of courtesy, which is the wedding of humility with dignity. He scoffed at such stories as that of the Black Prince[117] waiting like a servant on his helpless captive; and he thought he could not scoff at them more effectively than by saying they would be suitable to Kenelm Digby; or, as he put it, to "those who think, like the author of *The Broadstone of Honour*, that God made the world for the use of gentlemen." One is tempted to reply, in some moods, that there will always be enough bounders, even among the learned, to redress the balance.

Now Kenelm Henry Digby was, as his name implies, a member of an old Catholic family, established in Ireland; and, as with the other branches of such old families established in England, it would not be very unnatural if he did attach some importance to being a gentleman. If the weakness has sometimes been too apparent in the old Catholics of England, it is at least pardonable and rather pathetic. When you are an honest and perfectly patriotic squire, and all your countrymen regard you as a liar, a traitor, a poisoner and a devil-worshipper, it must be something of a sentimental comfort to you that they cannot deny you are a gentleman. Poor human nature being what it is, you may be excused if you come to think a little too much

[116] Digby (1800–1880) published the book in 1822.
[117] The Black Prince was Prince Edward, the eldest son of King Edward III, who ruled England from 1327 to 1377.

of it; and talked nonsense about gentlemen, as if God had made the world for them. But as a simple fact, it was not Digby who talked nonsense about gentlemen, but Macaulay who talked nonsense about Digby.

What would Macaulay have said if after writing his epigram about a universe created for the gentry, he had made the bold experiment of opening the book at random, as I did, and reading a paragraph like this:

"The noble Italian Arnigio shows how truly generous and heroic peasants and men of the lowest rank of life may become." "The glorious nativity of the Redeemer of the world," he observes, "was revealed to shepherds, as to men pure, just and vigilant When our adorable Saviour was to be born blessed Mary and the devout Joseph were so little possessed of worldly grandeur that the stable of an inn was their only place of refuge. For mark, says a holy man, the evangelists do not say that there was no room in the inn, but there was no room for them. Oh what a noble school is poverty! What a temple of sovereign honour! Pope Urban IV was so little ashamed of being the son of a shoemaker that he ordered the pulpit of the church of St. Urban, at Troyes, his native city, to be adorned on great festivals with tapestry representing his father's stall. There is even an example of legislation, on the principles of the romances, which places Chivalry before nobility; for the state of Pistoja, in the thirteenth century, ennobled men as a punishment for their crimes."

Do you think that perhaps even Macaulay would have felt slightly ashamed of himself?

Anyhow, the author of *The Broadstone of Honour* did not think the world was made only for gentlemen. He thought in his simplicity that it was made for man; and he could not escape from a prejudice in favour of brave men and honest men and (I am so antiquated as to add) men who felt a special consideration for women. The book has some of the faults of its type and time; in that sense it is now rather dated; nearly as much dated as Macaulay. We must read it, or at least parts of it, rather as we read a song of Tom Moore or a patriotic poem of Thomas Davis,[118]

[118] Thomas Moore (1779–1852) was a poet whose *Irish Melodies* (1807–35) made him Ireland's foremost lyricist. Thomas Osborne Davis (1814–45) was an Irish nationalist and poet.

or all that rather rhetorical yet very red-blooded tradition of talking and writing that derived from the mighty melodrama of Byron or was sympathetically satirised in Micawber.[119] But when we have allowed for variations in the taste for purple patches, a matter entirely relative in our taste as in his, the book is sustained from first to last by what can only be called a sustained energy of virtue. It does anybody good to meet a man so little ashamed of an enthusiasm for mere goodness. Many of his gestures are as noble as any of those that make the decisive moments in the Chansons de Geste.[120] Many of his concessions are as graceful as any that he himself praises in the chronicles of the tournament or the tented field. But he was very far from being merely an amiable old antiquary haunting Melrose[121] by moonlight; or even a dazed Don Quixote with his head hidden in folios about Arthur and Amadis of Gaul.[122] I cannot resist making another quotation, which will serve to show that Kenelm Digby was not by any means unconscious of what was going on in his own time—and, I will add, is still going on in ours.

After speaking of St. Francis and of many knights who would feed the poor and eat with them and carry their coffins, he says, "Oh! is it for the rich of the nineteenth century to talk of the inhumanity of the Middle Ages? To give alms, with them, is to encourage idleness. He is hungry, he is naked? Let him work. But he is old? There are employments for all. But he is a child? Do not teach him to beg. It is the mother of a large family? Perhaps she does not tell the truth. We have institutions on a new system. Yes truly, and woe to the unhappy ones who are doomed to receive relief from them! In order that the children of pleasure may not be incommoded by the sight of poverty the poor are shut up within high walls and condemned to confinement for the crime of being poor and miserable.

[119] Micawber is a character in Dickens' *David Copperfield.*

[120] The *Chansons de Geste* are epic poems in Old French, the earliest of which date from the twelfth century. The most famous of the *chansons*, which deal with chivalry, courtly romance and heroic exploits, is the *Song of Roland.*

[121] Melrose Abbey appears in Sir Walter Scott's poem *The Lay of the Last Minstrel* (1805).

[122] Amadis of Gaul is an eponymous protagonist of an Iberian romance written by Garcia de Montalvo in the late fifteenth century.

When they are thus secluded from the enjoyment of nature an odious Board of Governors takes care that they should be provided with what is sufficient to support life. And then they have to endure the countenances of ferocious barbarians who are the officers to administer this horrible humanity."

That is the testimony of Digby, as it is the testimony of Dickens, who did not presumably labour under the illusion that God made the world only for gentlemen. That is also the testimony of Cobbett,[123] of Carlyle, of Hood, of Ruskin, of everybody who actually watched the modern industrial movement with his eyes open; but the fact that Digby wrote that paragraph may alone be my apology for writing this note on his neglected name.

[123] William Cobbett (1763–1835) was an English political radical and agricultural reformer, whose best-known book was *Rural Rides* (1830).

REFLECTIONS ON A ROTTEN APPLE

Our age is obviously the Nonsense Age; the wiser sort of nonsense being provided for the children and the sillier sort of nonsense for the grown-up people. The eighteenth century has been called the Age of Reason; I suppose there is no doubt that the twentieth century is the Age of Unreason. But even that is an understatement. The Age of Reason was nicknamed from a famous rationalist book.[124] But the rationalist was not really so much concerned to urge the rational against the irrational; but rather specially to urge the natural against the supernatural. But there is a degree of the unreasonable that would go even beyond the unnatural. It is not merely an incredible tale, but an inconsistent idea. As I pointed out to somebody long ago, it is one thing to believe that a beanstalk scaled the sky, and quite another to believe that fifty-seven beans make five.

For instance, a man may disbelieve in miracles; normally on some *a priori* principle of determinist thought; in some cases even on examination of the evidence. But on being told of the miracle of the multiplication of the loaves and fishes, he is told something that is logical if it is not natural. He is not told that there were fewer fishes because the fishes had been multiplied. Multiplication is still a mathematical term; and a mob all feeding on miraculous fishes is a less mysterious or monstrous sight than a man saying that multiplication is the same as subtraction. Such a story, for such a sceptic, does not carry conviction; but it does make sense. He can recognise the logical consequence, if he cannot understand the logical cause. But no pope or priest ever asked him to believe that thousands died of starvation in the desert because they were loaded with loaves and fishes. No creed or dogma ever declared that there was too little food because there was too much fish. But that is the precise, practical and prosaic definition of the present situation in the modern science of economics. And the man of the Nonsense Age must bow his head and repeat his *credo*, the motto of his time, *Credo quia impossibile.*[125]

---

[124] Chesterton is referring to Thomas Paine's *The Age of Reason*, published in two parts, 1794–95.

[125] *Credo quia impossibile* is Latin for "I believe because it is impossibile."

Or again, the term unreason is sometimes used rather more reasonably; for a sort of loose or elliptical statement, which is at least illogical in form. The most popular case is what was called the Irish Bull; often suspected of resembling the Papal Bull, in being a supernatural monster bred of credulity and superstition. But even this old sort of confusion stopped short of the new sort of contradiction. If any Irishman really does say, "We are not birds, to be in two places at once," at least we know what he means, even if it is not what he says. But suppose he says that one bird has been miraculously multiplied into a million birds, and that in consequence there are fewer birds in the world than there were before. We should then be dealing, not merely with an Irish Bull but with a Mad Bull, and concerned not with the incredible but with the incomprehensible. Or, to apply the parable, the Irish have sometimes been accused of unbalanced emotion or morbid sentiment. But nobody says that they merely imagined the Great Famine, in which multitudes starved because the potatoes were few and small. Only suppose an Irishman had said that they starved because the potatoes were gigantic and innumerable. I think we should not yet have heard the last of the wrong-headed absurdity of that Irishman. Yet that is an exact description of the economic condition to-day as it affects the Englishman. And, to a great extent, the American. We learn that there is a famine because there is not a scarcity; and there is such a good potato-crop that there are no potatoes. The Irishman, with his bull or his bird, is quite a hard-headed realist and rationalist compared to that. Thus, the old examples of the fantastic fell far short of the modern fact; whether they were mysteries supposed to be above reason or merely muddles supposed to be below it. Their miracles were more normal than our scientific averages; and the Irish blunder was less illogical than the actual logic of events.

For it seems that we live to-day in a world of witchcraft, in which the orchards wither because they prosper, and the multitude of apples on the apple-tree of itself turns them into forbidden fruit, and makes the effort to consume them in every sense fruitless. This is the modern economic paradox, which is called Over-Production, or a glut in the market, and though at first sight it sounds like the wildest fantasy, it is well to realise in what sense it is the most solid of facts. Let it be clearly understood, therefore, that as a description of the objective social situation at this instant in this industrial society, the paradox is perfectly true. But it is not really true that the contradiction in terms is true. If we take it, not as a description but as a definition, if we take it as a matter of abstract argument, then certainly the contradiction is untrue, as every contradiction is untrue. The truth is that a third element has entered into the matter, which is not mentioned in this abstract statement of it. That element might be stated in many ways; perhaps the shortest statement of it is in the fable of the man who sold razors, and afterwards explained to an indignant customer, with simple dignity, that he had never said the razors would shave. When asked if razors were not made to shave, he replied that they were made to sell. That is A Short History of Trade and Industry During the Nineteenth and Early Twentieth Centuries.

God made a world of reason as sure as God made little apples (as the beautiful proverb goes); and God did not make little apples larger than large apples. It is not true that a man whose apple-tree is loaded with apples will suffer from a want of apples; though he may indulge in a waste of apples. But if he never looks upon apples as things to eat, but always looks on them as things to sell, he will really get into another sort of complication; which may end in a sort of contradiction. If, instead of producing as many apples as he wants, he produces as many apples as he imagines the whole world wants, with the hope of capturing the trade of the whole world—then he will be either successful or unsuccessful in competing with the man next door who also wants the whole world's trade to himself. Between them, they will produce so many apples that apples in the market will be about as valuable as pebbles on the beach. Thus each of them will find he has very little money in his pocket, with which to go and buy fresh pears at the fruiterer's shop. If he had never expected to get fruit at the fruiterer's shop, but had put up his hand and pulled them off his own tree, his difficulty would never have arisen. It seems simple; but at the root of all apple-trees and apple-growing, it is really as simple as that.

Of course I do not mean that the practice is at present simple; for no practical problem is simple, least of all at the present time, when everything is confused by the corrupt and evasive muddlers who are called practical politicians. But the principle is simple; and the only way to proceed through a complex situation is to start with the right first principle. How far we can do without, or control, or merely modify the disadvantages of buying and selling is quite another matter. But the disadvantages do arise from buying and selling, and not from producing: not even from over-producing. And it is some satisfaction to realise that we are not living in a nightmare in which No is the same as Yes; that even the modern world has not actually gone mad, with all its ingenious attempts to do so; that two and two do in fact make four; and that the man who has four apples really has more than the man who has three. For some modern metaphysicians and moral philosophers seem disposed to leave us in doubt on these points. It is not the fundamental reason in things that is at fault; it is a particular hitch or falsification, arising from a very recent trick of regarding everything only in relation to trade. Trade is all very well in its way, but Trade has been put in the place of Truth. Trade, which is in its nature a secondary or dependent thing, has been treated as a primary and independent thing; as an absolute. The moderns, mad upon mere multiplication, have even made a plural out of what is eternally singular, in the sense of single. They have taken what all ancient philosophers called the Good, and translated it as the Goods.

I believe that certain mystics, in the American business world, protested against the slump by pinning labels to their coats inscribed, "Trade Is Good," along with other similar proclamations, such as, "Capone Is Dead," or "Cancer Is Pleasant," or "Death Is Abolished," or any other hard realistic truths for which they might find space upon their persons. But what interests me about these magicians is that, having decided to call up ideal conditions by means of spells and incantations to control the elements, they did not (so to speak) understand the elements of the elements. They did not go to the root of the matter, and imagine that their troubles had really come to an end. Rather they worshipped the means instead of the end. While they were about it, they ought to have said, not "Trade Is Good," but "Living Is Good," or "Life Is Good." I suppose it would be too much to expect such thoroughly respectable people to say, "God Is Good"; but it is really true that their conception of what is good lacks the philosophical finality that belonged to the goodness of God. When God looked on created things and saw that they were good, it meant that they were good in themselves and as they stood; but by the modern mercantile idea, God would only have looked at them and seen that they were The Goods. In other words, there would be a label tied to the tree or the hill, as to the hat of the Mad Hatter, with "This Style, 10/6." All the flowers and birds would be ticketed with their reduced prices; all the creation would be for sale or all the creatures seeking employment; with all the morning stars making sky-signs together and all the Sons of God shouting for jobs. In other words, these people are incapable of imagining any good except that which comes from bartering something for something else. The idea of a man enjoying a thing in itself, for himself, is inconceivable to them. The notion of a man eating his own apples off his own apple-tree seems like a fairy-tale. Yet the fall from that first creation that was called good has very largely come from the restless impotence for valuing things in themselves; the madness of the trader who cannot see any good in a good, except as something to get rid of. It was once admitted that with sin and death there entered the world something that we call change. It is none the less true and tragic, because what we called change, we called afterwards exchange. Anyhow, the result of that extravagance of exchange has been that when there are too many apples there are too few apple-eaters. I do not insist on the symbol of Eden, or the parable of the apple-tree, but it is odd to notice that even that accidental image pursues us at every stage of this strange story. The last result of treating a tree as a shop or a store instead of as a store-room, the last effect of treating apples as goods rather than as good, has been in a desperate drive of public charity and in poor men selling apples in the street.

In all normal civilisations the trader existed and must exist. But in all normal civilisations the trader was the exception; certainly he was never the rule; and most certainly he was never the ruler. The predominance which he has gained in the modern world is the cause of

all the disasters of the modern world. The universal habit of humanity has been to produce and consume as part of the same process;
largely conducted by the same people in the same place. Sometimes
goods were produced and consumed on the same great feudal manor;
sometimes even on the same small peasant farm. Sometimes there
was a tribute from serfs as yet hardly distinguishable from slaves;
sometimes there was a co-operation between free-men which the
superficial can hardly distinguish from communism. But none of
these many historical methods, whatever their vices or limitions,
was strangled in the particular tangle of our own time; because most
of the people, for most of the time, were thinking about growing
food and then eating it; not entirely about growing food and selling
it at the stiffest price to somebody who had nothing to eat. And I for
one do not believe that there is any way out of the modern tangle,
except to increase the proportion of the people who are living according to the ancient simplicity. Nobody in his five wits proposes
that there should be no trade and no traders. Nevertheless, it is important to remember, as a matter of mere logic, that there might
conceivably be great wealth, even if there were no trade and no
traders. It is important for the sort of man whose only hope is that
Trade Is Good or whose only secret terror is that Trade Is Bad. In
principle, prosperity might be very great, even if trade were very
bad. If a village were so fortunately situated that, for some reason, it
was easy for every family to keep its own chickens, to grow its own
vegetables, to milk its own cow and (I will add) to brew its own
beer, the standard of life and property might be very high indeed,
even though the long memory of the Oldest Inhabitant only recorded
two or three pure transactions of trade; if he could only recall the one
far-off event of his neighbour buying a new hat from a gipsy's barrow;
or the singular incident of Farmer Billings purchasing an umbrella.

As I have said, I do not imagine, or desire, that things would ever
be quite so simple as that. But we must understand things in their
simplicity before we can explain or correct their complexity. The
complexity of commercial society has become intolerable, because that
society is commercial and nothing else. The whole mind of the community is occupied, not with the idea of possessing things, but with

the idea of passing them on. When the simple enthusiasts already mentioned say that Trade is Good, they mean that all the people who possess goods are perpetually parting with them. These Optimists presumably invoke the poet, with some slight emendation of the poet's meaning, when he cries aloud, 'Our souls are love and a perpetual farewell.' In that sense, our individualistic and commercial modern society is actually the very reverse of a society founded on Private Property. I mean that the actual direct and isolated enjoyment of private property, as distinct from the excitement of exchanging it or getting a profit on it, is rather rarer than in many simple communities that seem almost communal in their simplicity. In the case of this sort of private consumption, which is also private production, it is very unlikely that it will run continually into overproduction. There is a limit to the number of apples a man can eat, and there will probably be a limit, drawn by his rich and healthy hatred of work, to the number of apples which he will produce but cannot eat. But there is no limit to the number of apples he may possibly sell; and he soon becomes a pushing, dexterous and successful Salesman and turns the whole world upside-down. For it is he who produces this huge pantomimic paradox with which this rambling reflection began. It is he who makes a wilder revolution than the apple of Adam which was the loosening of death, or the apple of Newton which was the apocalypse of gravitation, by proclaiming the supreme blasphemy and heresy, that the apple was made for the market and not for the mouth. It was he, by starting the wild race of pouring endless apples into a bottomless market, who opened the abyss of irony and contradiction into which we are staring to-day. That trick of treating the trade as the test, and the only test, has left us face to face with a piece of stark staring nonsense written in gigantic letters across the world; more gigantic than all its own absurd advertisements and announcements; the statement that the more we produce the less we possess.

Oscar Wilde would probably have fainted with equal promptitude, if told he was being used in an argument about American salesmanship, or in defence of a thrifty and respectable family life on the farm. But it does so happen that one true epigram, among many of his false epigrams, sums up correctly and compactly a certain truth, not (I am happy to say) about Art, but about all that he desired to separate from Art; ethics and even economics. He said in one of his plays: "A cynic is a man who knows the price of everything and the value of nothing."[126] It is extraordinarily true; and the answer to most other things that he said. But it is yet more extraordinary that the modern men who make that mistake most obviously are not the cynics. On the contrary, they are those who call themselves the Optimists; perhaps even those who would call themselves the Idealists; certainly those who regard themselves as the Regular Guys and the Sons of Service and Uplift. It is too often those very people who have spoilt all their good effect, and weakened their considerable good example in work and social contact, by that very error: that things are to be judged by the price and not by the value. And since Price is a crazy and incalculable thing, while Value is an intrinsic and indestructible thing, they have swept us into a society which is no longer solid but fluid, as unfathomable as a sea and as treacherous as a quicksand. Whether anything more solid can be built again upon a social philosophy of values, there is now no space to discuss at length here; but I am certain that nothing solid can be built on any other philosophy; certainly not upon the utterly unphilosophical philosophy of blind buying and selling; of bullying people into purchasing what they do not want; of making it badly so that they may break it and imagine they want it again; of keeping rubbish in rapid circulation like a dust-storm in a desert; and pretending that you are teaching men to hope, because you do not leave them one intelligent instant in which to despair.

[126] The quotation is from *Lady Windermere's Fan* (1892).

SEX AND PROPERTY

In the dull, dusty, stale, stiff-jointed and lumbering language, to which most modern discussion is limited, it is necessary to say that there is at this moment the same fashionable fallacy about Sex and about Property. In the older and freer language, in which men could both speak and sing, it is truer to say that the same evil spirit has blasted the two great powers that make the poetry of life; the Love of Woman and the Love of the Land. It is important to observe, to start with, that the two things were closely connected so long as humanity was human, even when it was heathen. Nay, they were still closely connected, even when it was a decadent heathenism. But even the stink of decaying heathenism has not been so bad as the stink of decaying Christianity. The corruption of the best. . . .

For instance, there were throughout antiquity, both in its first stage and its last, modes of idolatry and imagery of which Christian men can hardly speak. "Let them not be so much as named among you."[127] Men wallowed in the mere sexuality of a mythology of sex; they organised prostitution like priesthood, for the service of their temples; they made pornography their only poetry; they paraded emblems that turned even architecture into a sort of cold and colossal exhibitionism. Many learned books have been written of all these phallic cults; and anybody can go to them for the details, for all I care. But what interests me is this:

In one way all this ancient sin was infinitely superior, immeasurably superior, to the modern sin. All those who write of it at least agree on one fact; that it was the cult of Fruitfulness. It was unfortunately too often interwoven, very closely, with the cult of the fruitfulness of the land. It was at least on the side of Nature. It was at least on the side of Life. It has been left to the last Christians, or rather to the first Christians fully committed to blaspheming and denying Christianity, to invent a new kind of worship of Sex, which is not even a worship of Life. It has been left to the very latest Modernists to proclaim an erotic religion which at once exalts lust and forbids

[127] The quotation is from Ephesians 5:3.

fertility. The new Paganism literally merits the reproach of Swinburne, when mourning for the old Paganism: "and rears not the bountiful token and spreads not the fatherly feast." The new priests abolish the fatherhood and keep the feast—to themselves. They are worse than Swinburne's Pagans. The priests of Priapus and Cotytto[128] go into the kingdom of heaven before them.

Now it is not unnatural that this unnatural separation, between sex and fruitfulness, which even the Pagans would have thought a perversion, has been accompanied with a similar separation and perversion about the nature of the love of the land. In both departments there is precisely the same fallacy; which it is quite possible to state precisely. The reason why our contemporary countrymen do not understand what we mean by Property is that they only think of it in the sense of Money; in the sense of salary; in the sense of something which is immediately consumed, enjoyed and expended; something which gives momentary pleasure and disappears. They do not understand that we mean by Property something that includes that pleasure incidentally; but begins and ends with something far more grand and worthy and creative. The man who makes an orchard where there has been a field, who owns the orchard and decides to whom it shall descend, does also enjoy the taste of apples; and let us hope, also, the taste of cider. But he is doing something very much grander, and ultimately more gratifying, than merely eating an apple. He is imposing his will upon the world in the manner of the charter given him by the will of God; he is asserting that his soul is his own, and does not belong to the Orchard Survey Department, or the chief Trust in the Apple Trade. But he is also doing something which was implicit in all the most ancient religions of the earth; in those great panoramas of pageantry and ritual that followed the order of the seasons in China or Babylonia; he is worshipping the fruitfulness of the world. Now the notion of narrowing property merely to *enjoying* money is exactly like the notion of narrowing love merely to *enjoying* sex. In both cases an incidental, isolated, servile and even secretive pleasure is substituted for participation

128 Priapus and Cotytto are fertility deities.

in a great creative process; even in the everlasting Creation of the world.

The two sinister things can be seen side by side in the system of Bolshevist Russia; for Communism is the only complete and logical working model of Capitalism. The sins are there a system which are everywhere else a sort of repeated blunder. From the first, it is admitted, that the whole system was directed towards encouraging or driving the worker to spend his wages; to have nothing left on the next pay day; to enjoy everything and consume everything and efface everything; in short, to shudder at the thought of only one crime; the creative crime of thrift. It was a tame extravagance; a sort of disciplined dissipation; a meek and submissive prodigality. For the moment the slave left off drinking all his wages, the moment he began to hoard or hide any property, he would be saving up something which might ultimately purchase his liberty. He might begin to count for something in the State; that is, he might become less of a slave and more of a citizen. Morally considered, there has been nothing quite so unspeakably mean as this Bolshevist generosity. But it will be noted that exactly the same spirit and tone pervades the manner of dealing with the other matter. Sex also is to come to the slave merely as a pleasure; that it may never be a power. He is to know as little as possible, or at least to think as little as possible, of the pleasure as anything else except a pleasure; to think or know nothing of where it comes from or where it will go to, when once the soiled object has passed through his own hands. He is not to trouble about its origin in the purposes of God or its sequel in the posterity of man. In every department he is not a possessor, but only a consumer; even if it be of the first elements of life and fire in so far as they are consumable; he is to have no notion of the sort of Burning Bush that burns and is not consumed. For that bush only grows on the soil, on the real land where human beings can behold it; and the spot on which they stand is holy ground. Thus there is an exact parallel between the two modern moral, or immoral, ideas of social reform. The world has forgotten simultaneously that the making of a Farm is something much larger than the making of a profit, or even a product, in the sense of liking the taste of beetroot sugar; and that the founding of a Family is something much larger than sex in the limited sense of current literature; which was anticipated in one bleak and blinding flash in a single line of George Meredith; "And eat our pot of honey on the grave."[129]

[129] The Meredith quotation is from *Modern Love* (1862).

ST. THOMAS MORE

Most would understand the phrase that the mind of More was like a diamond that a tyrant threw away into a ditch, because he could not break it. It is but a metaphor; but it does sometimes happen that the metaphor is many-sided, like the diamond. What moved the tyrant to a sort of terror of that mind was its clarity; it was the very reverse of a cloudy crystal filled only with opalescent dreams or visions of the past. The King and his great Chancellor had been companions as well as contemporaries; in many ways, both were Renaissance men; but in some ways, the man who was the more Catholic was the less medieval. That is, there was perhaps more in the Tudor of that mere musty fag-end of decayed medievalism, which the real Renaissance reformers felt to be the corruption of the time. In More's mind there was nothing but clarity; in Henry's mind, though he was no fool and certainly no Protestant, there was something of confused conservatism. Like many a better man who is an Anglo-Catholic, he had a touch of the antiquary. Thomas More was a better rationalist, which was why there was nothing in his religion that was merely local, or in that sense merely loyal. More's mind was like a diamond also in a power like that of cutting glass; of cutting through things that seemed equally transparent, but were at once less solid and less many-sided. For the true consistent heresies generally look very clear indeed; like Calvinism then or Communism now. They sometimes even look very true; they sometimes even are very true, in the limited sense of a truth that is less than the Truth. They are at once more thin and more brittle than the diamond. For a heresy is not often a mere lie; as Thomas More himself said, "Never was there a heretic that spoke all false." A heresy is a truth that hides all the other truths. A mind like More's was full of light like a house made of windows; but the windows looked out on all sides and in all directions. We might say that, as the jewel has many facets, so the man had many faces; only none of them were masks.

Thus there are so many aspects of this great story, that the difficulty of dealing with it in an article is one of selection, and even more of proportion. I might attempt and fail to do justice to its highest aspect; to that holiness which now stands beyond even Beatitude;[130] I might equally fill the whole space with the homeliest of the jokes in which the great humorist delighted in daily life; perhaps the biggest joke of all being the book called Utopia. The nineteenth century Utopians imitated the book without seeing the joke. But among a bewildering complexity of such different aspects or angles, I have decided to deal only with two points; not because they were the most important truths about Thomas More, though their importance is very great; but because they are two of the most important truths about the world at this present moment. One appears most clearly in his death and the other in his life; one, perhaps we should rather say, concerns his public life and the other his private life; one is far beyond any adequate admiration and the other may seem in comparison an almost comic bathos; but one hits exactly the right nail on the head in our present discussion about the State; and the other about the Family.

Thomas More died the death of a traitor for defying absolute monarchy; in the strict sense of treating monarchy as an absolute. He was willing, and even eager, to respect it as a relative thing, but not as an absolute thing. The heresy that had just raised its head in his own time was the heresy called the Divine Right of Kings. In that form it is now regarded as an old superstition; but it has already reappeared as a very new superstition, in the form of the Divine Right of Dictators. But most people still vaguely think of it as old; and nearly all of them think it is much older than it is. One of the chief difficulties to-day is to explain to people that this idea was not native to medieval or many older times. People know that the constitutional checks on kings have been increasing for a century or two; they do not realize that any other kind of checks could ever have operated; and in the changed conditions those other checks are hard to describe or imagine. But most certainly medieval men thought of the king as ruling *sub deo et lege*; rightly translated, "under God and the law," but also involving something atmospheric that might more

---

[130] Chesterton is referring to More, who was canonized in 1935.

vaguely be called, "under the morality implied in all our institutions." Kings were excommunicated, were deposed, were assassinated, were dealt with in all sorts of defensible and indefensible ways; but nobody thought the whole commonwealth fell with the king, or that he alone had ultimate authority there. The State did not own men so entirely, even when it could send them to the stake, as it sometimes does now where it can send them to the elementary school. There was an idea of refuge, which was generally an idea of sanctuary. In short, in a hundred strange and subtle ways, as we should think them, there was a sort of escape upwards. There were limits to Caesar; and there was liberty with God.

The highest voice of the Church has pronounced that this hero was in the true and traditional sense a Saint and Martyr. And it is appropriate to remember that he does indeed stand, for a rather special reason, with those first Martyrs whose blood was the seed of the Church in the very earliest pagan persecutions. For most of them died, as he did, for refusing to extend a civil loyalty into a religious idolatry. Most of them did not die for refusing to worship Mercury or Venus, or fabulous figures who might be supposed not to exist; or others like Moloch or Priapus whom we might well hope do not exist. Most of them died for refusing to worship somebody who certainly did exist; and even somebody whom they were quite prepared to obey but not to worship. The typical martyrdom generally turned on the business of burning incense before the statue of Divus Augustus; the sacred image of the Emperor. He was not necessarily a demon to be destroyed; he was simply a despot who must not be turned into a deity. That is where their case came so very close to the practical problem of Thomas More; and so very near to the practical problem of mere State-worship to-day. And it is typical of all Catholic thought that men died in torments, not because their foes "spoke all false"; but simply because they would not give an unreasonable reverence where they were perfectly prepared to give a reasonable respect. For us the problem of Progress is always a problem of Proportion; improvement is reaching a right proportion, not merely moving in one direction. And our doubts about most modern developments, about the Socialists in the last generation, or the Fascists in this generation, do not arise from our having any doubts at all about the desirability of economic justice, or of national order, any more than Thomas More bothered his head to object to a hereditary monarchy. He objected to the Divine Right of Kings.

In the very deepest sense he is thus the champion of Liberty in his public life and his still more public death. In his private life he is the type of a truth even less understood to-day; the truth that the real habitation of Liberty is the home. Modern novels and newspapers and problem plays have been piled up in one huge rubbish-heap to hide this simple fact; yet it is a fact that can be proved quite simply. Public life must be rather more regimented than private life; just as a man cannot wander about in the traffic of Piccadilly exactly as he could wander about in his own garden. Where there is traffic there will be regulation of traffic; and this is quite as true, or even more true, where it is what we should call an illicit traffic; where the most modern governments organize sterilization to-day and may organize infanticide to-morrow. Those who hold the modern superstition that the State can do no wrong will be bound to accept such a thing as right. If individuals have any hope of protecting their freedom, they must protect their family life. At the worst there will be rather more personal adaptation in a household than in a concentration camp; at the best there will be rather less routine in a family than in a factory. In any tolerably healthy home the rules are at least partly affected by things that cannot possibly affect fixed laws; for instance, the thing we call a sense of humour.

Therefore More is vividly important as the Humorist; as representing that special phase of the Humanist. Behind his public life, which was so grand a tragedy, there was a private life that was a perpetual comedy. He was, as Mr. Christopher Hollis says in his excellent study, "an incorrigible leg-puller." Everybody knows, of course, that the comedy and the tragedy met as they meet in Shakespeare, on that last high wooden stage where his drama ended. In that terrible moment he realized and relished the grand joke of the human body, as of a sort of lovable lumber; gravely discussed whether his beard had committed treason; and said in hoisting himself up the ladder, "See me safely up; coming down I can take care of myself."

But Thomas More never came down that ladder. He had done with all descents and downward goings, and what had been himself vanished from men's eyes almost in the manner of his Master, who being lifted up shall draw all men after Him. And the dark closed over him and the clouds came between; until long afterwards the wisdom that can read such secrets saw him fixed far above our heads like a returning star; and established his station in the skies.

THE RETURN OF CAESAR

Whether or no it be an example of first and second childhood, I sometimes have a whimsical fancy that I shall end as I began, trying to make some sense out of what is called Liberalism in politics. There is a Fleet Street story about me, which may be a fact though I have entirely forgotten it, that when I was asked if I was a Liberal, I answered, "I am the only Liberal." It will be agreed that, in these days, I should be very nearly the only Liberal. But I hope nobody will accuse me of wanting to be a Liberal leader. The Liberal Party now consists entirely of leaders — or rather misleaders. And all they want, all they have left to pray for, is one single simple solitary human being who is willing to be misled. On second thoughts, I rather doubt whether I will offer myself even to fulfil this humble office; whatever may be my qualifications for filling all the seats at a public meeting, and constituting the whole audience, while my five leaders address me from the platform, urging me to five urgent but incompatible courses of action. No, the sense in which I have again become conscious of the existence of purely political Liberalism is not so much due to what remains of it, as to what has vanished from it; not to what the Liberals say as to what they do not say. In the face of fashionable Fascism, and the toppling simplifications of the Totalitarian State, there really is a great deal that ought to be said for Liberalism; or, in clearer language, for Liberty.

Many things return; and thank God we live now in a time when we can talk once more about Church and State; though nowadays it generally means the Catholic Church and the Totalitarian State. But at least we have abolished the most illiberal of the illiberal limitations of Liberalism. We can recognise religion in history at the back of European ideas, including modern ideas; and in this connection the story of Church and State is very strange indeed. Of course, the one thing that has really confused the story of Church and State is the thing called the State Church. But that is a mere illogical interlude; in which God holds his authority from Caesar; instead of Caesar holding it from God. The normal relation between Church and State, through most of the varied phases of history, has not been exactly an establishment, but something more like what we have seen reappear in Germany. When there was not a conflict, there was a Concordat. It will be noted that the Church generally had a Concordat with her enemies rather than her friends. There was a dispute with Napoleon and a Concordat with Napoleon; a dispute with Mussolini and a Concordat with Mussolini; a dispute with Hitler and a Concordat with Hitler. And though the word would not perhaps have been used, and would not perhaps have been correct, something of the same paradox broods like a suspended storm over the State and Church in their relations in even earlier times. It marks the Church in her relation with the Roman Emperors; in her relation with the Greek Emperors; in her relation with the German Emperors. There was always some sort of Concordat, and there was never any complete concord.

It needs nearly a lifetime to trace the curve or orbit of the Church, and the rhythm of things returning. But to one growing up as a Liberal, and in many ways still a Liberal, the chief interest of the last days is in this. The Church, roughly speaking, almost always remains at about the same distance from the State and its experiments. There are exceptions, of course; when an Emperor persecutes the Church or the Church excommunicates an Emperor. The Church could hardly be expected to concord very much, even in the coldest manner, with Nero or the No-God Movement in Moscow. But it is most often found at about the same distance from the State as it is now from the Totalitarian State. Leo XIII stood at about that distance from the French Republican State. Few Catholics need originally have stood at any much greater distance even from the French Revolution. But the very names will serve to remind us of the vital point at issue. It is the State that changes; it is the State that destroys; it is nearly always the State that persecutes. The Totalitarian State is now making a clean sweep of *all* our old notions of liberty, even more than the French Revolution made a clean sweep of all the old ideas of loyalty. It is the Church that excommunicates; but, in that very word, implies that a communion stands open for a restored communicant. It is the State that *exterminates*; it is the State

that abolishes absolutely and altogether; whether it is the American
State abolishing beer, or the Fascist State abolishing parties, or the
Hitlerite State abolishing almost everything but itself.

Now suppose, for the sake of argument, that I did become again
merely an ordinary Liberal, as the term was understood when I was
active in Liberal politics. Suppose I thought the time had come to remind men that there really is an intellectual advantage in hearing all
sides; a help to order in a measure of liberty; a healthy irritation in
government by debate. Suppose I said (as I do say) that every government ought to be checked by an opposition; suppose I said (as I
do not say) that free international exchange is demonstrably better
than all this economic nationalism. Suppose I said that recognised
majority rule is better than random minority rule; suppose I said
that Democracy as a failure is better than Dictatorship as a success. I
could say all this, and much more, and remain a quite ordinary and
orthodox member of the ancient Church. But I could not say it,
over a great part of the modern world, without being punished by
the modern State. Rome with its religious authority would not silence me. But Fascism with its secular authority would silence me.
Bolshevism with its secular authority would silence me. Hitlerism
with its secular authority would silence me. When I began to live
and (alas) to write, all the other Liberals had inherited a huge legend
that all persecution had come from the Church. Some of them still
mumble old memories about the Spanish Inquisition (a thing started
strictly by the State); with the fact staring them in the face that the
actual persecution now going on in Spain is the spoliation of Spaniards, simply because they are Catholic priests and schoolmasters.
But anyhow, it was supposed that what was called superstition was
somehow the mother of persecution. I appeal to all my fellow-
Liberals to admit that the facts have flatly contradicted this idea.
Every Catholic enjoys much more freedom in Catholicism than any
Liberal does under Bolshevism or Fascism. I might have been a Liberal and belonged to the Centrum[131] in Germany or the Partito Pop-
ulare in Italy; it is not the Church but the State that would stop

[131] The Centrum refers to the Center Party, a Catholic political party established
in Germany in 1871.

me. For the State has returned with all its ancient terrors out of antiquity; with the Gods of the City thundering from the sky and, marching with the pageant in iron panoply the ghosts of a hundred tyrants; and we have begun to understand in what wide fields and playgrounds of liberty, the Faith that made us free has so long allowed us to wander and to play.

AUSTRIA

Last year, the representative of all that remains of the Holy Roman Empire was murdered by the barbarians. As an atrocity it has been adequately denounced; and it breeds in some of us rather a dumb sort of disgust, almost as if it had been done not by barbarians but by beasts. Perhaps the only further fact to be noted, on that side, is the fact that this is the only kind of effort in which these clumsy people are not merely clumsy. The Nordic man of the Nazi type in Germany is a very slow thinker, and incredibly backward and behind the times in science and philosophy. That is why, for instance, he clings to the word "Aryan," as if he were his own great-grandfather laboriously poring over the first pages of Max Muller,[132] under the concentrated stare of the astounded ethnologists of later days. He is slow in a great many things; as, for instance, in releasing prisoners who are admittedly innocent; or in answering questions put by foreign critics or Catholic bishops. We have good reason to know that he is slow in paying his debts; to the point of ceasing to pay them. He is very slow in bringing about the Utopia that he promised to the German people; the complete financial stability and the total disappearance of unemployment. He is slow in a thousand things, from the length of his meals to the lengthiness of his metaphysics. But in one thing he is not slow but almost slick. He is swift to shed innocent blood; he really has a certain technique in the matter of murdering other people; and the prospect of this sport alone can move him to an animation that is almost human. Hitler really killed quite a creditable number of people for one week-end holiday; and the assassination of Dollfuss did show some touch of that efficiency, which the Nazis once promised to display in other fields of activity.

But it is much more important to insist on the large human and historic matters mentioned at the beginning of this article. Dollfuss died like a loyal and courageous man, asking forgiveness for his murderers; and the souls of the just are in the hands of God, however much their

[132] Friedrich Max Muller (1823–1900) was a German-born Oxford professor and authority on philology, mythology and comparative religions.

enemies (with that mark of mere mud that is stamped over all they do) take a pleasure in denying them the help of their religion. But Dollfuss dead, even more than Dollfuss living, is also a symbol of something of immense moment to mankind, which is practically never mentioned by our politicians or our papers. We call it for convenience Austria; in a sense we might more truly call it Europe; but, above all (for this is the vital and quite neglected fact), it would be strictly correct and consistent with history to call it Germany. The very fact that the name of "Germany" has been taken from the Austrians and given to the Prussians sums up the tragedy of three hundred years. It was the tale of the war waged by the barbarians against the Empire; the real original German Empire. It began with the first Prussian shot in the Thirty Years' War; it ended with the shot that killed the Austrian Chancellor.

Whether we call it the Empire, or the Old Germany, or the culture of the Danube, what Austria meant and means is this. That it is normal for Europeans, even for Germans, to be civilised; that it is normal for Europeans, even for Germans, to be Christians; and, we must in historic honesty add, normal for them to be Catholics. This culture always incurred the hatred of the barbarians to the north-east; and in the nineteenth century a barbarian of genius, named Bismarck, actually managed to transfer to Prussia the prestige that had always normally belonged to Austria. That is the broad fact which is always left out in all modern enlightened discussion; for it involves two things; an elementary knowledge of history, which is rare, and an elementary knowledge of recent history, which is much rarer than a knowledge of ancient history. There is always a chance that about six politicians have heard of the Roman Empire; and perhaps two and a half politicians have even heard of the Holy Roman Empire. Among the scholarly leader-writers who have hitherto hardly noticed the existence of the Austrians, there are some who have read something about the Ostro-Goths[133] or perhaps (if they are very scholarly) really do know much more about Austriasians[134] than about Austrians. It is sometimes

[133] Ostro-Goths were the eastern division of the Goths, who invaded Italy in the late fifth century.

[134] Austriasians were the eastern division of the kingdom of the Franks.

possible to arouse faint interest in anything remotely historic; and always possible to arouse a fashionable fuss about anything prehistoric. But the facts which led up to the facts which stare us in the face, those are known practically to nobody in the age of newspapers. And perhaps next to nobody among our rulers will know what is meant by saying that the filthy butchery at Vienna was but the continuation of a policy, expressed in the invasion of Silesia and the victory of Sadowa.[135]

We have at least learned one lesson to-day; that old things return. This is simply that very old remembrance of our race; the barbarian invasion. This is not the Corporative State; or the Fascist Theory; or the thousand theories, including our own, for improving our ancient civilisation. This is the Turks besieging Vienna. If indeed it be not an injustice to the stately, the stable and the reverent religion of Mahomet to compare it with the feverish fads and fallacies that chase each other across the half-baked and half-baptized Teutonism of the North. This is at least, what all men meant by the Turks besieging Vienna. It is the centre of our civilisation in peril; it is the blow of the barbarian when for once, in his blindness, he happens to aim at the heart.

[135] Chesterton is referring to the invasion of Austrian Silesia in 1740 by the Prussian armies of Frederick II. The victory of Sadowa was the Prussian defeat of Austria in 1866.

THE SCRIPTURE READER

Mr. Bernard Shaw has written a very Protestant tract,[136] on the paramount duty of reading the Bible, and especially of re-reading the Bible; of course in the light of Private Judgment. For Private Judgment is never wrong, just as Private Property is never right. It is something of a triumph to have carried principles so entangled and contradictory, unchanged, untroubled and unenlightened, through a long and valuable life. Some technical difficulties may still prevent Mr. Shaw's Bible tract from being included in the literature of the British and Foreign Bible Society; but I should imagine that they would soon be overcome; now that the old stuff that calls itself the Modern Mind has become such a muddy amalgam of Puritanism and Modernism that it does not matter, so long as a man reads his Bible, whether he denies his God. But I, who love and admire Bernard Shaw, cannot help being sorry that he should have returned from the land of the Boers so completely transformed into a Baptist missionary beginning to have doubts about Habakkuk. Perhaps it is a judgment on him for having supported the Imperialists in the Boer War; because the Webbs had the truly wonderful notion that it was "practical."

Of course, like every other sectarian "Scripture-reader," Mr. Shaw re-reads the Bible and finds something different from what the last sectarian found. That is the whole fun and futility of this "Sunday game," which has now been played for nearly four hundred years, and is about played out. But the old sectaries, who discovered Calvinism or Quakerism or Mormonism in the Bible, at least had the tenacity to keep hold of what they found; and finish their programme logically. But, alas, Mr. Shaw is a true Modernist in the fact that he cannot complete even his own argument, for fear it should end by proving something. His new theory of Holy Scripture is broadly this; that the Old Testament Prophets were each of them dealing with a different God; though they seem to have been under the impression that it was the same God. Thus the God of Job is

[136] Chesterton is referring to the *Adventures of a Black Girl in Search of God* (1932).

better than the God of Noah; the God of Micah is better than the God of Job and therefore . . . therefore what? The obvious logical conclusion of the argument would be that the God-Man of the Christians, the Second Person of the Trinity, was better than the God of Micah; and rightly replaced him on progressive principles. But here, of course, Mr. Shaw goes all to pieces; wildly reverses the whole of his own theory of theistic improvement, and collapses, muttering some nonsense about the psychological misfortunes of Jesus. That is only one part of the book but it is typical of the whole of this jointless inconsequent modern way of writing. Pages upon pages are devoted to showing that primitive gods were leading up to something greater and more splendid; and it is perfectly obvious what they did actually lead up to. But the moment the Modernist sees it, he runs away from it.

The actual story of the Black Girl seems to be modelled on *Candide*; indeed much of it takes place in the famous garden of Voltaire. It was not really a very wide garden; indeed, it was a narrow garden, but it was a neat garden, according to the Dutch gardening of the period: and it is almost a relief after the jungle of journalese that is now called modern thought. Voltaire, unlike Shaw, had a straightforward and logical plan for his story. Candide is a youth brought up by a German professor in a very nonsensical philosophy called Optimism; like many nonsensical philosophies taught by German professors. It was to the effect that everything in this world fits in with our peace and comfort; whatever else it was, it was almost the opposite of Catholicism, or even Protestantism; for Christians had, if anything, rather exaggerated the truth that life is a vale of tears and a place of trial; that peace could only be found in the monastery or justice on the Day of Judgment. But Voltaire has no difficulty in showing how real life knocked this Teutonic heresy of Optimism to pieces. But it marks the more muddled modern mentality that we do not really know, at the end of Mr. Shaw's parable, what it is that has been knocked to pieces; or whether the Black Girl has found God, or failed to find God, or found that there is no God to find. Anyhow, she has found Mr. Bernard Shaw, who is acting as Voltaire's gardener, but has not yet learnt the lucid style and thought of his employer. It

must be a comfort to Mr. Shaw at least to know that he is truly a
Proletarian. Voltaire said that a man should cultivate his garden. It is
the measure of Progress that he has since apparently become a servant cultivating his master's garden.

For the rest, I know there are many simple people who will console and gratify my old friend by being duly shocked at various passages in his book. It would be almost cruel to deprive him of such
comfort; but I confess that I myself remained cold, and could not get
anything resembling a decent shock out of the whole business. It
always seems to me that we must face the question of whether we
are dealing with believers or unbelievers; and only a believer can be a
blasphemer. We Catholics must realise that by this time we are living in pagan lands; and that the barbarians around us know not
what they do. Of course, those who think Jesus was an ordinary
man will talk of Him in an ordinary way. What I complain of is
that, even then they cannot talk of Him in a sensible way. For instance, Mr. Shaw has a long dialogue in which his imaginary Jesus
feebly implies the idea that everything can be solved by love, and apparently love of any kind. Now there is not a grain of evidence that
the historical Jesus of Nazareth ever said that any such emotion,
selfish or sensual or sentimental, must be a substitute for everything
else everywhere. Rousseau and the Romantics, in the time of Voltaire, sometimes said something a little like it; and the Church
resisted it from the beginning, just as Bernard Shaw wakes up to
resist it in the end. It is much more important for us to point out
that the attack on the Faith breaks down, by its own folly on its
own ground, than to express our own feelings about some of the
random results of its invincible ignorance, when it stumbles upon
ground more sacred.

AN EXPLANATION

The last two essays in this collection have so obviously the character of
newspaper correspondence, that a word must be added about the circumstances of their appearance. At the request of the B.B.C., I gave
an address in their series on Freedom about the Catholic view of the
matter; an address which was very much criticised; but I sometimes
fancy that the most deadly criticism was involuntary and unconscious.
For I could not help feeling that some of my critics must have gone to
sleep, and snatched a brief respite from the recital, only to wake again
with a start and all the bewilderments of nightmare, to hear the ruthless infliction still going on. I should be the last to blame them; I
sometimes nearly go to sleep myself when listening to myself, let
alone to anybody so remote from me as I must naturally be from
them. But the actual effect, anyhow, was that most of the agonised
questions which they asked me afterwards I had already answered
before they were asked. At the beginning of the whole address, I explained the beginning of the whole business; that I had been specially
asked to speak as a Catholic and therefore as a controversialist. If they
asked Sir Oswald Mosley[137] to explain why he was a Fascist, it might
or might not be popular; but it would be a little hard on Sir Oswald
to complain that he had dragged the subject of Fascism into politics,
or the subject of politics into the B.B.C. Yet to read some of the innocent criticism I have read, one would really suppose I had been asked
to give a literary lecture on Milton or Shelley, and had seized the opportunity to deliver a wild eulogy upon Torquemada and Guy
Fawkes. If indeed, in this free country where (I am assured) all views
can be expressed, it is unpardonable to suggest that the Protestant
view of Freedom is wrong, some responsibility must be shared by
those who ask the Catholic to explain why the Catholic view is right.
For that peculiar diplomatic and tactful art of saying that Catholicism is
true, without suggesting for one moment that anti-Catholicism is false,
is an art which I am too old a Rationalist to learn at my time of life.

[137] Oswald Mosley (1896–1980) was the founder of the British Union of Fascists
in 1932.

The second legend that arose out of hearing, or not hearing, my wireless speech, was an extraordinary delusion that I made a speech about drink. Out of nineteen hundred words, the newspapers seemed to have selected three words, in the form of the polished epigram, "I like beer." Now I fear I am so constituted by cultural tradition, that I cannot for the life of me see anything more comic, or eccentric, or provocative, or sensational, about saying, "I like beer," than about saying, "I like bananas." But I do most certainly see that there would be something both egotistical and trivial about saying, "I like bananas," if it were not a part of an ordinary objective argument. And my remark was a part of an objective argument. Only I was arguing for the exact opposite of what they imagine. I said it was well to remember, to start with, that an ordinary poor man from Catholic countries would find what he regarded as ancient universal popular liberties forbidden in Protestant countries. The obvious instances are Prohibition and the veto on the Irish Sweepstake. I then said that these lighter instances were balanced indifferently for me, because "I like beer; there is nothing that bores me quite so much as horse-racing. But I have some sense of human rights." In short, it is self-evident that I only said I like beer in order to show that it did not matter a curse what I liked. Yet in face of this fact, an excellent cultivated weekly paper declared that I should not like Liberty if I did not like beer. The editor handsomely admitted the fact when I drew his attention to it, and my quarrel is not here with him. But further comments were made in the matter, which are the text of one of these two essays.

For the rest, if any one doubts that there is such a thing as Catholic liberty, I think it can do no harm to let him realise that there is such a thing as Catholic controversy; I mean controversy between Catholics. I have, therefore, included here my reply to some frank and friendly but very definite doubts about my action, that were expressed in one of the very best of the modern Catholic papers. For I feel it would not be fair to answer somewhat controversially a criticism in an Anglican organ, while in any way concealing the fact that I have been criticised also in an organ of my own communion. It will also be clear from the context, I think, that a distinguished Italian, Dr. Crespi, who speaks specially as an opponent of Fascism, attacked me at a slightly different angle. And this alone would illustrate the main fact; that the substance of my speech was concerned with all sorts of large modern problems, and had no more to do with my taste in beer than with my familiar appearance as a fashionable figure at Ascot. I pointed out that, by limiting liberty to preaching and printing, we had given a huge advantage to cranks over common Christian people; that we had lost a peasantry and were living under a plutocracy. Indeed, some critics combined the contradictory accusations; having proved that I was wholly concentrated upon booze and betting, they rushed on to rend the sky with cries against my sweeping slanders on the Press, the Parliament, the Landlord System and the British Empire. If they will try compressing all these topics into twenty minutes, they will understand how easy it is for the hearer (even if he manages to keep awake) to miss the proportion and the point.

WHY PROTESTANTS PROHIBIT*

It is with mingled respect and regret that I differ from a paper I admire so much as I do the *Catholic Herald*, or a critic for whom I have so much sympathy as I have for Dr. Crespi. I have already said that the *Herald* is nearly the best, or the only newspaper we have; and my confidence in Dr. Crespi's sincerity is so complete that I unhesitatingly accept his assurance that he has both read and heard my address on Liberty; for without that assurance, I might be tempted now and then to think he had done neither. But this distressing exhibition of mine seems to have been such a shock to him as to leave him with a strange impression that I uttered some sort of eulogy, or at least apology, touching Italian Fascism, or more generally, the new dictatorships in Europe. Now as a fact, I was very careful to explain that I did nothing of the sort. I said of such a system that I detested some forms of it, that I did not defend any form of it; that it practically proclaimed itself a tyranny, and that I was quite ready to treat it as a tyranny. What I said was that this tyranny, even if it was a tyranny, had not in fact torn up certain traditions of popular freedom in Catholic countries, which have been, and are being, more and more ruthlessly and rapidly torn up and uprooted in Protestant countries. If I say, "Even Nero never forbade people to grow corn," I am not uttering a eulogy on Nero; and that is the sort of thing I might say about the Prohibitionists who forbade men to drink wine. But there is indeed a curious irony about my two friendly critics on this occasion. My own friendly feeling for the *Herald* is largely founded on the fact that it does print solid blocks of information about what wicked foreigners have to say for themselves, including Fascists and Hitlerites; so that we can judge for ourselves how wicked the foreigners are. And my unfriendly criticism of British plutocracy is largely founded on the fact that its monopolist newspapers never do this; being owned by one or two millionaires ignorant of Europe and interested only in some silly stunt or slogan. In short, I only

* Letter to the *Catholic Herald*.

523

say that if dictators suppress newspapers, newspaper proprietors suppress news. And yet I am rebuked for disliking this, even by those who avoid it.

Similarly, I warmly respect Dr. Crespi for trying to free his country from what he regards as oppression and wrong. But apparently he will not allow me to do the same thing for my country. I fear, on this point, I must be firm with him. I respectfully refuse to allow my native land to be ruined by blindness and pride and hypocrisy, and its heart eaten out by corruption and the worship of wealth; merely in order that Dr. Crespi may have a wholly imaginary England to flourish in the face of Signor Mussolini.

I need not in this space destroy the delusion in detail; because for most English economists (especially Catholics) it is already destroyed. I will only say that his paean in praise of nineteenth-century capitalism would have been very welcome to the rich in the nineteenth century; and greatly encouraged those who laid on the millions a yoke little better than slavery. But I will give him a tip: from one who knows (I make bold to say) more about England than he does. *Whenever he sees our newspapers announcing revival of trade it simply means that employers have found out how to cut down the wage bill.* All recent industrial history here has been a scheme to lower wages; beginning with the triumph of the lock-out that crushed the miners, followed by vindictive laws against Labour after the general strike, and ending by taking advantage of the default on gold, to pay every workman a pound that is not a pound. That is how we do it here. I did not argue whether it is worse when done by a despot or by this anonymous conspiracy. But the tragedy (and to me despotism instead of democracy, even theoretical democracy, is a tragedy) is largely due to reaction against commercial conspiracies. For the rest, let not your Wireless Expert weep for me; or imagine that all will be bewildered who "have not the key." I happen to have stacks of letters from very poor people thanking me for pointing out how the small men are now crushed in England if they attempt independence. They are turned out of house and shop by the hundred, by modern monopolist aggression. They have the key all right; it is called in slang the key of the street. None of them has heard of the

Keys of Peter; but, being poor like St. Peter, they know how poor men are goaded in the House of the Governor; and what rage rises in them against the servant of Caiaphas. They support me sufficiently, thank you, in not encouraging the Englishman to play the Pharisee.

The fact is that Protestant tyranny is totally different from Catholic tyranny; let alone Catholic liberty. It is ineradicably rooted in a totally opposite motive and moral philosophy. You seem to suggest that, where Protestant restrictions are really excessive, it is but a part of the normal temptation of officials to magnify their office.

Under your favour, it is nothing of the sort. That is just the point of the whole business. Protestantism is in its nature prone to what may be called Prohibitionism. I do not mean prohibition of drink (though it happens to be a convenient comparison: that none of the ten thousand tyrants of Mediterranean history would ever have dreamed of uprooting the vine, since Pentheus[138] was torn in pieces); I mean that the Protestant tends to prohibit, rather than to curtail or control. His theory of Prohibition is rooted in his theory of progress; which began with expectation of the Millennium; but has ended in similar expectations of the Superman. I have no notion what Dr. Crespi means by my golden age: after Eden I know of no golden age in the past. But Protestant progress does imply a golden age in the future—and one *utterly* cut off or altered from the past. By now this Dawnism is deeply affected by Darwinism. Man is a monkey who has lost his tail and does not want it back. It is not a question of docking his tail, because it takes up too much room; or telling him to curl up his tail and only wave it on festive occasions; as in the Catholic view of discipline and recreation. No men need tails; so they need amputation.

Now the modern Protestant applies this absolute idea of amputation to all parts of problematical human nature; to all popular customs or historic traditions. He does not mean that men should be restrained in them just now; he means that men should drop them for ever, like the monkey's tail. When puritans abolish ritualism, it means there shall be no more ritual. When prohibitionists abolished beer, they swore that a whole new generation would grow up and never know the taste of it.

---

[138] In Greek mythology, Pentheus is the Theban king murdered by the female votaries of Dionysus because he attempted to ban the worship of their god.

When Protestants look to the solution of Socialism, most of them do not merely mean to attack the contemporary congestion called capitalism; they mean to abolish for ever the very idea of private property.

Thus there is a fanatical quality, sweeping, final, almost suicidal, in Protestant reforms which there is *not* even in Catholic repressions. Once Puritanism pervaded America, once Prussianism pervaded Germany, there appeared a new type of law; sterilization or compulsory eugenics, from which even the dictators of the Latin tradition would shrink.

There have been any number of good Catholics who might be called puritans, from Savonarola to Manning,[139] who made their little bonfires of the vanities; but they never mistook them for the everlasting bonfire. There have been any number of bad Catholics who might be called tyrants from Borgia to Bomba,[140] who drilled or destroyed from hate or ambition; but even when torturing men they never thought they were twisting or altering Man. Therefore their prohibitions were never so prohibitionist.

Mussolini may be wrong to suppress newspapers; but who can imagine Mussolini saying, "The world will never again be cursed with printed leaves," as Jennings Bryan would say, "We shall never again be cursed with alcoholic liquor"? I think some of the recent Fascist schemes for drilling children reach the ridiculous; but they do not reach the point of saying that children should be kept from their mothers; a point which numberless Protestant progressive followers of Wells or Shaw would reach in one wild bound. In short, apart from Catholic liberty, Catholic tyranny is either temporary in the sense of a penance or a fast, or temporary in the sense of a state of siege or a proclamation of martial law. But Protestant liberty is far more oppressive than Catholic tyranny. For Protestant liberty is only the unlimited liberty of the rich to destroy an unlimited number of the liberties of the poor.

The B.B.C., much to the credit of its own relatively sound sense of liberty, having asked me specially for what I thought about

[139] Henry Edward Manning (1808–92) was a convert to Catholicism who became archbishop of Westminster in 1865 and a cardinal ten years later.

[140] Bomba is King Ferdinand II of Naples, who earned this cognomen from his infamous bombardment of Messina in 1848.

Catholicism, I did certainly divulge the secret that I thought it was true; and that, therefore, even great cultures falling away from it, in any direction, had fallen into falsehood. I fully appreciate the desire to be fair or friendly that may lead anyone to deplore this disclosure; but I do not myself believe it will do an atom of good to anyone, least of all to the English, to whitewash or conceal the bad results of heresy in history. I was, therefore, a little puzzled when a contributor called it "a sectarian note." Somehow, I had not expected anybody on the *Catholic Herald* to call the Catholic Church a sect.

WHERE IS THE PARADOX?

A writer on a High Church paper, being full of the lyric muse, recently described me as a "prolix Papist professor of paradox"; a line which it is my firm intention to extend into a poem of no less than nine verses depending upon the letter p; by which alliterative industry the unaccountable absence of any allusion to polygamous Popes, poisoning Pontiffs, piratical prelates and pestilent peasantries, will be supplied and made good at my own expense. And though the editor very gracefully apologised for having been accidentally prevented, doubtless by my prolixity, from discovering what I actually said in the passage he criticised, another critic has since then broken out on the same paper in the same literary style; and described the same statement as going "beyond such terminological inexactitude as is permissible in the most putrid paradox"; and saying I devote myself to the propaganda of the gutter. I rather wish I knew what it is that makes the most distant prospect of me (of me, a mere dot on the crowded horizon) throw an honest gentleman at the Faith House, Tufton Street, into such astonishing convulsions. It is all the more mysterious because, so far as I am concerned, it is entirely unprovoked. I have never made any particular attack on the Anglo-Catholic theory, or the Anglican Church, or upon any Anglicans, as such. I know the Anglo-Catholic theory can be honestly held; for I held it myself for many years. I have the greatest respect for those who are in such a state of conviction; as well as the greatest sympathy for those who are in any stage of doubt. I still have a large number of Anglo-Catholic friends, who do not find me so very putrid and prolix, and, though of course I differ from them, I have always rather avoided mere dispute with them; partly because there are so many things much more in need of being disputed; and partly because I know from experience that it often does more harm than good. I used to read the paper in question because it was a good paper; and until quite recently a good-humoured paper. Why so innocuous a reader should have this extraordinary effect on the other readers and writers, I do not clearly understand. But the effect is so extraordinary that the critic falls back desperately on a sort of half-defence of Puritanism, of Protestantism and of Prussianism; though these are things which all the old Anglo-Catholics used to denounce, and which I used to denounce quite as much when I was myself an Anglo-Catholic. On a former occasion, for instance, in the same strained way, it picked a particular personal quarrel with me, merely because I joined with the whole civilised world in deploring the assassination of Dollfuss. If it were only a matter of personal quarrels, it would not be worth referring to again; for I am quite content with the admission already made about the facts in dispute; and all is gas and gaiters. But there are much more important quarrels, which concern all Christendom and especially this country, about which I can hardly leave an important organ of opinion under so false an impression.

Touching Mr. C. E. Douglas, the smeller out of putrid paradoxes, I need only record that he complains; of "an unhistorical use of the word Catholic," and assures us that we should be content with the fact that clergy of the national church are attached to nearly all our institutions, as a guarantee that "in theory, the Catholic religion is the official religion of the nation." I can only say that if he used his imagination about our point of view, as much as I try to use my imagination about his, it would, I think, dawn upon him that it is not altogether unreasonable in a real Catholic, or even a real Anglo-Catholic, to find this official reassurance a little thin. Certainly, in that sense, there are "Catholic" priests attached to all sorts of things; there is a "Catholic" bishop preaching that science has destroyed the whole original Christian scheme; there is a "Catholic" dean who booms Birth-Prevention like a quack medicine; there is a "Catholic" canon who is ready to "break bread" apparently with anybody from Mormons to Moslems; at least I myself should rather prefer the Moslems. But I cannot believe that either Mr. Douglas or the Editor of the paper really regards that retrospective breakfast as a substitute for the Blessed Sacrament. But though Mr. Douglas's view of our scruples is not highly sympathetic or discerning, there is one point on which Mr. Douglas endears himself to me, though I dare not hope that I am likely to endear myself to him. He may think what he likes about me, so long as he will go on thinking what he now thinks about Prussia. Because I classed Prussia with England among the Protestant countries, he protests against anything like a suggestion that they are the same sort of countries; and there I am warmly with him. They have certain negative things in common; but even in these it would be true to say that the Prussian prefers to be bullied where the Englishman only submits to be blinded. But England is a thousand times jollier and more human as a national culture than Prussia; the disease is milder and the mood more healthy. But it is a mood which is weakened by the absence of a militant creed of Christian morals, and the power to define and defend. The test could best be made by the introduction of some of the new abnormal laws already threatening the world in the name of science. Suppose something of the type of Compulsory Sterilisation or Compulsory Contraception really stalks through the modern State, leading the march of human progress through abortion to infanticide. If the heathens in North Germany received it, they would accept it with howls of barbaric joy, as one of the sacred commands of the Race Religion; the proceedings very probably terminating (by that time) with a little human sacrifice. If the English received it, they would accept it as law-abiding citizens; that is, as something between well-trained servants and bewildered children. There is a great difference; but not so great as the certainty that the Irish would not accept it at all.

Now the real reason why I have taken the text of these two High Church critics, is that their views happily cancel out upon a point of immense international importance. Mr. Douglas preserves his healthy instinct against Prussia, as being not improbably the source of Prussianism; though he might not admit my view that the error had its original source in Protestantism. But the other writer would protect Protestantism from any such criticism; and falls back on the jolly old catchword of calling Hitler a Catholic. Of course there are countless Catholics whom I think wrong in politics; and countless Catholics who think me wrong in politics. But I wonder if it is much truer to call Hitler a Catholic than to call Bertrand Russell an Anglo-Catholic. He was quite probably christened in an Anglican Church. But the much more important point is the historic and

cultural origin of the whole movement of the more admittedly hea-
thenish Hitlerism. The Anglican critic says that this tribal cult of
triumph began in Bavaria. It would be as sensible to say that it began
in England; because it was popularised, long before anybody had
ever heard of Hitler, by Houston Stewart Chamberlain.[141] In fact,
the movement began before the Great War; before the Franco-
Prussian War;[142] and has its origins far back in history, in the fact
that the Protestant edges of Germany only partly emerged from barbarism and soon relapsed into paganism. But in its present practical
form, it is simply the tail-end, we might say the rag-tag-and-bobtail
of the nineteenth-century Prussianism; the camp-followers of the far
better disciplined army of Bismarck. Nobody understands its very
rowdy revivalism who does not understand that it is merely a revival. To suppose it began with recent headlines about Hitler is
newspaper history, which is knowing no history but only news; and
that frequently untrue. The movement that has actually abolished
Bavaria, and left no State alive except the Bismarckian Empire, is but
the last phase of the Bismarckian plan to Prussianise Germany, by
crushing and outnumbering the Catholics of the Rhine; and stealing
the old Imperial Crown from the other Catholics of the Danube. In
short, he set up a new Protestant Empire, to dwarf and depose the
old Catholic Empire; and Hitler is his heir and his executor.

These things can easily be shown to be facts, to anybody who
knows anything of what happened before the newspapers of a few
months ago. We need merely ask what Bavaria was like when it was
Bavaria; before it felt the pressure from Prussia. When Bavaria was
allowed to be Bavarian, all sorts of things were said against the
Bavarians; that they were dreamy, that they were drunken, that
they were ridiculously romantic, that they were mad on music, and
so on. But nobody ever said that they were stiff or rigid or ruthless
or inhuman or mad on mere official centralisation and militaristic
discipline. That particular sort of cold brutality came from Prussian

[141] Houston Stewart Chamberlain (1855–1917) was an Englishman who espoused
Nordic racial superiority. He moved to Germany where, after his death, his theories
enjoyed popularity among the Nazis.

[142] In the Franco-Prussian War (1870–71) France suffered a humiliating defeat.

prestige; it could not possibly have come from anything else. And that Prussianism came from Protestantism; not of course, in the sense that it came to infect all Protestants, or that there are not millions of good Protestants free from this error, or suffering from other errors. But it was a historical fruit of Protestantism; and that is not merely a historical fact; it can also be clearly traced as a philosophical truth. The racial pride of Hitlerism is of the Reformation by twenty tests; because it divides Christendom and makes all such divisions deeper; because it is fatalistic, like Calvinism, and makes superiority depend not upon choice but only on being of the chosen; because it is Caesaro-Papist, putting the State above the Church, as in the claim of Henry VIII; because it is immoral, being an innovator of morals touching things like Eugenics and Sterility; because it is subjective, in suiting the primal fact to the personal fancy, as in asking for a German God, or saying that the Catholic revelation does not suit the German temper; as if I were to say that the Solar System does not suit the Chestertonian taste. I do not apologise, therefore, for saying that this catastrophe in history has been due to heresy; and I cannot see that even an Anglo-Catholic supports his own claim to orthodoxy by denying it.

*   *   *

Naturally, I have never expected that people would agree with these views. Among the remarks which I must have spoken so badly that hardly anybody heard them, was my preliminary remark that I would very much prefer to talk to my countrymen about the things on which we should agree, about Dickens or the great comic culture of the English tradition; but that any man challenged on his allegiance to a Church must disagree with those who definitely disagree with it. I said on that occasion: "If I say these things, I cannot ask most of you to agree with me; if I did anything else, I could not ask any of you to respect me." But it does strike me, in amiable retrospect, that the whole situation is a little amusing. We live in an age in which anybody may teach anywhere, by any scientific instrument of instruction, that such a trifle as God was tossed up out of a tribal quarrel about incest or parricide, and so religion poisoned the first springs of progress; in which the Communist can claim that humanity went wrong when private property first appeared among prehistoric men; when anything, however real in its beginning, however remote, can be called an enormous delusion darkening the whole history of man. But when I choose to think that one island, in one corner of one continent, took the wrong turning in thought at the end of one century, hardly four hundred years ago, when I attribute to that relatively recent and local fad the collapse and despair that has actually fallen on one commercial culture, a cry of protest goes up against an intolerable blasphemy; accompanied with the assurance that those who are thus horrified have, alone among all peoples, the power to tolerate all opinions.

I confess I found a faint whiff of paradox (though by no means putrid) in the fact of these few fanatics telling me in one breath that they were devoted to liberty of thought and that I had disgraced myself by saying what I thought so plainly. But they were only a few; and I ought not to close this episode without bearing testimony to the vast number of messages I received from Protestants, or even from Pagans, quite fairly recognising or quite fairly discussing, what I had really said. Above all, I know well that I could have proved my case, more clearly than appears in this hasty correspondence, if I had merely printed a correspondence far more valuable; the letters I received from very poor people, who had suffered the silent aggression and enslavement by modern monopoly; and who thanked me with only too much of the truly English generosity, for exposing the wrongs they endure with only too much of the truly English good humour.

THE WAY OF THE CROSS
1935

A COMMENTARY BY

GILBERT KEITH CHESTERTON

In this series of designs, one of the most masculine of modern men of genius, famous in every sense for the breadth of his brush and a glow of colour not only rich but robust, has dealt very individually with things which many would now associate rather with a certain type of crystalline severity in the Primitives; with the most awful austerity and renunciation and with the secrets of a more than human sorrow. It is necessary to note first that any commentary may be a matter of controversy; for there is now a general controversy about whether there should be any commentary at all. For some, any suggestion of spiritual significance in a picture is somehow entangled with the idea of treating it as a mere anecdote; or, what is often worse, as a mere allegory. The controversy sometimes becomes a comedy; the painters passionately affirming that their pictures are quite meaningless, and the other people, who are not painters, tenderly explaining to them what they really mean. But the difficulty really arises from there being too little rather than too much controversy in the modern world. A discussion seldom begins at the beginning or continues to the logical end; it consists of catchwords and curses and fragmentary phrases on both sides, and it drags on intermittently because it has never really begun. It is not so very difficult to state shortly a true or at least tenable philosophy of the matter. Certainly a criticism of art, which is a purely literary criticism, is not a criticism of art. If a man does not know that, for the artist, the line, the balance, the rhythm, the optical proportions, *are* the picture, he does not know what he is talking about; or is talking about something else. He may be a critic, but he is not an art critic if he does not understand that a mere line curling into a corner, or pausing at a point, or even a space left blank and apparently unused, may be by far the most important thing in the picture. It may, in a special sense, be the beauty of the picture. But if we ask ourselves what such beauty is, or why it is beautiful, we soon find that we have not (as we fondly hoped) escaped from thinking or from the world of ideas. That our pleasure is animal or accidental, or even a sight that pleases the eye as a taste may please the tongue, is inconsistent with the intensity and implicit infinity of the feeling itself. We may despair of prose and take refuge in verse, as did the poet who wrote: —

> What are the names for Beauty? Who shall praise
> God's pledge He can fulfil His creatures' eyes?
> Or what strong words of what creative phrase
> Determine Beauty's title in the skies?

But most of us have an instant inward conviction that it is a title in the skies; that is a reality, though not expressed in reason or speech; that it is the unfolding of a transcendental truth. It may often be disputed how far every artist, including some of the greatest artists of the past, knew exactly what he meant; in the rather narrow sense of wanting to translate it into words. It may often be disputed, and that somewhat violently, by the artist himself, whether the critic has even approximately translated it into words. But even then it is always possible that the critic has seen another part of the same cosmic pattern; if once we admit that beauty is real, in being part of the cosmic design. All that I write here is subject to the possibility, or probability, that I have missed or mis-stated the main part of the purpose; but I have not missed it by anything so crude and clumsy as not understanding that a picture is a picture, or supposing that literature, let alone journalism, can express what is expressed by art. The most original artists are those who come out of a tradition; and in the very broadest sense, Brangwyn[1] comes out of the great Flemish tradition; and is full of that peculiar fullness, something that might be called a Christian exuberance, which piled itself up to overflowing in the free cities of the Catholic Netherlands. It is a complete mistake, for instance, to suppose that the exuberance of Rubens is not a Christian exuberance. It may have some of the Paganism of the Renaissance; and, by that proof alone, not the Paganism of the Pagan world. The Christian who thinks that it is merely

---

[1] William Frank Brangwyn (1867–1956) was an English painter and etcher born in Bruges of Welsh parents.

Pagan is himself only the half-Christian, who is called the Puritan. But there is a difference between that Flemish flamboyance as it appeared in Rubens and as it appears in Brangwyn. And the more modern artist is also the more medieval artist. He is at least the more mystical artist; and less purely objective and rationalist than the most orthodox men of the Renaissance. The difference is chiefly seen in the artist's work in colour; for the Middle Ages saw a light shining through things, as through stained-glass windows; while the Renaissance saw a light shining on things, as on silver and gold; and sometimes, it must be admitted, on brass. Anybody must have noticed that the modern artist's tints are more transparent and his sunlight has more of sunset than the hard noonday sun of the sixteenth century. In these black and white designs this particular distinction does not arise; but there is another test which illustrates the same truth. We do sometimes feel in the Flemish Renaissance that the goddesses are too handsome to be beautiful. Rubens did not paint many ugly people; but he painted many good-looking people who are too good-looking to be good, even in an almost physical sense of good. When exaggerations on both sides are allowed for, there was something in the Renaissance that did cheapen bodily perfection. Under that sixteenth-century sun, there was something a little too like sun-bathing. There is something more medieval in the tradition of expressing vitality, and even exuberance, by the vast variety of ugliness; and even the ugliness of the crowd. Now these pictures are packed with exactly that sort of Flemish vitality and variety. Every face is different; and every face is vigorous, with an ugly energy that is more attractive than vulgar beauty. It is important to emphasise this crowded and tumultuous background of all the pictures, especially in connection with the grotesque distinction in every face and gesture, because it leads up to the point of the most decisive distinction of all. I have called the drawing exuberant; but it is the very reverse of careless. It would be possible to write a page about every face in that crowd. A face peering out of some dim corner is often in the exact sense surprising; to some it will often be puzzling. For though these masks of the mob are often extravagant in type, they are always subtle in intention. The mob is not a mob, in the sense of men merely turned into a man, still less into a beast. There is every shade of every passion, or lack of passion, that may go to make up a huge human blunder or crime; as if to emphasise the deeper doctrinal conception that every man has his own quarrel with God. To take one or two cases out of scores; notice the contrast between the two most prominent faces in the first scene of Christ falling under the Cross; the old Pharisee really gibbering with a positive and personal emotion, shaking with shrill and senile derision, gone ga-ga with hatred; and opposite to him the long, lined, patient, lifeless face of the soldier or official leaning automatically to lift the cross; cold, dull, quite callous, quite without cruelty; doing his job; the face of any tired workman bending over a carpenter's bench. Or note the delightful stiffness of the two children in the Eighth Station, who feel as if they were in church and who know how to behave there. All this motley mob has the special effect of throwing up the central figure; and it is touching that figure that discussion, and perhaps difference, will most probably arise.

Many people must have speculated on the possibility of expressing some special facet of the many-faced mystery of a divine humanity, under the symbol of a new version of the bodily presence of Our Lord. Not all, or possibly most people will immediately accept, or perhaps understand, the particular type which Brangwyn has taken as the image of such an idea. Andrea Mantagna[2] has somewhere a very fine figure of a dark and beardless Christ, rather like the traditional figure of the strenuous John the Baptist in his youth. I have sometimes wished that the experiment might have become an alternative tradition, as emphasising the aspect of the wrestler with evil, the deliverer of mankind. Brangwyn has conceived a type that may seem rather curious; its chief feature is a profile of the type called aquiline. Some may suggest that it is meant realistically as the type called Semitic. But though this would be quite defensible, I cannot entirely reconcile it with the scheme. For there is no pretence of any realistic racial treatment touching the rest of the human characters, especially of the populace of Jerusalem. They are, as I have said, drawn with every possible variety of human form and feature; the

---

[2] The correct spelling is "Mantegna".

general effect suggesting something like a Flemish medieval mob; the individuals in detail often suggesting any real individuals anywhere; including numbers of individuals whom we might meet in a train or a tram. It may be a dangerous, and in some cases almost a murderous simplification to be always saying that the Jews killed Christ. But surely it would not be a simplification, but simply a falsification, to suggest that the only Jew involved was the Jew who was killed. Nor, indeed, is the face strictly what is meant by a Jewish face; at least by those who have any real experience or understanding of Jewish faces. The nose might almost be called a hook nose, but it is not a Jewish nose; in many cases, it rather recalls the high-bridged nose of a Roman Caesar. I speak under correction, but I think it may have been drawn deliberately as what is called a falcon face; and that this may be connected with an idea which does really, I think, run through the whole design. First, it does really make the central figure distinguished, in the exact sense of distinct. And it sets it in a particular kind of contrast to the rest. For most are of that broad and burly, flat or bulbous Flemish sort, which is exactly at the opposite extreme for the aquiline type. In such a case, all comparisons are prosaic and almost profane; but the impression may be suggested by saying that the isolation of Christ is here rather stressed as the isolation of the artist or the idealist; the keen and sensitive spirit passing through the coarseness and carelessness of mankind. But it is keen as well as sensitive; and it is here perhaps that we touch on something, if not of the intention, at least of the impression, or the effect. We have the sense of something that cleaves its way like an arrow; that cuts through the crowd like a knife; even when disarmed and defeated, something that brought a sword into the world.

There is one scene specially in which this imaginative impression is to me so extraordinarily vivid, that I will venture to attempt a fuller description of it; all the more since I know that in this case the point may not be obvious or may even be repellent.

If the Gospel description of the Passion of Jesus Christ is not the record of something real, then there was concealed somewhere in the provinces ruled by Tiberius a supremely powerful novelist who was also, among other things, a highly modern realist. I think this improbable. I think that if there had been such a uniquely realistic romancer, he would have written another romance, with the legitimate aim of money; instead of merely telling a lie, with no apparent aim but martyrdom. We hear much in modern times of a realism which is apparently flattered by being called ruthless. I cannot say, as a matter of individual taste, that I am much more attracted to ruthlessness as a virtue of German novelists than of American millionaires. But if ever realism could be called ruthless, and ruthlessness could be called right, it is in the rending story of insult and injustice that has been imbodied in the Stations of the Cross. Christians are enjoined to think about it; but I must confess that I simply have not the courage to write about it. It is rather too real, or realistic, for one commonly in contact with the milder modern realism. Anything so grim in every detail as that would be recognised as beating all the moderns at their own game, if only it had been on what is called the modern side. Details like the repeated failure to carry the Cross have an inhuman horror of humiliation, that would make the fortune of a modern novelist writing on concentration camps to prove there is no God, instead of writing to prove that a God so loved the world. Now, through this trailing tragedy of torture, this Procession of Protracted Death, to use the phrase of one of our cheerful modern poets, Brangwyn has stuck grimly in the main to the grim old tradition of exhaustion and defeat. He almost exaggerates, if anybody could exaggerate, the paradox of the impotence of omnipotence and the hopelessness of the hope of the world. Christ appears again and again prone as a felled tree or a fallen pillar, faceless in that His face is already turned away to nothingness and night. And yet it all works up, as it seems to me, to one central design in which Christ lifts His head, looks sharply over His shoulder, and his eyes shine with defiance and almost with fury. And that one flash of fierceness is shot back at the Women of Jerusalem weeping over Him.

I doubt whether everybody will like it; I am not sure that I like it. But I am quite sure it is the most powerful scene in a powerful series; and that there are many thousand more things in it than meet the eye; either my eye or anybody else's. Since this is the sharpest relief and revelation of that pointed profile, against the multifarious faces of the mob, it will seem to many to show only that sharpness of the Semitic edge, of which I have written already. I can imagine people saying that it looks like Shylock throwing a curse over his shoulder as he leaves the court. Well, there is a dark inverted truth even there; there is that double contrasted aspect, of light and darkness, in the same sensitive spirit of Israel. But in the highest example there is always this high paradox; that He has prayed for his foes, but is protesting against His friends. Jesus is not in the least like Shylock; but there is some symbolic parallel between Jesus and Job. It is not recorded, I think, that Job went out of his way to curse the robbers who had raided his flocks and herds; he could endure everyone except his comforters. But in the higher example—in the highest example—there is a riddle to be solved by a principle much more profound; and depending indeed upon that central mystery of the human and the divine united, which is the tremendous theme of the whole. The theme of the Greek tragedy is the division between God and Man; the theme of the Gospel tragedy is the union of God and Man; and its immediate effects are more tragic.

The figures of the weeping women will also puzzle the spectator; or, at any rate, the superficial spectator. It is here, I think, that the peculiar value of that variety of portraiture, with which the pencil of the artist has played upon the many-faced mob, has produced some of its most delicate and original effects. For they are a rather curious group of mourners, these mothers and maidens of the holy city. I do not mean that many of them, or even most of them, are not perfectly sincere in their pity for an unfortuante prisoner going to punishment. But I do mean that there are singular shades and degrees, even in that sincerity, and that in some cases it is curiously mixed with curiosity, and in some even sinks into vulgarity. One elderly woman (characteristically) in the background, is realistically torn to the heart. She is only a face half thrust out of the shadow, into which the more energetic have elbowed her; but I feel that I know all about her; she is almost exactly like a Margate landlady with a heart of

gold—which is broken. One younger woman is quaintly sentimental; she has an eye off, with some suggestion of a tear in the corner of
it; but I cannot help feeling that she was wondering whether they
will show the Crucifixion on the Pictures. Another woman is an utterly stolid and probably sensible mother, laden with trailing children; doing her duty in a dazed way; but I rather suspect it is chiefly
the duty of taking the children to the show. Behind, and a little
apart, a few strokes indicate a woman who is also a lady; but I am
not sure whether she is tragic or only dignified. And as I looked at
this confusing crowd, I suddenly had a collective impression about
them, whether it was the impression intended or no. All these people
are looking at a man who is going to be hanged. Most of them are
really sorry for him because he is down and out; none of them has
the slightest doubt that he is entirely down and out. They have read
all about it in the Sunday papers; and the Home Secretary would not
interfere. They not only could not conceive of there being any hope
for him; still less could they conceive of there being any case for him.
But they are sane and cannot deny that it is sad that he should die
and disappear, when their own daily lives will go on in security and
even prosperity. And it is upon them that the victim turns back, in
sudden and burning anger, the face of an eagle.

The original words of the New Testament have a crushing com-
pression which can never be expanded without being weakened. But
because their meaning is sometimes understood conventionally, or
not understood at all, and because we all feel that every short sentence seems to say a thousand things at once, there is always the
temptation to adumbrate, however vaguely in a verbal sense, the implications and applications that may not be immediately seen; and
there is a stream of thoughts flowing through the single sentence
here recorded, which the merely human mind can only very ten-
tatively trace: ". . . and this is the last portent of the darkness; that
you are sorry for me. That part of me in which you never believed,
the madman's dream of deity—you need waste no tears upon that.
But that part of me that is part of you; that ancient and achieved
thing in which you do believe, that tradition that was mine as well
as yours; the Blood; the Household; the Great Story—if you are

wanting something to weep for! Because I was born Man, I was born patriot; of a place and of a people; and if you would compassionate me for anything, compassionate me for that; for the Tables and the Temple and Solomon in all his glory. Do you imagine that a dream has come to an end; if you knew what reality has come to an end! If you knew the real tragedy that shall trail after you across the world, century after century; the wrongs you do, the wrongs you suffer, the endless wrangle about wrongs. And you who stand on the very crest of the stooping wave of this awful and pitiable catastrophe—you do not even know what to pity." I cannot exaggerate my sense of the vivid inspiration of the artist who made that last look backwards as fierce as a flash of lightning. "Daughters of Jerusalem, weep not for Me; but weep for yourselves and for your children."

It would, of course, be thoughtless to dwell on the particular effect, of this particular example, without allowing for the general fact that the artist's method would in any case give the look of something motley and even fantastic to any particular group of the dreadful pageant. Pictorially, as well as poetically or spiritually, nobody would expect Brangwyn to draw the group of the weeping women as classic mourners, veiled in Greek draperies or lamenting round the Roman urn. That would be to misunderstand even the technical treatment, and the personal use of the medium of black and white. There runs through the whole, as I have said, a changing pattern of Flemish and medieval grotesque; the background is in any case conceived as a sea of homely or ugly faces; and much of the individual variety, even here, is probably incidental and possibly accidental. But I do not think that the concentrated irony of that particular scene can be entirely accidental. There are other places where critics with other tastes may well complain that this style of the Flemish Gothic runs too much to gargoyles. It goes very far, as did all the most medieval humour, in avoiding the sentimental. There may well be many, for instance, who will faintly plead for the possibility that St. Veronica may have looked a little more like the beautiful Christian maiden of conventional art. A yet deeper and more vibrant note is necessarily struck, in touching the topic of the image of the Mater Dolorosa. For though almost every possible type of woman has been glorified by being given that part in the pageant of painting, there are some of us who can never avoid a thrill, both of hope and fear, when a fresh figure is added to the procession. In this case, I venture to think, the choice is connected with certain conditions which also operated in the choice of a human model for her Divine Son.

It will be only too obvious that all this is guesswork and gossip rather than criticism; but I still feel that the figure of Christ in this particular artist's vision expresses an idea; which may have been reached by a sort of process of elimination. There are two great traditions of Christian art which the artist might have followed. There is that which insists on a luminous purity almost ethereal; a tradition which is not only mystic but almost monastic. It is always associated with the most orthodox and theological painters, like Fra Angelico; though, in fact, the theory of the thing, if it becomes too thin and transparent, is always in some peril of the Gnostic heresy of the bodiless Christ. On the other hand, there is the other extreme, which made such a very solid appearance at the Renaissance. I feel somehow that Brangwyn, if he had been content with the Christ of Rubens, would have felt that he missed something of the sort of distinction and isolation, that he wished to stamp upon the entirely unique face and figure. In that sense, he may have feared something commonplace in the emphasis on a rather too Flemish Christ; a mere bearded Hercules from Antwerp. This is what William Blake felt,[3] when he expressed that amusing but fanatical rage against Rubens:

> "I understood Christ was a carpenter
> And not a brewer's drayman, my good Sir."

Between and beyond these two traditional types, the modern artist has certainly invented a third and thoroughly original type; which seems to be meant to suggest something that cleaves its way with a shining sharpness; the thrust of a sword or the flight of an eagle. The same conjecture may be made about his conjectural conception of Our Lady; only that there were even more extremes of interpretation between which to steer than in the traditional interpretations of Our Lord. The Blessed Virgin has also been shown as very ethereal

[3] The quotation is from Blake's *Notebooks, 1808–11.*

or very human and emotional; and the conception suggested here is not exactly either. Rather one might interpret it in the sense of strength; something of the peasant woman who toiled through the deserts to Egypt, and something, also, of the daughter of queens who stood erect singing the *Magnificat*. But it is strength under the strict conditions of that Flemish candour and humour, which some would think almost harsh. And this is no more than another illustration of the unity of this humour or tone, which is a consistent harmony, even where stiff classicists or slack sentimentalists might think that the harmony consist of discords.

It is symbolic that the figure in the drama, which is sacred but entirely human, has been more of a magnet of controversy even than that which is both sacred and divine. For these rambling remarks must end, as they began, upon a note not always welcome; the note of the inevitable controversy. I have dealt in nothing but adumbrations of criticism, or of answers to criticism, touching the technical genius of the artist; or, in other words, with the treatment of the theme. But it is impossible to avoid the abiding challenge of those who object to the theme rather than the treatment. The tremendous tradition to which Brangwyn has here added an extension, essentially unchanged in its challenge to all those who pass by, the same challenge repeated through the Roman decline, through the Dark Ages, through the Middle Ages, through the Renaissance and through the modern world even more loudly than in the Renaissance; that is the fundamental theme and thing round which the world now revolves as much as it ever did; "Is it nothing to you, all you who pass by? Was ever sorrow like unto my sorrow?" But there has been in recent times a whole rally of protest, which really protests against the thing because it is sorrowful. There are any number of people now who would say, sincerely if superficially, that it is morbid to stand at all under the Stations of the Cross. As I have noted, they are not altogether consistent. While accusing their fathers of being morbid about faith, they have not even rebuked their contemporaries for being much more morbid about doubt. They have tolerated modern literature which is even darker with defeat and despair; on condition that it contains nothing except defeat and despair. Swinburne wailed in melodious versification against the morbidity of martyrology; "the ghastly glories of saints and dead limbs of gibbeted gods." But the very next phase of versification[4] showed the turn of the modern taste; by which anything is allowed to be ghastly so long as we are certain it is not glorious; and anybody may dwell on the dying agonies, if it is quite certain the god is dead. If there was one man of a later generation who did manage in a new way to be as musical as Swinburne, his melodies may be found running like rivlets through the play of *Hassan*.[5] Yet that play practically turned upon a prolonged episode of torture, far more morbid than anything in the martyrology of Christians. What seems to have reconciled the modern mind to it, is that it describes the triumph of the tyrant, and not the triumph of the hero. Yet again it would be to play the hypocrite to pretend that it is only a question of the hero. Those who mock or misunderstand the great painters of the Passion, would have something a little more like a case, if it had only been the perpetual repetition of the particular sufferings of a particular hero. There would be some meaning in the complaint, if there had been quite so many pictures depicting the torments of Regulus.[6] It would be possible to understand the unrest, if classical artists had all dwelt with such detail on the bodily effects of the hemlock upon Socrates. By a grim irony, the answer to the complaints of the modernists and humanitarians is itself a complaint against modernism and mere humanitarianism. If any modern man should say, "You make too much of the sufferings of Jesus of Nazareth," it is a strictly logical answer to say, "It might or might not be too much for the sufferings of Jesus of Nazareth; it is not too much for the sufferings of Jesus Christ." If *his* theory were true, that Jesus was not merely a human being but

[4] A group of poets active in the 1890s tried to renew poetry in violent opposition to the world-weariness of the times and especially to the aestheticism and hyper-refined style of the "Decadents" (Swinburne is sometimes considered among them). The leading representatives of the new style included Robert Louis Stevenson and Rudyard Kipling. Later members of this group included Chesterton and Hilaire Belloc.

[5] *Hassan* is a verse drama by James Elroy Flecker (1884–1915), published posthumously in 1922.

[6] Marcus Atilius Regulus, a Roman general in the First Punic War (264–41 B.C.), suffered a crushing defeat at the hands of the Carthaginians in 256.

almost a historical accident, then indeed we might seem to be making too prolonged a lamentation over such an accident. But if *our* theory is true, that it was not an accident, but a divine agony demanded for the restoration of the very design of the world, then it is not in the least illogical that the lamentation (and the exultation) should last as long as the world. The sceptic, who is also the sentimentalist, is engaged in his usual game of arguing in a circle; he is merely saying that if the Passion was what he thinks it was, it is very wrong of us to treat it as what we think it was. Certainly, if Christ was not of the very substance of omnipotence, it becomes relatively pointless to point to the paradox of his impotence. But we do not necessarily admit we are wrong, merely because our version of the story is the only version that gives it a point. That there has been a dreadful and even deadly insistence upon that point is perfectly true, and for us perfectly consistent; there has been an everlasting energy in driving in that point; in pressing upon it as upon the thorns; in hammering at it as at the nails. But we are not bound to consider the critic who is merely annoyed by the hammering or puzzled by the pressure, without even seeing the point. This book is but the last contemporary witness to the fact that the very recurrence and reality of the subject depend on the dogma which some would call the most doubtful or the details which some would call the most diseased. But for such fundamental facts, both mystical and material, such imagery of the Passion would long ago have faded with the dusty and stilted engravings of forgotten statesmen on the scaffold, or now neglected stoics falling on antiquated swords. In every century, in this century, in the next century, the Passion is what it was in the first century, when it occurred; a thing stared at by a crowd. It remains a tragedy of the people; a crime of the people; a consolation of the people; but never merely a thing of the period. And its vitality comes from the very things that its foes find a scandal and a stumbling-block; from its dogmatism and from its dreadfulness. It lives, because it involves the staggering story of the Creator truly groaning and travailing with his Creation; and the highest thing thinkable passing through some nadir of the lowest curve of the cosmos. And it lives, because the very blast from this black cloud of death comes upon the world as a wind of everlasting life; by which all things wake and are alive.

FIRST STATION

JESUS IS CONDEMNED TO DEATH

SECOND STATION

JESUS IS MADE TO BEAR THE CROSS

THIRD STATION

JESUS FALLS FOR THE FIRST TIME

UNDER THE CROSS

FOURTH STATION

JESUS MEETS HIS AFFLICTED MOTHER

FIFTH STATION

THE CROSS IS LAID UPON SIMON OF CYRENE

SIXTH STATION

VERONICA WIPES THE FACE OF JESUS

SEVENTH STATION

JESUS FALLS THE SECOND TIME

EIGHTH STATION

JESUS SPEAKS TO THE
DAUGHTERS OF JERUSALEM

NINTH STATION

JESUS FALLS THE THIRD TIME

TENTH STATION

JESUS IS STRIPPED OF HIS GARMENTS

ELEVENTH STATION

JESUS IS NAILED TO THE CROSS

TWELFTH STATION

JESUS DIES UPON THE CROSS

THIRTEENTH STATION

JESUS IS TAKEN DOWN FROM THE CROSS

FOURTEENTH STATION

JESUS IS PLACED IN THE SEPULCHRE

The text of this book has been set in Bembo by the Neumann Press of Long Prairie, Minnesota. Printed on Warren's Sebago paper by Thomson Shore, Dexter, Michigan. Bound in Kennet cloth by John H. Dekker & Sons. The cover and jacket design are by Darlene Lawless O'Rourke.